MOVING BOARDERS

SPORT, CULTURE & SOCIETY

DAVID K. WIGGINS, SERIES EDITOR

OTHER TITLES IN THIS SERIES

MOVING BOARDERS

SKATEBOARDING AND THE CHANGING LANDSCAPE OF URBAN YOUTH SPORTS

Matthew Atencio ▪ **Becky Beal**
E. Missy Wright ▪ **ZáNean McClain**

The University of Arkansas Press ▪ Fayetteville ▪ 2018

ISBN: 978-1-68226-078-4 (cloth)
ISBN: 978-1-68226-079-1 (paper)
eISBN: 978-1-61075-653-2

22 21 20 19 18   5 4 3 2 1

Designed by Liz Lester

⊛ The paper used in this publication meets the minimum
requirements of the American National Standard for
Permanence of Paper for Printed Library Materials
Z39.48–1984.

Library of Congress Cataloging-in-Publication Data

Names: Atencio, Matthew, 1975–   author. | Beal, Becky, author. |
  Wright, E. Missy, author. | McClain, ZáNean, author.
Title: Moving boarders : skateboarding and the changing landscape of urban
  youth sports / Matthew Atencio, Becky Beal, E. Missy Wright, ZáNean
  McClain.
Description: Fayetteville : The University of Arkansas Press, 2018. | Series:
  Sport, culture, and society | Includes bibliographical references and index.
Identifiers: LCCN 2018015289 (print) | LCCN 2018040223 (ebook) | ISBN
  9781610756532 (electronic) | ISBN 9781682260784 (Cloth : alk. paper) |
  ISBN 9781682260791 (Paper : alk. paper) | ISBN 9781610756532 (eBook)
Subjects: LCSH: Skateboarding—Social aspects—United States. | Skateboarding
  parks—United States. | Sports for youth. | Urban youth—Social conditions.
Classification: LCC GV859.8 (ebook) | LCC GV859.8 .A84 2018 (print) |
  DDC 796.22—dc23
LC record available at https://lccn.loc.gov/2018023706

CONTENTS

FOREWORD

My time on a skateboard is limited, but my son and daughter spent considerable time on their boards as they sought challenging physical activities between the mid-1970s and the mid-1980s. I would watch and talk with them and their friends who skated on local streets and neighborhood parking lots. These young people were part of the new urethane-wheels generation that enjoyed skating experiences seldom achieved on the steel roller skates and clay wheels used during the 1950s and '60s.

Our garage became a workshop, as skateboards and wheels were modified, repaired, and replaced, and as Sting-Ray bikes were customized for jumps and tricks in the street. Ramps were built and put in the street in front of our house. We were at the bottom of a gentle hill that gave skaters and Sting-Ray riders a relatively controlled opportunity to hit ramps and try tricks at speeds that made me nervous. Fortunately, muscle and bone bruises and road rash were the worst injuries I treated during those years. Since the 1970s, I've watched with interest as skateboard cultures have faded, returned, and taken multiple forms depending on local conditions and the young people who created them. If you've ever had questions about skateboarding, the authors of *Moving Boarders* provide a sense-making framework for understanding its social significance and impact on culture and the environment. The research done by Matthew Atencio, Becky Beal, Missy Wright, and ZáNean McClain puts skateboarding into historical, social, cultural, and community contexts as it highlights the processes through which today's skaters give meaning to skating experiences and shape environments through their activities. Those of us who study the social aspects of sports often focus our attention on the organization and dynamics of sport experiences, the meanings given to them, and how people integrate those experiences and meanings into their lives. We distinguish between many sport forms as we study their social dynamics and significance. For example, we may distinguish between sports as recreational or competitive, informal or organized, action/alternative/extreme or mainstream, amateur or professional, individual or team, and developmental or elite, among other ways of categorizing them.

A distinction I've found useful is between *prolympic sports* and *people's sports.* The former refer to formally organized competitive physical activities based on a merger of professional and "Olympic" models. They are controlled and sustained by governing bodies that establish and enforce rules and generate resources that come from spectators, sponsors, and media companies. Because they focus on outcomes, *prolympic sports* tend to exclude participants who don't meet certain skill requirements. *People's sports,* on the other hand, are process-oriented and participant-controlled physical activities based on local traditions and movement cultures. Although they may be associated with a local group or club, they are created, controlled, and sustained by participants through their social networks and personal resources. Inclusion is valued, but it is mediated by those networks and the norms they create. *Prolympic sports* emphasize entertainment and keep official records, whereas *people's sports* emphasize experiences, relationships, and authenticity.

For most of its history, skateboarding has been a people's sport. It was created by and for skaters, with its popularity ebbing and flowing with the interests and efforts of young people, primarily young men who used it and surfing as signature activities and expressions of antiestablishment rebellion. Participation during the 1950s and '60s was largely confined to southern California and limited by the risks of skating on unforgiving steel or clay wheels attached to DIY decks. Wipeouts were a regular occurrence and hitting concrete surfaces produced more serious injuries than hitting surf. The move from ocean waves to streets and empty, bowl-shaped swimming pools took a toll on skaters' bodies and led them to be defined as troublemakers.

Seen as a dangerous activity performed by scruffy-looking surfers on quests for endless summers, skateboarding declined in popularity until the mid-1970s, when new urethane wheels were combined with flexible wood and composite decks. Like the introduction of shorter, user-friendly Alpine skis, and bikes designed to handle off-road terrains, the easier-to-control boards attracted new participants seeking challenging physical activities without controlling coaches who blew whistles, ran drills, and punished players with laps and wind sprints. At the same time, the deviant, devil-may-care image of skateboarders was perpetuated in magazines—a fact that attracted many young males and worried their parents.

A slalom and freestyle contest held in Del Mar, California, in 1975 attracted attention as top skaters were introduced to a wide audience. The first skate parks were built during the late 1970s, but liability issues and insurance costs slowed the growth of both public and private skating venues at that time. As skaters continued to use sidewalks, streets, and other hard surfaces, they clashed with cars, pedestrians, businesses, and pool owners. This intensified their reputation as troublemakers and perpetuated the antiestablishment subculture of skateboarding, but it also slowed its growth.

The invention of VHS technology and widespread access to video cameras during the 1980s gave skaters opportunities to create videos showing their signature moves. As these videos were copied and shared, the visibility of skateboarding and its creative possibilities spread world-wide. Top skaters earned reputations that led to endorsements. Skateboard and apparel companies fueled growth as they marketed products to young males, a targeted consumer demographic in most wealthy countries. Board shapes and designs became increasingly diverse and individualized as skaters sought new experiences on a range of surfaces and terrains.

The antiestablishment culture of skateboarding was supported during the 1990s as many skaters embraced punk and other raucous rock music. But when ESPN sponsored the first X Games in 1995, skate-boarding received a major boost as people began to see it as a legitimate sport. This marked a turning point and propelled it into the mainstream of popular physical culture. As more young people saw skateboarding as an alternative to formally organized, adult-controlled competitive sports, it grew in multiple directions across a range of age cohorts. Helmets, protective pads, and improved board features led parents to be more sup-portive of their children who experimented with skateboards and spent time with other skaters.

As communities became willing to deal with liability issues during the first decade of the twenty-first century, they funded a growing number of skate parks. Skateboarding video games further hooked young people and recruited them into the sport. Boards also came to be seen as a handy, efficient mode of transportation that fit in school lockers and were easily carried on unfriendly surfaces. Skateboarding grows and *Moving Boarders* enters the scene. Atencio, Beal, Wright, and McClain team up to describe and explain local examples of the *institutionalization* of skateboarding. They trace the processes though which skateboarding and the relation-ships that constitute it are being organized in the Bay Area to meet the interests of participants, sponsors, emerging grassroots leaders, and others impacted by the sport. As readers move through the chapters, they learn that these processes occur on multiple levels from local skate parks to neighborhoods and communities. The processes described by the authors are grounded in and mediated by social, economic, and political forces, as skateboarders and their advocates lobby for access to spaces where skaters can learn skills, express themselves though their moves, and participate in contests that bring them local and even regional recognition.

Moving Boarders gives us a preview of the institutionalization of skateboarding that also occurs nationally and internationally. For example, the Tokyo 2020 Skateboarding Commission is planning and will manage the Skateboard Street and Park Terrain events during the 2020 Olympic Games. The Commission, formed with assistance from the International Olympic Committee (IOC), encouraged the merger of the Fédération Internationale de Roller Sports (FIRS) and the International Skateboarding Federation (ISF). These two federations (FIRS and ISF) recently formed World Skate, a new organization that governs and manages the officially recognized disciplines in skateboarding and roller sports worldwide. World Skate will oversee the global development of these disciplines, create standardized processes for judging competitions, and monitor the rules and rule enforcement for national skateboarding and roller sport federations.

As institutionalization occurs on the local and international levels, skateboarding undergoes changes that please some and upset others. As it makes the transition from a *people's sport* to a *prolympic sport*, equipment is standardized, scoring schemes are developed, judges are trained and certified, performances and tricks are ranked by difficulty, performance styles are evaluated, and skaters worldwide seek to imitate the performances of medal winners. At the same time, local, regional, and national contests are developed and sponsored as communities seek to cash in on sport tourism and as corporations recruit new consumers of skate-related products.

Skateboarding as a *people's sport* will not disappear, but it will fade as parents become involved and local competitions are planned by non-skaters. Skills will continue to be learned informally, but skateboarding classes and coaches will become increasingly common. Pedagogies for teaching skateboarding will be developed and explained in articles and books read by skate entrepreneurs wanting to make a living in the sport they love. Age-segregated classes and competitions will gradually erode the age-integrated participation that has long been an attractive feature of skateboarding. Among skaters, the unregulated search for hard surfaces, edges, slopes, and jumps will give way to the regulated use of skate parks and other venues.

As this transition occurs, the IOC-sanctioned governing body for skateboarding, World Skate, claims that it will provide "direction and governance to the sport of skateboarding worldwide while upholding the *culture, authenticity and lifestyle of skateboarding that is freedom of self-expression, passion and creativity*" (italics added).[1] But achieving this goal be a never-ending challenge. One issue is how skateboarding competitions will be judged and who will create the standards used to evaluate aspects such as fun, freedom of expression, creativity, innovation, and progression. These elements constitute skate culture and have attracted so many people to the sport. Another concern is that World Skate oversees skateboarding and nine other roller sport disciplines (artistic roller skating, roller freestyle, inline alpine, inline downhill, inline freestyle, inline hockey, roller derby, rink hockey, and speed roller skating). They will want to distinguish each discipline so there is no significant overlap between them. To do this, they will standardize each one and position themselves to be the official enforcer of those standards. This will empower their executives and keep them in line to benefit from the revenue-producing potential of each discipline.

As a sociologist, I will look to *Moving Boarders* as a benchmark of current skateboarding organization and use it to track changes as skateboarding transitions from a *people's sport* to a *prolympic sport*. My hope is that many members of the skating culture resist this transition and maintain the self-expression, passion, and creativity that have long existed in the sport. Additionally, it would be encouraging to see the sport become increasingly inclusive with respect to gender, ethnicity, social class, and ability.

The skate parks that I've visited over the past few years attract far more people than the chronically empty baseball and softball fields and tennis courts that still occupy prime physical activity spaces in communities. This, along with information in this book, should serve as a wakeup call for parents, community leaders, and others who wonder how to foster regular physical activities among young people. It is clear that many young people seek activities that allow them freedom of expression and opportunities to be creative. If there is a sequel to *Moving Boarders* in 2028, it would be heartening to see that skateboarders taught us an important lesson about the experiences that will motivate people of all ages to be physically active.

Jay Coakley

SERIES EDITOR'S PREFACE

Sport is an extraordinarily important phenomenon that pervades the lives of many people and has enormous impact on society in an assortment of different ways. At its most fundamental level, sport has the power to bring people great joy and satisfy their competitive urges while at once allowing them to form bonds and a sense of community with others from diverse backgrounds and interests and various walks of life. Sport also makes clear, especially at the highest levels of competition, the lengths that people will go to achieve victory, as well as how closely connected it is to business, education, politics, economics, religion, law, family, law, family, and other societal institutions. Sport is, moreover, partly about identity development and how individuals and groups, irrespective of race, gender, ethnicity or socioeconomic class, have sought to elevate their status and realize material success and social mobility.

Sport, Culture, and Society seeks to promote a greater understanding of the aforementioned issues and many others. Recognizing sport's powerful influence and ability to change people's lives in significant and important ways, the series focuses on topics ranging from urbanization and community development to biographies and intercollegiate athletics. It includes both monographs and anthologies that are characterized by excellent scholarship, accessible to a wide audience, and interesting and thoughtful in design and interpretations. Singular features of the series are authors and editors representing a variety of disciplinary areas and who adopt different methodological approaches. The series also includes works by individuals at various stages of their careers, both sport-studies scholars of outstanding talent just beginning to make their mark on the field and more experienced scholars of sport with established reputations.

Moving Boarders: Skateboarding and the Changing Landscape of Urban Youth Sports is an insightful examination of skateboarding and its increasing acceptance as an action sport that has contributed to positive youth development and community health promotion. Matthew Atencio, along with his colleagues Becky Beal, E. Missy Wright, and ZáNean McClain, provide an ethnographic study centered in the San Francisco Bay Area that makes clear the changes in local skateboarding culture and the importance of new skate parks developed in this region's urban neighborhoods. Based on 62 interviews, including 26 with parents (and grandparents), 19 with children and youth, and 17 with people associated in some way with skate parks, the authors paint a vivid picture of a multilayered skateboarding culture involving parents, community leaders, private industries, city governments, and nonprofit groups who immersed themselves in the sport for a variety of reasons and purposes. Among these stakeholders, it is parents who have become especially avid supporters of skateboarding, believing that it can potentially help their children acquire certain benefits and forms of capital.

David K. Wiggins

ACKNOWLEDGMENTS

We could not have written this book without the support of many people. Firstly, we appreciate the institutional support we received from our Department of Kinesiology and the College of Education and Allied Studies at California State University, East Bay. Some financial support for this work was provided by the Division of Academic Affairs at California State University, East Bay through a Faculty Support Grant. Additionally, we had several of our students contribute to this project as Research Assistants, through activities that included doing field observations and interviews, conducting literature searches, and editing and referencing the manuscript. These include Ebow Dawson-Andoh, Liem Tran, Jessica Ji Hyeon Lee, Anastasiya Stebikhova, Havalind Farnik, Colleen Swafford, Adrienne Bugglin, Jasmine Jow, and Laura Greene. Furthermore, Leanne Perry provided invaluable editorial support as well as referencing assistance over the entire manuscript. Also, Tod Wright provided critical comments that helped shape the introductory book chapters.

We have met many amazing adults who have given time and energy to their neighborhoods and youth. Many are featured in *Moving Boarders*, yet we cannot name them all because of our need to ensure anonymity. We sincerely appreciate the time they gave to us. Additionally, we are grateful to the photographers who were willing to share their photos for this book, including Todd Fuller, Keith "K-Dub" Williams, Kim Woozy, and Bethanie Hines. The cover photo was provided to us by Sariah Adviento.

Dr. Jay Coakley's outstanding youth-sports research has greatly influenced the ideas found in this book. We are very pleased that he provided the forward to *Moving Boarders*. We would also like to thank Dr. Oliver Laasch for pointing us to the literature on social enterprise and sport. In addition, Dr. Carolyn Nelson first suggested that we investigate the phenomenon of public-private networks that are making positive social contributions in the Bay Area. The editorial staff and production team at University of Arkansas Press has provided tremendous guidance and support throughout the process. We especially want to thank Dr. David Wiggins, our Editor, for providing such prompt and insightful feedback throughout the book project; his guidance enabled us to tell the skateboarding stories that we wanted to tell.

Finally, we are grateful to our friends and families for their continued support during this four-year project. Matthew Atencio would like to thank his wife, Lyndsey, and daughter, Eilidh, for their immense support, understanding, and sacrifice. Many family trips were tied in with visits to skate parks, and book writing took precedence for over three years. In addition, Matthew would like to thank members of the Atencio family for sharing their youth sports insights about participating, coaching, and parenting. Becky Beal would like to thank her partner, Jennifer Sexton. ZáNean McClain would like to thank several members of her family, including mother Jacqueline Haynes, sisters Gwendolyn McClain and DáFona Jackson, nieces Jurnee and Jaxin Woodward, and daughter Jazzlyn McClain, for their constant support and dedication. They attended and participated in numerous skate-park events, gave feedback, and kept things positive. Missy Wright sends her appreciation to Alaine Karoleff and Anne Schmitt for their support around the house during the long days and nights of writing and editing. Missy's parents have also been a continued source of encouragement, which she values greatly.

MOVING BOARDERS

Picture of urban skateboarders and their supporters.
Courtesy of Todd Fuller.

Youth Sports and the Urban Skateboarding Landscape

Robert is a forty-nine-year-old father of two children. In conversation at a local skate park near Northern California's Silicon Valley, he articulated how his son and daughter, now both teenagers, first became involved in skateboarding: "You know, when the kids were little, between like three and five, we exposed them to almost every sport. Every one we could think of; that we had some knowledge of. So, that included baseball, soccer. I was a soccer player so I coached their soccer. I thought they were both going to be soccer players. Football, basketball, swimming; they did all of those in group form. [I] took them skiing." Robert went on to finish his thought, recalling his son's avid participation in skateboarding rather than traditional youth sports: "He never really liked the group sports. And we had just got him a skateboard . . . some cheap thing from Target or whatever." Over a decade since buying his first low-priced skateboard, Robert's son Brady is now sponsored by a surf shop and Vans shoes.

Another parent, Gloria, revealed how her son Trevor was spurred on to skateboard after he went to the opening of a skate park and saw people "skating in the big bowl." After he received two skateboards for Christmas at the age of six, Trevor started practicing on the living-room rug. As we continued to talk in a local skate park, Gloria lamented that she preferred that her son play "America's Game." A parenting tug-of-war was going on over whether Trevor should hit baseballs or ride the skateboard. She told us, "The difference is that we wanted him to play baseball. He wanted to skate. This is kind of his thing. Baseball is kind of our thing." As we talked during the interview, Gloria went on to suggest that her son prefers "skateboarding because it's the freedom that he can go off and do his own thing" whereas in baseball, "he doesn't have as much freedom because he's on a team." She ultimately conceded, "I had to let him do it. He's a boy, he's going to do it."

Over three and a half years of research, we heard many stories like these while talking to parents about their skateboarding kids. *Moving Boarders: Skateboarding and the Changing Landscape of Urban Youth*

Sports concomitantly tells us how skateboarding has begun to challenge the preeminent position of traditional youth sports in the United States. The fact is that many team and organized youth sports have recently lost a foothold in the lives of children and their parents. Taking up this premise, our book exemplifies how American youth sports, a major rite of passage for so long, must now take into account the huge popularity of *action sports*.[1] In parallel with this shift, *Moving Boarders* tells the story of how skateboarding, once condemned as a pursuit for mostly "raw" boys and young men, is now being taken very seriously by many American families.[2] Today, tremendous momentum is behind the notion that skateboarding is an accessible and beneficial activity for all kids. And this popular view goes far beyond appreciation for the skills needed to maneuver a board, and involves perceived positive learning and socialization elements. Furthermore, skateboarding has burst into mainstream view, "on a wave of multimedia appeal," if you believe the *New York Times*.[3] Take, for instance, Tony Hawk, who is known both for his billion-dollar video-game franchise and regular appearances on the globally televised X Games.[4] Not surprisingly, Hawk was recently distinguished as the most recognizable athlete in the United States among the youth demographic.[5] Then, there is the MTV favorite Rob Dyrdek, who can be considered a mega celebrity with his "mainstream fan base" that props up an eight-figure business empire.[6]

Further testifying to its popular standing, skateboarding is now synonymous with the Olympic spirit. In fact, the International Olympic Committee (IOC) has unanimously voted to include skateboarding as an official event in the 2020 Tokyo Summer Olympic Games. The official Olympic Channel promotional site on Facebook already has a tagline for this change: "From broken bones to big dreams."[7] This sanctioning, reliant upon skateboarding's "vast youth appeal," will surely captivate a wider international audience, to the elation of corporate sponsors everywhere.[8] Market-research projections already indicate that by the time Tokyo 2020 comes around, the skateboarding equipment market will exceed over $5 billion (U.S.) in value. And it is projected that skateboards, along with shoes and protective equipment, will become must-have items.[9]

And skateboarding is not just for the youth. It is to the point where the American Association of Retired Persons (AARP) is promoting the benefits of skateboarding for retirees:

> Seeking activities that brought her joy, Odanaka decided to revisit her childhood hobby of skateboarding, which she gave up at the

age of 13 to focus on running track. Soon enough, Odanaka found so many moms interested in joining her at the skate park that she started Moms Who Skate, a club for women in their 40s, 50s, and older who enjoyed skating. Despite the scrapes, bumps, and bruises that come along with skateboarding, the women cheer each other on and support each other to overcome their fears.[10]

Older adults on boards is an important example; this phenomenon illustrates how skateboarding is now considered appropriate for all segments of society.[11] The legitimization of skateboarding, for both young and old, is something that we wanted to study. We felt that the everyday experiences and motivations of its expanding participant base needed to be understood. With this goal in mind, *Moving Boarders* contributes to our knowledge of skateboarding, and youth sports more generally, by examining diverse stakeholders located across several skate scenes. This book provides a closer examination of various meanings and belief systems that now accompany involvement in skate activity. In particular, a key premise that we address is that American families are now fueling the current youth skateboarding explosion. As a matter of fact, a skate shop owner from Harlem observes, "Now a kid comes in my shop and he's like, 'Yo, Mom, can I get a skateboard?'"[12] Parents are actually on board with the idea that skateboarding is important to their children's lives. Consider the following social network testimonial provided by a parent in response to a Bay Area community's proposed skate park[13]:

Dear Council Member,

I am a Danville dad and business owner who has been living here for close to 20 years . . . I grew up in Southern California where skateboarding was my go-to activity as a young kid and I still skate today. Over 30 years on a board and I absolutely love it. (Don't try to guess my age.) My son, like many sons, has lots of team sport activities to choose from in Danville (soccer, baseball, basketball, etc.) which offers a great sense of community for those boys and girls that enjoy team sports. However, there is a large group of kids, as well as adults, who enjoy action sports who are not interested in playing team sports and we are forced to travel to do it. It really is sad when my son says he wants to go skating and we are forced to plan it for the weekend because of the 30-minute drive to get to a decent skate park. What happens to the local kids whose parents just don't have the time to drive that far for them? It's sad to think about. We put so much time into our local kids but disregard a large segment of our own population. It's just not right. These are great kids. For me as a kid, skating had its own sense of community that changed my life. We were misunderstood alternative sport kids, but action sports tends to bring in a different class of unique personalities and fosters out-of-the-box thinking and creativity. (References upon request.) Looking back now, the kids I skated with are now scientists, school principals, artists, doctors, firemen, policemen, financial planners, and founders of companies. So when people say skate parks create a culture for misguided youth, it infuriates me. It couldn't be further from the truth; it actually helps guide people and helps people challenge their personal fears to become better versions of themselves. So, next time you see a somewhat sketchy looking character at a skate park, go up and say hi; you might be surprised. They also may be the next Silicon Valley hotshot or pull you out of a fire someday. You never know . . . If the skate park DOES exist, we have a single epicenter for activity where lives will move forward, connections will be made, personal challenges can be overcome, lifelong bonds will be made and ultimately the love for Danville will be furthered into the next generation.

Throughout the course of this book, it will become obvious that skateboarding fluently traverses mainstream sport status and its older reputation as an underground activity. The current state of skateboarding is not only being influenced by parental support, but also by corporate, government, and nonprofit bodies that are spreading their particular visions of urban and youth development. These additional supporters seek to advance their own unique projects which eventually create new forms of urban space. To examine and explain the social dynamics of these skate spaces, we focus on four neighborhoods in the San Francisco Bay Area. This community-based approach is warranted by the belief that rich, local descriptions can reflect the nuanced "cultural politics" of youth-sports participation.[14] Importantly, even though we focused on community issues, key social debates at the local level don't exist in isolation. Many of these local concerns mirror national debates about contemporary American youth sports. Our approach, therefore, is to use evidence-based analyses in order to explain certain social patterns and shifts taking place specifically through urban skateboarding practice. We want to push current thinking regarding how modern youth sports like skateboarding may profoundly impact America's urban landscapes. This aim led us to move away from providing a more generic, "one-size-fits-all" portrait of youth-sports participation and instead focus upon explaining the multifarious skateboarding practices found within diverse urban communities.

Adults, Professionalization, and Traditional American Youth Sports

To understand the place that skateboarding has now in the American imagination, we describe the broader societal context of traditional youth sports. Compiling the exact number of American kids playing youth sports is a tough task, even for experienced researchers; still, available studies clearly indicate that *most* kids have played youth sports *at some point* in their lives.[15] This statement is telling, in that it illustrates the grand stature of youth sports in the United States. It is "almost a national obsession," according to one recent NBC news report.[16] Indeed, a view that is widely held in this nation is that youth sports *have never been more important* to the lives of children and their parents.

Despite the currency of such views among Americans, it is indisputable that many youths are avoiding traditional sports as they are now offered. Youth sports participation numbers have been consistently falling for the six-to-twelve age bracket since 2008, according to the latest statistical data provided by the Aspen Institute's Project Play.[17] Notably, severe participation losses have been found in the "big four" youth sports of baseball, basketball, soccer, and football.[18] Directly highlighting this perhaps unforeseen downtrend, the *Wall Street Journal* starkly posits that "Fewer Children Play Youth Sports."[19] With regard to "dropout from organized sport," researchers have found several key contributing factors, including injuries, lack of enjoyment, as well as social pressure often due to adult interference.[20] This last idea will be particularly salient to our exploration of new coaching and parent involvement in skateboarding.

Given the competitive state of many youth sports, it is not unexpected that sociologist Michael A. Messner calls out "authoritarian coaches who treat kids like Marine Corps recruits."[21] Messner goes on to capture the essence of coach as well as parent intervention with the sardonic declaration, that in youth sports, "it's all for the kids."

The American youth-sports phenomenon is in fact unique in the world, in the sense that adults are so deeply ingrained in its fabric. Indeed, American adults feel compelled to integrate within youth sports like it's some kind of cultural duty, with their participation symbolizing moral effort and value. Parents, for instance, perceive that they are accountable for their child's success or failure in youth sports.[22] In this regard, a parent supporting two children on travel lacrosse teams from Portland, Oregon, admits in a 2017 *Time* magazine cover story, "You say to yourself, am I keeping up?" and that "there's pressure." In the same article, a soccer parent from San Diego concedes, "This sports lifestyle is crazy. But they're your kids. You do anything for them."[23]

Nevertheless, despite many good intentions, what has transpired in our society is the noticeable trend of adults controlling youth sports, which, as Project Play's Tom Farrey reminds us, "sends the message to kids that they aren't really part of the structure."[24] There is an emerging critique that well-meaning adults may, in many cases, be fostering negative experiences and outcomes for youth across many traditional sports.

At this point in the chapter, we are building the case as to why skateboarding, as a historically youth-driven activity, perhaps represents a new, viable option in the youth-sports world. Does skateboarding offer something different from the other sports described above, in terms of youth influence and participation? Or is it, too, becoming led by adults? For now, let's continue to probe further into concerns surrounding broader American youth-sports practice, because there is another major factor that strongly underpins the decline of traditional youth-sports participation. A dire prognosis is that American families "can't afford summer" anymore due to high participation costs.[25] Today, many families just cannot afford to pay the money needed for uniforms, coaching, transportation, lodging, and league fees. One commentator, for example, gives us a glimpse into this problem, highlighting "the out-of-state hotel rooms and $300 graphite bats" that are required for traveling teams nowadays.[26]

Furthermore, the problem of cost is obviously more acute for families with lesser financial resources. Project Play's 2020 Report weighs in on this concern, once again, by showing us that children from homes in the lowest income bracket remain at significant disadvantage compared to those from wealthier households, in terms of their opportunities to play sports. And this participation discrepancy seems to be increasing, as we can see in the following statistical discussion: "In 2013, the gap between kids in homes with incomes under $25,000 and those with $100,000+ households was about 23 percentage points. In 2016, the gap had increased to 32 percent percentage points."[27] As a result, American youth "have separated into sport haves and have-nots" with the lesson being that "if you don't have money, it's hard to play."[28] Families with more resources undoubtedly have a major advantage when it comes to their children's participation in youth sports.[29]

But why exactly are America's youth sports becoming so expensive to join? In her book on parenting trends, sociologist Hilary Friedman describes the current professionalization of activities like soccer:

> Since the 1980s it is not only the costs of participation in competitive children's activities that have grown, but also the level of professionalization. As more children compete in more activities for more money at higher levels, the result over the past three decades has been the growth of hypercompetitive youth sports programming.[30]

A 2017 cover from *Time* magazine therefore unsurprisingly announces, "Kid Sports Turned Pro."[31] The point being made here is that hyper-expensive youth sports modeled after the professional versions have replaced their barebones "ball and stick" predecessors.[32] Today it is not far-fetched to say that there is an ongoing "arms race" in an increasingly privatized youth-sports scene. For example, parents are enrolling kids as young as two in private "toddler soccer" classes linked with elite clubs.[33] Also, a 2016 thread on Quora, an online "Q and A" forum, opens with the following query (presumably from an overenthusiastic parent): "How can a 4-year-old join the FC Barcelona Academy?"[34] This question is perhaps not so outlandish as it seems: the *Washington Post* also tells us that kindergarteners are now being ranked by basketball analysts.[35]

The upshot here is that because of our highly professionalized youth-sports culture, American parents must perform cost-benefit analysis when determining how to support their children's participation. How much time, effort, and resources are needed to get just the right pay off? And let's keep in mind that parenting the next Lionel Messi or Serena Williams is only one perceived outcome out of many; parents often want to ensure that their children benefit through their participation socially and educationally, too. In fact, from the parental point of view, youth-sports participation can lead to a plethora of possible outcomes for youth.

To underscore the changing nature of American youth sports, with significant adult involvement now dovetailing with the privatization of participation, this book relies upon the concept of neoliberalism. It is indisputable that a shift toward private-industry thinking has occurred since the latter decades of the twentieth century. Our next chapter will spell out this neoliberal concept with much more depth. For now, we can turn to sport sociologists David L. Andrews and Michael Silk for a preliminary working definition:

> The basic prescription of neoliberalism is . . . purge the system of obstacles to the functioning of free markets; celebrate virtues of individualism (recast social problems as individual problems, such as drug use, obesity or inadequate health insurance) and competitiveness; foster economic self-sufficiency, abolish or weaken social programs.[36]

What's more, social critic Henry Giroux avers that "neoliberalism extends into all aspects of daily life" whereby "the boundaries of the cultural, economic, and political become porous and leak into each other."[37] In simple terms, this means that private industry logic now prevails, and determines life in not only economic and political spheres, but also within cultural realms such as youth sports. Neoliberalism, we thus show, gives rise to unprecedented adult intervention in American youth sports activity.

The Mainstream Appeal of Skateboarding

We have outlined that the seemingly sacrosanct fare of traditional, organized youth sports has been called into question on a national scale. Concerns about adult dominance and the trend of privatization have arisen in the contemporary youth-sports dialogue. In this context, we now turn to speculate how skateboarding may represent a viable sporting alternative for American youth, as well as their families. Indeed, it is worth speculating about traditional youth sports' current stasis or even decline to contextualize skateboarding's newfound appreciation in American family life. How might skateboarding offer something different from traditional youth sports? And, yet, at the same time, how may today's version of skateboarding come to resemble these activities?

At this point in time, it cannot be denied that activities like surfing, snowboarding, and skateboarding have gained much cultural traction. Today, these activities can no longer be thought of as niche, extreme, or alternative pursuits, as they are regularly integrated within people's everyday lifestyles and identities.[38] Because of certain intrinsic elements, it could be argued that activities like skateboarding are especially befitting to youth. For instance, scholar Emily Chivers Yochim, in her award-winning book *Skate Life*, suggests that "the relative lack of organization, rules, routines, coaches, playing fields, game times and so on in most types of skateboarding is appealing to many skateboarders."[39] What's more, she says that having fun is a key motivational factor that drives youth to become skateboarders.[40]

Now vying to capture the imagination of youth, skateboarding also, in part, addresses the need for more affordable participation. Skateboarding has a relatively cheap entry point, with Chivers Yochim breaking down the cost in these terms: "skateboarding can be practiced virtually anywhere with relatively small entry fees. A skateboard costs between 20 and 120 dollars, requires no special clothing, and can be practiced on any paved street, sidewalk, or driveway."[41] In our own study, an ex-professional skateboarder who coaches newcomer youth told us, "A lot of kids, they've come with Walmart boards or Target boards."

Skateboarding at the youth level is clearly an enjoyable, low-cost sport. Thus, underlying *Moving Boarders* is the premise that skateboarding has gained popular youth interest. But, simultaneously, parents are increasingly coveting the potential benefits of this activity, helping it to become such a fast-growing youth sport. One expert even concludes that now, "the soccer mom has become the skate mom."[42] This type of "family-friendly" skateboarding makes us wonder how youth and adults coexist in skate parks and evolve this activity.

Parent appreciation actually dovetails with skateboarding's exploding transnational presence, as this activity's "ideas, images, and styles" have global reach.[43] Statistics are important when examining the scale of skateboarding's recent popularity. At a domestic level, in 2007, it was reported that skateboarding was easily the most popular action sport with 12 million American participants, including 4.7 million frequent participants skating over 30 days per year. Most of these participants were young, "between the ages of 7 and 17 with an average age of 14."[44] Sport sociologist Holly Thorpe adds that, as recently as 2008, skateboarding was considered *the* fastest-growing sport in the United States.[45] The most up-to-date statistics report that skateboarding participation still remains robust, especially for "Generation Z" youths born since the mid-1990s, both in terms of frequent and casual participation.[46] Attesting to its popular status, skateboarding now has its own national Go Skateboarding Day and even a Skateboarding Hall of Fame is now up and running.[47] Further, as previously noted in this chapter, skateboarding for the first time has been officially included in the Summer Olympic Games.

The cultural coveting of skateboarding is also reflected in its vast industry and consumer base.[48] Crystallizing this belief, one skateboarding coach in our region told us that "it's now more 'trendful' within the economy." Skateboarding's acceptance as serious business can be seen in a recent master's degree course, Skateboarding and Action Sports in Business, Media, and Culture, at the University of Southern California.[49] This type of course is timely, given that skateboarding supports a thriving multi-billion-dollar industry.[50] *Fortune* magazine, for instance, reports that Vans, "the highly popular, eternally youthful skater footwear brand," reached $2.3 billion in shoe sales during 2016.[51] Other affiliated soft goods such as skate lifestyle clothing are also now in high demand. Skateboarding is even fusing with high fashion; a recent *New York Times* article notes that "skate enthusiasts" can now partake in the "elevated aesthetic" confines of a Lower Manhattan clothing showroom.[52]

It is thus well-established that, with mainstream cultural assimilation, skateboarding is no longer under the exclusive purview of niche, rebellious youth beholden to countercultural beliefs and maverick personae. Today, skateboarding's popular status clearly resonates with at least some traditional mainstream sports values. Increasing adult and corporate involvement, in particular, challenges us to consider who supports and controls skateboarding activity.

The Diversification of Skateboarding Participants

This book demonstrates how skateboarding attracts people from from all walks of life. Skateboarding indeed has a rich history of cultural diversity, despite popular perceptions that it is mostly a white person's sport.[53] Legendary skateboarder Stacy Peralta once made the following claim: "Street skating opened up ethnicity in a huge way. It made it possible for impoverished inner-city kids to skate, because all they needed was a skateboard and surrounding architecture."[54] And with the return of skate parks, which we discuss later on, it is now undeniable that, from coast to coast, skateboarders of color are now *even more* involved and visible.[55] It has thus been claimed that contemporary skateboarding represents "a hotbed of culturally-rich, diverse participants."[56] This assertion rings true particularly in diverse, multicultural urban environments such as the San Francisco Bay Area, as we will see in the chapters of *Moving Boarders*.

In fact, skateboarding's newly acquired marketability and cultural cachet is often derived from its inextricable association with urban-based racial and ethnic identities. *Entertainment Weekly* recalls that urban musicians such as Pharrell Williams and other hip hop MCs are "taking cues from ghetto-fab celeb skaters like Stevie Williams and Marcus McBride."[57]

At the turn of this century, multinational corporations such as Reebok, Levi's, and Nike began to portray skateboarding as a form of urban expression to sell their goods.[58] In regards to this branding approach, a skate-park leader in our study once told us that "so many musicians and hip hop artists, the young independent cats are all wear skateboarding stuff, a lot of them all skate. . . . And it's just really interesting to see it kind of come to the inner city and have them be hip and be considered cool." *Moving Boarders* speaks to this attribute of racial and ethnic diversity that now underpins skateboarding's rising popularity. What's more, we will demonstrate that this type of social diversity is being recognized and accounted for by many urban families, community groups, and corporations. We also invoke more critical views regarding the elements of race and ethnicity in the skateboarding scene.

Related to this phenomenon of social diversity, there has also been a definite uptick in female skateboarding participation. The female presence in skateboarding first became overt with the iconic Patti McGee handstand on a *Life* magazine cover in 1965. Women remained prominent until the beginning of the 1980s. Female skateboarding in the past included a roll call of famous names like Ellen O'Neal, Vicki Vickers, Laura Thornhill, Robin Alaway, Kim Cespedes, and Peggi Oki. Oki was on the Zephyr Team of *Dogtown and Z-Boys* fame. Largely centered in California, the women's scene was comprised of traveling teams and contests. Ellen Berryman, known for her choreographed gymnastic-style skating, described this era as "mostly surfers (who) were innovatively applying their art to the skateboard and taking advantage of the urethane wheel."[59]

However, once punk-rock and skateboarding cultures merged in the 1980s, Duane Peters's "Master of Disaster" style of in-your-face masculinity came to exemplify skate culture. Female participation was at its lowest point during the 1980s, when skateboarding was generally construed as an *urban male street activity*. However, women reestablished a presence as professionals beginning with skaters such as Cara-Beth Burnside and Elissa Steamer in the 1990s, with the latter featuring in several *Tony Hawk's Pro Skater* video games. Regarding women's participation today, we can see that "there are plenty of sick new pros you should know."[60] For example, skaters such as Vanessa Torres, Samarria Brevard, Nora Vasconcellas, and Lizzie Armanto are just a few of the female names currently advancing the sport.

Even younger girls are becoming part of the rising female skate scene. Skateboarding since the age of three, Sky Brown has been dubbed a "pint-sized badass skating prodigy."[61] Similarly, a local Bay Area skater, Minna Stess, made history by becoming the first girl to win the California Amateur Skateboard League (CASL) series, and also took an event title at the King of the Groms contest in Minneapolis.[62] She was the youngest person to ever go down the twenty-seven-foot Woodward West mega ramp in Northern California.[63] Stess also now features in several Lego television commercials.[64]

Beyond these individual success stories, female skate crews are also coming onto the scene. An all-female skate group from New York known as "the Brujas" (which in Spanish means "the Witches") regularly whizzes through the streets of the Bronx, where "they still tend to turn heads."[65] Over on the West Coast, there is the Pink Helmet Posse. These three girls were invited guests on *The Ellen DeGeneres Show* and also featured in promotional advertisements for Gap Kids. This particularly hyperbolic incarnation of the recent skater-girl phenomenon is described below:

> The newest skateboarding sensations to hit the scene in Southern California are crazy talented, crazy daring, and also crazy adorable. You can spot them by their pink helmets, fluffy tutus, and funky knee socks. Their names are Relz Murphy, Sierra Kerr, and Bella Kenworthy. They're 6 years old.[66]

Discussion about skateboarding's increasingly diverse gendered, racial, and ethnic constituents will accordingly take place throughout this book. Social class is another related factor influencing skateboarding that we address in our chapters. This type of sociocultural discussion also directs attention to the actual spaces where these participants skate and socialize. We must therefore take into consideration the actual skate parks that are being prolifically used by American youths. Skateboarding's mainstream popularity, this book argues, now relies upon the superabundance of multi-million-dollar skate parks that are being constructed around the world.[67] This phenomenon has been dubbed as the "skate infrastructure building boom."[68] It is not surprising that skateboarding, as one parks and recreation supervisor excitedly told us, has "become so mainstream" that now "everybody's got one [skate park]!" This claim is backed up by one story in *Parks and Rec Business* magazine, which states that "Skateparks are quickly becoming the darling of a city's recreational needs, as opposed to 20 years ago when they were considered a frivolous waste of public funds. Why the change? Skateparks have proven to be the most used park, per square foot, in the parks and rec portfolio."[69]

Picture of females at a skate park event.
Courtesy of Kimberly Woo.

But how exactly did skate parks become so fundamental to skateboarding practice? Below, we address this question, and reveal how the proliferation of urban skate parks currently shapes modern skateboarding practice.

Skateboarding and the Rise of American Skate Parks

Following decades of ebbs and flows in participation, skateboarding experienced a resurgence in the mid-1980s due to its reinvention as an aggressive, street-based male subculture.[70] Immortalized nationwide in historic hotspots such as San Francisco's Embarcadero, Portland's Burnside, as well as Philadelphia's own skate mecca, LOVE Park, we can see that skateboarding has often been done in unsupervised, organic city spaces.[71] Over several decades, however, this grassroots male street practice has increasingly been juxtaposed with municipal skate parks constructed by city governments, and in many cases, corporate sponsors.

But how did the skate park emerge in the first place? The rise of sanctioned skate parks nationwide can be traced back as early as 1975, when governing bodies and private companies began catering to skateboarders seeking a more controlled and less dangerous experience.[72] These spaces were most often pay-to-play, with skate park entrepreneurs taking full advantage of heightened skateboarding interest. At the same time, as mentioned by Jay Coakley in this book's foreword, skateboarding's growth was being influenced by the invention of polyurethane wheels that allowed for more traction and a softer feel than clay or steel.[73] However, because of skyrocketing insurance premiums grounded in lawsuit concerns, skate parks shut down by the beginning of the early 1980s. Skate parks briefly regained popularity again in the mid-1980s, buoyed by key individuals such as Tony Hawk's father, Frank Hawk, a former World War II Navy fighter pilot. The elder Hawk helped to form a skateboarding league and association. Skate park contests were held where his now-famous son showcased his burgeoning *vert* skills, rolling up and down the ramps.[74]

Eventually skate parks became more established in the mid-1990s due to industry investment, change in liability laws, and popular events such as the Extreme Games. These televised contests later became known as the X Games by the end of the 1990s. Further support for skateboarding's resurgence came from a variety of new stakeholders and investors, with corporations like ESPN and Vans getting heavily involved. Other organizations, such as the International Association of Skateboard Companies and the Skate Park Association of the United States, were also created to support what has become known as skateboarding's "fourth wave of popularity."[75]

Today, skate parks have expanded participation in this sport, several decades after the original building trend began. Over a relatively short recent period, skate parks have been constructed across many American communities. Architectural scholar Ocean Howell once revealed that there were over 2000 skate parks in the United States by 2008, representing an increase from just 200 skate parks in the early 1990s.[76] The "Skaters for Public Skateparks" advocacy group has claimed that, in just 2011 alone, over 100 skate parks were constructed across the United States.[77] And these skate parks are now getting a positive reception in communities that are both big and small. Take Carthage, Missouri, for example, which has a population of approximately 15,000 people. A local newspaper story hailed the construction of its new skate park, next to Mark Twain Elementary School, as "a home run."[78]

This current skate-park boom reverberates globally, as major projects have been completed in London, Marseilles, Calgary, Tokyo, Shanghai, Barcelona, Montreal, and the Cayman Islands, to name only a few places.[79] In one ostentatious example of skate-park construction, the Chinese Government in 2005 constructed a skate park that was considered the world's largest at the time.[80] This location was three times the size of the largest skate park in the United States and it came at a cost of more than $8 million (U.S.).

In one sense, the reestablishment of skate parks followed public concerns with street skateboarders, typically males, and their perceived anti-social behavior. "They [street skateboarders] are a pain. They scare little old ladies ... everybody," once claimed a police chief from Los Angeles.[81] "Moral panic" surrounding "unsavory types" associated with street skateboarding's subculture led to the advent of regulated skate parks.[82] But increasingly, skate parks are becoming viewed as useful city infrastructure catering to a burgeoning recreation base and a multi-billion-dollar market which includes tourism. City leaders across the nation are now highly motivated to construct skate parks, with these spaces being labeled "zones of economic activity."[83] The private industries have also played a key role in building new skate parks. The behemoth 30,000-square-foot Vans skate park based in an Orange County shopping mall serves as a glaring example of this corporate involvement. And, intriguingly, many new skate parks have been built with support from skateboarding celebrities including Tony Hawk, Rob Dyrdek, Steve Berra, and Eric Koston.

Going forward, what we will see in *Moving Boarders* is that families are paying immense attention to the skate park building boom. Indeed, skate parks have typically been the places where parents get involved, according to one skateboarding advocate we interviewed:

> [Historically] parents brought them [kids] to the skate park. They brought them to the YMCA. They bought them pads and helmets and they bought them—a lot of the skate parks do have the more, I don't know, I guess traditional environment of dropping your kids off at the pool or something. You have to pay to get in and you have to sign a waiver, too, but maybe some parents I think feel safer because it's not like any random drug dealer can walk in.

Clearly, families have had an affinity for skateboarding that occurs within the more controlled confines of a skate park. Parents continue to consider these spaces as vital contexts to raise their children. This fact required us to further explore the perceived benefits of skate activity for America's families. With skate-park construction becoming a massive, global undertaking, we speculate next how these skate parks closely align with youth development as well as health and well-being principles. Below, we illustrate that an abundance of government and private groups, in addition to families, have latched onto the idea that skateboarding makes a considerable difference in young lives.

Skateboarding for Social Change: Ideals of Youth Development and Health Promotion

At this point, we have demonstrated that urban skateboarding has grown in terms of demographic reach due in part to new skate parks. In parallel with this view, this section details how skate parks in many communities are considered to be the perfect environment for social intervention to occur.

In one sense, skateboarding's broader acceptance is reflected in its newfound positioning as a teaching and learning tool. In a blog posting titled "Skate Park Pedagogy," a former teacher recounted a visit to his son's skate park. "What I saw was kids taking calculated risks, developing skills and confidence, approaching daunting elements in a systematic way and most of all enjoying themselves." He then concluded by stating that "schools should be like skate parks" because they foster cooperative learning, adaptability, a sense of fulfillment, and increased self-confidence.[84] Indeed, skateboarding has already been infused within some school physical education curricula, with one such program called Skate Pass. Furthermore, an elementary school in Corrimal, Australia, has a skateboarding "interest pod" held twice a week. According to teacher Paul Thompson, in the local newspaper, "The students are challenging themselves, learning about safety, thinking about how to balance and use their bodies and how to take care of themselves."[85]

This recurring belief that skateboarding benefits youth, especially in terms of their character, is a recurring theme throughout *Moving Boarders*. This idea follows the long-standing idea "that sport is a powerful and positive developmental force."[86] Further advancing the belief that action sports, in particular, are positive social forces, sport sociologist Holly Thorpe has developed the concept of "Action Sports for Development and

Peace" (ASDP).[87] ASDP encapsulates how action-sports initiatives featuring activities like skateboarding, surfing, and snowboarding can contribute to youths' health and wellbeing. It is with good reason, then, that social activists regularly use activities like skateboarding "as a force for social good."[88] The perspective that skateboarding is not destructive, but actually a good thing, especially for kids, has spread around the world. It is our belief that this perception correlates with the large number of new skate parks that have been recently erected on a global scale. Academic research already begins to support this idea that skate parks specifically offer "considerable potential for positive youth development."[89] We will revisit this theme many times in this book's chapters, where we feature numerous pro-social skate-park programs functioning in the San Francisco Bay Area.

Meanwhile, multinational corporations are increasingly coming on to the ASDP scene. The makers of Levi's jeans, Levi Strauss and Company, have recently started building skate parks around the world in under-served, developing regions. "Levi's" has constructed skate parks in locations such as La Paz, Bolivia; Bangalore, India; Oakland, California; and the Pine Ridge Indian Reservation in South Dakota as part of their community partnership program. According to one community leader who worked with Levi's in the Pine Ridge Indian Reservation project, skateboarding actually improves young people's lives. "You are that spirit on a human journey, you are meant to be here to enhance and make life better, that's Lakota way of life," says Walt Pourier. "That's what our kids need to see and move with again and literally they feel that when they're dropping into the bowl."[90]

As a matter of fact, proponents of skate-park construction often refer to the potential health benefits for adolescents.[91] A Seattle skateboarding master plan, for example, characterizes skateboarding as a healthy community activity. Under the heading "Why a Plan Now?," the Seattle Parks and Recreation department strategy details how they "adopted a Skateboard Park Policy in 2003, recognizing skateboarding as a healthy, popular recreational activity and a legitimate use to integrate into the parks system."[92] In the San Francisco Bay Area, a website petitioning for a new skate park in the city of Newark features a young man claiming, "I would rather skate than play video games, just sit around, you know."[93] The same website states, "Obesity is a problem in our youth. What do you call an obese skateboarder? A beginner. A free sport is an excellent way to encourage physical fitness, get them away from the video games, give them access to fresh air and exercise!"[94] It thus seems to us that skate-boarding, particularly within a skate park, is now envisioned by communities as a healthy outlet for youth.[95]

Long derided as a public nuisance, skateboarding is no longer considered as such. Its status has shifted dramatically as it is now increasingly characterized as a youth activity that has social, educational, and even health and well-being benefits. Below, we theorize how these purported benefits are specifically offered in the San Francisco Bay Area skate parks that we researched.

Envisioning Urban Skate Parks as Sites of "Capital" Generation

Skate parks have expanded through the incorporation of youth-development and healthy-living ideals, implicating an array of new skateboarders and affiliates. To ascertain how these stakeholders constitute diverse skate park milieus, we draw on sociological theory that explains how emerging new, diverse stakeholders have arisen. Subsequently, we theorize how these social networks foster certain benefits, or what we call "capitals," for those involved in urban skate parks.

Once again, one of our key assertions is that individuals and groups invest in skate-park activity according to a neoliberal ethos that pervades American society. In this regard, we argue that the concept of *social enterprise* is insightful; we utilize this concept frequently, as it sheds light on how public and private citizens, as well as organizations, are supporting urban skateboarding. What now brings these previously divergent public and private interests together is their desire to make positive social change. Researchers from Stanford University in fact suggest that today, "innovative social solutions cut across the traditional boundaries separating nonprofits, government, and for-profit businesses."[96] For these social-enterprise coalitions, which we recognize in the context of urban skateboarding, the "goal is to achieve a social mission."[97] *Moving Boarders* consequently illustrates how social-change agendas in urban skate parks are underpinned by "the free flow of ideas, values, roles, relationships, and money across sectors" on an unprecedented scale.[98]

Certainly, social-enterprise networks and their projects cohering around youth-development agendas have an impact upon skateboarding families. This book consequently explains how parents and their children utilize skate parks set up by social-enterprise entities to capture numerous benefits. These benefits were alluded to in our earlier discussion of ASDP;

sociological scholarship treats these benefits as "capitals", as originally outlined by French scholar Pierre Bourdieu in his classic treatise *Distinction: A Social Critique of the Judgment of Taste.* Adapting Bourdieu's conceptual framework, we contend that each skate park acts as a network of various people that interact according to the prevailing social codes and meanings that have been established over time.[99] Social status and value is conferred in a skate park according to how individuals take up and represent preferred codes and meanings. In this way, each stakeholder can potentially accrue benefits, or capitals, as Bourdieu calls them. And, as explained in the next chapter, Bourdieu suggests that these capitals are diversified, reflecting a range of economic, social, and cultural benefits.

This conceptual approach regarding capital acquisition has been incorporated in numerous sports studies.[100] Within skateboarding, surfing, and snowboarding, to name just a few relevant action-sports examples, individuals have benefitted from participating in the social networks supporting these activities.[101] The corollary for *Moving Boarders* is that social networks such as those found in skate parks also hold potential value for participants. These skate-park participants, including parents, children, and other community and industry members, strive to benefit from skateboarding by making certain choices and investments that lead to social, cultural, and economic capital gains. In our chapters, we will demonstrate how, due to local social-enterprise practices, each skate park is actually designed to provide these diverse capitals to participants.

With these ideas about capital generation in mind, we now outline the research questions that guided the study featured in *Moving Boarders*:

- How do urban skate parks reliant upon social-enterprise practices privilege certain knowledges, missions, and belief systems?
- How are skate-park participants using these social environments to create new meanings, relationships, and experiences?
- Given the conditions found in four urban skate parks, how do participants benefit socially, culturally, and economically?

Our study site, in the San Francisco Bay Area, is intriguing because it was once distinguished by its "skate and destroy" reputation, as we describe next in chapter 1. This famous, rebellious skate scene once distanced itself from Southern California's more glamorous surfer and Hollywood skateboarding vibe. But times have changed, as we will explain. Today, families, government bodies, and corporate organizations have collaborated in the development of new skate parks in Bay Area urban neighborhoods. This sea change in the local skateboarding culture compelled us to evaluate its new participants, meanings, and practices. Next, we articulate our study's methods and the specific communities where we conducted our research.

Research in Urban Skateboarding: Studying the Social Logics and Practices of Skate Parks

DESIGNING AND CONDUCTING THE STUDY

Our research team first became embedded across several skate-park locations in fall 2013. Altogether, the research study lasted over three and a half years, until spring 2017. While the skate culture based in the San Francisco Bay Area could be understood as our overall research focus, a few individual case studies underpinning this broader context were specifically identified, including two skate parks in San Jose (Lake Cunningham and Roosevelt skate parks), Bay City's skate park,[102] and Town Park housed within West Oakland's historic De Fremery Park site. In addition, we also researched skate-park activity in other skate parks based in Berkeley and Hayward, although our engagement in these sites was less extensive. Although these skate parks are occasionally referred to in this book, as they sometimes contextualize our overall research findings, they are not prominently featured. In a more collective sense, our individual cases from San Jose, Bay City, and Oakland were pooled together into one larger case-study that captured the social practices and dynamics of this region. Each researched skate park thus fused into a broader research context allowing us to understand: (1) the minutiae of specific skate-park life; and (2) a more integrated portrait of how these skate parks functioned when compared with one another in a broader sense. We describe at length the rationale for using this case-study method, and our research involvement, in the Methodological Appendix.

The aforementioned case-study skate parks were purposefully selected based on several criteria: (1) they were newly built and thus reflected the pattern of urban skate-park development unfolding across the world; (2) these skate parks, due to neoliberalism's influence, were largely driven by indispensable leaders, organizers, and supporter groups representing both government and private-sector interests; and (3) they were each imbued with unique socioeconomic and cultural markers that influenced local skateboarding practice. In regards to the latter line of thought, the San Francisco Bay Area is fascinating from a research perspective because it embodies some of the richest demographic diversity in the United States within a metropolitan area. Several local communities in this region are ranked near or at the top in the nation when it comes to ethnic, racial, and linguistic diversity.[103] These attributes warranted the use of specific case-study locations that could similarly echo these distinctive demographic trends.

Australian professor Jan Wright, among others, has suggested that scholars conducting physical activity research should reveal their own backgrounds and assumptions, as these critically impact the research process.[104] Perhaps surprisingly, then, we note that none of the authors of this book are actually skateboarders. Rather, we have been steeped in traditional organized-sports experiences, including soccer, tennis, softball, and running. What's more, we work together in the same academic department of Kinesiology and share interests grounded in youth sports and physical activity, with a particular interest in promoting social justice. Indeed, all of us are currently involved with the Center for Sport and Social Justice, which aims to use sport as a vehicle for enacting social change. Originally, our collective interests cohered around an increasing awareness that urban skateboarding was becoming very popular in our local area. Over time, we began to see evidence that the landscape of skateboarding was changing in a demographic sense. At our own commuter university, distinguished as one of the most racially and ethnically diverse in the United States, we noticed more people riding skateboards than ever before.[105] We also observed a wide range of age groups skateboarding in local neighborhoods and skate parks. Additionally, we became aware that in our local communities, more and more parents were getting involved in skateboarding. We saw an increased parental presence in local skate parks and noticed that they were regularly watching and even coaching their children.

Although we work in the same academic department and hold similar ideals about the role of sports in society, our unique academic journeys and sub-disciplines mean that our theoretical ideas differ somewhat from each other. Becky Beal initially began her study of skateboarding over twenty-five years ago, drawing upon critical sociological theory with a focus on gender relationships. Her doctoral thesis, from 1992, has been characterized by one fellow scholar in this manner: "[It is] on the cusp of two eras—concerned with the resistive potential of skateboarding but still able to connect with the increasing mainstreaming of skateboarding. This tension has since been a consistent topic in much skate scholarship."[106] Beal started working with Matthew Atencio in 2004 after meeting him at a North American Society for the Sociology of Sports (NASSS) conference in Tucson, Arizona. Atencio was then studying "pickup" and "street" sports, including basketball, soccer, and skateboarding. Using post-structuralist ideas from French philosopher Michel Foucault, Atencio focused upon how these informal activities provided identities and life meanings for urban youth. ZáNean McClain's background is in physical education pedagogy, where she has addressed issues of social equity and diversity, as well as youths' perceptions of enjoyment within school-based lessons. Missy Wright came into this study with knowledge of social psychology, with her research focusing upon youth's sporting engagements in underserved urban contexts. She was once part of Michigan State University's Institute for the Study of Youth Sports, whose mission is to transform sports "in ways that maximize the beneficial physical, psychological, and social effects of participation for children and youth."[107] *Moving Boarders* subsequently incorporates this spectrum of academic interests and experiences in analyzing and interpreting the study's findings.

Ethnographic research is commonly used to excavate the microscopic meanings and experiences embedded within specific case studies. Implementing an ethnographic approach, we employed multiple qualitative methods in order to generate fine-grained insights regarding skate parks and their social dynamics. These qualitative methods include semi-structured interviewing; in total, we conducted 62 interviews, including 26 interviews with parents (and grandparents), 19 interviews and/or focus groups with children and youth, and 17 interviews with individuals associated with skate-park organizations and programs. These interviewees were quite diverse in terms of their profiles and backgrounds. Also, interviewees ranged in age from child skate prodigies to a grandfather who watched skateboarding from his pickup truck in the parking lot. In addition, we utilized other helpful methods of collecting data, including focus groups (often with younger children as this seemed to be more comfortable for them), and field observations conducted in skate parks, town-hall meetings, and other community events like skate contests, camps, fundraisers, and informational events. We even attended one art exhibition dedicated to skateboard artists held at a local gallery. Moreover, it was also important for us to examine social media, given its usage as an instrument for creating and promoting skate parks in our study area. One researcher, Steph MacKay, contends that digital media is an important resource for skateboarders.[108] She believes that digital media arguably maintains skaters' identities, reinforces certain beliefs, and fosters group participation. Platforms of digital media, she suggests, now include websites, blogs, and social media platforms such as Facebook, Twitter, Instagram, YouTube, and Vimeo. We concurred with this idea, and thus closely examined these data sources. Additionally, we examined documents such as brochures and other promotional materials such as event fliers. These textual-analysis procedures were utilized in order to understand prevailing assumptions and belief systems, thus shedding more light on the workings of local skate-park cultures.

SCOPE AND STRUCTURE OF THE BOOK

> *What one's view of the culture is of skateboarding, to another it's completely different. Skateboarding culture in itself is broad. It is fragmented. It's not like we're all in it as one, [or] in one way.*
>
> (Mike, ex-professional skateboarder)

Especially germane to skateboarding's rise is the fact that it is a fun, low-cost, and social activity that appeals to youth. This made us wonder whether skateboarding may provide a contrast to traditional youth sports that are now being marked by adult involvement. Yet, as mentioned, a growing adult presence also hoists new rationales and mechanisms upon skateboarding activity that was once hailed as a rite of passage for youth seeking participant control, non-conformity, freedom, and a creative outlet. With more and more adults becoming involved in skateboarding, this activity has expanded and thus requires fresh investigation. Consequently, the following chapters in *Moving Boarders* will show that skate parks have added new dimensions to skateboarding, with these spaces becoming vehicles for modern parenting, youth development, and community renewal.

Chapter 1 begins by telling the story of the San Francisco Bay Area's world-famous skateboarding culture. We link this discussion to current socioeconomic conditions in this region that have fostered severe lifestyle, recreation, and health disparities. We directly identify the neoliberal climate, manifest so prominently here, as creating major social divides and conflicts. We thus intend to show that the widening gap between rich and poor residents also influences the nature and provision of skate parks.

Another takeaway here is that public and private stakeholders, including families, community leaders, nonprofit groups, city governments, and private industries, work to install new visions of skateboarding within urban skate parks. This type of collective involvement is for largely instrumental reasons, that is, in order to generate certain benefits or capitals. A key concept that we therefore introduce here is the *Urban Platform for Capital*. We will show that parents are especially avid participants in urban skate park "platforms." These parents hope to satisfy various ambitions and investments by using new skate parks. This line of thinking follows the view that American parents are keenly aware that youth-sports participation can be used to cultivate their children. We will thus frame how parents utilize urban skate parks so that their children can obtain various forms of capital.

Chapter 2 illustrates the range of social-enterprise groups that conduct their social-change work through skateboarding, including within the San Francisco Bay Area. With the ascendancy of the neoliberal ethos, we show how several unique coalitions have entered into the arena of youth sports in order to fill gaps left by the public sector. What this means is that nonprofit and even entrepreneurial social-change groups are embedding themselves within urban skateboarding culture. The community groups featured in this chapter directly operate in all of the local skate parks that we visited. At the same time, these groups are guided by specific sociocultural concerns that influence their work across a wide variety of projects. And, in this chapter, we also show that social-enterprise groups integrate business and corporate sponsors in order to conduct their work. With recent scholarship around action sports and youth development used as context, this chapter directs attention to whether these groups are able to achieve their stated missions, given their current visions, practices, and resources.

Chapter 3 is situated in Bay City Skate Park. This skate park is located in a more suburban area of the San Francisco Bay Area that borders Silicon Valley. The chapter begins with a contextual description of how this skate park evolved out of adults' desires to provide a safe and legal place for youth to skateboard. Indeed, we show how a highly visible supporter group has worked closely with parents, a skate coach, and the city government to overcome neighborhood opposition to the skate park's construction. Then, we demonstrate how parents have taken up the prevailing family-friendly vision of this community space in line with their own desires to be good parents. Bay City's adults in fact had quite strong views about what constitutes appropriate parenting through skateboarding. These views ranged from unabashed helicopter parenting to more free-range approaches; sometimes this discrepancy brought parents into conflict with one another. This chapter thus brings to light the presence of divergent and even contested parenting strategies as they affected youths' skateboarding experiences.

Chapter 4 describes West Oakland's Town Park, a new skate park housed in a larger city park where the Black Panthers formerly ran their revolutionary community activities. With this history in view, we illustrate how this eclectic space was designed by Keith "K-Dub" Williams, an art educator who also invented a youth festival called Tha Hood Games. Town Park, as we shall see, is indeed K-Dub's unique brainchild. He uses this space to mentor underserved, local young men of color, although all youths are in principle welcomed here. Framed in this manner, Town Park directly supports Oakland youths' personal- and social-development opportunities. This type of work, we argue, is contextualized within an increasingly gentrifying neighborhood that is undergoing massive economic and cultural changes. As such, chapter 4 also describes how Town Park promotes neighborhood pride and self-determination through an emerging, organic youth culture. Narratives from adults presented in this chapter indicate parents' support for Town Park's mission.

In Chapter 5, we articulate how San Jose, officially dubbed the "Capital of Silicon Valley," simultaneously uses ideologies around public health and perceptions of at-risk youth to finance and program several skate parks. This case context is unique in the sense that the recent influx of high-tech money has built up the city's financial capacity to resource parks and youth programming. As a result, the city has created a unique set of rationales for skate-park development, in line with the mission of its Parks, Recreation, and Neighborhood Services department. This city department actually has a full-time employee with the title of Action Sports Specialist to fund, oversee, and promote various skateboarding projects. In California's largest skate park, Lake Cunningham, we demonstrate how tight regulation and surveillance has created an exclusive family- and tourist-friendly environment. It is often used by white, professional-class parents and their children. In comparison, the case of Roosevelt Skate Park is compelling for its largely low-income, youth-of-color neighborhood base. This skate park is not far from Lake Cunningham, but, in contrast, it is placed within a neighborhood park location where a Latino gang coexists with many homeless residents. As we shall see, the city uses skateboarding here to reclaim a seemingly at-risk urban space and transform local residents. San Jose's dual strategies when it comes to skate-park provision prompts a discussion about the role of adults and youths in determining prevailing practices and goals.

Finally, in chapter 6, we discuss how our research study contributes new ideas about family, community, government, and private-sector participation within urban youth sports. The specific attributes of each case-study location are revisited, but, crucially, we also bring these skate parks into conversation with each other. This integrated, cross-case analysis is used to highlight divergences as well as consistencies emanating from youths' skate-park participation. Considering all four of the skate parks, we ultimately propose that skateboarding is expanding through innovative social-enterprise entities, while becoming increasingly meaningful to families. We discuss this pattern of social-enterprise support for skate parks, and the major effects this has upon families, by returning to the concept of *Urban Platforms for Capital.* It is our contention that families are especially motivated to invest in skate parks (and other youth-sports contexts) because they want their children to gain certain character values and life skills to be successful. Yet, we also contemplate how youth may circumvent this adult conception of skateboarding and instead use skate parks in ways that are more personally meaningful and enjoyable to them. We end the book by speculating how skateboarding holds particular ramifications for urban youth sports, as well as society more broadly. Several key takeaways from our research findings are thus offered to the reader in this conclusion.

ONE

Neoliberalism and the New
Urban Spaces of Skateboarding

The pervading influence of various private stakeholders in skateboarding reminds us that youth sports no longer exist, in nature and scope, as they once did. Indeed, while recently listening to a local radio feature story, we were reminded of a foregone era when public oversight was actually given to local youth sports:

> The days of simply playing ball with your friends is over and the age of the youth sports industrial complex featuring pay-to-play leagues is here. . . . Growing up in Oakland, I played in the police athletic league. The cops picked us up in a paddy wagon on the corners where my friends and I lived. They dumped us off at any number of dirt baseball diamonds in Oakland. The coaches were volunteers. The equipment was donated by sponsors. After our games, we found our own way home.[1]

We are indeed living in a new, different era in which youth sports are greatly shaped by the broader societal trend of what writer Lisa Duggan describes as "The Incredible Shrinking Public."[2] This involves the degradation of state regulation and the consequent prioritization of private-sector control and values to determine both social and economic realms, according to Duggan:

> The primary strategy of turn-of-the-millennium neoliberalism is privatization, the term that describes the transfer of wealth and decision-making from public, more-or-less accountable decision-making bodies to individual or corporate, unaccountable hands. Neoliberals advocate privatization of economic enterprises, which they consider fundamentally "private" and inappropriately placed in any "public" arena. They go further than this, though, in advocating that many ostensibly public services and functions also be placed in private profitmaking hands.[3]

Underneath the widespread authorization of free-market logics at this point in the twenty-first century, new sophisticated public-private working relationships structure youth-sports provision. Following on this, one of our main premises is that the private sector can significantly enact its philosophies, and in some cases its overt control, over youth skateboarding.

The neoliberal influence on youth-sports practice, including skateboarding, is not new. Since the end of the twentieth century, youth sports have been deeply associated with big business. A book called *Young Athletes, Couch Potatoes, and Helicopter Parents*, by scholars Jessica Skolnikoff and Roger Engvall, offers the blunt assessment that "sports teams are not only a place for children to play and have fun; they have become a moneymaking industry."[4] Sociologist Jay Coakley provides a complementary view, highlighting that the "bare bones" cuts to publicly funded youth-sports agencies over recent decades have coincided with the emergence of "new youth-sport organizers, entrepreneurs, and hustlers."[5] Clearly, there is now significant pressure on public servants working in their communities to "do more with less" under the neoliberal values of efficiency and self-sustainability.

So, it is not unexpected that public agencies have created new working arrangements with private groups in order to address the needs of sporting youth and their families. Government entities, including parks-and-recreation departments, are often reduced to simply issuing permits to private organizations; as such, these government agencies largely function as gatekeepers to public property instead of directly funding and running their own youth-sports operations.[6] We will regularly see this approach at work in the *Moving Boarders* skate parks.

It is to the point that multinational sports corporations are even fighting each other over access to what used to be considered public recreation space. An example will illustrate this claim: In 2015, *The Oregonian* newspaper proclaimed that "the simmering turf war between Nike and Under Armour got political this week as Portland mayor Charlie Hales and commissioner Amanda Fritz sparred over corporate sponsorship of city parks."[7] Eventually, the city of Portland, which has long relied upon Nike to renovate park spaces including its neighborhood basketball courts, accepted Under Armour's offer, much to Nike's chagrin. The city's Under Armour deal was subsequently characterized as "the latest example of city officials' willingness to commercialize park facilities to help pay for improved fields."[8]

Moreover, we will show that the divorce of youth sports from municipal oversight has also engendered a new type of private-sector social activism. By using social-enterprise mechanisms, many groups and programs aiming to support urban skateboarding utilize the privatization principles of neoliberalism. This form of social activism, exemplified by both nonprofits and corporate initiatives, often appears in America's urban communities, "where a new form of racialized urban poverty" has taken hold due to "a rapidly changing global political economy."[9] Sociologist Douglas Hartmann also significantly adds to this discussion with the case study he presents in *Midnight Basketball*. His book convincingly illustrates how a unique conglomeration of religious, correctional, industry, and governmental supporters epitomize how neoliberal social activism structures urban sports provision.[10] His assessment is that private-market logics are now thoroughly enmeshed in pro-social urban sports infrastructure and programming.[11] In *Moving Boarders*, we will show that this model also underlies skate-park programs explicitly targeting urban youth of color.

Looking ahead in this book, we can see that urban skateboarding is now poised at the juncture of nonconformity and mainstream acceptance. And this is occurring during a time of rapid free-market expansion that simultaneously promotes great social disparities. Despite the sanctity of the view that youth sports are public, by now it is clear that public resources and investment have generally eroded and that the purveyors of free-market capitalism now greatly permeate and even lead youth-sports practice. While this idea has been fleshed out since the end of the last century, how neoliberalism structures youths' skateboarding has not been explained. *Moving Boarders* therefore focuses upon the shift under neoliberal conditions toward private-sector mechanisms and social-enterprise relationships that affect contemporary urban youth skateboarders. Our study will show that government bodies often rely upon social-enterprise coalitions representing private industries and citizens. We shall demonstrate how this trend unfolds within several local Bay Area communities where newly built skate parks have come to exist.

In the next section, we further contextualize neoliberalism as it pertains to skateboarding at a broader level. Then, we briefly trace out the history and importance of skate culture in our local area to exemplify this phenomenon. What follows is an illustration of how neoliberalism produces both significant opportunities and meaningful consequences for various stakeholders. The neoliberal trend, we argue, significantly influences how modern youth and their families experience youth sports like skateboarding. The prevailing form of skateboarding, we conclude, influences parents to be highly engaged supporters as part of their expected parental duties.[12]

The Transformation of Urban Skateboarding in Neoliberal Times

We have demonstrated that skateboarding now has currency in the mainstream. It has, we strongly believe, expanded greatly from its niche, subversive origins. This is especially true since the turn of the last millennium, when "everyone had jumped on the extreme bandwagon," selling everything including cheeseburgers, shaving razors, and hair coloring as part of "extreme" sports marketing campaigns.[13]

In parallel with this free-market exposure, neoliberal practices have been identified as endemic to contemporary urban skateboarding culture. This might seem strange, given that skateboarders have long prided themselves on making their own skate spots, cultures, techniques, styles, and regulatory structures, with limited official oversight. This is known as the "do it yourself" (DIY) ideal. However, this belief in skater DIY directly aligns with neoliberalism, as it privileges the idea of a self-sufficient, entrepreneurial citizen.[14] Here is a convincing example of this proposition: A recent article in *Wired* magazine was headlined "Silicon Valley Has Lost Its Way. Can Skateboarding Legend Rodney Mullen Help It?" This piece illustrates how one famous skateboarder, Mullen, is now consulting big-wigs in Northern California's tech industry. According to the writer, "More than 30 years after he invented most of the gravity-defying maneuvers that still form skateboarding's basic vocabulary, Mullen is enjoying a strange sort of second act. He has become a sought-after speaker on the Silicon Valley conference circuit, making the rounds at PopTech, Foo Camp, TEDx, and myriad other events where technology bigwigs gather to feast on ideas."[15] The extent that Mullen is considered valuable in top corporate and entrepreneurial circles indicates skateboarding's affinity with neoliberal principles. Scholar Emily Chivers Yochim further reinforces the belief that skateboarders are often beholden to the neoliberal mindset.[16] She contends that skateboarders create new cultural codes, ways of being, and modes of communication that resonate with the American entrepreneurial spirit. *Moving Boarders* significantly draws upon this line of thought, to illustrate how urban skateboarders and their support networks embrace private-sector, entrepreneurial mechanisms and ways of thinking.

The urban skate park is indeed the perfect site for skateboarding's participants and supporters to implement neoliberal practices. This idea has been thoroughly covered in the works of scholar Ocean Howell. Because skate parks, Howell argues, are not just about skateboarding per se, they also operate in close alignment with free-market capitalism, public disinvestment trends, as well as individualistic, entrepreneurial practices.[17] Today, private supporters and organizations attempt to serve their communities via skate parks; this rationale strongly propels the development of skate parks in terms of their design, policies, and programming.[18] Howell in fact outlines a wide range of "public officials and their staffs, parks and recreation professionals, architects and landscape architects, and increasingly private businesspeople" who now have great influence in skate-park provision.[19] Given this high degree of privatized involvement Howell suggests that skate parks instill neoliberal values pertaining to ideals of "personal responsibility, self-sufficiency, and entrepreneurialism."[20]

The latest research, provided in the previous chapter, tells us that youth are now gravitating to skateboarding like never before. In the section above, we explained how an abundance of private stakeholders, working with local government officials, are now beholden to the idea of making social change through skateboarding. Together, these private and public stakeholders are indicative of social-enterprise practice. It is our belief that these stakeholders have tremendous power to define "what counts" in skateboarding and for whom. Ahead, we articulate how intricate public-private coalitions underpin newly built skate parks in the San Francisco Bay Area. This line of thought requires us to first detail the historical antecedents and contemporary skateboarding conditions in our study location. We will ultimately reveal how our local skate scene truly exemplifies the logics of neoliberalism, which holds particular consequences for youth and their families.

"One of the Rawest Skate Scenes Around": The San Francisco Bay Area Skate Network

As one local skate-park developer in our study told us, "skate shops are the hub" within the community. In this way, skate-shop owners are uniquely positioned to comment about local skateboarding. They interact on a daily basis with the city's skateboarders, while their businesses ride the ups and downs of local skate trends. Meanwhile, these individuals are often imbued with a passion to support the city's skate scene. And so, in order to contextualize our description of the San Francisco Bay Area skate scene, we intersperse the voices of local skate-shop owners throughout this section.

In San Francisco, we can point to numerous cultural institutions of skateboarding, with global reputations, such as For the City (FTC) skate shop. In operation since the mid-1980s, FTC has sponsored many of professional skateboarding's biggest names, including Chico Brenes, Jovontae Turner, Jim Thiebaud, and Mike Carroll.[21] Kent Uyehara, owner of FTC, describes the local scene in this manner: "When I moved to San Francisco, it was a skateboard mecca. It was this big fucking deal to be a skateboarder in San Francisco. Not to the mainstream, but to skateboarders, SF was kind of the hub of what was going on." These comments begin to show how San Francisco and its associated urban region, known as the *Bay Area* (see fig. 1), can rightfully claim to be one of *the* most iconic skate locales in the world. In fact, Uyehara has gone on to assert that "San Francisco is dubbed the skate capital of the world."[22]

It does not take much to justify Uyehara's lofty characterization. Indeed, during the emergence of street skateboarding in the mid-1980s, the first professional street contest was held in San Francisco's Golden Gate Park in April 1983.[23] The Embarcadero, located in the city's financial district on Market Street, was called *EMB* by skaters, and it "became an epicenter in the late 1980s and early '90s when pro skaters including James Kelch, Mark Gonzales and Mike Carroll began capturing their groundbreaking tricks on video here" and, as one article went on to note, "During EMB's heyday, you could have seen nearly 100 skaters per day getting in on the action."[24]

Another famous skateboarder born and raised in San Francisco is Tommy Guerrero, once a key member of the iconic Bones Brigade team sponsored by the Powell Peralta company. Guerrero received the 2013 Transworld SKATEboarding "Legend" award. Also, the fifth and sixth X Games were held in San Francisco in 1999 and 2000, respectively. In 1999, Tony Hawk famously became the first skateboarder in history to land a 900-degree spin on a half-pipe. This act was once characterized as being equivalent to breaking the four-minute-mile barrier in running.[25] Going further, there is the locally founded skate-media institution *Thrasher* magazine. *Thrasher* was founded in San Francisco in 1981 as the quintessential "skate and destroy" skate magazine of our times; it was

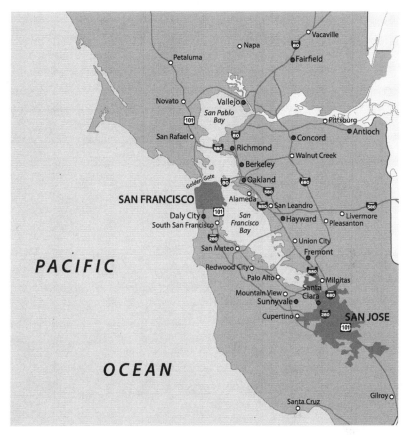

San Francisco Bay Area. *Courtesy of Rainer Lesniewski/Shutterstock.com.*

founded locally by Kevin Thatcher, Fausto Vitello, and Eric Swenson.[26] A recent feature article notes that *Thrasher* magazine has been the "bible for skaters for more than two decades."[27]

Across the Bay Bridge in the East Bay, Oakland has been host to numerous DIY spots, such as Bordertown and The Spot. These organic, skater-made spaces have been torn down by California state transportation officials over the past decade due to their illegal placement near major freeways.[28] Lower Bobs is the last remaining DIY spot in Oakland, although it, too, is under threat of closure.[29] In adjacent Berkeley, the owner of the seminal 510 Skateboarding shop, Jerry Harris, further contextualizes the history of skateboarding in the East Bay, saying that it had "no epicenter, no meeting place" because "it was just really spread out."[30] Indeed, Berkeley's skate spots once comprised an eclectic mix, including half-pipes that were once well skated or "ripped" on a daily basis, as well as tennis courts, pools, and even the art museum. In Berkeley, it was said that skater Tim Marring "blew minds when he introduced the maneuver known as the 'Rock 'n' Roll' to pool skating," while other skaters have "contributed many different approaches to freestyle and vertical skating, in addition to being masters of downhill skating."[31] 510 Skateboarding owner Harris consequently sums up the scene:

> [Berkeley] has always been a lot different from San Francisco, but kind of linked at the hip at the same time. It definitely has its own distinct feel. . . . It's still grimy, it's still dudes in warehouses and all they give a shit about is skateboarding and building cool places to skateboard. . . . It's definitely kept a pretty strong indie feel. The skateboard industry has grown up and gotten all huge around us, but the scene around here has stayed pretty grimy [*laughs*], pretty authentic.[32]

Just down the I-880 freeway, San Jose stakes a definite claim to being a skateboarding hotbed, too. This city has produced numerous professionals and top amateurs in recent decades. In a 1983 *Thrasher* magazine article, writer Craig Ramsay provides the following assessment of San Jose's emergence on the skate scene:

> The Pit (as it is fondly referred to by some) might be considered a perfect example of the total skate environment. A post–World War II baby boom and ensuing suburban sprawl of the '50s and '60s saw to that. Lush apple, cherry, and prune orchards were bought, sold and developed with no concern for city planning. Places where one used to hunt for lizards and ride Sting Rays through creek beds are now being ridden in a different way on skateboards. The terrain is now made up of drainage ditches, pipes, loading docks and empty pools. Billions of tons of concrete, asphalt and plaster have been poured into the valley floor to accommodate the massive flow of auto and pedestrian traffic.[33]

Ramsay's nostalgic article goes on to list a roll call of natives, a veritable who's who of skateboarding, who were at that time carving local San Jose skate spots. This famous list includes Lance Mountain, Jim "Bug" Martino, and Steve Caballero. On the eve of the millennium in 1999,

Caballero was even given the title of Skater of the Century by *Thrasher*. "Cab" once reminisced about San Jose's scene, in a local article:

> Whether it was a ramp in a warehouse, whether it was the Raging Waters ramp in the '80s, whether it was Winchester Skatepark in the '70s. So we've always had something pretty cool that attracted people to the city. And we'd get other people from different cities and even different states coming over to San Jose to skate the spots that we made famous in the magazines and videos.[34]

San Jose's skateboarding scene is supported by yet another famous skate shop. Circle-A Skate (directly referencing the popularized anarchist symbol) was founded in 1985 by Bob Schmelzer, who once performed in the movie *Back to the Future*. As one native in a local skate park reminded us, "You know whenever Marty McFly is riding a skateboard, Bob is the stunt double for that. Bob is the guy that did that." Schmelzer once characterized the local scene in a Transworld SKATEboarding story in this manner: "There's a huge concentration of amazing professional and amateur skateboarders downtown—it's the skateboard energy here that's the lure. From the new breed to the old guys, there's just a lot of energy, period."[35] San Jose's unique blend of skateboarders, skate spots, and skate shops indicates why, like San Francisco, San Jose has also been considered "the 'skateboard capital of the world'" and "still remains home to one of the rawest skate scenes around."[36]

A main premise in *Moving Boarders* is that skate parks have now become vital sites for youth skateboarding in America's cities. Over recent years, then, we can see how the iconic San Francisco Bay Area skateboarding scene also embodies this same cultural shift. In tandem with the street scene, purpose-built skate parks remain vital spots for local skaters.

Local skate parks arguably emerged because of government and residential concerns. For example, San Francisco in the early 1990s began to extensively regulate skateboarding activity on the street, according to one local writer. The excerpt below details a local skater's perspective on how police started patrolling the Embarcadero or *EMB*, to ward off skaters.

> San Francisco cops began encroaching on the various back alleys and benches where skateboarders plied their trade. . . . By 1994, a beat cop was hanging out there every day. "We called him 'Officer Squirrel' because he'd try and ambush you," Thompson says. "He was like the worst, awful, cliche-looking cop— this white ginger guy with

a little mustache and glasses. Such an asshole. He took so much joy in taking our skateboards."[37]

During the dot-com boom in the late 1990s, urban skateboarders in San Francisco began playing cat and mouse with the authorities in order to avoid arrest. These skaters scoured the city for new haunts, as they were effectively barred from skateboarding in tourist areas and other locations that were considered lucrative and earmarked for development.[38] Eventually, organic skate spaces, including Embarcadero, became prohibited through anti-skate architecture and legal codes. The city of San Francisco eventually compromised by building several skate parks at the cost of several million dollars each.[39] This was, in essence, "a multimillion-dollar olive branch from the city to its skaters, in the hope that they'll cause less trouble if they're kept inside a fence," according to one local writer.[40] Clearly, then, city skate parks were meant to placate local skateboarders, essentially "to pacify [the city's] thrasher subculture."[41]

This example reveals how local skateboarding regularly takes place in city-sanctioned urban spaces. But these skate parks have taken on new meanings that go beyond simply trying to domesticate seemingly outlaw youth.[42] As we noted earlier, in today's world, skate parks are conceptualized as valuable spaces for physical and social development. This perspective is described here by the former director of a local parks-and-recreation department:

> Of course it used to be years ago, I'd say fifteen to twenty years ago, that it [skateboarding] was one of those things that nobody wanted to touch because it was associated with bad behavior. That in my mind has turned around greatly. It's more associated with a great place for kids to go to be active, it is now centered around health, kids sweating, kids getting out and being physical, socializing as well—doing bad things, doing good things, but that's what you do when you grow up. These parks offer all of those kinds of things. Back in the day again it was like taboo, "We don't want that. It's a bad thing, don't bring it to our neighborhood."

Given this rationale, the fact is that many new skate parks have been purposely built for youth consumption within the Bay Area. In our vicinity alone, many new skate parks have been constructed over the past ten years. Indeed, according to one local media source, "California boasts more than one hundred skate parks, and about twenty-five of them are in the Bay Area."[43]

In its entirety, the San Francisco Bay Area skate scene can be characterized as one of the most vibrant in the world. The prominence of this skate scene made us want to probe deeper into how it was being affected by the returning presence of skate parks. We applied the idea that new participants held certain belief systems, motivations, and resources while supporting this form of urban skateboarding. This line of thinking also compelled us to investigate how specific local conditions influenced the lives of these skate-park participants.

The San Francisco Bay Area: A Unique Mixture of Non-conformity and Neoliberalism

In the previous chapter, we told the story of an evolving paradox: once considered an exclusive subcultural activity, skateboarding is now being championed within urban neighborhoods as a vehicle to benefit youths' lives. We have emphasized that the activity of skateboarding, once condemned by adults, is now considered a good thing, so to speak, for youth as well as their families. Supporting this idea is the belief that neoliberal conditions now encourage the free-market treatment of urban youth sports such as skateboarding. The privatization of skateboarding is also reflected in its evolution into a capital-rich activity, with potential to improve the lives of participants. To develop these ideas, we next examine how context makes a difference, in terms of shaping how people participate, invest, and build relationships in local skateboarding. Concomitantly, we speculate below how the prevailing social, economic, and political conditions of the San Francisco Bay Area forge particular new meanings in its skateboarding scene.

The San Francisco Bay Area, once widely revered for its bohemian "hippy" lifestyle, is now held up as *the* global economic success story. Global cultural icons, including Facebook, Google, and GoPro, were conceived and nurtured in the Bay Area. In fact, it has been suggested that the technological experimentation occurring in places like Stanford University actually melded with 1960s countercultural ideals to spawn Silicon Valley.[44] Clearly, this region embraces economic and technological innovation by doing things differently.

Today, the San Francisco Bay Area's financial engines are generating astronomical profits. A recent story in *The Guardian*, for instance, reports that Facebook CEO Mark Zuckerberg sees $6.4 billion in quarterly revenue to be merely the tip of an iceberg.[45] This type of financial success provides a few select residents, often associated with high-tech industries, with unbelievable salaries and therefore an unparalleled spectrum of life opportunities.[46]

The reality for most local residents, however, is not so idyllic. Nowadays, even Bay Area professionals making healthy salaries face an existential crisis. A recent thread in a community advice forum, Quora, opened with this non-facetious question: "How can I survive in the Bay Area with $400k family income?"[47] And where else could you find people making six-figure incomes complaining that they have been sold a false dream, or people discussing the merits of "$8 toast"?[48] The vast majority of residents with more down-to-earth salaries here struggle to pay the bills amidst the rising cost of living prompted by the infusion of technology money. The *San Francisco Chronicle* recently deemed this situation as "the fade of S.F.'s middle class," noting that many of the city's residents have simply given up and moved out.[49] What's more, a recent research report commissioned in Silicon Valley further articulates how "since 1989, [income] inequality in the Bay Area has increased at a more rapid pace than in California or the nation." This stark prognosis is explained more comprehensively in terms of severe income discrepancy:

> Since the rise of the semiconductor industry in the 1950s and '60s, the San Francisco Bay Area has been considered a high-income region. . . . This view of the Bay Area as a relatively rich region focuses on the top of the income distribution, while a more complete view of incomes in the region presents a very different picture —one of extreme income inequality.[50]

A report from *USA Today* subsequently describes the emergence of two divided social groups within the Bay Area, the "haves" and "have nots"; this is actually considered a place where "fences and roads divide the rich from poor, the powerful from the powerless."[51]

The New Yorker further highlights this growing socioeconomic divide, revealing the erasure of established neighborhoods in San Francisco where people of color once lived. A story in the magazine contends that tech workers are "pouring into the formerly working-class immigrant neighborhoods, driving up the cost of housing, and giving the landlords increased incentives to evict longtime tenants from rent-controlled apartments."[52] Major demographic changes are unfolding in the city, this article tells us, reflected in how between 1990 and 2011, "the Mission District lost fourteen hundred Latino households and gained twenty-nine hundred white ones; during the same period, the black population of the city was cut in half."

It is our belief that these major social changes now permeate local urban sports provision, too. In order to understand this connection, let's turn to a recent popular example. In a viral video emanating from a soccer field in San Francisco's Mission District, a turf war erupted, pitting young men of color against white male professionals. This latter group, employees from both Dropbox and Airbnb, and thus sporting "tech-company logos," are deemed by one observer as "the perfect avatar of the incoming population that's transformed the city's demographics."[53] The tech workers had rented this field through the city's parks-and-recreation department and were attempting to play their own soccer match. This occurred much to the dismay of the regular park users who arrived at this soccer field for their regular afternoon pickup game. A heated discussion ensued between the leaders of each camp:

> Kai (leader of the pickup group): This field has never been rented. How long have you been in the neighborhood?
>
> Tech worker: Over a year. [Crowd of local boys guffaw and laugh]
>
> Kai: How long have you been playing here? My whole life . . . I have been born and raised here for 20 years. And my whole life, we've been playing here.

Ultimately, the tech workers produce a $27 park permit given to them by the city. This means that the local boys and their leader, Kai, will forego their regular game on the field. Kai's animated plea, "Just because you got money and can pay for the field, doesn't mean you can book the field, for an hour, to take over" thus goes in vain.[54]

The crucial takeaway from this video, which has been viewed online over 800,000 times, is that youths of color from low-income urban communities have fewer opportunities to participate in sports compared to those wielding more capital. This fact was statistically supported in the previous chapter. And, we contend, this situation is being exacerbated by neoliberalism, and specifically gentrification, as we see in this particular case. In fact, Kai and his family have been evicted from two apartments since 2005. In a follow-up story, he points out a new "luxury restaurant, and right above it, brand new luxury condos" before turning his attention to Mission Park, stating, "I think a lot of Americans right now can relate to issues of space, and [the question of] 'whose space is it?' and the fight over

Confrontation in Mission Park. *Courtesy of YouTube.*

who belongs here."[55] Indeed, the original incident was once characterized as reflecting a "fight over San Francisco's public spaces."[56]

Kai's question "whose space is it?" and his concern with "who belongs here" receives close scrutiny in this book. The increasing application of free-market logics to sports, exemplified in the practice of public-park rentals to private groups, raises questions about the nature of urban space itself. Under neoliberalism, are these types of spaces fundamentally public, or are they actually privatized? And depending on how one thinks about private involvement in what used to be considered urban public space, citizens are either given more opportunities to participate or they are being restricted in an unprecedented manner. We thus drill down into issues concerning the constitution of urban space for specified purposes and users. Eventually, we examine how certain youths may or may not be authorized to use urban space to skateboard. This is important because we know that youth can potentially gain social, cultural, and material benefits from using urban skate parks. This discussion will implicate the potential for skate parks to serve as *Urban Platforms for Capital*. We outline this original concept of *Urban Platforms for Capital* in the next section in order to frame how skate parks have been intentionally set up as new types of urban space, leading to particular forms of usage.

Urban Platforms for Capital

Skate parks are now being designed as vehicles to support a range of adult concerns, including urban regeneration, youth development, and appropriate parenting. During our research, it soon became apparent to us that these rationales were being extensively used to create new skate parks in our area. In one of our early interviews, Oakland's skate park leader, Keith "K-Dub" Williams, told us, "My whole thing is just providing the platform." This use of the term "platforms" made us realize that *all* of the skate parks we researched were essentially urban platforms created to address the aforementioned adult concerns. We were also reminded of Pierre Bourdieu's theories of capital reproduction, as described in the previous chapter. Eventually, we came to see that urban skate parks were meant to be urban platforms that generated capital for youth, families, and communities.

We know that capital comes in different forms. Bourdieu tells us that these capitals are: social (e.g., social relationships that enhance individuals and their communities); cultural (e.g., culturally valued styles, attributes, and ways of being that translate internally and externally to skateboarding); and economic (e.g., financial or material gain). We now turn to outline these different capitals as they pertain to urban skateboarding.[57] First, regarding social capital, this book will show that skate parks act as key sites where youth gather, establish trusting relationships, and become civically involved. Susie Weller's study of London's South Bank skate scene is one useful example of how social-capital networks emerge in and through skate parks.[58] In another study, this time from the Newcastle region in England, Adam Jenson and colleagues provide another case that challenges the perception of skateboarders as antisocial:

> The one constant in Tyneside's skate playspace is the sociability of the scene and the social capital the skaters create. The Tyneside skateboard scene represents an asset to the wider cityscape. The skaters are not a problem; their scene is sociable, entrepreneurial, and protective of spots in the city they value.[59]

Delving into these researched ideas about social capital, this book explains how local skate parks have been created by municipal agencies, and also non- and for-profit supporters, to impart meaningful social capital opportunities for youth.

Then, we further contend that urban skate parks have been constructed by certain parties to privilege cultural and economic capital, as well. In the cultural sense, youths may work to obtain specific traits and skills through skateboarding that translate into local and broader cultural appreciation. This cultural capital, like social capital, may benefit skaters in their local skate scenes, while also potentially transferring across educational, community, and employment realms. With regard to economic capital, skate parks create chances for some youth to profit from their distinctive performances and personae. Economic benefits could include sponsorships, equipment, contracts, and website incomes. Skateboarding scholarships are now even being offered to youth by organizations such as the College Skateboarding Educational Foundation.[60]

In simple terms, skate parks are considered vital for youth because they seem to provide diverse, broader types of life benefits that go beyond simply learning tricks on a skateboard. Our umbrella concept *Urban Platforms for Capital* is meant to capture the important processes of capital reproduction found in urban skate parks. Going forward, then, this book features four skate parks that were each uniquely designed to benefit local participants. In fact, we will see that a range of people saw value in these skate parks and became encouraged to participate accordingly. The idea that skate parks act as networks of capital provides a window into how youths and families, as well as community groups, are investing considerable time, energy, and even money in skateboarding.

Urban "Social Spaces" that Generate Capital

In the past, it was suggested that, unlike traditional youth-sports participants, skateboarders were continually inventing new spaces and ways of using them.[61] It is even said that skateboarders source and utilize urban space like no other group in society does, based on criteria such as accessibility, design, and ability to make social relationships.[62] In this regard, famous skateboarder Stacy Peralta once avowed that "skateboarders in a sense operate like viruses, because they go into places where they're not really welcome, and not only use those places, but make them their own places."[63] Moreover, skateboarders were once deemed "urban guerrillas" by film producer and former leader of the Zephyr skate team, Craig Stecyk, because "they make everyday use of the useless artifacts of the technological burden, and employ the handiwork of government/ corporate structure in a thousand ways that the original architects could never dream of."[64]

City landscapes are therefore vital to being a skateboarder. The ways in which urban spaces are produced and subsequently utilized are important facets of skateboarding that we thoroughly examine in this book. Within this urban spatial analysis, our main concern is how skate parks can be envisioned as social as well as physical in nature. That is, we conceptualize skate parks as being physical in terms of crucial layout and design features while also sustaining dynamic social networks that impact upon participation.

Henri Lefebvre's seminal work *The Production of Space* is a useful starting point for understanding the concept of "social space" more specifically. Lefebvre demonstrates how spaces actually function according to how people uniquely create and inhabit them.[65] Cultural geographer Doreen Massey likewise reminds us that spaces are social in the sense that people "are constantly engaged in efforts to territorialize, to claim spaces, to include some and exclude others from particular areas."[66] This idea of politicized, social spaces has been judiciously used in the work of urban geographers, planners, and designers, as well as sport sociologists, to show how certain practices and identities are created during spatial usage. Developing this concept, we wanted to find out how social meanings and practices in skate parks are "constantly produced, reproduced, contested, negotiated and reconfigured" by local people.[67]

The idea of *Urban Platforms for Capital* directly relies upon this perspective that skate parks are social spaces that propagate new, diverse, and sometimes conflicting meanings and practices. It is thus worth speculating how these social platforms reinforce certain neoliberal ideals "as they pertain to the desired personal qualities of young citizens."[68] This raises several questions that are addressed later in this book: Which youth are being targeted by these skate parks? And based on what criteria? What kinds of people are they expected to become? It will become obvious that adults, including parents, municipal and community leaders, as well as corporate investors, play key roles in determining appropriate behaviors and identities in skate parks.

This extensive intervention by adults in skate parks to create ideal versions of youth activity and citizenship mirrors the increasingly privatized usage of urban space. It is crucial to realize here that the simple dichotomy that used to exist between public and private urban space is now much more convoluted. Below, we can see how this idea, regarding what constitutes public or private spaces, has been energetically discussed in the scholarly literature. This discussion frames how San Francisco Bay Area skateboarding participants incorporate new types of urban spaces into their social lives.

The End of Public Space? Neoliberalism and the Shaping of New Urban Space

Since the end of the twentieth century, scholars interested in the urban condition have contemplated the potential end of public space. In particular, these scholars are preoccupied with the rising influence of the private sector in determining public life.[69] Geography scholar Andrew Kirby, for instance, identifies this scholarly focus upon the "privatization of public space," which he deems as "one of the more important changes to occur in the contemporary American city."[70] Kirby goes on to consider how many parks or streets that were once considered open, public spaces have been ceded over to private entities. This practice, Kirby tells us, has key social ramifications. Indeed, Kirby summarizes a critical view emanating largely from urban and geography scholars, "that explicit re-mapping of capitalism on the urban landscape has in turn been linked to various social outcomes."[71] This statement raises questions about how individuals may lose their rights to participate "and interact freely with others" in our cities. There is thus concern here regarding the potential demise of what we often consider public space. In particular, this could mean that "those whose appearance is different in some manners due to poverty, gender, age, ethnicity or religious observances may be singled out for scrutiny and may be denied entry."[72]

And yet, Kirby as well as other scholars augment this debate by suggesting that the end of the previous century ushered in new types of urban space. Another scholar, Roman Cybriwsky, characterizes this period as "the age of *private public spaces*."[73] This latter viewpoint goes directly to the heart of the public space idea itself, as it questions whether urban spaces have ever been purely public in the first place.[74] Can the sports stadium or concert hall be considered a truly public space? What about a shopping mall or sidewalk café? And now, what about skate parks? Given the fuzziness of the public-space concept, we are thus left to contemplate a new conceptualization of how urban space is actually designed and taken up, akin to Cybriwsky's private-public space characterization.[75]

Our argument, here and throughout our book, is that possessing a more complex view of public space is necessary to go beyond a simple public or private spatial dualism.[76] Especially under neoliberal conditions, we contend, urban skate parks are formulated by *hybridic* public and private interests. These spaces are constantly in a state of flux reflecting diverse stakeholders and their agendas. We must therefore unpack how these new spaces operate in the lives of youth, families, and their communities. The following chapters recognize the new public-private nexus underpinning skate parks, while attending to how these new articulations of urban space engender certain social beliefs, identities, and relationships.[77] But concerns about who can access and participate in these new forms of urban space remain important. We should recall how Kai and his soccer friends in San Francisco's Mission Park could not play when the soccer field incorporated privatized mechanisms. *Moving Boarders* thus engages with issues of access and inclusion that are found within various public-private skate spaces.

What's more, given that city spaces like skate parks have been constituted by new public and private forces, we are led to consider the impacts of gentrification. Gentrification profoundly shapes West Coast American cities from Seattle to Los Angeles, impacting local neighborhoods in terms of housing affordability, resident displacement, and cultural and demographic shifts.[78] Gentrification undoubtedly factors into how urban skate parks have been created through both private and public means, especially under the logics of urban renewal. Even the iconic Burnside skate park, once the epitome of Portland's DIY and countercultural ethos, is being influenced by luxury-apartment builders. "Well, it's kind of a weird situation spaces like Burnside and spaces . . . made by the artistic creative community are often the forefront, the first step of gentrification," recently commented one of Burnside's leaders.[79]

This view of skate parks as part of urban gentrification processes has specific consequences on social life, which we shall address throughout this book. But how is gentrification expected to improve city life in the first place? Many critical urban and geography scholars hold Richard Florida's 2002 book, *The Rise of the Creative Class*, to account for promoting a vision of urban regeneration that relies upon gentrification by creative individuals. To understand the popularity of Florida's vision, let's hear from urban scholar Jamie Peck: "From Singapore to London, Dublin to Auckland, Memphis to Amsterdam; indeed, all the way to Providence, Rhode Island, and Green Bay, Wisconsin, cities have paid handsomely to hear about the new credo of creativity, to learn how to attract and nurture creative workers."[80]

This call to entice creative new residents arguably works in tandem with "'neoliberal' development agendas."[81] Peck sums up Florida's compelling yet controversial view that cities should cater to the tastes of potential transplants who want "exciting" and "creative" amenities, including "extreme sports," "art," and "music." [82] Essentially, urban areas are expected to reflect the "geographies of 'cool.'" It is thus easy to see how skate parks have become valuable under urban neighborhood regeneration projects aiming to install specific "cool" conditions suitable for new urban clientele. Indeed, skateboarders have even been called the "shock troops of gentrification."[83]

But we also take critical pause here. Because the belief that cities should refashion creative, cool districts to regenerate urban areas must also be viewed alongside deep-rooted social inequalities and divides. In fact, there is arguably great need for longer-term solutions and social supports to overcome these problems in our cities.[84] Major criticisms have been leveled at Richard Florida's thesis, questioning how sustainable and equitable urban regeneration actually occurs just by introducing new, creative residents.[85] In fact, Florida himself has just come out with a new book, which highlights rising socioeconomic inequality, lack of affordable housing, and gentrified "re-colonization" of neighborhoods. Revisiting his original thesis, Florida admits that "seemingly overnight, the much-hoped-for urban revival has turned into a new kind of urban crisis."[86] Later on, we revisit these more critical lines of thinking. We shall discuss the ramifications when community and industry leaders use skate parks to lure certain new participants, in order to promote a particular vision of urban social change.

In summary, there is much evidence to suggest that public-private partnerships now guide most youth-sports programs and spaces in our cities. Indeed, we shall see that all of the *Moving Boarders* skate parks are complicit in privatized practices. These practices include cultivating private-citizen and business donors, soliciting corporate sponsorships, charging admission fees, and hosting pay-to-play events such as camps and lessons. And when copious amounts of public funding are actually used to build skate parks, cities like Bay City and San Jose actively court additional private funds on a regular basis to drive their operations. The terms *cost neutral* and *cost recovery* are thus regularly invoked in these respective locations.

Skaters using a newly created park in Oakland. *Courtesy of Todd Fuller.*

The Place of Skateboarding Youth in Urban Space

Drawing on the work of urban and geography scholars, we can see how the principles of free-market capitalism so consonant with life in the San Francisco Bay Area drive urban skate park activity. The fact that these spaces are so closely identified with neoliberal practices, including urban renewal and gentrification, made us wonder how these sites directly impact participants. In one sense, this means examining how youth experience skate parks that have been designed for them under public-private logics. Privatization often operates in sync with youth development agendas based in the urban core; we thus need to thoroughly consider how this effects youth skateboarders. In fact, scholars have already noted that youth are generally considered by adults as being "difficult, deficient, and at risk."[87] This has often meant that the urban space is "produced as an adult space," which engenders specific consequences for youth as they are often considered a detrimental presence.[88] And youth have accordingly been subjected to adult regulatory mechanisms, including surveillance and restrictions. Practices to control "undesirable 'others'— notably youth," have been especially prevalent under privatization efforts intended to "revitalise or aestheticise" urban space.[89]

We thus wonder how urban skate parks, essentially created for youths' benefit, simultaneously utilize certain privatization mechanisms within broader urban-change initiatives. And what are the consequences here for youth? Scholar Jeremey Németh provides an intriguing and related example regarding Philadelphia's LOVE Park skate scene. In its original heyday, LOVE Park, gritty and neglected as it was, existed as "a space where youth could escape the clutches of regimented school or home life and enter the exciting stage of Center City."[90] However, over time, this space became increasingly subjected to corporate and munic-ipal development projects that basically rendered young skateboarders unwanted. This example challenges us to consider how youth negotiate new private-public spaces that are under adult control. How might youth actually use this type of urban space to meet *their own needs*?

These critical ideas speak to the capacity of youth within skate parks to envision and construct their own forms of social capital. Indeed, it has been suggested that most studies looking at social-capital generation reveal adults' abilities to create value for themselves; what is arguably missing from these studies is how youth themselves may constitute more favorable social relationships to support both individual and commu-nity wellbeing.[91] The capacity of youth to create social capital, and other related capital types, within urban spaces is highly important. Already, we know urban spaces can potentially foster diverse social exchanges, a sense of community, meaningful relationships, improved health and wellbeing, and enhanced quality of life.[92] Our case-study chapters will discuss how *Urban Platforms for Capital* might support youth in the social-capital process. In the next section, we identify how parents, too, are deliberately incorporated within urban spaces that produce capital. These parents, we explain, encounter skate parks while holding certain beliefs that mesh with normative parenting ideals.

Skateboarding as an Indicator of Good Parenting and Positive Youth Development

We don't go to Disneyland, but we go to Vans (skate park) in Anaheim

—Carl, parent in San Jose

There is a rich diversity of interests and experiences for parents who now support their children's usage of city skate parks. The scene described below was captured in one of our field notes. It reveals how parents and their families are now seamlessly blending in with skate park culture:

It's President's Day. This is a school holiday and the park is teeming with youth and parents. Teenaged guys are playing country music on a stereo from the middle of the skate park. Nearby, an African American boy is sitting on the bench sipping on a soda while rolling his skateboard under his feet. A white guy with a skate shop T-shirt follows a group of several young men on their skate runs while making videos on his phone.

The parking lot is full to the brim, parents and children constantly pull up and enter the park.

Some boys wear headphones as they skate. Another five guys line up and eye a bowl, watching and waiting for their turn. A girl wearing a pink T-shirt practices in the middle of the park on a small ramp.

"Johnny Cash helped me get out of prison" blares out from the stereo.

A thirty-eight year old Asian dad is with me:

"Growing up we didn't have this." His daughter came out last year for the YMCA skate camp. One of his work colleagues, a woman, told them about her experiences learning to skate here.

He says, "I admire her [the colleague] because she started when she was forty." He then points to all the young men and teens in this park. He calls them "groovy dudes." "These are younger cats who can skate."

The mom then comments: "I love the fact that there were so many females."

"Even that was just awesome to see, especially having a daughter, having an interest. I want her to see people that look like her doing the things she wants to do, that role model type thing."

"She is six years old."

A guy in his twenties wearing black plug earrings screeches hard on a stop, and then an awestruck girl goes up to him and shrieks "You scared me!" Now, she tries to hang out with him and his friend. She is wearing running shoes with bright pink laces. She seems quite curious; "wow" she exclaims as they skate. She bangs her board slowly on the concrete in approval as the guys skate a small concrete bowl below them. The girl keeps talking to them—they look bemused with hands placed on hips. But they keep talking to her in a friendly manner. Meanwhile, the guys scan over the scene and seem to be planning their next run.

Ice Cube's song "No Vaseline" now pumps out, almost a signal that the park dynamic has changed, with more people trying their tricks. It is 2:15p.m. on a school holiday and the skate park is in full swing. No more stories of Johnny Cash, because funky bass lines and hard lyrics now blasting out from the stereo: "The bigger the cap, the bigger the peelin' who gives a fuck about a punk ass villain."

A Mexican ice-cream cart rolls up and about ten kids immediately line up to get one.

A dad is here with his daughter and son. During our impromptu interview at the skate park, he says that he grew up in this city, skateboarding fifteen years ago. He says that the city "never really embraced skateboarding like it has today."

"We had to travel to find skateboard facilities. Because we didn't have a skate park, we took the hammers and nails built our own stuff, we had quarter pipes, launch rails, camel humps you know we made our own rail slides. . . . And the city would have enforcement officers come out that put enforcement notices on our skateboard ramps, telling us if we didn't move them how the garbage company would come out and pick it up and then send us the bill for it. That actually happened several times . . . 'course we were pretty pissed."

He says that he used go skate at the Santa Cruz teen park in San Jose, in an indoor warehouse. This made his daughter suddenly declare, "I want to go there, I want to watch you skate there!" Meanwhile, the son is skating around wearing a Teenage Mutant Ninja Turtles T-shirt and a helmet resembling an alligator head.

An older white guy in a pair of navy slacks and beard and hat expertly navigates the park terrain, but he suddenly trips up as an inexperienced boy steps right in his way. They both wipe out. But rather than curse, the older guy looks over and asks the kid "Hey are you okay?" in a calm voice. They quickly go their separate ways.

A young boy rolls up and sits next to his mom and dad, who are sitting under a tree watching from above the skate park. This is a pit stop. He takes a breath and checks in with his parents, then he is off to skate again. The mother is wearing an Islamic hijab. Their young daughter is also here, her eyes constantly transfixed by the unfolding commotion. Finally, she moves down to the edge of the skate park. She is now holding up and shaking a teddy bear at everyone as they roll past.

The scene above illustrates the pronounced presence of youth and their families as we regularly noticed them in urban skate parks. This consistent finding made us curious as to why parents, such as those revealed above, felt that skate parks were an integral facet of family life.

The advent of urban skate parks that have been designed and programmed by other adults in the community has certainly piqued the attention of parents. And as neoliberal values such as individualism, self-responsibility, and entrepreneurialism increasingly take root more broadly in youth sports, parents beholden to these same American values see youth skateboarding as a legitimate child-rearing mechanism. The overriding role played by these parents now is summed up by the claim that "sports parenting is an art."[93] And this fact provides an entry point to explore how skate parks are being designated by parents as critical child-raising environments.

Parents now value skate parks with adult mentors. *Courtesy of Kimberly Woo.*

Once more, the idea of *Urban Platforms for Capital* suggests that there is also an explicit connection made between families and capital reproduction; today's parents, we believe, are motivated to translate their children's sports participation into multiple benefits. As we have already shown, much more is at stake now when it comes to youth-sports participation, besides athletic performance per se. Given the range of potential rewards on offer to families through the professionalized environment of youth sports, parents are now quite savvy about the nature and scope of their engagements. Again, neoliberalism sets up a free-market model that invites parents to become strategic agents. We thus demonstrate in this book's chapters how many parents leverage youth sports to instill specific values, attitudes, styles, and traits in their children. These attributes are indeed considered transferrable within American meritocratic society more broadly. Neoliberal ideologies that prevail in our society have influenced new modes of parenting, as explained below.

Under neoliberalism, societal ideals of what it means to be a proper parent have engendered certain preferred practices and styles. Arguably, the new "cultural script" of parenting implies that "parental actions should be organized around what is presumed best for the individual child, in isolation from wider family or social considerations. By a similar token, these strategies endorse the conceptualization of childrearing as a highly privatized, rather than generational, responsibility."[94] The upshot is that parents often feel personally responsible to do their "best for the individual child"; this means immersing their child within activities that will provide them with necessary "cultivating experiences."[95] Scholars Carl Vincent and Carol Maxwell affirm this view in their research paper, stating "we are moving towards the normalisation of concerted cultivation as a parenting strategy for all" which means that "parents not able to or willing to engage in such activities will be positioned as offering inadequate parenting."[96] It is certainly true that today's parents are expected to invest in their own children's activities, at great monetary and labor costs.[97] This essentially means that youth activities have become societal indicators of individual parenting abilities.

Children should have some measure of freedom as well as autonomy while under conditions that are safe and supportive; this is another facet of today's parenting expectations. Scholar Jennie Bristow is instructive in explaining this belief:

> Parents recognize that children need some freedom and independence and that these are good things to have; but this recognition

takes place within a culture that emphasizes the need for safety and protection above all. Parents thus find themselves under contradictory pressures, not only to avoid stifling their children but also to keep them safe from possible harms to their physical safety or emotional well-being.[98]

There is thus a tension here in terms of how adults support their children's independence while also constructing certain conditions for this to occur. This idea is important when considering the element of risk-taking inherent to youth sports, especially with skateboarding. Could it be that parents see skate parks as environments to teach their children about both physical and social risks? And how might this view of appropriate risk-taking work to create numerous parenting approaches? The case-study chapters will explore a spectrum of parental practices, ranging from "free range" type practices to more "helicopter parenting" styles. This latter approach of course implies that parents excessively shield and problem solve for their children, instead of allowing them to experience challenge or failure on their own.[99] And then, we speculate how some parents may actually take up a balanced approach that incorporates both of the above parenting visions.

Next, we further illustrate how broader parenting trends in our society impact the domain of youth sports directly. As alluded to above, parents are implicated in their children's participation in these activities. There is a prevailing assumption that "behind every good young athlete, there is a good parent."[100] And once again, this means that youth-sports parents "can receive recognition through their child."[101] Youth sports, like other child-rearing activities, thus clearly indicate "proof of parental moral worth."[102]

But what are the substantive elements of youth sports that parents covet? Sociologist Hilary Friedman's book *Playing to Win: Raising Children in a Competitive Culture* gives insight into how youth sports provide competitive outlets that reinforce family social status. Parents in her study wanted to give their children the best opportunities, she reports, which could perhaps give these children personal and social advantages over others. Activities such as soccer were thus used by parents to cultivate competitive acumen, which she calls "Competitive Kid Capital," in order "to succeed in various educational tournaments through childhood and early adulthood."[103] Friedman's work perfectly illustrates that youth sports, including skateboarding, are regularly used by parents to give their children translatable benefits that lead to social advantages. We will return to this idea below, when discussing how social class may determine the nature of youth-sports parenting.

But skateboarding is not just about competition. We can thus segue from Friedman's work into another parenting concept illustrating how capital reproduction is used for social purposes. A key premise in this book is that parents often envision their children's sports participation with positive youth development (PYD) outcomes. According to scholars associated with Michigan State University's Institute for the Study of Youth Sport, the concept of PYD refers to the development of desirable competencies or outcomes through sports that can generally aid a young person. These scholars conclude that PYD encompasses the development of specific life skills including "those internal personal assets, characteristics and skills such as goal-setting, emotional control, self-esteem, and hard work ethic that can be facilitated or developed in sport and are transferred for use in non-sport settings."[104]

This view of PYD, often invoked by what sociologist Jay Coakley calls private-industry "sport evangelists" is often taken up by parents; the reproduction of this belief system is based upon "the assumption that for young people, sport has a *fertilizer effect*—that is, if it is tilled into their experiences, their character and potential will grow in socially desirable ways."[105] PYD thus provides a conceptual lens through which we can understand the propensity of American parents to avidly participate in not just traditional, competitive youth sports, but also skate parks. This phenomenon of skate-park parenting has hitherto been neglected by researchers. Looking ahead to the case chapters, we will see how several PYD pillars closely align with skate-parent belief systems. In fact, we will demonstrate how these PYD principles have "received a major boost" due to private intervention, with parents becoming sold on the idea that skateboarding can "produce useful skills and quantifiable achievements leading to social and economic success."[106]

Social class, we further argue, does make a major difference in terms of how certain youth sports principles are taken up by some parents more than others. Not simply pursued for athletic performance, then, youth sports are also used by wealthier parents as a means to preserve their social advantages.[107] Returning to Hilary Friedman's book, *Playing to Win*, we can see that "the extensive time devoted to competition is driven by parents' demand for credentials for their children, which they see as a necessary and often sufficient condition for entry into the upper-middle classes and the 'good life' that accompanies it."[108]

Attributes that reinforce a family's high social status include "internalizing the importance of winning, learning how to recover from a loss to win in the future, managing time pressure [sic], performing in stressful environments, and feeling comfortable being judged by others in public."[109] These traits are considered useful not only for youths' sporting engagements, but they are also linked to success in future academic and employment endeavors, as we alluded to earlier. For further evidence of this sentiment, that sports reify one's class distinction and social status, consider a recent story from *The Chronicle of Higher Education*. A former Ivy League basketball player from one of Boston's low-income neighborhoods recounts how some wealthier players on the Yale team actually "played basketball simply to pad their résumés."[110]

Furthermore, Friedman rightly concedes that many American families "cannot afford to cultivate Competitive Kid Capital."[111] It could easily be the case that lower-income families must focus upon more tangible and immediate markers of their children's success. Indeed, it has been argued that these families attempt to secure upward mobility for their children through everyday youth-sports participation, with each practice and game constituting an aspirational "pipeline."[112] In conjunction with this view, youth-sports participation is regularly used as a vehicle to transform the lives of urban young men of color, in particular. It is assumed that sports are a medium that will enable these youth to learn positive life lessons, establish new social relationships, and make better decisions in order to be responsible and resilient citizens.[113] PYD, in this form, thus remains a priority for various urban community sports, recreation, and activity programs intervening in the lives of low-income youth. As a matter of fact, over the past thirty years, this perspective that sports participation can rescue "at risk" and "in need" youth has gained tremendous currency.[114] Scholar Douglas Hartmann reveals that since the 1990s, a new generation of urban sports-based initiatives has appeared; "touted as innovative, inexpensive, and remarkably effective approaches to crime prevention and targeted typically at racial minorities," these initiatives exist in "a variety of types and sizes."[115]

Social class thus plays a major role in determining adults' outlooks toward the provision and uptake of youth sports. This fact made us wonder how skate parents, too, might approach youths' development in different ways, according to distinctions of social class. This line of analysis nuances our analysis of parental investments in urban skate parks. And these adult investments, we shall see later, are in fact meant to give both low-income and wealthier youth new opportunities for capital enrichment.

A Gendered and Racial Perspective of Urban Skate Park Participation

We contend that social discrepancies in the San Francisco Bay Area influence the experiences of local youth sports parents and their children. Despite prevailing rhetoric in America that characterizes sports as a neutral endeavor or even a social equalizer, we contend that the world of youth sports is definitely not immune to societal divisions and injustices.[116] Because what we think of as the domain of youth sports also reflects widening lifestyle, educational, and opportunity gaps that are quite prominent in society. We have previously accentuated that social class strongly influences how families are motivated to approach and engage in youth sports. Simultaneously, social class factors into how urban youth sports like skateboarding are facilitated and run by social-enterprise groups. In addition to social-class concerns, this book also investigates how racial, ethnic, and gender issues likewise manifest across skate parks, as described below.

Many scholars, including the authors of this book, have documented the difficulties females regularly face in becoming recognized as legitimate skateboarders or being involved in its core culture.[117] Tyler Dupont's ethnography of two different skate cultures in Buffalo and Phoenix is highly revealing. Dupont found that both of these skate contexts were male dominated, as "skaters rarely accepted women outside of their traditional supportive role."[118] This meant that the women's abilities were not recognized or leveraged to gain capital in the local skate cultures. A 2009 paper by the first two authors of this book further identifies how women are often considered "inauthentic" participants, labeled as groupies or posers, and thus may have little opportunity to benefit from skateboarding.[119] We also reveal, in the next chapter, how popular media and the industries surrounding skateboarding have symbolically portrayed females in demeaning ways.

At the same time, as part of skateboarding's new mainstream trajectory, gendered practices underpinning this activity could be changing. In fact, a recent local magazine article declares, "In the male-dominated sport, female skaters in the Bay Area and beyond are creating their own cultures, challenging stereotypes, and inspiring others along the way."[120]

Moreover, *Forbes* magazine recently explains that "if you ask industry insiders about the future of women's skateboarding, they will tell you that interest levels have shot up. It is the fastest growing demographic in action sports, and younger girls are starting to skate."[121] Our findings therefore also speak to this new pattern whereby females are increasingly participating within skateboarding. For instance, a fifty-three-year-old female skateboarder once told us during an interview that girls "have more opportunities now." She elaborated, "I'm telling you, I've had little pools that I've been afraid to drop in. I had a three-year-old pass me and drop in and start skating. It's just pretty awesome. A lot of young ones, really young ones, and girls." In addition, we provide examples of social-activist groups working in communities to improve the place of females in skateboarding. *Moving Boarders* thus closely looks into how new gendered practices may directly influence the operation of skate parks and even the urban skateboarding trend more broadly. This line of analysis is important to update previous research focused upon the state of gender relations in skateboarding culture.

Alongside gender, the sociocultural dimensions of race and ethnicity are also vital to examine in urban skateboarding. Scholars have previously explained that action and lifestyle sports cultures often promote irreverent yet politically conservative versions of white masculinity.[122] Sport sociologist Belinda Wheaton provides much insight here, with her idea that these sports have historically functioned as contexts for imagined "white tribes," and where racial and ethnic differences and mechanisms of exclusion are never contemplated.[123] Scholars Mihi Nemani and Holly Thorpe further claim that the body of scholarly work focused upon action sport cultures fails to engage with the roles and experiences of people of color.[124] The prevailing assumption that activities such as surfing and skateboarding take place in fundamentally "white" contexts has also been expressed by Amy Sueyoshi, an ethnic-studies professor from San Francisco State University. Sueyoshi identifies the Asian American historical and cultural influences of skateboarding that have been largely obscured.[125]

Now, in our daily interactions at skate parks, we regularly observe youth of color doing their thing. Our local-level observations indeed match up with a national trend. The urban skateboarding phenomenon has in fact been noticed and even marketed previously as the "skurban" trend (combining skateboarding with the urban). Skurban confronts the dominant belief that skateboarding is the "domain of suburban white boys."[126] A 2015 article from the *Huffington Post* likewise claimed that skateboarding is "more than a white dude's sport."[127] Recently, high-profile skateboarders of color such as Samarria Brevard, Nyjah Huston, Eric Koston, and Paul "P-Rod" Rodriguez, to name but a few, have become popular.

As skate parks continue to proliferate in these neoliberal times, skateboarding has become important to females and people of color in unprecedented ways. *Moving Boarders* thus pays attention to how these participants and their families utilize and perhaps benefit from new *Urban Platforms for Capital*. This line of thinking also involves unpacking how social-enterprise networks are creating and operating these platforms under social-change agendas that directly reference gender, social class, as well as race and ethnicity.

Conclusion

Contextualized within one of the world's most recognizable and innovative skateboarding destinations, the following chapters reveal how neoliberalism, with its market-oriented social philosophy, is one of the main drivers powering the current popularization of skate parks. In many cases, we will see that there is an instrumental perception that skate parks offer positive developmental experiences for youth and also promote broader social changes. This view is held strongly among skate-park supporters, and thus it largely determines adult efforts to resource and operate these spaces. Likewise, parents in an increasingly competitive and unstable neoliberal economy are attracted to the notion that their investments will help their children succeed in various life domains. Further, in explaining the nuances of how skate parks operate, it will become clear that racial, ethnic, gender, and social-class factors affect how youth, families, and communities approach urban skateboarding in different ways. These sociocultural factors also shape how social-enterprise groups, which fluidly merge for- and non-profit principles and methods, develop skate parks under specific rationales. Looking ahead, we will see that these public-private social-enterprise groups utilize skateboarding to make a raft of social changes pertaining to gender discrimination, urban poverty, gang prevention, youth marginalization, as well as neighborhood regeneration. Chapter 2 thus illustrates the rising presence of these social-enterprise groups that are making social changes and creating new societal values in urban environments.

TWO

Social-Enterprise Skateboarding Organizations

The Installation of New Public-Private Spaces for Youth and Community Development

A major insight we gained from our research is that under neoliberalism, a new array of stakeholders regards skate parks as promising spaces to create positive social opportunities for American youth. The field note–based narratives provided below are from the Oakland Skatepark Summit, which lasted three hours and was held in a local brewery on March, 18 2017. This gathering indicates how individuals representing philanthropic foundations, nonprofit groups, city government, businesses, and major corporations all coalesce in order to promote youth- and community-development goals.

During this particular meeting, these individuals shared information and advice about building and programming skate parks to help local youth develop new skills, relationships, and character values. Importantly, as part of this conversation, these adults highlighted the necessity of deliberately constructing new types of urban space where youth and adults in the community could integrate and generate social capital.

We first illustrate the conglomeration of diverse individuals present at this meeting, reflecting extensive social-enterprise networking:

> Two members of the research team and one research assistant are attending a community event held in the Old Kan brewery located in Oakland. Approximately sixty individuals are here (these include parks and recreation employees, city employees, industry people, and local advocates) to discuss the development of skate parks and skate culture. The theme of this meeting is Public Skate Park Development and it is being sponsored by the California Endowment foundation and hosted with Keith 'K-Dub' Williams representing Town Park, Ashley Masters who is the program director of Skate Like a

Advertisement for the Oakland Skatepark Summit community event.
Courtesy of Keith Williams.

Girl (SLAG), and Peter Whitley who leads Tony Hawk Foundation
(THF) programming.

The meeting starts with Whitley and K-Dub welcoming audience members. Whitley gives shout-outs to other THF members
in attendance (including Steve Hawk, who is Tony's older brother
and one of their board members). K-Dub then adds that there are
many industry people in the room, including people from a local
skate shop, the new head of Oakland's Park and Recreation department, a former Levi's employee who sponsored the deal to sponsor
Oakland's Town Park, and San Francisco native and skate legend
Tommy Guerrero.

Furthermore, turning to the next field-note excerpt from this event,
we can see how Peter Whitley, from the Tony Hawk Foundation, advocates that social relationships involving diverse community members are

fundamental to developing urban skate parks. In line with the social-capital concept, we see below that urban skate parks can foster trusting relationships between diverse urban residents, both young and old. It is hoped that eventually more and more community members come to gain a sense of pride and ownership over these spaces; this will also negate the need for intensive municipal regulation, including law enforcement.

Peter Whitley opens with a presentation that deals with how neighborhoods can obtain skate parks. In particular, he addresses the support and development aspects. Whitley suggests that people often focus on securing money before gaining support, but emphasizes that building a base of support is key to ensuring success of the park. Long-term relationships, he says, will lead to trust and ongoing communication, whereas fundraisers aren't as effective because activities such as local T-shirt sales rarely make much money and they don't focus on cultivating neighborhood support. To illustrate his point, Whitley describes how a group of skaters once volunteered at a senior citizens' home, picking weeds. Their goal was to build support for a proposed skate park to be located across the street. The skaters made a good impression and the skate park was approved. In addition, some of these skaters, he says, maintained a relationship with the senior citizens beyond the building of the park. Whitley's strategy of building a sense of community to support parks coincides with his goal: to use skate parks as a means of integrating skateboarding youth within their communities. Continuing on, Whitley suggests other strategies to promote advocacy including communicating with city staff and getting them involved on a steering committee. Ultimately, he argues that skate parks need to be embedded within city master plans.

Whitley offers some metrics for skate-park development that include the number of them and where they should be located. He asserts that there should be a skate park in every neighborhood. The THF defines a neighborhood as 25,000 residents. Serving this size of a neighborhood requires at least a 10,000-square-foot skate park. Whereas for dense urban areas like the Bay Area, the metric is 40,000 residents for this type of skate park. He then describes the best characteristics for skate-park locations. He addresses these in terms of comfort, activity, access, and sociability. When addressing what constitutes a viable site, he states that they are frequently used by different groups and accommodate diverse activities. He then notes that the litmus test for safe and active sites is when they are used by single women and the elderly. Skate parks should be in a very visible space, he says, with lots of eyes on them, and ideally close to public transportation. In other words, for skate parks to be successful, they need to be integrated into broader community recreation elements.

Next, at this event, we heard from several individuals working directly with youth in the field. They believed that local youth need more activity spaces to develop, because these spaces are typically ignored under urban-regeneration projects. It was then suggested that skate parks could be used to raise awareness about specific social issues, and simultaneously create new allies for causes such as gender inclusion. Furthermore, it was posited that adult support for skate parks would show youth that they were valued and trusted community members.

> At this point in the meeting, the audience was able to discuss programmatic concerns with members of SLAG and K-Dub. When these people talked, most of it focused on creating spaces that youth are invested in where they can build self-confidence and a sense of teamwork. The women of SLAG discuss changing the culture at skate parks from fear to comfort, making them more inclusive for all genders. Considering the future of skateboarding, SLAG envisioned personal benefits to skaters, such as self-discipline and confidence. SLAG also addressed more social benefits such as building friends and community through social justice and inclusiveness. Masters notes that SLAG welcomes male allies, so that they are not creating a female-only space, but rather a gender-inclusive space. Some specific activities to reach their goals include skate lessons and other job skills, such as interviewing and resume writing.
>
> In addition, all panel members agree that now is the time to build skate parks because these spaces could potentially disappear through urban privatization and gentrification. Discussions of how skaters are currently being pushed out of their DIY spots soon follows. There is some further discussion about potential strategies to share spaces with the encroaching private sphere. However, all agreed that in many urban centers, land is at a premium, and open spaces for youth should be a priority.
>
> K-Dub then talks about the need to develop allies around youth space. He says that working to establish community connections, in order to build trust and support, is vital in order to effectively program these spaces. The Levi's representative then chimes in to say that this was how Oakland's Town Park was built. K-Dub encourages non-skaters to come to skate parks and see what is going on, stating,

"Skating is not so foreign." He says there is a great need to invest in public spaces, especially for young people lacking other resources. K-Dub further states that young people should be "stakeholders in our community" and have pride in their community spaces. He contends that there is a need for more youth-oriented public space. K-Dub declares, "Give them a world-class facility, so they believe they are supported by community." K-Dub continues by noting that one can go to the local skate parks and run into her/his hero, but the same person cannot go to the basketball court and run into her/his favorite National Basketball Association (NBA) player.

We can see that the Oakland Skatepark Summit participants, representing diverse affiliations and responsibilities, shared stories of success and difficulty with each other and local attendees. This event demonstrates how diverse social-enterprise stakeholders like these often work in sync to prioritize skateboarding as a medium for supporting youth and their communities. Over the course of this book, we demonstrate how this type of adult networking and intervention has led to the creation of new urban spaces across several Bay Area communities. These skate parks, we will see, are intentionally designed under specific social-change visions, so that different forms of capital can be generated for youth and community benefit. Below, we delve further into this discussion by outlining the social-enterprise concept as it currently influences the processes by which skate parks are being built and subsequently utilized.

Social-Enterprise Practice in the Neoliberal Era

Investment in skateboarding, as in other sports, does not reflect a simple binary of either serving the social good or maximizing private profit. In fact, organizations involved in supporting sports frequently blend for-profit business structures with their social-service missions. As first revealed in the introduction to this book, this hybrid social-change model is often referred to as social enterprise.[1] Sport management scholar Daniel Bjärsholm proposes that under conditions of neoliberalism, with reduced government expenditures for public activities, social-enterprise organizations have expanded to fill the void left by the state.[2] This social-enterprise model has been characterized as a continuum that fluidly incorporates public and private attributes as well as mechanisms.

This typology breaks down the traditional boundaries between the nonprofit and private sectors and reflects a more hybridized vision of business and social-change values. "In doing so, the typology explores how institutions have combined a mix of social values and goals with commercial business practices. . . ."[3] Furthermore, it has been identified that social-enterprise practice "can take different forms, including public-private partnerships incorporating elements from state, market, and civil society logics."[4] The Oakland Skatepark Summit is indeed an overt example of how "ideas, values, roles, relationships, and capital now flow more freely" amongst social-enterprise networks, eventually leading to a "cross-sector fertilization" effect.[5]

Taking up this idea, we argue that local skate-park coalitions from the Bay Area represent different models in the social-enterprise continuum. Indeed, the groups featured later in this chapter differ from each other in terms of how they flexibly incorporate social-service, entrepreneurial, brand-marketing, fundraising, and profit-making goals. But while their mechanisms may diverge, the primary social values being promoted by these social-enterprise groups cohere around youth- and community-development ideals.

In some cases, we will see that social-enterprise representatives work more "on the ground," so to speak, in order to directly confront the traditional social norms of skateboarding within difficult and complex environments. This can be arduous work, as noted in the following description based on one of our research observations. During one visit to a skate park in Berkeley, we saw two twenty-something female skate activists cajoling a small crew of young girl skateboarders during a special skate event. It was a searing day, and the heat was exacerbated by the concrete and lack of shade in this skate park. Because the male skaters were utilizing most of the space for themselves, the girls and their mentors were stuck in a small corner in the back, penned in by a metal fence. A few parents also squeezed in, trying to watch and make videos of their daughters. Meanwhile, numerous guys in tank tops and jeans blitzed through the bowl at high speeds. Oblivious to the amount of space they occupied, and the girls' predicament, the men cut a wide swath through the skate park while downing tall cans of beer. At the skate-park entrance, a couple sat on a bench sharing a marijuana joint, its strong odor wafting through the skate park toward the kids. Even the research group, including two of the authors and their two student research assistants, felt somewhat cautious and claustrophobic walking into this caged-in skate park scene. We left this scene with newfound appreciation for the volunteers leading these events on a weekly basis.

We can see from this example that being a skateboarding activist at the grassroots level is not your typical youth-sports-team coaching job; it often requires tremendous energy, adaptability, and patience in order to advance one's social cause. And it is often the case that this type of youth mentoring goes unpaid. We will further demonstrate how this type of daily commitment to youth is also complemented by the presence of more "behind the scenes" supporters. Together, these organizational leaders regularly work on behalf of youth that have been identified as being "less visible" in skateboarding culture, like the women and girls in the skate-park scene described above.[6]

Next, we will identify the range of social-enterprise skate-park groups that are structuring local skateboarding experiences for youth and their families in our area. Intersecting youth- and community-development principles, we suggest, *always* run through the missions of these groups. Later, we will demonstrate that these social-enterprise organizations usually embed their strategies in privatized practices, even as their mechanisms and approaches diverge from each other. As we alluded just above, some of these groups employ a more behind-the-scenes approach, while others are more committed to working directly on the ground, at the neighborhood level. We then ascertain how these social-enterprise groups are creating new sets of social relationships and practices within urban skate parks. From the standpoint that social-enterprise groups intend to change society, we discuss how newly created skate parks are meant to tackle embedded social problems and inequalities. Local skate parks, we contend, are explicitly set up to address social concerns related to race, ethnicity, gender, and social class. Throughout this entire discussion, we will see that new types of urban spaces, citizens, and relationships are being envisioned through social-enterprise networks supporting skate parks.

Using Sports to Make Social Change:
Action Sport for Development and Peace (ASDP)

But, in the first place, how does sports practice correspond with ideals of creating social change? One historical example of social-enterprise practice in sports is known as "Sports for Development and Peace" (SDP). According to Canadian scholar Bruce Kidd, SDP "has become a recognised strategy of social intervention in disadvantaged communities throughout the world, with an array of proclamations, endorsements, programmes, organisations, specialists, students and researchers."[7] The

SDP movement has in fact evolved since the 1960s and specifically draws attention to diverse causes, including apartheid, women's equal participation, and civil rights.[8] Today, SDP is even positioned as a key mechanism to achieve the United Nations' Millennium Development Goals (MDGs), which pertain to gender inclusion and youth's health outcomes, among other goals.[9] At the same time, established sports organizations including the International Olympic Committee (IOC), national-level organizations, as well as "hundreds of NGOs, big and small, from every corner of the globe," have also implemented SDP programs worldwide.[10]

In our introduction, we discussed Holly Thorpe's premise that the SDP model also resonates with contemporary action-sports practice. She describes this concept as "Action Sports for Development and Peace" (ASDP). In fact, it has been revealed that "since the mid-and late-1990s, action-sports participants have established nonprofit organizations and movements relating to an array of social issues, including health, education, environment, anti-violence and female empowerment."[11] This scholarly view is supported by numerous program examples. Indeed, there is a sizeable list of organizations juxtaposing social causes with board sports.[12] For instance, a recent *Huck Magazine* article entitled "Bangladesh's Teenage Surf Girls are Dreaming of a Better Future" includes the provocative subtitle "Paddling Through Patriarchy."[13] This article declares that a surfing program enables young women to become more independent and confident. Further demonstrating the global reach of board activism, for youth, there is another nonprofit initiative called Cuba Skate, which "hopes to foster a constructive environment for Cuban youth that will have a positive impact on the greater community." What's more, Cuba Skate purports that it "expands the future for these skaters by creating a chance to continue skateboarding, and developing, year round."[14] In addition, we have already identified the famed Skateistan project that, since 2006, has provided young women in Afghanistan, Cambodia, and South Africa, "with opportunities to participate in sport, education and employment."[15]

These real-life examples support the scholarly idea that action or lifestyle sports such as surfing and skateboarding are now being utilized in line with other SDP activities to potentially help youth. Certainly, then, these board sports can no longer be simplistically categorized as "hedonistic, thrill-seeking, anti-authoritarian, individualistic" activities.[16] Scholars Holly Thorpe and Megan Chawansky also remind us that there is a spectrum of different groups involved in these social issues. Groups identified here range from locally based grassroots programs to some entities whose work is becoming globally recognized by "mainstream social justice and humanitarian organizations."[17] We will draw from this understanding of different ASDP models and goals in order to illustrate the variety of programs operating in the Bay Area. Our belief is that there are similarities and contrasts found amongst these local ASDP-type social-enterprise groups. These groups create new youth and community values via new skate parks, based upon positive youth development (PYD) principles. A key part of our discussion thus pertains to the unique scope and approach of each featured group in line with their specific mission and access to resources.

Important to this discussion is the fact that some of these ASDP groups "have flourished in the contemporary moment" under neoliberal conditions.[18] This follows a global trend that involves the "privatization of humanitarian and social justice groups," since governments have often "absented themselves" from addressing pressing social needs.[19] Focusing once again on the idea of social enterprise, we can observe how recent skate-park projects may utilize government support but nonetheless employ private-sector strategies, too. As we shall see, these groups make fundamental links with businesses, corporations, and individual donors to achieve their goals.

We now turn to describe several social-enterprise groups and their leaders that intend to impact urban skateboarding through their espoused social-change goals. We detail their contributions in terms of specific backgrounds and rationales, as well as the key social values and practices that they enact. In this discussion, we further explain how each group attempts to develop new sources of capital for youth, families, and communities. Our discussion of these groups is often contextualized by the voices of program representatives, as found in digital outlets including organization websites, online news reports, and social-media posts. Semi-structured interviews and field observations, recorded when activists were present and conducting their work, are also incorporated.

At first, we illustrate the presence of celebrity skate-park foundations, led by famous skateboarders Tony Hawk and Rob Dyrdek, that primarily support the building of skate parks in low-income neighborhoods.[20] Then, we highlight how there are additional local groups that focus upon the racial, ethnic, and socioeconomic dimensions of skateboarding. Featured groups here include Rob "Skate" Ferguson's various entrepreneurial projects, as well as a unique religious/government entity from

San Jose called SJ 180. Furthermore, with female inclusion underlying their social-change agendas, we explain how MAHFIA.TV, Girl Riders Organization (GRO), and Skate Like a Girl (SLAG) have become active in our local region.

The groups showcased in this chapter regularly conduct their work flexibly across several skate parks. As we shall see, this attribute offers some benefits for reaching a wider and more diverse clientele, while there are some disadvantages to being at the whim of various skate-park operators. The subsequent *Moving Boarders* case-study chapters (3, 4, and 5) will provide additional accounts of how these social-enterprise groups and their representatives work in specific skate-park locations.

Social-Enterprise Groups Addressing Low-Income Urban Youth

TONY HAWK FOUNDATION

The Tony Hawk Foundation (THF) is an organization set up under the namesake of the most recognized skateboarder in the world. Tony Hawk started skating in the 1970s and was a champion vert skater during the 1980s and 1990s. Hawk has parlayed his skate achievements into lucrative business ventures, including his line of best-selling video games, *Tony Hawk's Pro Skater*, and he co-owns a skate brand, Birdhouse. His foundation was established in 2002 with the primary aim of helping build skate parks across communities in the United States. The THF board of directors is comprised of various experts from the fields of real estate, retail, music and entertainment, law, action sports, and social media.[21]

The mission of the THF is "to foster lasting improvements in society, with an emphasis on supporting and empowering youth."[22] Moreover, the THF deliberately targets at-risk youth based on the assumption that skateboarding can be utilized to serve them in their communities, giving "priority to communities that can document a high degree of social problems among teens and pre-teens, such as drug use, high drop-out rates, high arrest rates, childhood obesity, teen pregnancy, free or reduced school lunches, and the like."[23] Consequently, the THF issues grants to low-income communities in order to build skate parks. These grants range from $1,000 to $25,000 and have been awarded to cities in all fifty U.S. states. To further aid local communities, the THF has developed a public-skate-park development guide outlining five steps in creating and operating a skate park.[24] Moreover, demonstrating the overlapping work of social-enterprise groups, the THF supports international programs such as Skateistan. Complementing the THF, Hawk developed Stand Up for Skateparks, which has raised over $9.3 million to support the THF's mission.[25]

During the Oakland Skatepark Summit described earlier in this chapter, programs director Peter Whitley highlighted the key areas that THF focuses upon. Another field-note extract from this event describes some of Whitley's explanations to the audience:

> Whitley states that the THF's goal is to support the health and the character of the city. Nonetheless, he mentions that cities frequently will not initiate the building of skate parks because they don't see benefits, and often hear about drawbacks. Whitley then points out that individuals oppose skate parks because of issues associated with skateboarding and especially teenaged males (e.g., noise, perceived delinquency). Whitley even states that resistance to neighborhood skate parks originates from the fear of fifteen-year-old boys. He notes that although there is some evidence to support these concerns, skate parks are actually good places for teen boys to become part of the community. To appease naysayers, he says, one must address noise levels, youth engagement, and parks' architectural designs. Doing so may help persuade those people who support skate parks in principle, yet take a "not in my backyard" (NIMBY) stance once talk of construction begins.

The THF's goal is thus to stimulate community engagement and provide organizational skills for youth who are expected to lobby for and use a skate park. For instance, the THF website states that youth should create advocacy groups, promote the proposed skate park to other community members, obtain necessary approval from local leaders, and allow other local youth to be part of the process. Ultimately, the THF says to youth, "We can help you do those things, but you need to understand that you'll be doing the local work."[26]

We learned through our research that the THF actually influenced Jane, the leader of Bay City's skate-park supporter group described at length in Chapter 3. Here, Jane recalls working closely with the THF to develop the supporter group's strategy for securing a new skate park in Bay City:

> [I had] gone to a few of Tony Hawk Foundation events, and, sort of, my entry into the whole skateboard universe was through doing volunteer work and going to events and doing some volunteer work

at the Tony Hawk Foundation. That was really helpful because when we were building the park, they [THF] were able to help us to get things like noise studies and testimonies from police departments where they'd seen graffiti and trespassing go way down. Tony Hawk Foundation was able to help us with that kind of stuff, so that was cool.

The THF contends that "there are social benefits" for urban, at-risk youth when they are provided with safe places to "pursue an athletic activity that they love." And, as we noted before, the controlled environment of a skate park, as opposed to the street, is viewed as most appropriate for youth to develop: "There are public health benefits in having a safe place for young people to develop active lifestyles away from the risks found in the streets."[27] To achieve these aims, skate parks, according to the THF, should be built in areas that fulfill the following criteria: they can be used by a broad segment of the community; they are free and accessible; and they can be easily seen. Regarding this last standard, Peter Whitley noted in the Oakland Skatepark Summit that skate parks should not be built down an alley hidden from public view; otherwise they become exclusively used by teenagers instead of the general population. If the chosen site is right, the THF believes, then more community members will feel attached to the success of this space, to the point that they monitor local behavior. Crucially, this means foregoing official security mechanisms such as guards and city supervisors:

> An outdoor, open, highly visible location—as most skateparks are—is not the place to bully kids, use drugs, or be a nuisance. Skaters are there for a reason, and are generally very good at policing each other about behavior that interferes with their enjoying the park. . . . (On the other hand) supervised skateparks can undermine progress made in natural stewardship by superseding that feeling of ownership with a "sanctioned" authority figure.[28]

Importantly, following this view of community stewardship, we can see in the next field-note extract, once again from the Oakland Skatepark Summit, that the THF wants to develop new social networks through the provision of free, inclusive skate parks.

> An interesting dialogue between Peter Whitley and a middle-aged white woman took place later in the Q and A session. The woman said she has enjoyed paying a fee to get into a skate park as she finds them cleaner and safer than free public skate parks. She asked

what was his opinion about endorsing this type of skate park. Whitley responded that they [THF] do not endorse pay-to-skate parks because they limit who can skate at the park. This limitation removes the social aspect that organically happens between different types of people who come to the skate parks. After checking with another THF representative, Steve Hawk, Whitley adamantly reinforces his earlier claim that the THF does not under any circumstance financially support parks that are pay-to-play, as they see this as dividing communities instead of building them.

Our overall belief is that the THF facilitates localized public-private partnerships in order to create skate parks that benefit low-income, underserved youth in their own neighborhoods. The THF, in part, wants to serve as a resource, in terms of providing information, organizational support, and initial funding. And while it functions on a national scale, the THF also directly engages with local city master plans and parks-and-recreation departments. Programs director Peter Whitley's appearance at the Oakland Skatepark Summit also demonstrates how the THF engages with locally based skateboarders and community supporters when necessary. Because it is these local stakeholders who will eventually lead the process of obtaining a new skate park and also determine the nature of future participation.

"STREET LEAGUE FOUNDATION" AND "ROB DYRDEK FOUNDATION"

Similar to the THF, the Street League Foundation and the Rob Dyrdek Foundation were both created by famous skateboarder-entrepreneur Rob Dyrdek. Originally from Ohio, Dyrdek eventually moved to California as a teenager to start several companies and obtain numerous sponsorships. Notably, he was involved with popular brands such as Alien Workshop and DC Shoes.

Rob Dyrdek subsequently applied his skateboarding prowess and entrepreneurial skills to creating and producing several hit MTV shows, including *Rob & Big*, *Rob Dyrdek's Fantasy Factory*, and *Ridiculousness*. His production company, Straightjacket, has produced shows for several other cable television networks. In addition, Dyrdek has funded and acted in films such as *Street Dreams*, and has been featured in video games. Altogether, these endeavors clearly indicate how Rob Dyrdek embraces and promotes entrepreneurialism via skateboarding.

As a matter of fact, Dyrdek's website describes him as a "renowned storyteller, systematic entrepreneur, venture capitalist, pop-culture personality, ex-professional athlete, retired stuntman, brand ambassador, and groundbreaking media impresario all wrapped into one."[29] In terms of his style, scholar Emily Chivers Yochim characterizes Dyrdek as "adopting hip-hop (read black) and working class signifiers such as heavy gold chains, oversized clothing, 'trucker' hats, and scruffy facial hair."[30]

Dyrdek has notably established a professional skateboarding circuit called Street League Skateboarding, which initially aimed to award the most prize money to skateboarders and take precedence over competing events such as the X Games and the Dew Tour.[31] According to its website, "Street League Skateboarding was created to foster growth, popularity, and acceptance of street skateboarding worldwide."[32] Dyrdek's Street League Skateboarding, including its tour and championship events, has recently been sanctioned as the main path to qualification for the Tokyo 2020 Summer Olympic Games. In addition, several global Street League events merged with the skateboarding contest portion of ESPN's X Games beginning in 2013; these events became branded as "Street League at X Games," with Dyrdek proclaiming, "There is no better opportunity to elevate Street League globally than our new partnership with the X Games."[33]

In addition to his numerous business ventures, we describe below how Dyrdek has supported two foundations that have built street-style skate parks in several American communities, called *skate plazas*. These skate plazas are often based in underserved urban neighborhoods, with several based in Los Angeles alone. Indeed, one recent press report quoted Los Angeles councilmember José Huizar as saying, "Rob Dyrdek and I know that kids on the Eastside like to skateboard as much as anybody else and this skate plaza is an incredible gift to the young people of this community."[34] In 2014, statements on the Rob Dyrdek Foundation's former website called for "a skate plaza in every community," to be used by "everyone" from "the most advanced pro to the youngest novice."[35] Referring to its creation in 2003, this foundation claimed that its purpose was "to create healthy communities by promoting and providing the inherent benefits of skateboarding to all facets of society."

Much like the THF, the Rob Dyrdek Foundation championed public-private ways of working, thus mirroring social-enterprise practice. Its vision statement reported that it wanted to "encourage construction of legal street skating areas, be that through large urban skate plazas or single skate spots."[36] Partners that were accordingly sought out to build these skate parks included "governments, park and recreations departments and local urban renewal and community improvement commit-tees" as well as "major corporations and organizations . . . who wish to give back to their communities through funding, land donation or other means of support."[37] In fact, one skate park built in Los Angeles's largely Latino Boyle Heights area was championed by the Diamond Supply Company, several government leaders, offices including the Department of Recreation and Parks, as well as the California Endowment, a founda-tion which aims to improve health in poor communities.[38]

In 2015, the Rob Dyrdek Foundation link on his Street League Skateboarding website disappeared and a newer incarnation, the Street League Skateboarding Foundation, appeared in its place. This newer foundation echoed its predecessor's intention to "foster healthier com-munities by promoting and providing access to skateboarding to all lev-els of society equally," while also giving out skateboards.[39] As elsewhere, extensive youth- and community-development rhetoric was used to frame the need for these new skate spaces: "Skateboarding is a proven way to instill self-confidence, promote self-expression, and encourage an active lifestyle. Through continuous outreach to local governments, parks and recreation departments, and local urban renewal and community improvement committees, we hope to show how designated skate plazas can invigorate and enrich their communities."[40]

It is clear that Rob Dyrdek sees himself as a social entrepreneur who is building an urban brand aligned with his various popular, media-driven personae. In addition, Dyrdek ostensibly supports youth and community development across several American cities. The community skate plazas seem to be quite connected to his lucrative, competitive skate circuit, with one of his webpages stating that "the 'SLS Foundation' launched in 2013 as a way to extended the SLS mission to increase global participation in street skateboarding."[41] Dyrdek actually hosts "events at SLSF public pla-zas that bring Street League Skateboarding Pros to meet and skate with the local communities."[42] One skate park in Fresno, California, was even renovated in order to resemble a Street League skate course, according to one news report: "The new plaza will replace the current park with a design that mimics the courses set up for professionals in the Street League competitions—with a series of ledges and stairs, planter boxes, curbs and the like. . . . The plaza is already getting buzz for its connec-tion to Dyrdek and Street League Skateboarding, which will bring sev-eral of its pro skaters to the plaza's grand opening."[43] Within this story, a representative of Dyrdek's foundation claimed, "It's a pro-skating version of a little league field. It's building the next generation of professional skater." Furthermore, in 2010, it was reported that cities hosting major Street League events would receive the used obstacles and also obtain $50,000 from Dyrdek's foundation for design and construction costs that would help build a new skate plaza.[44]

When compared, we find that the THF and Dyrdek's foundation have similarly stated social aims, as they draw on public-private alliances to help build skate parks to help at-risk, underserved youth. However, our assessment is that the THF's model is more explicit in terms of fostering sustainable social networks that can provide for active youth citizenship and social-capital generation. The THF intensively assists local DIY efforts by providing seed funding, development and organizational strategies, alongside research illustrating the positive impact of skate parks. The THF advocates for local skateboarding under an umbrella vision of creating free and accessible skate parks that prominently feature in neighborhood life. THF program director Peter Whitley once provided a useful example of how diverse community members can work and live together in society, when he shared the story of skaters befriending local senior citizens during the building of a THF skate park.

Drydek's twin foundations have commendably worked with companies and philanthropic groups to build skate parks in areas where youth need this type of facility. Yet, our critique is that these skate plazas also seem quite deliberately placed to support Dyrdek's various for-profit endeavors. Without doubt, these urban spaces serve to increase the visibility of the Street League skateboarding style and also expand the consumer base for Dyrdek's skate tour and his various products and projects.

We therefore question how Dyrdek's skate plazas actually foster sustainable social change. In terms of his strategy for promoting health and social change, we did not find evidence that sophisticated, committed advocacy was provided, and that sustainable, intentional working relationships were being fostered on the ground level, as we saw with the THF. As a result, there is a simple yet problematic assumption being made here, that positive social values and relationships will organically arise from how youth approach and utilize new skate plaza infrastructure. And, as we will explain throughout *Moving Boarders*, this top-down, hands-off approach, while perhaps well-intentioned, does not frequently lead to significant social change, particularly for female skaters who have historically been precluded from participating fully in skateboarding.

Groups Focusing on Racial, Ethnic, and Economic Issues in Local Skate Parks

Besides the celebrity-run ones, there are other skate-park groups reliant upon local individuals supporting urban underserved youth of color and their neighborhoods. The two groups outlined below were led by what scholar A. James McKeever recently deemed local "community heads" that use city parks to mentor youth.[45] Next, we will see that Danny Sanchez and Rob "Skate" Ferguson used their grassroots organizations to aid youth in our region's skate parks. Both of these youth mentors had actual sports skills that gave them entry and respect within neighborhood youth skate cultures, even as they were not high-profile professionals like Tony Hawk or Rob Dyrdek.[46]

SJ 180'S COMMUNITY: "A LITTLE BIT OF SKATEBOARDERS, A LITTLE BIT OF GANGSTERS, AND A LITTLE BIT OF PEOPLE THAT ARE JUST HANGING AROUND"

One group hoping to make skate parks relevant to communities where youth of color reside is SJ 180 in San Jose. Since 2016, this organization has worked under the auspices of the city government to help youth in their neighborhood skate parks. SJ 180 is headed by local resident Danny Sanchez, a self-identified skateboarding pastor. Sanchez explained the origins of SJ 180 to us during an interview at San Jose's Roosevelt skate park, which is featured in Chapter 5:

> Interviewer: SJ 180. So, tell me about SJ 180.
>
> Sanchez: So SJ 180 was birthed out of connecting with skate parks. As a pastor, being a part of a local church, I would come out for years and bring water to the kids and talk with them and just try to engage them more. A few years later, I started working with the Mayor's Gang Prevention Task Force in San Jose and this community is kind of a mixture, you know what I mean? You have a little bit of skateboarders, a little bit of gangsters, and a little bit of people that are just hanging around, you know, getting high.

During one summer evening, as a skate contest was about to begin, Sanchez told us that adults could utilize skateboarding to engage youth in neighborhood parks such as Roosevelt. His desire was thus to transform Roosevelt in a 180-degree direction, he said, by turning it into an engaged "community family." Speaking hypothetically toward youth, he once stated, "You're a part of this family and we want to invest in you and what your passion is"; he considered this passion to be skateboarding.

In Chapter 5, we illustrate how SJ 180's approach to youth development comes under the city's broader intervention of "place-making." This model is employed by San Jose to advance urban redevelopment efforts within low-income areas where people of color live, under the view that the local youth are living "at risk." Sanchez, operating in conjunction with the city, provides the following description of SJ 180's public-service model and intended participants below:

> So, you know, the city sometimes gets complaints about who's hanging around the skate parks, the environment of skate parks, the graffiti. They have gang graffiti and regular graffiti and sometimes it can be seen in a negative light so we got to talking with the city of San Jose and we started to, we're piloting this program, we did it last year also. We're piloting this program, SJ 180. The 180, the SJ of course [is] San Jose, but the 180 is a trick. It's doing a 180 on your skateboard, but it's also changing a direction, right. So, what we want to do is change the direction of the park from a negative view everybody has of it to a positive view. We do that by engaging the youth, connecting with them, doing contests, providing food. . . . Some of the people that hang out here, they're hitting some ruts in their life and they need a little bit of support and help, so that's what we do. We provide contests to build community with them, we want to draw families. We have a lot of young kids that are here.

The SJ 180 program is integrated within skate jam sessions held in these particular San Jose neighborhoods. In conversation with us, Sanchez said that skate jams feature several competition brackets: "We have a ten-and-under bracket, we have an eleven-through-seventeen, eighteen-and-over, and we have a female bracket." These contests are held in conjunction with the city's Viva Parks! summer program; this is a series of events which focus upon the provision of health and wellness resources, physical activities and community engagement.

SJ 180 directly receives support from the city of San Jose as well as two faith-based organizations, including the Whosevers, a Christian outreach program working with Californian high-school students, and the City Peace Project, another Christian program that assists youth and families impacted by gangs and violence. Sanchez is the founder and director of the City Peace Project, which is based in San Jose. He also spends considerable time fostering links between SJ 180 and the local police department, the Boys and Girls Club, and Silicon Valley tech companies in order to give San Jose's youth further networking and learning opportunities.

Like other locally based activists we met in our research, Sanchez was frequently observed in the skate park making a concerted effort to engage the local youth. He told us that he drew upon his own skateboarding background and then tapped into city resourcing, as well as his other nonprofit community service organizations. Essentially, Sanchez used skateboarding as a point of entry in order to meet youth and then assist them through these various public-private support mechanisms. This social-enterprise approach is revealed in the next interview quote:

> It [skateboarding] was just something that's been a part of my life since I was twelve years old. I didn't have, I wasn't very good at sports, I wasn't very connected in other ways and it really connected me with a community of people. . . . They know I could skate and they respect that, you know what I mean? Like, I'm coming as one of them to meet them right where they're at, to say, "Hey you know what? I have the resources to support you." Through the city, through my nonprofit, through other organizations that are willing to give.

It became obvious to us that Sanchez's visits to Roosevelt and other neighborhood skate parks reflect his passion and care for youth. But, they also served to provide the youth here with tangible opportunities. For example, SJ 180 offers a six-week program through community centers, such as Roosevelt's, that involves weekly workshops for youth job-seekers. This was a "SJ 180 job training program," Sanchez once told us, "to get them re-engaged in the community and change their current circumstance." In fact, during one weekday afternoon visit, we saw Sanchez sitting on a skate bench inside Roosevelt, hanging out with a group of several local young males and one female. Together, they observed the other skateboarders practicing their tricks. A short time later, Sanchez had ended up standing in front of them and offering tips for obtaining city jobs. We observed that the youth listened even as many drank beer. Sanchez later explained that his ultimate aim was to provide youth like these with a sense of value and also opportunities to improve their lives:

> It's more informal. I walk up to people, individuals, and I talk with them about the program and I invite them. Some will come, some won't, and some it takes a little while, but I give everyone the opportunity to be involved. It's just where they're at in life. Are they ready

to make that change? I know for me it took a while so that's why I never give up hope. That's why I keep investing in these guys here, and gals, at this park, because they are vital members of our community and they are important.

On a regular basis, we noticed that Sanchez was given respect and time from the Roosevelt youth who otherwise seemed reticent about adults in their space. During one Viva Parks! skate jam event we watched, Sanchez was seen talking and shaking hands with many boys and girls from the local neighborhood; we could see that he knew many of them personally. Indeed, he told us later that he knew their families and where they went to church and school.

Through Sanchez's casual yet committed mentoring approach, SJ 180 is one means for San Jose youth to feel that the city supports them and their activities. This social-enterprise program, reflecting a unique blend of religious, private-industry, nonprofit, and city-government components, invites San Jose youth to become more integrated into their community. But social integration here reflects the terms that the city prefers; the underlying goal is that youth should gain a sense of personal integrity and become more skilled, employable citizens. As part of this process, SJ 180 and the city provide the youth with access to more mainstream contexts including job training and opportunities. As the story in *Moving Boarders* unfolds, we will see that this mission—to provide youth with new types of benefits and social identities—aligns with our concept of *Urban Platforms for Capital*.

ROB "SKATE" FERGUSON: "PLAYING BOTH SIDES OF THE FENCE" TO HELP YOUTH, PARENTS, AND COMMUNITIES

Rob "Skate" Ferguson likewise heads numerous social-change organizations that collectively exemplify social-enterprise practice. Like Sanchez, he also utilizes his skateboarding background and experience in the local scene to work as a youth mentor. Ferguson embraces this idea of being a mentor, to the point of resembling a father figure or big brother, as he told us in conversation. "So, as a father figure, especially in different communities, a lot of the individuals, especially the youngsters, they see me coming out and giving back to the community in so many different ways. They look to me for different types of advice. I'm, if not father figure, I could be classified as a big brother type of guy to them."

Ferguson uses the term "platform," borrowed from his own men-

Rob "Skate" Ferguson working at a community event. *Courtesy of Todd Fuller.*

tor Keith "K-Dub" Williams, to characterize each of his projects, which include the Rob Skate Skateboarding Academy, 4141Corp nonprofit organization, and Cali Am Jam free community skate events.[47] Through this portfolio of community projects, Ferguson supports free skateboarding events in underserved areas while also overseeing a cadre of youth skate coaches who generate income through skate coaching. Altogether, his organizations serve a wide range of skaters, including both boys and girls hailing from low-income as well as wealthier suburban neighborhoods.

Ferguson takes a much more entrepreneurial approach compared to San Jose's SJ 180 program. Without city government and religious benefactors, Ferguson embraces a for-profit model that is simultaneously committed to serving the public good. In fact, he was once dubbed a "Skateboarding CEO" by a local writer.[48] Furthermore, in our conversations, Ferguson often referred to himself as an "industrialist." This phrase has connotations from early American corporate philanthropy and originally meant that "those who had made fortunes were responsible for redistributing this wealth to be good citizens."[49] And, further revealing this mindset, one of Ferguson's project websites directly states, "Our firm is dedicated to taking care of our customers and partners."[50] The name of this particular project is called the 4141Corp which he dubs a "people's corporation . . . with a focal point on youth empowerment and teen development."[51]

We can thus see that Ferguson and his roster of skateboarding projects both have private-sector connotations. Some of his projects do not seem to generate much personal income: free community contests, public appearances in schools, and volunteer contributions such as fixing up park black-tops. But these social causes directly end up promoting his persona and vision to new audiences, in a manner similar to Rob Dyrdek's approach. And, likewise, this public exposure eventually leads to further interest in his profit-making endeavors. The interwoven nature of Ferguson's non- and for-profit projects is apparent in the following two quote segments from our interview.

> Within the skateboarding scene, I have a production side that makes the boards, has a skateboard team, does all the hard and soft goods, and it goes out—there's that whole side of it. The next side of it is a skateboard camp. I run a lot of paid-for or free programs all throughout the United States, mostly here in California, then trickling a little bit in Colorado, going as far over as Atlanta. That's the other side of it. Another aspect is the private one-on-one lesson, which parents just absolutely love. . . .
>
> Then, on the other side of everything, with all of that, I ended up being tight knit in with a lot of cities so I then coordinate either building new parks or also setting up community events for countless cities across, all around.

Ferguson's various social-enterprise activities, reflecting both philanthropy and entrepreneurialism, thus directly complement each other, as we saw in the case of Rob Dyrdek's foundational work. Yet in contrast to Dyrdek, we observed that Ferguson utilizes an everyday, hands-on approach as he attempts to foster social change, by closely mentoring youth skateboarders and his own coaching staff. At the same time, in regards to families, Ferguson once told us that he wanted parents and their children to see that "skateboarding is okay" and that it is actually a supportive, developmental outlet, that "it's all one big love," as he suggested. Ferguson consequently sought to create a supportive learning environment for youth being introduced to skateboarding, as revealed in the following interview commentary: "Say it's a kid at the skate park for the first time. They're seeing all these other kids out there doing great things. They want to learn. They're hungry. They then ask other individuals out there, 'Hey, how did you do that?' That then begins a conversation, which then begins learning how to get out there and go talk to other people." We will see in chapter 3 that another skate coach, Mike, similarly taps into this newcomer family participant base. And, in both cases, engaging with this new client base also supports these coaches' various entrepreneurial projects.

What's more, Ferguson also wants to provide capital to youth through the acquisition of certain life skills, like many other programs featured in *Moving Boarders*. In this regard, he told us that skateboarding enables youth to "learn lots about themselves" and provides youth with a range of transferrable skills, including perseverance, self-expression, and relationship-building. These positive youth development outcomes are further reiterated on Ferguson's skateboarding academy website, which claims that skateboarding promotes goal-setting, confidence, self-esteem, and positive social interaction, eventually leading to success in other contexts. According to the website, "When channeled properly the act of skateboarding can literally be the medium to enhance a student's adaptations to almost any challenge or experience they may come across in life."[52]

Ferguson consolidates a wide variety of both public- and private-sector interests to create youth-development opportunities. To illustrate this unique combination of interests, we recall one event from the Cali Am Jam skateboard contest series that we attended. These contests are meant to raise awareness and funds to support a range of social causes including diabetes, health and fitness, autism, and cancer. According to one event handout, the Cali Am Jam utilizes a "jam-style" format (both street and bowl) where up to four skaters simultaneously showcase their skills. During this specific event held in one East Bay community skate park, we observed Rob as he emceed the event from dawn to dusk, giving positive shout-outs to the crowd all day long in X Games fashion, while handing out prizes to contest winners. The skate park itself was overwhelmingly filled with young men of color who participated in the skate contests and also freely skated during intermissions. Once again, it was notable to us that Ferguson was able to attract support from so many diverse entities. The Make a Wish Foundation offered a free trip to Hawaii for one young man, while some skate-contest winners received Chipotle-branded skate decks and Zumiez (a skate-oriented apparel company) gift certificates. The park was full of vendors handing out goods, ranging from reggae-themed iced coffee to lemonade, while other organized groups such as the Hayward Parks and Recreation Department, a local skate shop, and even the United States Marine Corps were also present and met with the public.

Ferguson told us that this entrepreneurial, networking approach "makes it easy for things to happen." He admitted that he wants his social projects to be "picked up by a lot of sponsors" and he deliberately uses his own knowledge, background, and immersion in the local scene to succeed: "That's also why it spreads out as far as it does versus many other companies."

Both Danny Sanchez and Rob "Skate" Ferguson are committed youth mentors who focus upon creating new social values and contexts with respect to underserved youth of color in their urban neighborhoods. They see the social worth of skateboarding in terms of teaching life skills, even though their mechanisms are quite different. Sanchez sees the need to respect skaters and their youth activities in order to gain trust which, in turn, is used to draw these skaters into more mainstream forms of civic engagement supported by religious, nonprofit and municipal bodies. By contrast, Ferguson enacts a free-market, entrepreneurial vision, which involves developing new, synergistic social networks comprised of quite diverse and perhaps disconnected supporters, in order to reach and expand his youth base.

Social-Enterprise Groups Focusing on Gender Issues

Although none of the groups outlined above explicitly limit their work to males, we found that they did not intentionally create more opportunities for female skateboarders, except in the case where Ferguson targeted females for his youth coaching program. Coinciding with skateboarding's rising global popularity, there have been a number of new organizations that advocate for more female access and visibility. Social activism directed at improving the participation and experiences of females is occurring globally. In fact, scholars Indigo Willing and Scott Shearer contend that "despite their lower numbers, female skaters globally have been proactive in pushing for more recognition of their engagement in skateboarding, as evident by the emergence of girl skate groups, networks, competitions, and films."[53]

Consequently, in this section, we highlight several of the groups addressing basic inclusion issues for females while simultaneously challenging existing gender stereotypes. Many of the female youth mentors we studied were encouraged by the skateboarding industry's recent endorsement of female skateboarders. However, these mentors were still concerned that industry interest did not always translate into real "on the ground" social improvement. Indeed, women have mostly been afforded limited everyday acceptance within the male-dominated skateboarding world. We thus explore how social-enterprise groups in our area are attempting to alter the gendered landscape of skate parks and the skate industry. This type of intervention intends to go beyond simply creating a "goodwill" factor to actually diversify the members and the values found within this sport.[54]

PROMOTING THE PLACE OF GIRLS AND WOMEN IN SKATEBOARDING: GIRLS RIDERS ORGANIZATION (GRO), SKATE LIKE A GIRL (SLAG), AND MAHFIA.TV

Girls Riders Organization (GRO), MAHFIA.TV, and Skate Like a Girl (SLAG) are three feminist skateboarding organizations that we researched. All of them were operating in the San Francisco Bay Area during the time of our study. To give more context to the concurrent emergence of females as well as feminist social activism in skate culture, we present the experiences and motivations of four women with ties to these three organizations. Rachel works with the San Francisco branch of GRO, while Mandy and Evie once held volunteer leadership roles with the San Francisco chapter of SLAG. Kim Woozy is the director of MAHFIA. TV. Woozy has also very recently taken over leadership duties for SLAG.

From our conversations with these women, we learned that GRO, SLAG, and MAHFIA.TV have similar missions in trying to increase the number of women skateboarders in the San Francisco Bay Area. They have a shared belief in combating sexist gender norms often found in the skate media and industry. And they want to create new social networks in skate parks to effectively achieve this goal. In fact, these individuals can often be seen working together and supporting each other's events in local skate parks. By targeting the participation levels of women, these four leaders believed that, if successful, there would be a concomitant change in the attitudes and behaviors of those at skate parks. This approach would also let other females know that they have a legitimate place in skate parks and, more broadly, in skate culture. To attract more women and girls to skate parks, these activists usually dedicated a time

Girls getting a lesson during a female-centered skate session.
Courtesy of Kimberly Woo.

and place for female skateboarding to occur, usually on a Saturday or Sunday morning. The subsequent field note describes our experiences at one such skate session.

> We are at a girls' skate session that takes place monthly in Bay City Skate Park. This event is hosted by a nonprofit group that wants to increase the presence of girls in skate parks across America. An older woman who is skateboarding comments that "you'll get one guy that's like, 'oh God, girls.' . . . There's just got to be one douche bag who has a problem with girls being in the skate park." The session feels casual with no signage or check-in table. There are pockets of young girls milling around on new skateboards, occasionally testing their budding skills on this bright California morning.
>
> Parents have brought their own portable chairs that they set up on the fringes of the skate park. The parking lot is filled to the brim

with large family vehicles, with a few parents still remaining inside them, trying to catch sight of their daughters through the crowd.

A few parents actually skateboard with their daughters, albeit awkwardly in their newly purchased pads and helmets. It is obvious that some of these moms and dads are beginners, just like their kids. One mom with the group even proclaims that "skateboarders are wild," adding, "Without my kids I won't do skateboarding. I won't be in the park. I will be having coffee in my house or going shopping." Another newbie skate mom tells us about becoming a skateboarding casualty. She recently fell and smashed her orbital bone (just near the eye). And she did this right in front of her daughter. The injury shocked the daughter so much she stopped skateboarding for a while, the mom says.

While the male veterans dropped into the large pool bowl at the back, most of the girls in the female skate event maneuvered in the front end of the park, where their parents were watching. Around 12:30 p.m., the park picks up with more male teenagers who finally turn up as the younger girls begin to go home. Suddenly, one teenaged boy zooming at high speed crashes into a young girl wearing shiny green Puma shoes. She is skateboarding with her dad, who turns out to be a competitive skateboarder. With the dad standing nearby and glowering at him, the exasperated teenager proclaims "There are so many kids!" and speeds away in a huff with his male buddy.

As we can see, new female skateboarding groups are making an impact on daily skate-park life. These groups promote social-change activities such as female-specific skate days that have attracted new participants and supporters. We now turn to illustrate the missions and practices of three specific groups involved in supporting new female skateboarding activities.

"WE'RE TAKING OVER THIS BOWL. THERE'S NO IFS, ANDS, OR BUTS": GIRL RIDERS ORGANIZATION (GRO)

On the evening of February 17, 2017, NBC Nightly News presented a story about GRO excerpted below:

(A group of young girls are shown taking turns zooming up and down an indoor skate ramp)

Narrator: At 10 years old, Zoe Harrington is a daredevil on wheels. But she wasn't always that way.

Interviewer: Tell me about the first time that you went to a skate park.

Zoe: I just saw a bunch of boys, I was like, "Why am I the only girl here?"

Narrator: Pretty intimidating for a first-timer [Zoe is shown wiping out on her skateboard]. But then Zoe joined GRO, the Girls Riders Organization, an encouraging environment where girls of all ages can learn to skateboard.[55]

The commentary in this nationally televised report identifies the mission of GRO, which is "to inspire, educate, and support girls through action sports to be active in life and confident leaders of positive change in the community around them." Although a national organization, GRO is structured to have a coach/leader working at the local level who coordinates activities such as the girls skate session described above. GRO is working toward the goal of having an all-girl skate crew in each state.[56]

We met Rachel at one of the local GRO sessions. She agreed to talk with us about her role with GRO and her views and experiences of female skateboarding. At the time of our study, Rachel was the local chapter representative. She told us during our interview that the primary role for GRO was to create new social networks for females and to simultaneously challenge skateboarding's hegemonic masculine orientation. These potential social networks, she explained, could empower females and give them new opportunities. Rachel oversaw two-hour female skate sessions one Saturday per month in a local skate park. These free sessions were well organized, with announcements posted on their national website months in advance highlighting the numerous sponsors for the session. These announcements also conveyed the idea that sessions were for "all girls/all ages/all abilities."

During our research observations, we saw anywhere from two to about a dozen girls attending each event with Rachel volunteering to organize and coach at these events. As a matter of fact, "it's all nonprofit," Rachel told us during our interview at one event. "And it's all just about supporting women and letting other girls come and create a network," she added. Rachel then recounted, "We even had new riders today. Every time, we have new riders, and they all say the same thing. It's all about, when you skate with other girls it's just about having a network of other girlfriends because it's just hard to find."

During these events, Rachel tried to have older and younger females work together, in order to help each other skate, as seen in the commentary below.

> First, I'll have them do a little race, or something where I can assess their level, and then I'll pair them up into little groups and have them teach each other. Then I have little tickets, so I'll give them tickets, and I'll say, "If you taught someone today, come see me and I'll give you a ticket," or a sticker or something to keep track. At the end of the day, whoever taught someone the most is the person that gets the board or the mega prize or whatever. So, it's not who was ripping the most, and I think that just helps with their attitude. It's like, "Yeah, I taught people. I helped everyone else, and everybody was rad and I won a prize for it." It helps them support each other.

Rachel also felt that the young girls who often attended these GRO events had limited power to change the current masculine domination found within skate parks. In this regard, Rachel believed that her adult presence as well as her own skateboarding experience could be used to help new female skateboarders. "Sometimes we take up . . . if we just barge on a bowl, I'll do that," she emphasized to us. "I'll just barge on a bowl and be like, 'Oh, we're getting in here right now, because it's this little girl's first time skating ever. She's about to have the time of her life and skate for the rest of her life. We're taking over this bowl. There's no ifs, ands, or buts.'"

All of the female skate leaders that we met indicated that the limited yet hypersexualized portrayal of females in skateboarding drove them to be involved. Rachel once described this negative trend as follows: "Now that women are starting to be promoted in skateboarding, they're being promoted [in] this hypersexual way, and it makes me look like I'm some hypersexual, cheap, dirt-bag girl. . . . Then you see the ten-year-olds doing the twerking on their skateboards and stuff." She thus envisioned her work in the skate park as one means of contesting the sexist depiction of female skateboarders. Rachel thus advocated for a more "healthy" and "professional" vision of skateboarding, as she characterized it. Achieving this vision, she stated, ultimately meant increasing critical awareness about male domination in the skateboarding industry and everyday culture:

> I just try to increase the awareness to other girls then it's up to them, because women's skateboarding is being defined right now. It's up to them to decide how they're going to portray it, and if they're going to say "yes" to some company that says, "Can I portray you like this?"

That's why I do it, for awareness of "what is women's skateboarding?" and of course to help it grow.

GRO, like many other nonprofits featured in this chapter, relies heavily upon private businesses and donors based in the local community. Rachel felt that this private backing, often from males and their companies, was given with full knowledge of GRO's activist mission to contest negative, sexualized portrayals of young females.

Probably 75 percent of the local skate companies have sponsored GRO—all of the skate shops except maybe two. I'll send out a mass email and then they all say "Yes. Oh, we want to support the girls. Yes." They don't ask for anything back. It's kind of weird, because they don't . . . of course they don't ask . . . I think they know what I represent, and they don't ask me for photos of the girls holding their product in any weird way. That's where I feel that maybe I'm making a difference, because they know better than to ask me to get a shot of the girls doing some sexual pose with their product.

Rachel also believed that females could become part of skateboarding's associated creative industries as they became further involved in this sport. In fact, as we will see, many adult skateboarding leaders described in *Moving Boarders* shared this view. Rachel clearly speaks to this perspective in the following two interview extracts.

Well once you're in the skate community, they start to work together and you never know, you might get hired at the skate shop. It helps them out. It's major networking. You can go anywhere.

They can start filming . . . pick up a camera, get paid $100 from a sponsor, pick up a camera, start filming, start sending to the magazines, start working for the magazines. There's a million different ways you could go with it.

Returning to our concept of *Urban Platforms for Capital*, it is apparent that GRO strove to use skate parks in order to provide female skaters with more life opportunities and ways of contesting prevalent masculinist practices. And yet, it seemed to us that the activist practices of this organization were unsustainable. That is, despite having the support of local skateboarders and private backers, GRO had difficulty remaining financially viable. While GRO could leverage private connections in order to obtain "freebies" and "flow product," as Rachel once told us, this did not readily translate into regular funding and other resources that were required to sustainably program and staff events. In fact, a recent check on the GRO national website does not show the existence of a San Francisco Bay Area chapter anymore. We have heard from other members of the local community that GRO has gone quiet on the local skate scene.

"DOING IT OURSELVES AND HAVING A PLACE IN THIS WORLD": SKATE LIKE A GIRL (SLAG)

SLAG has a more regional presence than GRO, as it is largely based on the United States' West Coast. Seattle hosts its most visible and well-funded chapter. SLAG has established key working relationships with various other female-focused social-activist groups. These associated groups include the Women's Skateboarding Alliance, Reel Grrls media training program, and MAHFIA.TV (we explore this last group in the next section). SLAG's extensive private-industry links include: the Clif Bar corporation, an indoor skate park in the Seattle area, a gluten-free cookie company, and various skate businesses selling products such as helmets, socks, and clothing. These connections are used to support SLAG's operations across several chapters, rather than for strictly entrepreneurial or profit-making reasons. In fact, one local leader suggested to us that "We are about building community. So, that goes with the way that we're organized, too, and everything. Nobody's here to make money. There are a couple of paid positions now, but it is not for the money."

SLAG's core mission is to foster "confidence in girls and women to skateboard and take leadership in their communities."[57] To achieve this mission, SLAG hosts numerous sessions held in various local skate parks, including SoMa West, Town Park, Berkeley, and Bay City. We attended six of these open skate dates, with observations at these events revealing an average of roughly a dozen girls and women from beginners to seasoned skaters in attendance. Through our research visits, we became acquainted with two leaders, Mandy and Evie, whose voices are featured next. Although, more recently, we have seen Kim Woozy take on primary leadership duties in SLAG.

Evie had been with SLAG for several years, working as the programming co-director for the San Francisco chapter. Mandy used to run all of these SLAG skate dates in person, although she sometimes enlisted support from other mentors. She was often observed coaching small groups and offering tips to girls. At the same time, Mandy herself skated during these events, blending into the regular skate crowd; she seemed to use this practice to show new, younger female skaters how to be confident in using the skate park. This practice also modeled appropriate social etiquette and how to perform certain maneuvers. Mandy once told us that the San Francisco chapter of SLAG was more of a "loosely affiliated group of people," with programming ebbing and flowing based on the schedules of the volunteers involved.

Much like Rachel from GRO, Mandy and Evie told us that negative skate experiences influenced their work. In this regard, Evie told us about her previous stressful experiences of skateboarding as a female. "When I was learning it, it sucked because I was the only girl most of the time and I was representing how girls skate, feeding into this stereotype that they suck because I was learning." She then mentioned in conversation, "I think that you feel like all the eyes are on you and that discourages a lot of people from going and learning."

In another interview, Mandy reflected upon the belief that females were made to feel as if they did not belong in the skate park. "I felt like I couldn't take up space because I wasn't good and I'm a woman," she said. "And when you're not good then you feel less confident and [less] like taking up space in the skate park, even though you're entitled to be there, you know, it's just this kind of cultural thing." Mandy further expanded upon her viewpoint that skate parks tend to exist as male spaces. This belief, honed by personal experience, motivated her to try and create a new type of female space where women and girls could feel comfortable and help each other learn to skate.

> We just make space at skate parks for girls and women to come and, like, feel safe to try something and also to empower other girls [who are] really shy coming to skate parks. And when it's your first time stepping into there, you're terrified because you don't know, like, what's happening, who's looking at you, who's judging you, but I feel kind of good to be, like, this is our space, too, like we can be here. Everyone starts at square one, you know? Like, it's okay to suck, like, whatever. And I was in their position too, but it feels good that, like, I feel empowered to have this as my space too.

Although some men were open-minded about female skateboarders, Evie conceded, the typical belief held by males was that they had ownership of the skate park. According to Evie, "It is weird because it's like open but yet . . . it is hard for girls to enter that space. So, it's open but yet there's still some of these barriers." Consequently, she felt that men could thus use skate parks to bond with and learn from each other. To counter this phenomenon of male-controlled social space, Mandy also suggested to us that her ideal SLAG event "would look like a bunch of girls, like fifteen or twenty or twenty-five girls, and then we'd skate and teach each other tricks and we'd have, like, some younger ones maybe, teach some younger ones." She felt that this type of presence would eventually counteract the regular presence of "white dudes," as she called them, whom she felt were mostly controlling skate parks.

SLAG, much like GRO, wanted to create opportunities for females to learn skills that could transfer to work in affiliated creative industries. And, similarly, it was hoped that having more females in these industries would advance the female skateboarding cause. In this regard, Evie once told us:

> Maybe someone doesn't want to continue skateboarding, but we like to provide a support system and platform for people to pursue the kind of things they want to pursue. If someone helps us with our clinics we can recommend them for jobs teaching skateboarding or if they want to do a 'zine, then we can promote that and help them put it together and be part of that. . . . So they can be a part of these projects that help them to be involved members of society and the community, for them to get jobs and to try to be that support system.

And yet, similar to the local chapter of GRO described earlier, one of the primary challenges that SLAG encountered, during most of our study, was a lack of consistent local programming due to their inability to directly fund programs and pay women to operate them. In this regard, Mandy commented to us in November 2015, "I hope to see more volunteers, [it] would be nice to have grant writers and expand to free programs after school for kids, maybe more organized—because we are all busy people, we all have jobs." In comparison, a large-scale, high-profile organization such as the Tony Hawk Foundation actually has personnel devoted to this type of grant-writing.

SLAG maintained an active schedule in 2015, with several regular skate sessions being hosted per month across several skate parks. We saw this program downsize in 2016 only to be resurrected in 2017, when SLAG began co-hosting several events with the MAHFIA.TV social-media platform. MAHFIA.TV's leader, Woozy, took up a concurrent leadership role in SLAG at this time. As we shall see next, MAHFIA.TV represents another version of social-enterprise practice, as it utilizes consistent funding streams linked with its social-media presence as well as private industry connections.

Advertisement for girls skate session at Oakland's Town Park.
Courtesy of Kimberly Woo.

"JUST BEING STRONGER AS A UNIT AND REALLY HAVING EACH OTHER'S BACKS": THE MAHFIA.TV MEDIA "ECOSYSTEM"

MAHFIA.TV's leader, Woozy, has a corporate background steeped in the sports-business and media professions. Consequently, with private-industry resources and expertise to draw upon, MAHFIA.TV has a sustainable, visible presence in local skate parks. MAHFIA.TV aims to become the "global destination for girls action sports," with both virtual and on-the-ground programming, according to Woozy:

> We post videos that we just come across on YouTube or Facebook or Instagram. We still create our own original content, and the goal is to just expose, to really give the spotlight to the women and expose media to inspire girls. Then, on top of the actual digital content,

we've been doing physical events, too, because we've seen the need for and success of that.

Woozy actually began to skateboard by participating in SLAG sessions after she moved to the San Francisco Bay Area from Southern California several years ago. She was inspired by SLAG's approach to creating a supportive atmosphere where female skateboarders could learn from each other. During our interview, Woozy recalled her entry point into skateboarding:

> The most I ever skated was when I moved back up to the Bay Area and found Skate Like a Girl, because even in Southern California, I was in the industry and at skate parks all the time, but I wasn't skating because it wasn't an environment that was inviting to me. Oftentimes, I'd be with the pro girls when I would want to shoot them, because that's my passion, too, is photography and video, but there was never an opportunity for me to learn because the pros are at the level and I'm a beginner and then with Skate Like a Girl, everyone was just there to have a good time and teach each other. So, I really understood more about what we needed in our community when I found Skate Like a Girl and experienced that for myself.

As someone who picked up skateboarding later in life, after playing many competitive sports, Woozy believed that skateboarding offered a unique type of sporting opportunity for young women. "That's one of the most amazing things about skateboarding, there's no wrong or right way to do it. . . . There's not really an end objective," she told us. "It's just really, like, have fun, like, be outside, be creative." Yet even as she transitioned into the skateboarding world as a practitioner, she was surprised to see that women were being treated as second-class citizens in the industry. She also articulated her belief that females had internalized their oppression by males, and were satisfied with taking up secondary roles. What's more, Woozy saw that women were often pitted against each other in the sports industry. "They all had to fight with each other for some tiny sliver of a pie that really wasn't even being given out." These experiences all contributed to Woozy's eventual creation of MAHFIA.TV. She wanted to use skateboarding as a means to empower females and form a new political bloc in order to confront the current male-dominated politics of action sports. "Because then we'd be stronger . . . going to the table of a company that is all males making decisions."

Indeed, we saw that Woozy was highly collaborative and hosted materials from other female skateboarding-activist groups on her social media platform. Woozy's participation in the Oakland Skatepark Summit also illustrates her intention to work with others in order to support the female skateboarding cause through grassroots daily programming. In this regard, Woozy told us that "leveraging support through existing institutions is great." This comment indicates her social-enterprise involvement, as she brings together numerous interests and parties in order to create what she calls an "ecosystem" that will benefit female skaters.

> On the women's side, we are trying to create our own ecosystem, so regardless of what happens over here, if this whole thing blows up and falls apart, which it has for women's [skate products and endorsements] in the past, like during 2008–2009, like everything [women's skate products] just got fully removed. So, it's like if we create our own ecosystem and our audience, [it] is about catering to be inclusive to the new participants as well as catering to the existing participants.

Woozy thus felt it was important that women and girls work together to build a more sustainable cultural presence that would ultimately help all female skateboarders, including new ones. As she explained to us, "The last thing you want to do is to go to the skate park by yourself as a beginner and be the only girl there. That sucks." And, like other female skate groups featured in this chapter, Woozy believed that increasing the participation of females would disrupt dominant gendered stereotypes and sexist practices. This also meant providing space where women and girls could express and exemplify diverse, non-traditional versions of femininity, outside of the prevailing "girly" stereotype.[58]

> So, I think there just needs to be multiple types, diverse role models, because no [two] girls [are] the same. Everyone identifies with different things. I think it's best if we live in a world or community where there are so many different types of girls, every ethnicity, age, body type, all that stuff, because then girls will be like. "Okay, yeah. It's for me because literally anyone could do it."

We have seen that the landscape of female skateboarding now involves several groups that are using social-enterprise mechanisms to develop missions and practices that contest gendered norms and relationships. Other social-enterprise organizations described in this chapter wanted to effect social change by developing new infrastructure and programming for urban skateboarders, in a broadly inclusive sense; the female-oriented organizations were more deliberately engaged in creating new social contexts and relationships to specifically help female skateboarders. The work of these latter groups finds sympathy with current research advice that calls for developing appropriate "girl-friendly program features." In fact, it has been recommended that urban sports programs should provide opportunities for safe, supportive, and open interaction to occur between females, including both participants and mentors.[59] All three of the groups that we researched did in fact attempt to instigate this type of social experience, even as each group utilized a different variant of social-enterprise practice to achieve this aim.

Conclusion

This chapter has identified key social-enterprise groups that currently advocate for youth skateboarding in urban communities. These groups conduct their work differently, from regional to international levels. All of these groups represent variations of social-enterprise practice, whereby the logic of providing social change clearly coincides with the practices of both entrepreneurialism and profit generation. In fact, all of the groups featured above clearly cultivated and made links with private- and public-sector sources to promote positive social experiences in youth skateboarding. These featured groups directly sought to influence social life across several local urban spaces, in order to foster positive youth experiences. The groups promoting youth development more generally in urban, underserved neighborhoods, often took up causes underpinned by the traditional American citizenship values of personal growth and transformation through sports. By contrast, it became apparent to us that the groups focused on addressing the plight of women and girls were more apt to contest the specific values, institutions, and practices that have marginalized female skateboarders. These latter groups were most explicit about installing inclusive yet subversive skate communities to disrupt prevailing male skate traditions and values.

The following three case-study chapters detail how these social-enterprise groups interact with other stakeholders, including families, in order to bring forth new *Urban Platforms for Capital* in specific skate locations. The upcoming analyses specifically explore life in four new Bay Area skate parks created by public-private partnerships that purportedly offer up new social benefits to participants. These parks operate in line with current ideologies about acceptable youth behavior and citizenship.

THREE

"They Were All About Police, Police, Police ... We Don't Need Police, We Need Parents"

Bay City's Adult-Organized Social Space

Legendary skater Stacy Peralta once recalled his formative skateboarding experiences in the following manner: "I chose this activity that didn't get parental support. It didn't even get parental *interest*."[1] Peralta's statement clearly identifies how skateboarding has long been constituted as an activity that forgoes parental support. But, as we have explained so far in *Moving Boarders,* skateboarding has become mainstream through the pronounced involvement of adults, including parents. Indeed, it is adult intervention that strongly determines what it means to be a youth skateboarder in Bay City Skate Park, which is featured in this chapter.

Examining life in Bay City Skate Park, we argue that skateboarding can be understood here as an unfolding spatial, political project that brings together an emerging mosaic of stakeholders, including plenty of adults.[2] Insofar as urban space is socially dynamic, we shall see in this chapter how these adults, in particular, enacted "collective campaigns to produce and format space according to identifiable logics and strategic goals."[3] Our consequent belief is that skateboarding in Bay City Skate Park reflects deliberate "goals and techniques" implemented by the adults to greatly contour youths' experiences in this urban space.[4]

In terms of its significant adult presence, Bay City Skate Park stood out among the sites that we visited in our research. A prevailing adult vision here was manifested in various forms of programming, including skate events, coaches, camps, the use of park rangers, and the presence of parents in person or via social media. Parents and community leaders alike held to a vision of a safe and inclusive park predicated upon consistent adult programming and surveillance. These space-based control techniques thus served specific adult functions that fell in line with municipal and private-sector interests.[5] Collectively, these adult-instigated techniques filtered much of the activity that we observed, especially when it came to younger children. It should also be noted that there was a parallel, older youth scene reflecting more traditional skate elements that coexisted in this space. These latter youth typically had less to do with adults such as parents, skate coaches, and community leaders.

Once again, the key research idea behind *Moving Boarders* pertains to *Urban Platforms for Capital* that are spreading via social-enterprise missions. The idea that skateboarding now gets major adult attention made us want to investigate how these adults went on to enact different belief systems and investments, in specific skate parks. In this chapter, we first outline the agenda that was used by several local leaders to create Bay City Skate Park. Then we proceed to explain the prevalence of parents using this type of skate park for a variety of child-raising purposes; the voices of parents are especially prominent in this chapter.

Research has shown that family structures and the relationships constituting them exist in a state of flux.[6] This implies that what we think of as family life is actually composed of diverse parenting styles, habits, and belief systems. With this complex view of the modern family in mind, this chapter highlights a range of parenting modes influencing youth skateboarding. We often asked Bay City parents why they were motivated to participate in local skateboarding; they responded that they were attracted to this supportive and community-like skate environment. An atmosphere like this one, we heard, would especially enable youth to acquire valuable life skills. It was intriguing, then, how the parents were beholden to ideas of risk-taking, autonomy, and social diversity, although they still wanted to exert control over these kinds of experiences. In addition, skate parents here, like many other youth-sports parents nationwide, also wanted their children to learn alongside their peers, make meaningful friendships, and gain a sense of teamwork and community.[7]

Bay City Skate Park:
A Social Network Constituted by Adult Visions

Our main premise in this chapter is that Bay City Skate Park encapsulates how adult-inspired mechanisms can be used to influence youth within an urban social space. The opening proclamation "We don't need police, we need parents" was offered by Jane, one of Bay City Skate Park's most outspoken and active advocates. Searching for a space where her teenage

Adults participating in Bay City Skate Park. *Courtesy of Kimberly Woo.*

son and his friends could legally skateboard, Jane went on to spearhead a community network that was integral to building the skate park in Bay City. Her statement from above reveals how this skate park was created largely under the vision and commitment of adult volunteers; they sought to create a welcoming, safe space that youth would enjoy. Indeed, Jane and other adults featured in this chapter constituted a highly noticeable and committed supporter group. This group, the Bay City Skate Park Group (BCSPG), greatly influenced the youth behaviors and experiences that we observed in the skate park. This group's intervention created the widespread belief that Bay City was a family-friendly location even though it simultaneously accommodated a more typical male skate culture.

In reality, then, Bay City Skate Park often teemed with all kinds of skateboarders, both young and old, reflecting multicultural attributes and gender diversity. It could reasonably be said that Bay City's participants reflected the most diverse mixture of people that we found in our study. The next field observation attests to this diversified skate culture.

On this sunny Saturday morning, we can see a few shirtless teenaged boys wearing jeans and Velcro wrist guards jump down stairs and rails. They are filming each other with their cellphones.

One of them mutters "shake that shit off" after another wipes out hard.

The sounds of an African finger instrument emanate from a white, middle-aged father sitting on a park bench, watching his son skateboard. This music blends into the pumping bass coming from nearby speakers. The source of the bass is a female skate event hosted by the MAHFIA.TV organization. They are set up under a black tent, where girls wearing helmets with party hats on top—like upside down ice cream cones. A pink, blue, and yellow piñata hangs inside the tent while Skate Witches (girls' skate zines) are spread on the floor. "It's kinda casual," says one event host as she hovers around the group, "We hand out a few things, we give people hype."

Two African American twin boys come in and skate in front of us, with one wearing Teenage Mutant Ninja Turtles kneepads. Another boy comes toward us wearing a Steph Curry Golden State Warriors T-shirt, he checks his cell phone and burps, while his friend hangs out with him. They find a Skate Like a Girl organization sticker on the ground, and one of the boys turns to the other and says "girl power" with a mocking tone. But he earnestly asks "where should I put it?" before putting it on the bottom of his skateboard.

In the back of the skate park there is a skate session where the older, experienced male skateboarders come to drop in the deep pool. One man making his skate run wears a shirt that says "Skate Dad: Don't Stop." He wears worn-out black skate shoes held together mostly by cellophane tape. An ice cooler sits on the ground with an ironic sticker slapped on it proclaiming "Don't do it" in a riposte to the famous Nike slogan.

Nearby, there is a young twenty-something man performing moves quite slowly on his skateboard. He is being videoed closely by someone, and it is obviously meant to be a "how to skate" tutorial. Eventually, these videos are going on a YouTube channel, one of the older skate guys tells us. "He's making money by kids going to his website" he growls. "He's a street skater, he never drops in, we just laugh." As usual, these regulars pack up and roll out around noon. They have family commitments and weekend jobs, one of them reminds us. In the parking lot, one of them says that he has a kids' birthday party to attend. At the same time, the MAHFIA.TV leaders walk past us with boxes of multicolored cupcakes to hand out in the skate park.

This description of a typical Saturday morning session reflects the rich tapestry of skate-park life that can be found in Bay City. We will discuss below how this burgeoning skate scene arose from the foresight of Jane and her cadre of adult supporters. Our research shows that this skate park, neither homogenous in composition nor reducible in activity, was deliberately created to sustain an unprecedented array of skateboarders representing diverse identities, styles, and beliefs. And while you might think that Jane was an ex-skateboarder or someone steeped in skate culture, we felt that her earnest demeanor and highly organized approach easily resembled the stereotypical soccer "team manager."[8] Later on we will describe how she was in fact new to skateboarding and had other professional interests and duties. Almost by coincidence, Jane became the point person of Bay City's supporter group.

It will become evident that Jane and her supporter group's enthusiastic adults formed an important bridge between government entities, such as the parks-and-recreation department, and private parties like skate coaches, social activists, nonprofit organizations, and parents. This pronounced adult immersion, reflecting social-enterprise practice once again, further demonstrates the erasure of skateboarding's previous subcultural boundaries that once determined the distinctions between legitimate and inauthentic practices. In this case, it took a coalition of interested adults, many of whom were newcomers and outsiders to "core" skate culture, to create a thriving skateboarding environment.

Twenty-First-Century American Parenting Modes and Youth Sports

This chapter provides a case story of how parental involvement largely determines the skateboarding lives of children in one skate spot. This parental presence added numerous layers to the social life in Bay City Skate Park, as it does across many of America's ball fields and gyms. In chapter 1, we revealed how the phenomenon of youth-sports parenting in the United States has emerged over the past thirty years. More than ever before, we explained, today's parents see their children as assets that need to be managed properly; in this context, youth-sports participation is one of our society's most heavily utilized outlets to develop children. As it stands now, youth skateboarding is considered by parents to be another valuable youth-sports opportunity. Although skateboarding is often known as an unregulated street activity, we will see that in locales such as Bay City this activity constitutes an important youth-development opportunity; positive youth development (PYD) principles, outlined below, were especially resonant with parents in this skate park.

Accordingly, this chapter touches upon several motivators related to PYD that underpin the investments of local parents. In terms of PYD, it has been argued that parents appreciate when children are immersed in engaging activities that offer them a sense of belonging. Parents also prefer when children can develop attributes such as initiative and resilience. In addition, the twin concepts of *external* and *internal assets* are both potentially useful to understand parental involvement in this skate park. On one hand, then, parents seem to appreciate the external supports that can be found, involving the presence of adult organizers, caring mentors, a helpful community, and the element of parental monitoring; these are key factors that Bay City parents want to have in place when their children participate. On the other hand, it will become clear that parents want to leverage this skate park in order develop their children's more internal assets, related to positive identity formation, social competencies, character and values acquisition, self-responsibility, and even an appreciation of diversity and social-justice issues.[9] Altogether, these various PYD benefits will be revealed as this chapter unfolds; these benefits attract many parents to this particular skate park.

Furthermore, the element of risk in youth sports further preoccupies today's parents, including those we found in Bay City. Research has found that modern parents often attempt to minimize conditions of risk through their adult intervention. This next quote from scholars Ellie Lee, Jennie Bristow, and Charlotte Fairchild exemplifies how parents see their children as exposed to risk and in need of intensive parenting:

> Children are today seen as more "vulnerable" to risks impacting on physical and emotional development than ever before. As a corollary, parents are now understood—by policymakers, parenting experts, and parents themselves—as "God-like," and wholly deterministic in an individual child's development and future. This has inflated the social importance of the parent role, precipitating a range of "intensive" styles of parenting (readily understood through such

tags as "Gina Ford," "Tiger Mothers," "Attachment," or "Helicopter parenting").[10]

These scholars further contend that neoliberalism contributes to adult anxieties about good parenting. In essence, they argue, society is now preoccupied with the idea of self-management. This implies that parents are expected to control their own children's exposure to risk while simultaneously giving them appropriate developmental experiences. The aim here is for children to eventually develop into acceptable and useful citizens. In this regard, researchers Sinikka Elliot and Elyshia Aseltine discuss the tension parents typically feel when trying to support their children's wellbeing. It is especially difficult, these scholars contend, for parents to balance children's exposure to risk while developing their sense of autonomy. The authors deem the resulting balancing act *protective carework*, which involves "gauging potential threats to children's well-being, determining how much autonomy to allow them, and employing strategies to monitor children's activities, peers, and surroundings."[11] This practice of protective carework often features within youth sports including skateboarding, as we will see later. In this context, parents often conceptualize children as "precious and valued commodities" who need help in navigating the youth-sports terrain; this can result in some parents perhaps taking on overly involved roles.[12] Adult-organized activities like Bay City skateboarding have become popular with parents who consider them a safe means of cultivating opportunities for their children.[13] And this type of parent support and involvement during these activities is actually considered an important facet of "good" parenting practice.[14]

Below we explore how parents gave diverse meanings to the daily challenges and social interactions that their children experienced in Bay City Skate Park. Building from our previous explanation of how various social, cultural, and material benefits are provided through urban skate space, it will become clear that parents identified certain attributes and relationships as vital to their children's experiences of skateboarding. Broadly speaking, parents registered that three elements were critical for their children's development: autonomy, risk navigation, and safety. In some cases, parents told us they were quite concerned about risk-taking behavior in terms of physical injuries and antisocial practices. Nonetheless, other parents saw skateboarding as the perfect venue to dialogue with their children about social disagreements and antisocial behaviors like public drinking and smoking marijuana. In fact, rather than protecting their children from exposure to "risks," these parents felt that this type of experience was necessary to be successful in life. Collectively, the parents in Bay City Skate Park brought immense attention to bear on their children's skateboarding in line with societal expectations regarding appropriate, moral parenting.

The next section provides a contextualization of Bay City as it influences the skate park. There is no doubt that this skate park evolved through the reproduction of youth- and community-development narratives directly tied to this city's unique sociocultural and economic conditions. This discussion is followed by an extended conversation demonstrating how key constituents, including members of the community group and the parent culture, ultimately created a multicultural and family-friendly skate scene which regularly constituted social life in Bay City Skate Park.

"We're so Bay City, You Know? We Really Are, and the Park Is, Too": Developing a Skate Park in the City's Own Image

The following interview quote reveals community-group leader Jane's passion for trying to build an inclusive skate-park culture that would mirror the city's demographics.

> I love that about this place. There's everybody here. Well, that's Bay City. Okay, so this is a good story. . . . Mike [a skate coach] is Muslim. He just came back from his pilgrimage to Mecca last weekend. Lisa, who's the other woman who's helping us, is Jewish, very involved in the Jewish community. She works for a Jewish nonprofit. She runs Jewish nonprofits. We're [referring to herself] recovering Catholics here. We're so Bay City, you know? We really are, and the park is, too. You have girls, that's really important to me, is to have girls and women. We have a pretty high percentage of Asian, Afghan in Bay City, so I think this just reflects the city, yeah.

Jane enlisted an ex-professional skateboarder named Mike, mentioned above, to support the skate park in a coaching role. We talked with Mike once about his views on youth skateboarding and how he envisaged his role in the skate park. He told us that the skate industry historically shaped this sport to be edgy, meaning that skateboarding has been dominated by male skaters glorifying sexism, drug-taking, and making profit. Mike told us that he wanted to open up both physical and social-media spaces to enable more people to benefit from skateboarding and simultaneously change the core skateboarding industry. "I'm really interested to have that community of parents and kids come together," he stated. "Something that everyone can kind of share ideas and how this can permeate through the whole industry and the goal, I think, essentially five or ten years down the road, is that we see a shift in the industry."

The fact that Bay City Skate Park often operates under the family-friendly concept, as advocated by Jane and Mike, was frequently reiterated by parents and other skate-park leaders. Yet, amidst this seemingly family-friendly environment, some adults who patronized this skate park actually expressed different opinions about how skateboarding could support young people's well-being. Below we provide commentary highlighting these differences, as expressed during an open-forum community meeting. A year after the park opened, the BCSPG hosted this town-hall meeting to reflect on the first year of operation and address any issues in the community. The meeting was held at a community center close to the skate park. Jane and Mike led the conversation with support from a city parks-and-recreation representative. Most individuals in attendance were parents or even grandparents, while a few had brought their kids along (although most of the kids were actually skating at the nearby skate park during the meeting). In fact, it soon became apparent to us that this meeting was essentially catering to adults in Bay City, as youth were not directly questioned or engaged. Our discussion of the meeting illustrates a range of concerns that were raised and addressed by the meeting's leaders and parents in the audience. We start this discussion by providing an extended field-note excerpt.

> Jane starts with introductions and introduces herself as a "park mom," and then asks the other twenty-five attendees to introduce themselves. After the introductions, Jane discusses how she organized the meeting to focus on upcoming events, what was going well, and future plans for developing the skate park. Then it was time to hear from the parents themselves. We hear that those attending the meeting are very positive about the climate of the skate park. One father explains, "It was so much more family oriented, more than you could ever believe. I recommend this to every kid or parent I see." Another mother chimes in, "I was there for the grand opening, and I love this place. Everybody watching out for each other, I'll hang out all day." Jane pressed the point by asking, what brings you back to the park? One dad responds: "The atmosphere. I like it; it's open to everyone. I have never seen anyone laugh at other kids." Another dad adds, "The older kids are supportive." Most of the attendees were nodding in what appeared to be agreement. But then concerns

start being expressed and the celebratory mood dissipates. Several parents of young children raise issues about pot-smoking, graffiti, swearing, and bullying at the park. Suddenly there is a groundswell of calls for having more formal enforcement of rules.

At this point, a self-identified "grandma" with a deep tan, raspy voice, tank-top shirt, and USA heart tattoo on the arm speaks up and argues that "skateboarding has an eclectic bunch of personalities, [and that you] can't dictate...don't turn this into a white middle-class country club . . . freedom of speech is not . . . that's all part of it. [Skaters are] a great bunch of people."

This statement elicits defensive responses from the concerned parents, who felt that, actually, more "policing" was necessary. Jane and Mike step in to reframe the conversation on how to create a welcoming environment that is simultaneously safe. Mike then provides a personal testimonial describing his childhood as troubled, sharing that both of his parents were drug addicts, and he was not an ideal kid. He claims that skateboarding was his home and that one needs to be careful about who is getting kicked out as this may be their only place to go. He emphasizes that parents need to be the stewards of the park and also that communication among parents is key. He finishes his comments by claiming that more programming also helps to keep the park safe and more open to all.

Mike's earnest testimonial and obvious concern for developing a unique skate-park community refocuses the conversation toward some collective goals. The meeting continues with a discussion about next steps. Some ideas are to hold workshops on teaching kids/parents about proper equipment, setting up a drop box for donating used equipment, handing out free helmets, and conversation about expanding the park. Jane ends the meeting by asking people to address the best things in the park. The two main responses are that this skate park was open to all and appreciation of Mike for being a good role model for their kids. One dad tells Mike, "You've been a very good influence. . . . You're a good presence. . . . Those [skate] classes have made a difference . . . and [the kids will say] this is a guy who knows the culture."

Although this meeting eventually ended somewhat cordially, our conversations with some of the parents immediately after the meeting illustrated ongoing tensions. One dad that we talked to felt like he was the brunt of backlash because he was a white male. "The lady that said that [don't make the skate park a white middle-class country club] was staring at me the whole time even though I'm not the one who made the statement that set her off. . . . I guess I was the white guy within her field of view." Another parent suggested that concerns about drugs and foul language were not intended to make the park a "white country club," but were instead intended to reiterate how some adults needed to "take parental responsibility." Looking back at the meeting itself, it is clear that the concept of parental responsibility featured in much of the parents' talk and reflected social expectations of being a "good" parent; this was often equated with high involvement and supervision.[15] This town-hall meeting example indicates how the integration of adults, including parents and community leaders, was essential to the new skate park's emerging social dynamics, as we will see throughout this chapter.

The Contested Origins of Bay City Skate Park

According to the Public Skatepark Development Guide, these concrete urban structures "are not your average tennis court."[16] On one hand, there are usability concerns, pertaining to the flow of people and traffic, speed of riders, difficulty and style for certain disciplines. On the other hand, functional concerns arise, which means that attention must be paid to capacity, access, safety, aesthetic appeal, as well as resources needed for regulation and maintenance.[17]

This substantial list of requirements reminds us that concrete urban skate parks are expensive and complicated structures. In fact, building skate parks often requires millions of dollars from public and private sources. In this case, Bay City Skate Park's location, conveniently located next to Silicon Valley, enabled the skate park's proponents to access major public funding. Indeed, Bay City's economy as well as its tax base are augmented by the presence of its professional population, with nearly 50 percent of residents having at least a bachelor's degree. Bay City currently has poverty rates well below the regional average and a high per capita median income of over $114,000. Healthcare as well as both established and start-up technology companies comprise the major employers that are bolstering the local economy.

Over the past thirty years, Bay City's reputation has evolved, from a city that was viewed as predominantly white and working-class to now being characterized as a hub of newly immigrated residents, which includes a heavy East Asian and Indian presence. Many of these new residents are employed in the nearby technology sector. Consider the following excerpt from a local feature story.

The Singh family rode from Toronto to the Bay Area on the high-tech job wave in the mid-1990s. They looked for housing they could afford, good schools, decent commutes and, as devout Sikhs, religious tolerance. They found it in Bay City, once a network of townships linked by two-lane roads through cherry orchards, then a blue-collar suburb that built Chevies and now an ethnically diverse and affluent Silicon Valley technopolis of 200,000 people.

A data-based report from Harvard University backs up this description, pointing out that "Bay City's diverse ethnic and religious communities contribute to the life of this city. . . . Today, Bay City is one of the nation's most diverse cities for its size." In alignment with this demographic contextualization, we found that the adults that went to Bay City were usually multicultural, with parents being solidly middle-class with aspirational educational and professional desires for their children. This demographic breakdown diverged from some of the other skate parks we researched, as we shall see when other case-study locations are presented.

At one time, Bay City had a wooden skate park. But over time it became dilapidated and needed replacement. The eventual process of building a replacement skate park did not unfold overnight, nor was it straightforward. In principle, the city government was supportive of the need to create a new permanent, concrete skate park. Still, as we shall see, in practice, it took over ten years to secure the funds and to fight off legal complaints before the skate park was finally built.

Early on, the city was able to draw from its capital improvement funds to provide over $2 million for the design and construction of a concrete skate park. Eventually, several public workshops were held to get feedback on the design and placement of the skate park. It was during this time that a vocal group of citizens halted the skate park's construction. A small group of residents in the neighborhood adjacent to the proposed site formally complained and delayed construction for over two years. The regional media outlets covered the citizens' complaints, which mostly centered on the specific location of the skate park. For instance, one resident said, "We'd like a skate park in a less residential area, rather than right in our front yards." Another added, "We don't understand why, when they have a great alternative, that they would put it here in front of a community that doesn't want it."

These local residents then took the city to task over matters including potential environmental and noise concerns as well as lighting issues. In each case, the city responded and reapproved the site. Yet, even after these issues were addressed, the local residents were still not appeased. Several parents in Bay City later told us that unstated concerns were at the root of this challenge. In particular, they said, these other locals were concerned about potential crimes being committed by teenagers, which coincides with the long-held stereotype that skate parks engender negative social behavior, with a potential negative impact on local property values. One parent claimed that the people contesting the skate park held certain misperceptions and feelings of mistrust about groups of skateboarding young men:

> The main argument against building a public skate park is that people do not want too many young men gathered in one place for any reason, period. "You're just scary." You can get past the noise and you can get past the traffic and the graffiti, and it comes down to a fear. It's a fear of a lot of young sixteen- to twenty-five-year-old males in one place, period, and so you've got to get past that.

As Australian scholars Myra Taylor and Ida Marais once pointed out, community members that object to skate parks typically consider these "hang outs" to be rife with antisocial or deviant behaviors. "Consequently", they argue, "the skate-park objecting faction tends to perceive nonconforming young people's activities to be a threat to their own preferred lifestyle." Furthermore, these scholars suggest that "sustained community opposition of this nature contributes to the labelling of young people's boisterous and non-conforming activities as being antisocial. In turn, the label leads to the stereotyping of adolescents as trouble-makers."[18] In terms of proposed skate parks, then, suspicions and fears about social change motivates some local residents to try influencing policies that may counter skate-park construction.[19]

Constructing a Family-Friendly Social Network: The Bay City Skate Park Group

The neighborhood's initial resistance to the permanent skate park actually became productive in the sense that it galvanized other community residents to initiate a support group. The leaders of BCSPG articulated a vision and narrative about the value of the skate park that went beyond simply providing recreational opportunities. Below we describe these skate-park leaders and their visions, and discuss how they worked together in social-enterprise fashion.

In essence, the BCSPG was led by Jane and Mike, the skate coach, who both shared the vision of creating a family-friendly skate environment. This family-friendly designation of the skate park underpinned the struggle to secure a new facility. Quite simply, this characterization was used to help the skate park gain community acceptance. The initial role of the BCSPG was for advocacy purposes, as Jane once recalled to us. "[We] started the Facebook page because we were going to the City Council when we were trying to get the park built. . . . We created this page really to get people to say, we need to be at the city council at seven o'clock tonight and here some letters to the editor and why don't you write your own? That kind of thing and it sort of grew from there."

One strategy that the BCSPG used was to counter the prevailing assumption that skateboarders were just teens with criminal inclinations. The suggestion here, according to Jane, was that when done right, skate parks could be a positive social space. And Jane's approach was to address negative assumptions head on. She said, "I tried to counter the neighbors with respect and data to get over the stigma and use facts."[20] The quote of hers that opens this chapter, regarding the need for parents not police, was made because the city council originally wanted intensive policing of this space. During public hearings, Jane drew upon information from the Tony Hawk Foundation (THF) which indicates that crime does not increase in areas where skate parks are located.[21] Reproducing further ideas from the THF, Jane noted that skate parks should be inclusive and visible to all community members, including families. "Parks in open, accessible areas located near other family activities are going to be more attractive to families," Jane declared during a news interview. "That means the location of the new park is just about perfect."[22] This type of advocacy played a major role in the skate park's eventual construction. Simultaneously, the supporter group expanded into a broader network of adults, including many parents, that became committed to the idea of a safe and family-friendly skate park. The composition of this group was actually described as "skaters, parents, and community members who work with the City . . . to ensure our free, public skate park is safe, welcoming, and inclusive for skaters and their families."[23]

Mike played a key role in shaping the skate park's supporter group's mission. As illustrated in the annual town-hall meeting, Mike was quite open about his own conflicting experiences with skateboarding. He has said publicly that as a young person, skateboarding provided a needed sense of community and place to escape family problems. Nonetheless, as he became more immersed in the skate culture, he began to party and abuse drugs. Recalling these darker times, he once told us, "I think a lot of that initial sickness [his earlier issues] came from [these kinds] of bad elements of skateboarding and being around the wrong people and drugs and just that stuff." Mike told us that he now lives a clean life and wants to give back. He said that he aimed to help youth and their families engage with the positive aspects of skate culture. He thus saw his role as "just trying to infuse in one's life just very healthy things that are from a spiritual, mental, and physical standpoint." To expand his reach with youth and families, Mike eventually led skate camps throughout the summer and also provided personal skate lessons throughout the year.

Referring to his own ups and downs, Mike told us that his aim was to make a space where youth could enjoy the healthy benefits of skateboarding. He wanted "to mentor kids in such a way, to help them kind of avoid what pitfalls and mistakes I made in the past or others have been making." To this he added, "I don't like anything that undermines a young person's healthy development." At the same time, Mike was up-front about his need to make a living through his efforts, "I think my spirit is very entrepreneurial. Don't get me wrong, I'm running [a] business." But, like other social enterprisers, Mike's for-profit organization was designed to enhance the lives of skate-park members: "I think entrepreneur is a very bold quest for someone. You can build a brand that's founded on integrity, honesty, trying to actually deliver product or service that is something that you would want as a client and you want to give someone."

Mike's ideas about branding and profit-making indicate how he, like others in this book, tapped into the logics of entrepreneurialism to create new social values in a local skate community. His insider knowledge of core skate culture, reflecting some of his negative experiences as a professional, provided impetus to assist youths' healthy development:

> My hope is to create, slowly, over time, a community of parents like me and just how we can create this raised—without sounding corny—kind of a raised awareness of what's going on out there in the culture that we call skateboarding—well, parts of it. How can they do this? How can they engage in it in a public space in the most healthy manner without having to go to a private facility, and how can they get the training or guidance or how can we be the resource? We want to be the resource people come to ... [providing information] from lifestyle to nutrition to the proper equipment to the safety to the skate-park etiquette, so everything that has to do

with all the healthy practices of skateboarding. The goal is to create a community around that.

We could see that both Jane and Mike, who were both middle-aged with children, were well-received by local parents. The skate park's parents seemed to trust them because they knew what it was like, so to speak. Mike was also respected for being steeped in knowledge since he was a former professional skateboarder. Jane, the coordinator of the group and its associated Facebook page, was a longtime resident of the city. She possessed knowledge about the city, including its political and social environment. Along with having worked in county support services, Jane was also involved in helping local schools.

Leveraging their collective experiences and skills, Jane and Mike created a unique family-oriented skateboarding environment that served as an *Urban Platform for Capital*. This skate park, as we shall see, was directly meant to offer resources, information, and positive social relationships that would benefit families, many of whom were coming into skateboarding for the first time. Exemplifying this model was the consistent presence of parents and other adults, including female skate activists, as we will see below. This grassroots approach refrains from using formal policing, according to these next comments from Jane.

> Well, we don't want police coming by and giving people tickets and hassling the skaters. We need a community of parents and skaters that give the skate park that sort of a vibe, so that you don't have people vandalizing and . . . people still smoke pot up on the hills and stuff like that, but the whole presence of parents, and more of a family atmosphere just keeps those kind of people out so we get serious skaters and people who just want to enjoy the park.

Adults in this skate park were thus expected to set the tone, in other words. And, in the majority of cases, parents we met appreciated the safe and controlled surroundings fostered by the regular adult presence. In fact, parents often told us that they wanted a safe environment for their children to skate instead of the street. They thought of this skate park as a well-monitored space for their children to learn the necessary skills of skateboarding. In general, then, parents found high value in their children's skateboarding within Bay City Skate Park. Gloria, a fifty-year-old mother who regularly attended the skate park with her son, summed up this perspective: "He's in a controlled environment where he can skate around this whole thing and I don't have to worry so much." She later disclosed, "I know the goal of this skate park is to be more family-oriented and stuff like that, I think that's fantastic." Next, we discuss how Bay City Skate Park was explicitly programmed by adults to provide socially inclusive skateboarding. Then, we explore how this particular framing supported various parenting practices in this urban space.

"Kids Should Have Fun Here . . . It Shouldn't Be a Thug Place": Family-Friendly Skateboarding and Adult Programming

Countering the view that all youth have equal access to participate, sociologists contend that many sports spaces actually need intentional recruitment and programming in order to be truly socially inclusive.[24] Contrary to public belief, the "if you build it they will come" approach does not often work. This implies the need for adult leaders to put in place certain mechanisms to facilitate more inclusive youth-sports participation. In the case of Bay City, we observed that Jane and Mike worked closely with the city's parks-and-recreation department to create programs that would facilitate a more inclusive, welcoming, and socially conscious environment. Rather than being hands-off about the skate park once it opened, these leaders purposely enlisted Girls Riders Organization (GRO), Skate Like a Girl (SLAG), and MAHFIA.TV, who were all considered essential to the leaders' goals. As discussed in chapter 2, these organizations held regular sessions where female newcomers were given free skate lessons in park space that was set aside for them, most typically on weekday mornings. What's more, the BCSPG tried to host A.Skate, an organization that introduces skateboarding to individuals with autism. But without direct financial help from the city government, the BCSPG was unable to secure the necessary funding to host this event. Mike further identified an expansive list of activities and programs that were used to counteract certain "liabilities" that he believed were associated with male skate culture.

> Programming would be anything having to do with the camps, lessons, group lessons that aren't specific times, but outside of the skateboarding instruction whether it be in the form of camps, lessons, private or group. The other aspects of programming like having the stewardship, the cleaning crew of the park, having the weekly barbecue, having the parent town-hall skate meeting once a month, having the public forum online where parents can come and give their input, essentially. That's not necessarily programming but it's part of the extension of it. So, anything that has to do with corralling

the park with meaningful activities to kind of help with the hope to offset some of the other liabilities.

Of course, this type of programming caters to a family-friendly user base. In fact, the skate lessons provided by Mike were often considered valuable entry points for newcomer families. During our interviews, these parents frequently commented on how access to professional lessons, which taught safety and skills, was a main reason that they started to use this skate park and involve their children in skateboarding. Gloria, for instance, stated that she felt obligated to help her young son skate properly and safely. "It's either, I had to support him or he was going to do it without the proper gear or without the right protection. . . . That wasn't okay." A Filipina mother, Amy, who has an eight-year-old son and a nine-year-old daughter who skate, agreed with this sentiment in her interview: "At least if they have the proper way of dropping in, being taught by a professional then I'll feel confident they could do it." The availability of organized lessons was viewed by Toral, a forty-three-year-old Indian mother, as a key reason why she came to accept her child's participation in skateboarding. "I'm like, 'I'm not going to let him skateboard unless he really knows how to do it.' I saw a broken something [body part] in my future." Toral subsequently described to us how she searched online and was excited to find Mike's skateboard lessons and camps. She promptly signed up her eight-year-old son for the last week of camp.

Early one Saturday morning, we spotted a middle-aged Indian man awkwardly navigating the park's elements on a skate deck while his daughter attended a free lesson led by a female activist group. Later on, this forty-five-year-old father, named Cal, came over to us and agreed to be interviewed. Standing on the outer rim of the skate park, Cal later explained how he and his two kids frequented the skate park. Still wearing his newly purchased helmet, he matter-of-factly stated that he would have preferred that the city use public funds to build a new library. However, since the skate park had already been built, and was generally free to use, he was going to take advantage of this facility. Consequently, he wanted his daughter to take lessons with a female coach during the special sessions; he appreciated the female mentorship that this program provided.

We can thus see from the examples above how adult-led programming became a drawing factor for many parents to bring their children to the skate park. These programs taught valuable skateboarding skills for many newcomer youths. We later discuss how many parents, including Cal, also wanted their children to directly obtain certain skills that could help them in other life realms.

Skate coaches, it was observed, would not only teach their own personal clients. These mentors engaged and supported other youth who happened to be in the skate park, too. Several of the young children we talked with stated how these coaches would check in with them during non-coaching sessions. These kids told us that skate coaches would ask them how school was going and if they were learning how to skate new tricks on their own time. This type of extended interaction—outside of the actual lesson format—helped consolidate the feeling of community that Mike and Jane originally wanted. Summing up this view, one parent commented about Mike's role in the skate park as follows: "I'd say teacher, mentor, you know, someone [my son] really looks up to." This parent continued by saying "[Mike's] great. I mean he basically is a mediator if anything comes up and needs to be addressed; he has no problems about going up to anybody and saying, 'Hey, you know, keep that out of the park.'" Academic research backs up these parents' positive views regarding multigenerational interaction. According to several sport psychologists, positive relationships between youth and adults like this are a key factor in youths' psychosocial development.[25]

In this same vein, Kelly, a thirty-five-year-old mother, further described Mike's central role in developing the positive, supportive skate park culture:

> I think it [success of the family friendly park] really is because of him. I really do. He's bringing so many families here by his classes, his demeanor. When you meet him, he's really easy to talk to, he's got this patience about him. . . . Most of the kids that come here learn from him, maybe went to his camp, or maybe, he has free sessions sometimes on the weekend, they joined the free session and got into it. After Christmas, he hosted a free class from nine to twelve or nine to one, a free class. "You got a new board, bring it down." I think he's a huge influence on making this park about family.

While Jane and Mike were the undisputed adult leaders of the skate park, they also incorporated the city-employed park rangers to be a part of the supervision and mentoring system. Jane told us that these rangers would drop in to the skate park on their regular rounds and established a solid working relationship with the skaters. Michael, a fifty-two-year-old father of two young skaters, explained the key role of the rangers in maintaining a family-friendly environment.

> The rangers here, they've come up to my wife and I both and most of the other parents around here. They gave us cards. They said, "If you see people smoking pot, if you see bad behavior, if you see this, call us, we're right down here, we'll show up in a second." We did [call the rangers] in the beginning. They patrol it regularly without being over the top. Kids should have fun here, even the older kids, but it shouldn't become a thug place.

In fact, one ranger named Jim is an accomplished skater himself. Like Mike, his authentic reputation in skate culture seemed to win over both the parents and youth. Jeff, a forty-three-year-old ex-skater who had a nine-year-old son named Kevin, described how rangers like Jim were central in maintaining the park's parallel family-friendly and traditional "core" skateboarding cultures.

> Yeah, the other rangers are really cool actually. They're all . . . I was really surprised when I initially saw them because in most places any authority figure contact for skateboarders is usually a bad thing. So, I was really shocked and also it was really cool to find out they were super involved in the culture and everything and Jim's done, I think a good job of making sure that all the other rangers understand kind of what's going on here and don't . . . in a realistic way, just that they have some respect for what happens here and they're not just looking at it as a bunch of kids who are . . . whatever society expects of skateboarders who are making trouble or messing stuff up.

The use of skate-park rangers who understood and allowed for multiple types of skateboarding to occur diverges from the usual municipal practice of contracting a security guard. A security guard is often considered by skateboarders to be an external crime-control figure. And some might say that skateboarding's security guards regularly alienate youth and provoke strong acts of resistance. Scholar Kara-Jane Lombard even claims that "the most apparent instance of resistance in contemporary skateboarding occurs in relation to the figure of the security guard."[26] In this case, we can see that the Bay City skate rangers were more sympathetic in their understanding and treatment of different skate behaviors. Observations indeed showed that rangers would either sit in a city truck to observe or they would walk around the skate park and converse with people in a friendly manner. We never witnessed instances of conflict or citation-issuing during the times we visited, although this may have occurred at other times.

It is noteworthy, too, that all these efforts to program and influence skate-park life were communicated via social media. One vital strategy used to develop an inclusive and family-friendly skate park was the use of a BCSPG Facebook page. Jane ran the page, where information was posted about the skate park and its programs. Information was also given regarding safety tips. What's more, this social-media platform offered general news about the culture of skateboarding, especially examples of skateboarders or other action-sports figures making positive social change. For example, Mike's skate camps and many pro-social stories were posted along with news about upcoming competitions and festivals taking place in other skate parks. Crucially, the site was also used to address issues at the park and to encourage adult intervention to resolve problems, as revealed in the following post: "I got a report that there were people shooting paint balls at skaters at the park tonight. The Rangers are aware of it. Parents and older skaters, please look out for the younger ones. It's OK to non-aggressively ask people making trouble to leave."

We can see, at this point, how Bay City was largely created and operated through the committed efforts and inclusive visions of Jane and Mike. These two private citizens and the community organization they facilitated tapped into the fiscal resources and infrastructural support provided by the city. With this social-enterprise coalition in place, specific goals and associated techniques were used to facilitate a unique adult-driven spatial project. This social-enterprise network in fact created an attractive, safe environment that eventually garnered significant parental and youth support.

"If Everyone in the World Would Function Like a Skate Park": Parents and the Perceived Benefits of Skateboarding

At this point in the chapter, we have established that parents supported Bay City Skate Park largely because of formal management from the city that engendered strong private-citizen oversight. But why else were parents so fervently committed to the city's skateboarding mission? One key explanation is that parents believed that important forms of child development were taking place within a safe, user-friendly skate spot. The pronounced engagement of families in this social space thus reflected parents' desires to facilitate the generation of youth capital.

Next, we can see how this skate park, which was originally designed in a family-friendly manner in order to promote specific life skills, served as an *Urban Platform for Capital* for local families.

The belief that children could markedly benefit from skateboarding at Bay City was especially important to the parents. As a matter of fact, the vast majority of parents here had very little knowledge of skateboarding. Some parents admitted that they were "not even skateboarders." But after their initial introduction to the skate park and the sport of skateboarding, many parents grew more familiar with and appreciative of this activity. Of course, we would expect that parents new to skateboarding would be wary of experienced, core male skateboarders. But some parents here noticed how proficient males, including young guys and middle-aged veterans, both helped children to learn and be comfortable in the park. Later on, we explain that this finding was tempered by a few parents' reservations about potential antisocial behavior, usually pertaining to when teenaged and "twenty-something" male skaters socialized with each other inside the park or on its periphery. And parental appreciation for skateboarding, while sincere, often seemed related to perceived health and wellbeing benefits for youth, rather than knowledge and respect for its traditional "core" culture.

Despite their individualistic reputations, skateboarders are known for helping each other. This practice is especially common among males who regularly mentor each other in skate parks. In some cases, parents witnessed this type of practice occurring, as proficient male skateboarders encouraged and taught their younger children. These parents noticed how the more experienced skaters were willing to informally coach their children, give advice on equipment, and generally keep a watchful eye on these younger kids. Mark, the father of an eight-year-old son, said that he sometimes saw the older kids in the park helping out the younger ones. Gloria, the fifty-year-old mother of a skater, reiterated this sentiment when talking about the skate park. "Everybody embraced [my son]. Out here a lot of people just watch everybody's back. I don't have to worry about my eight-year-old and his buddy skating out here."

These male skateboarders assisted children by teaching them technical skills and offering general guidance in an informal manner. It is also fair to say that these men sometimes served as role models. Kelly, a mother of two skateboarders, shared her thoughts on this practice. "There are some really good guys. This group of guys up here are pretty good, very respectful towards kids. When I see them—you know you have your regulars that you know are really great, they can be role models. I mean, look at them, they're not swearing, they're being really respectful of the little kids. Maybe my kids will pick up that." Other parents (and even grandparents) of girls especially appreciated the support they observed at the skate park. Jimmy, a grandfather of a young girl, talked about the support he saw his granddaughter receiving from others. "I say the first time she dropped into the bowl she fell here, and there was probably three guys in the bottom making sure she was all right. She was crying. Yeah, like I say, all the guys are real supportive of her, protective of her, and I feel real safe here with them." Another poignant example comes from Celia, a mother of a six-year-old boy skater. In conversation, Celia claimed to be hesitant about taking her son to a park because she assumed that there would be teenage bullies. However, she quickly realized her fears were unfounded. She went on to become a staunch advocate of skateboard- ing. "Everyone's so excited and it just seemed so—such a healthy positive environment.... If everyone in the world would function like a skate park we would have more peace because of sharing the space with each other."

We observed that the middle-aged male skateboarders who used the deep bowl in the back of the park often helped the younger boys who dared to skate with them. As he was packing up his cooler and loading up his car to go home one Saturday afternoon, an older skater told us that he wanted to give back to the skate park and its participants. In fact, his friends all liked helping kids learn how to skate, he said. These men, often with established skate backgrounds, kept an eye on youth while acting as stewards of the skate park. In fact, according to park leader Jane, "Whoever gets here first, cleans. The city staff, obviously, they don't go down there and clean the bowl (a ten-foot deep pool). You notice the guys [older male skaters who frequently use the bowl] have their brooms and stuff. Whoever gets here first cleans the bowls."

Furthermore, parents of girls told us that their daughters enjoyed seeing and engaging with other females in this space. This was consid- ered a positive reason for these families to visit Bay City Skate Park. This type of practice most often occurred during organized girls-only skate events that were hosted by groups such as SLAG, MAHFIA.TV, and GRO. During these events, adult women would often mentor younger girls. Cal, the Indian father we mentioned earlier in the chapter, said that he appreciated this practice and didn't want a "beardy-beardy" guy teaching his daughter. Cal felt that his daughter would learn better and enjoy the experience more when taught by a woman. Ashley, who had both a son and daughter who skated, shared how her daughter was encouraged by other females to join in and skate with them, "so, yeah . . . I did try and point the girls out [in the skate park] for her benefit. To let her know, yeah, go out there and do it."

Overall, we can see how inclusive social practices, encouraged and supported through sustained adult involvement, assuaged some of the new parents' initial fears about skateboarding. We found that this appreciation of Bay City skateboarding translated into adults, including parents, taking on more engaged roles in the skate park. Scholar Adam Jenson and his colleagues in Australia refer to this type of skateboarding as reflecting *high sociability.* This involves the sharing of space without conflict, mixing across different age groups, and the willingness of skaters to look after and teach each other. Other research has additionally recognized that social development and social capital both emerge from this type of peer-to-peer interaction.[27]

The parents' positive experiences in the park over time reinforced a strong commitment to their children's skateboarding. We saw this dedication play out in a variety of ways. In some cases, parents used skateboarding to connect and spend quality time with their children. For example, one mother who took her son to the skate park on a regular basis told us, "I figure if I support him and listen to him and I know what an ollie is and I know what some of these terms are, that's a connection that we have. That's a connection that we'll always have as long as he's into skateboarding." Michael discussed interacting with his son, and his son's friends, by taking on the role of videographer. "They want to have videos on YouTube of them skating. They don't want to film each other, they want me to film it." Robert, whose teenaged son is an advanced skater, goes on trips and documents the skateboarding. "So, I drive them around—trips with this filming buddy who brings two cameras for two different angles and stuff and they set it up and they film." All of these behaviors were seen as important ways that parents could connect with their children via skateboarding.

Parents thus appreciated the emotional bonds that they could make with their children in Bay City Skate Park. The youth-sports literature indeed indicates that this type of bonding experience is an important motivator for parents to become involved.[28] Furthermore, it has been established by research that parents enjoy interacting with their children when transporting them to and from practices or competitions, as we saw above with some of our skate parents. Research has also found that parents value being able to observe their children while simultaneously providing emotional and instructional support. We contend that skateboarding, with its fluid nature, offers the perfect context for these kinds of familial interactions to occur.

A unique aspect of skateboarding is that parents can synchronously skate with their children for long periods. In fact, several of Bay City's parents revealed that they tried out skateboarding because their children became interested in it and they could spend time together. Michael, for example, noted that he didn't skate before "but once I started coming here it's like we're spending a lot of time. I have no ability to watch that much, so I got helmet, pads, the whole nine yards." Amy, a forty-nine-year-old mother of a boy and girl who skate at the park, claimed that parental involvement in skateboarding was one way to spend quality time with their children. It was not, she said, to do with becoming more involved in the traditional skateboarding culture: "We all have the same reason; [it is] basically more because of our kids. It's not because this is something we want to do as [a] mom." She further explained, "You'll meet the other parents; I believe they will have the same reason. Their interest in skateboarding came from their sons' or kids' interest in doing it themselves." Over time, we heard many similar comments from other parents at Bay City Skate Park.

This latter line of commentary reveals how family time was directly associated with the shared act of learning how to skateboard. This practice of adults modeling sporting behavior is considered by scholar Thomas Quarmby to be a positive means of increasing youths' sports participation.[29] It has thus been advocated that parents "engage in sporting activities with their children wherever possible."[30] Skate-park activity is truly suited to support this particular type of parent-child interaction, especially when contrasted with popular team sports that have competitive team formats that create distinctive roles for adults and children. And yet, later on we will see that there were some problematic cases when family skateboarding time was used by parents essentially to monitor and control children's social experiences.

"Every Time You Get on Your Board, You're Pushing Yourself": Self-Confidence, a Sense of Belonging, and Feelings of Achievement

Much of the parent discussion so far orbits around the central belief that Bay City Skate Park was a place where children could safely skate while learning with peers and adults. At the same time, we are developing the picture, at this point, that parents at Bay City Skate Park held an instrumentalist view of skateboarding in terms of its impacts on their children. These parents, once again, were mostly self-identified outsiders and newcomers that wanted their children to gain valuable forms of capital. In essence, these parents were seeking tangible returns on their investments in youth skateboarding.

As we discussed in chapter 1, much has been written about parents' views regarding children's life-skill development through youth-sports participation. A critical component here is often the element of competition, with foremost scholars in PYD stating that "the unique demands of competitive sport may provide a context for teaching certain life skills—when sporting experiences are structured and delivered appropriately."[31] Parents in many youth sports thus tend to value competition because it seemingly prepares their children for future interactions and experiences.[32]

However, in our study, we found that Bay City parents were not particularly interested in this aspect of competition. In fact, only one parent bought into this perspective. Robert relayed to us what he told his son who had already quit other sports. "If all you want to do is skateboard, you need to figure out a way to compete at it." He subsequently stated, "We felt strongly that that's part of what kids should learn with sports. So, [my son] did some research and found some competitions to go to." This same parent subsequently gave poignant examples of the life skills that his son had gained through skate competitions.

> [He has learned] how to deal with success and not be arrogant or rude to people. How to deal with failure and not be mean or rude or be a bad sport. How to deal with disappointment. You work preparing for a contest for two weeks, you work really hard, and then the contest happens and you just don't happen to skate well that day. Or you get hurt right before the contest. Or you skate amazingly well and you should have won, everyone there thinks you should have won, but it's a subjective judging thing and you didn't win and you have to deal with life's not always fair. So, there's that lesson, too. Lots of lessons like that I think are consistent across all sports that he's learned through competing in skating.

Once again, this perspective was an outlier in our data set; the overwhelming majority of parents were uninterested in competition. Yet, it was still important to them that their children use skateboarding in order to enhance their futures. Earlier in this book, we outlined how parents in our neoliberal age are expected to help "children to gain the skills and credentials that would bring them future success."[33] We likewise found that this belief system underpinned many of the parents' actual investments at this skate park. Forthcoming parental comments reveal that children were expected to use skateboarding in order to gain new life skills.

In one sense, it was suggested that Bay City gave children regular opportunities to display their confidence and abilities. In this regard, the noncompetitive nature of skate-park usage was valued by these parents, as many of them had children that did not particularly succeed in or enjoy typical competitive youth sports. This view was expressed by park leader, Jane, who commented, "It's just a great culture, I think. It's such an outlet for kids who maybe aren't as comfortable with organized sports."

Scholars have noted the benefits of this type of sporting environment in terms of youths' self-esteem and self-worth; social environments such as Bay City Skate Park provide kids a sense of belonging, especially when their learning preferences are not compatible with competitive or traditional sports.[34] In fact, skateboarding was seen by one father, Michael, as a good alternative to traditional sports for his ten-year-old son. And, Paul, a father of two young children, noted that skateboarding has no rules, which means that kids were essentially free to innovate. In comparing skateboarding to other team sports he told us, "Everybody learns the basic stuff; but then it's like how crazy can you get?" Paul felt that skateboarding therefore gave his son more confidence and a greater sense of competency.

> Just the self-confidence he gets out of this that he's not going to get from team sports. The way that when somebody, if somebody were to say something to him at school about you can't do this, it's like, "Hey, you're right, I can't, [but] come with me sometime to the skate park. I've got a board for you. I've got a helmet, let's [see if you can] do it." He was not the most confident kid before this. It really changed a lot.

Jeff, another father, echoed this belief. He suggested that the skate park was good for youth "who are not the team sport kids and who aren't participating in a lot of social stuff." He was pleased for his son, "knowing he'd always have a place just to go that he would fit in. I think that's big to know that you have a place where you can fit in . . . a sense of freedom and accomplishment."

Instead of emphasizing competition, then, what we found instead was that most parents wanted their children to develop without being competitive with their peers. For example, Kelly, the mother of two young boys, once stated, "I think every time you get on your board, you're pushing yourself. Every time. You're not really competing, but when you're hanging out with your friends like that, I don't know if competing is the right word, but, you kind of are. You're pushing yourself more." In fact, she once told her son, "It's not a competition, you're supposed to just go out there and enjoy it. . . . If there's somebody out there that knows more than you, you try and get as much information from them as you can." This perspective was echoed by Paul, who said in conversation, "I love skateboarding," before then adding, "we're not about performance enhancement. We're about opportunities and positive learning environments."

Going further, parents often referenced perseverance as another key life skill that could be learned through noncompetitive skateboarding. This belief is exemplified in the following statements from a mother: "Nothing about skateboarding is easy. Nothing. It takes a lot of perseverance. I think that's really big character-building right there. Watching them try to ollie over and over and not give up. Just keep on that board, pick it back up and try again. I think that in general will [help them] pass through life." Another father, Mark, told us how his son was learning perseverance and commitment through skateboarding. Mark thought this would translate into other facets of his son's life. "So, he'd try something and give up early. Now the fact that he sees that he's improving with effort he's willing to put more effort in other activities that he would have given up on earlier." Mark provided an example of this, relaying a conversation he had with his son about "instant gratification."

> Mark: Well, how long did it take you to learn to drop into the bowl?
>
> Son: Well, it took like three weeks.
>
> Mark: Okay, well then maybe it's going to take you three weeks to have to read this book and write your book report.

Parents also mentioned other purported benefits such as task focus, creativity, and dealing with success, failure, and fear. Often times, many of these skills and attributes were related to the concept of calculated risk-taking. Consider this observation from Paul regarding situations his son would encounter at the skate park.

> "Okay, I'm looking down this thing, this run. Am I next in line? Is there a guy coming in the side? Is there somebody down there already and working his way back up?" That awareness, I think, is

important. Looking forward and then kind of planning for response and recourse. I think it's really, really good stuff. You don't really get that, I think, in team sports as much.

Paul strongly believed that these types of skills, gained by skateboarding in the park, were required to be successful in life. Likewise, another dad said that he was especially impressed with his eight-year-old son's rapid skateboarding progress. "At his age, in less than a year, I can say he's better than I ever was on a ramp because he's dropping in—he's dropping in off of high—that would have scared the crap out of me when I was in junior high." This dad thus appreciated how his son learned to overcome fear and find solutions to perform a difficult technical move.

In terms of risk-taking, all of the parents we met were concerned with their children's physical safety. Nonetheless, a few parents provided their child with opportunities to be independent while navigating this risk. These parents, we learned, allowed more risk-taking for a variety of reasons.[35] Below is an interview excerpt about one couple who did not require their son to wear a helmet, even though they were uneasy about this decision. This is recounted by the father, Robert.

> At some point, within a week, my wife and I decided that [Brady's] old enough and he knows how to skate and he's a good skater and he needs to learn to fall and not hit his head. At first, I think we had a rule for a while that he couldn't do any tricks down six stairs or bigger without a helmet. But then within four months we said "alright." Even though I'm inside feeling terrified that he might get hurt, my trick to calming my own nerves is I Google the closest hospital and the directions to it so that at least if he gets hurt I know exactly what to do.

Another set of parents explained how risk-taking was a key transferable life skill gained through skateboarding. Paul reveals in this regard how he tried to let his kids make their own decisions with regard to physical risk-taking.

> A lot of people are risk-averse by nature and they never learn how to take risks, so they never get anywhere in life. They just kind of become little automatons or zombies as they go through life. I think that most extreme sports require 100 percent commitment and focus. If you're dropping in on a pool, you're dropping in on a big wave, whatever. You're either on the edge and you're surfing and you're pushing over, well there's a point where if you don't actually

commit you're going over anyway. Or you'll just never catch a wave. So, I think it's really important. To be successful in life, I think, requires focus and commitment. So, I think that skateboarding or surfing—more so than some—skateboarding and surfing teach you that kind of commitment and the reward built right in there. It teaches you to take calculated risks.

In another vein, many parents saw the skate culture in Bay City as having many culturally diverse participants especially when compared to team sports. They appreciated the positive interactions that occurred when skateboarders from different backgrounds came together. Thus, like other skate park parents that we researched, Bay City parents felt that this type of diversity had a positive influence on their children. Ashley, a woman of color, grew up hanging out with skaters and noted, "Skateboarders who, for me, in my world, they weren't into drugs. They stuck together. They were an interracial group and I've always liked those qualities." Gloria talked further about her son's useful interactions with skaters who were older and had different ethnic backgrounds.

> I think it bridges age gaps and cultures all that stuff. It bridges all those things. The dude was twenty-two years old, black dude from [another city], my son's an eight-year-old white boy. It bridged it, they had a connection. . . . I wanted [my son] to experience more of a cultural diversity, and you definitely get that here. I love it because they look at what you can do on a skateboard, not what you look like on the outside.

This type of social environment, which brought together skaters from diverse backgrounds, was thus seen as conducive for youth development. This indeed reflects an important benefit that is known as *bridging social capital*.[36] This type of social capital reflects the creation of important new relationships between people that are usually divided from each other. It has even been referred to as "sociological WD-40."[37] Yet, while diversity in term of age, race, and ethnicity was regularly seen as a positive attribute, it became noticeable that parents did not talk about gender diversity being important to youth development.

Replete with social diversity, while providing noncompetitive yet risk-based learning opportunities, Bay City Skate Park was viewed by some parents as a critical site for youth to develop. We can thus see how urban skateboarding, like other action sports, offers up "opportunities for children and youth to gain a sense of achievement without having to compete against, and beat, another team or player. Rather, participants can learn alongside one another and gain a sense of accomplishment based on their own skill development."[38] Moreover, parental accounts of this skate park are consonant with the scholarly belief that activities like skateboarding are beneficial; they help youths acquire more self-confidence and develop meaningful peer relations and friendships.[39]

"He Is Six, But I Will Be Out Until He's Twenty-One": Parenting Strategies that Serve to Mitigate Risk

The parents discussed above noted that the skate park culture could function as a diverse, supportive and developmental space, for younger children. Yet, on some occasions, parents could also enact different forms of protective care work to address social risks.[40] Bay City parents sometimes believed that drinking, smoking, and bullying could still occur in the skate park, despite the generally positive social atmosphere. This type of behavior worried them to the point that a few of these parents became directly involved in correcting risky social behavior that they felt was inappropriate around their children. These parents would make their presence known even to the extent of initiating direct confrontations, as we will see below.

Therefore, some Bay City parents did not allow their children to play freely; for these parents, controlling the social riskiness of urban skateboarding became more imperative. This meant being in close proximity to the skate scene in order to reduce their children's exposure to certain behaviors and attitudes. For instance, Nori, mother of a twelve-year-old boy and eight-year-old girl who are both new skateboarders, appreciated the ability to closely monitor her kids within this skate park. "So when you're talking about risk with kids, at least things happen in front of me or close enough." Many parents who were new to skateboarding and had younger children, usually under nine years old, held similar views. Their comments exemplify a desire to control social risk, as this was an expected parental duty. Amy simply offered the view that the parents in this skate park could be placed into two camps: "I see two kinds of people here. One is wild and one is being protected. So, we're on the protecting side of it." This dualistic typology, regarding two opposing camps of parents, underpinned some of these parents' desires to directly monitor their children through close interaction. Amy's comment clearly illustrates how being an involved, protective skate parent was equated with good parenting practice. It was thus not unexpected that Amy went on to mention how she was worried about her son learning new, bad behaviors through skateboarding.

> The bad words, sometimes they call bad words and they're not comfortable about that. He gets really offended even only hearing it because he doesn't hear it in the house. So that's one thing. You see this environment of people who are drinking, taking drugs, having foul languages, the only thing I'm asking [my children] is to not do what [others are] doing. They know that. [I tells my kids], "The moment I see doing something you're not allowed to do normally in the house, you're off the board."

Amy also mentioned in conversation that her husband did not support their children being in Bay City because of potential exposure to undesirable behavior. But Amy allowed their children to skate, albeit with her close presence, to ensure their well-being and safety. She even took up skateboarding herself, and we saw that other parents in her social circle joined, too. We observed that these committed skateboarding parents formed a supervisory presence, keeping a close eye on their children.

Not very capable as skateboarders and hardly interested in traditional skate culture, parents like Amy were motivated by other perceived benefits. Interestingly, these parents, usually mothers and a few fathers, directly benefited from their children's skateboarding in Bay City Skate Park. We found out that some of the parents we met, especially the more intensive ones, formed a friendship group that would meet up in the skate park. They would also socialize elsewhere, for instance at someone's house. These parents therefore created a new social network around their children's skateboarding that gave them further reason to be in the skate park. Toral offered a detailed description of this group.

> We've been here for a long time. I mean I definitely feel, you know, there's definitely a little mom culture going on or a little parent culture going on here, too, right? I mean, like there's a bunch of us that are here on Saturdays and Sundays. You know, Gloria and Kelly and, you know, everybody, and we'll sit over there on the benches or we'll all bring our little chairs, you know, Gloria says "bring some chairs." And we'll sit there and we'll watch each other's kids, you know, and stuff like that. So, we all know who each other's kids are and that actually kind of helps, we're all together on Facebook and we know when each other's going to be at the park so we'll kind of plan so the boys always can have time together because sometimes it's more fun even being with each other, even though it's an individual sport,

right? Sometimes they just have fun skating together and trying new things and stuff like that. So, I call that the mom culture—the skate-mom culture that's here because I see the same, like, five ladies every time I'm here.

Intensive parental involvement in youths' skateboarding was also described by Toral, who previously lamented that she saw a broken bone in her son's future. She admitted to being a "helicopter mom." In this role, she regularly monitored her child's surroundings and searched for risky situations and behaviors. She would even directly intervene and admonish youth about their behavior when it contradicted her own family values. "I'm candid, like, 'Look, I don't really care, but you're smoking in front of my child, you know, I can make a choice and you're taking his choice away. And so, do whatever you need to do but do it in the parking lot.'" Toral further spoke about the need to monitor and filter skate park activity for her son, given that she had concerns about urban skateboarding and some of its cultural elements:

> Just the culture as a whole. You know, like my son asks a lot more questions at his age that I wasn't expecting, like, you know, about the cussing and the drugs . . . not ready as a mom of an eight-year-old to really answer those questions. I expected those in junior high, so I'm like, "What?" And it's because of the people that he meets here, what he sees when he's here, and those are, you know, some of the—I think that overall there is so much more positive than that negative, so it won't make me stop bringing him here.

Gloria, a fellow participant in the so-called "mom culture," would regularly visit the skate park to watch her son skate. And she liked how some of the park's skaters helped her son. So, during these visits, she took on a less direct strategy when she saw behavior that could perhaps negatively influence her son.

> You know, you get a rapport with some of the people that are drinking or whatever and I've gotten a rapport with them and I love them, that they're skating with my kid. And I said, "But you all have to take that all away because if you do that at the park, it's going to affect the park. It's going to affect how people perceive it, it's going to bring more people to do drink and drugs in here, which is not okay." They respect that. I said, "I get you want a beer, I get you want to smoke your stuff, whatever, that's your choice, but you don't need to bring my kid into it." They respect that. I can't control what everybody

else does, it's not my call. I can control whether or not I call the cops on them.

Celia, the mother of a six-year-old, told us that she appreciated the existing skateboarding culture, too. But she qualified this view, stating that an adult presence was required to create a safe social environment. "So, I think the other reason that parents are out, I'm out, [is] for the safety of my child. I mean he is six, but I will be out until he's twenty-one. I'll be the mom sitting in the parking lot, and his friends will know I'm in the parking lot, so if something happens—that there's somebody close and they know somebody knows what's going on. I just feel like a parent presence makes a whole huge difference."

Michael, the father of two skateboarders who picked up the activity himself, as mentioned before, even claimed that he wanted to shape the new family-friendly skate culture materializing here. In Bay City, he wanted to create a "critical mass" of like-minded parents to challenge traditional skate-culture elements.

> We can either say "yeah, we don't like the organization and what they stand for" or we can try and change it from the inside. We can do the same thing with street skating. We can stand by and say, "*Thrasher Magazine* is junk, nobody should look at it, and street skating is the bridge to the devil" or we can say "look, street skating can be fun and it can also be a positive experience" and change it from the inside out. It doesn't take a lot of people to hit a critical mass in a movement, especially in a small community like this.

This type of earnest involvement in children's skateboarding reflects strong parental dedication regularly found within American youth sports. In some cases, these examples above indicate intensive, helicopter-type parenting strategies, involving parents who went to great lengths to organize and shape their children's experiences.[41]

Looking back at the contentious town-hall meeting described at the beginning of this chapter, we can see how adults invested in an intensive-parenting approach could clash with others who utilized a more hands-off strategy. And, in fact, a few Bay City parents did not see cussing, smoking, and drinking as behaviors to control or eliminate; they instead saw these behaviors as part of a social world their children would at some point need to experience and learn to navigate. These parents viewed potentially negative situations found in skate parks as useful teaching opportunities. In response to concerns over foul language and pot-smoking at the park, they stated very similar sentiments to Jimmy, who often accompanied his granddaughter to the skate park. In conversation, Jimmy commented, "What are you going to do? They're going to be exposed to it sooner or later. It's part of the everyday culture. For the most part, the kids, everybody's good from what I've seen." A parent named Jeff echoed this belief system.

> I hope that we talk to him enough about . . . we come up here and see kids doing stuff that we know they're not supposed to do and we talk about—and hopefully he comes away with it understanding that all these people in the world they all do things different ways. Sometimes they make bad decisions and sometimes there is consequences for it and hopefully he can just be himself and that's not an impact.

Likewise, Ashley, a mother of two young kids, explained to us, "The people I know who are serious skaters, yeah, they smoke pot, yeah, they drink here." But Ashley said that she didn't interrupt these behaviors. Instead, her approach was to educate and enable her son and daughter to make their own decisions. She felt that her children were therefore learning a new, positive life skill. "I just tell my kids about drugs and hopefully they'll make the right choices." Although, she conceded that this approach would quickly change if the drugs in question were different: "If they're doing meth, we're going to have a huge problem."

Conclusion: A Social Space Featuring Adult-Driven and Family-Friendly Skateboarding

A running belief throughout *Moving Boarders* is that skate parks function as unique *social spaces* that have been deliberately designed to allow diverse forms of social life to proliferate. With regard to skate parks like Bay City, the social-space concept prompted us to examine who creates and uses these spaces and how participation here is related to mechanisms that are used to achieve certain ends.

Just like other skate parks featured later in this book, Bay City Skate Park relied upon a social-enterprise network constituted by multiple private and public stakeholders committed to a social cause. In Bay City, this network was authorized by the local government to create new, regular skate opportunities for diverse racial and ethnic groups, beginners, girls and young women, those with disabilities, as well as older individuals. But, alongside this finding, what truly sets Bay City Skate Park apart from some of the other *Moving Boarders* skate parks is its reliance upon adult oversight. A heavy adult presence here links with the presence of many younger children in the park.

Accordingly, there was a range of seemingly positive and negative behaviors that were identified and described to us by the parents we researched. In response, some parents formed social clusters and even participated in the oversight group, the BCSPG. Parental investment here often took into consideration skateboarding's social and physical risk factors, with some parents providing evidence of intensive parenting while others enacted a more hands-off approach. And we also saw that many parents appreciated the noncompetitive aspect of local skateboarding, as it benefited children who did not want to participate in team sports.

Taken together, this chapter's analyses indicate that many parents here wanted to enact what they considered to be good, socially valued parenting practices. This approach falls in line with the neoliberal idea that parents should be highly engaged and provide regular opportunities for their children to gain capital; this is considered an appropriate role for parents and part of their expected duties within a productive, normative society. Simultaneously, it has been argued that youth in sports are held responsible for obtaining certain socially-accepted values and attributes considered necessary for their success.[42] We can thus see why many of the Bay City parents ended up becoming so influential here.

At the end of the book, we will further explore how certain forms of intensive Bay City skate parenting raise questions about how youth skateboarders can develop their own sense of identity and agency. Often, Bay City parents hoped that their involvement in skateboarding could transform their children's lives, in line with their own adult expectations. There were fewer instances here where parents supported youths' self-determination by giving them more freedom and decision-making capacity amidst social risk.

Looking ahead to chapter 4, we will further explore this idea of youth engagement in urban space. This next chapter features West Oakland's Town Park, which was largely created by a private citizen, Keith "K-Dub" Williams, and support from a major corporate sponsor. Over the course of several years, K-Dub led a social-enterprise coalition that constructed yet another *Urban Platform for Capital* in our region. K-Dub's unique vision and its influence on youth, parents, and the community of West Oakland are the focus of the next chapter.

FOUR

"I Want the Platform and Everybody's Welcome"

Oakland's "Hood Cred" and Skateboarding Scene

There is a buzz in Oakland's "Town Park" this Saturday morning. A skate contest for youth is gathering steam. In contrast to your typical weekend youth soccer tournament, today's skate event feels more loosely organized. Altogether, there are about 20 kids and older teens competing, reflecting diverse racial and ethnic backgrounds. Approximately fifteen parents are hanging around. As the skaters compete one at a time on a half-pipe, an MC announces the type of moves being performed just like we see on television's X Games. Meanwhile, the older boys who are in the contest have become the judges for the younger divisions. We speak with a father who happens to be a research scientist at a local university. We have noticed him tailing his son wherever he goes in the skate park. Another dad, who tells us that he is an ex-skater, is sporting a Thrasher sweater and black sunglasses. He tells us about two types of parents that he regularly observes—those who were skaters from before that "got it," and then others that approached this like any youth sport and just wanted their kids to become pro skateboarders.

The dreadlocked Keith "K-Dub" Williams is the organizer of today's event. We observe him talking with two African American teenagers who say they cannot pay the skate contest entry fee. K-Dub says he will lend them five dollars, but with a catch. He asks them, "What are you going to do for me, then?," with one boy immediately replying, "Whatever you want." K-Dub jokes that he needs the tires on his truck changed. But what he really means is this: how would they give back to the skate park? One of these boys would eventually feature in a Levi's jeans skateboarding documentary that was filmed about Town Park.

Spectators watching from above the half-pipe occasionally burst out with *woo-hoos*. Skaters bang their boards on the ground to show

A diverse mix of young male skaters at Oakland's Town Park.
Courtesy of Todd Fuller.

appreciation for the tricks being landed. One of the local boys that was talking to K-Dub earlier is watching a six-year-old white kid perform his run. He exclaims that this young boy "is hella good!"

At one point, the event's MC bellows out "Goodbye Bay City, hello Oakland!," which elicits a loud roar from the crowd. This shout-out is not meant to dis Bay City's new skate park, but rather it signals that Oakland youth now have their own skate spot. K-Dub tell us that Levi's is going to spend over half a million dollars to renovate Town Park by pouring in concrete.

K-Dub then says that he will keep some of the wooden ramps emblazoned with graffiti art. But he will burn other wooden pieces in an edifice "like Burning Man," he says. At one point, surveying the buzzing scene in front of us, K-Dub professes that "there is a method to the madness."

The narrative above, from a field note, poignantly illustrates the proliferating skate life that evolved out of one man's mission to give Oakland's skateboarders a place of their own. This chapter will show that there was indeed "a method to the madness," as K-Dub put it, in terms of how this skate park was originally designed for youth and its subsequent metamorphosis into a globally recognized skate spot. In chapter 3, we explained that Bay City Skate Park came into existence through adult organizing at the ground level and in social media; this occurred in conjunction with official recognition and support from the city government. Bay City's adult coalition thus directly intervened in order to provide a safe, family-friendly youth-sports experience. Bay City Skate Park functioned as an *Urban Platform for Capital*, and the prevailing view among participants was that individual children could develop personally and socially by skateboarding in an adult-directed facility.

This chapter likewise delves into the political constitution of urban space. We will show how Town Park, based in Oakland, was also deliberately created by adults to serve youth and their families as an *Urban Platform for Capital*. And yet, this urban space has a different mission, involving the generation of a more politically conscious and communal skate scene; the development of neighborhood youth serves as its focus. Town Park skateboarding, we will explain, strongly incorporates Oakland's local history, politics, and culture.

This chapter once again illustrates that social-enterprise practice, which involves both private and public stakeholders working to create sustainable social change, takes up many forms in the neoliberal era.[1] Town Park lacked a committed parent presence supported by city government resources, as found in the aspirational, more professional enclave of Bay City. In Oakland, by contrast, it mostly came down to K-Dub, following in his mother's urban social-work footsteps, to determine the nature of youth skateboarding in Town Park. With limited municipal support, as well as ingrained cultural skepticism about city intervention and control, Town Park was molded largely according to K-Dub's personal vision. In true social-entrepreneur manner, K-Dub collected supporters ranging from individual donors to a multinational corporation. Thus, despite its grassroots, populist leanings, Town Park undoubtedly relied upon private-industry support, too.

The *Moving Boarders* case chapters clearly demonstrate that life in each skate park is shaped by unique local conditions. Likewise, context is especially critical when telling the story of Town Park and its original artistic, street vibe. Ensconced in the heart of West Oakland, within the confines of the historic De Fremery Park, this skate park was deliberately set up to reflect erstwhile political struggles. It was no coincidence that Town Park emerged on revolutionary ground, within a park that was once the locus of the Black Panther Party's community outreach programs. Indeed, this site in West Oakland was once considered a "hotbed of social struggle in the 1960s and 1970s," as part of the Black Liberation movement combating both inner-city decline and political marginalization in Oakland.[2]

Today, a flood of economic refugees reflects Oakland's reinvention as a prime lifestyle destination.[3] Quite simply, Oakland has become known as the epitome of West Coast urban cool. The mayor indeed proclaimed in 2016 that Oakland was attracting outsiders because it had a "secret sauce" comprised of "progressive values, creative energy, and a gritty authenticity borne of Oakland's deep blue-collar roots."[4] We will accordingly see that this skate park, unique among our case studies, was intentionally designed to capitalize on the rising value of urbanness, or even *hood cred*, as K-Dub once dubbed it. Twisting Oakland's newfound popularity to his advantage, K-Dub created Town Park to work as a social "platform," in his own words, that could provide valuable skills and networking opportunities for participants. We will see that this practice especially applied to local African American young men whose presence in the park exemplified Oakland's urban-cool factor.

The city government and private sector have recently been working to refashion Oakland into America's trendiest urban enclave. In this context, we will ultimately see how urban skateboarding "can create a cool, youthful buzz which many cities crave as part of regeneration."[5] Town Park without a doubt reflects Oakland's newfound high cultural status. At the same time, it is important that we reveal the voices of parents we met in Town Park; they serve as an important barometer of K-Dub's social-enterprise vision. Many parents, we will show, were attuned to Town Park's inherent sociocultural diversity. They actually came away feeling positive about the evolving mixture of youth inhabiting this new social environment. Simultaneously, we argue that some parents, especially established local ones, felt that skate life here was marked by a certain communal ethos. Town Park, they believed, reproduced the history and cultural makeup of the surrounding neighborhood. We conclude by highlighting the lack of girls and women in this skate park observed at the beginning of our research. This finding is complemented by more recent evidence that reveals how female skaters are now being systematically incorporated to a greater degree in Town Park.

Political History of De Fremery Park and West Oakland

As noted above, Town Park's underlying history is vital to know, as it sheds light upon this skate park's current mission and practices. Historian Chance Grable provides an excellent account of West Oakland's De Fremery Park, where Town Park is now based. This park, Grable explains, was initially conceived in the mid-nineteenth century as a pastoral getaway for the San Francisco elite, who grew weary of the city's rapid industrialization.[6] By the advent of the 1940s, military mobilization and resultant wartime jobs in Oakland began to attract African Americans from the southern states to this area.[7] At the conclusion of World War II, this park came into its own as a social-organizing hub, particularly for local African American youth. Grable offers the following description of De Fremery park during its post-war "golden years" of youth development.

> During this time, De Fremery also provided a space for youth to express their political will and challenge the color line that discriminated against them and their community. Most notably the youth organized a successful boycott of Coca-Cola, which resulted in the hiring of the first African American. During these golden years of youth development (1947–1964) De Fremery was transformed into a space which nurtured West Oakland youth both socially and politically.[8]

By the mid-1960s and early 1970s, social life in De Fremery Park could be characterized as becoming more overtly revolutionary. It was during this time that the park became a focal point for Oakland's African American community as it protested against institutionalized racism. These protests coalesced into the Black Power Movement. This movement's evolution is described by Grable as follows: "After years of superficial liberal allegiance and consistent rejection from white institutions, an increasing number of people from the African American community began to emphasize community control and building power within the community."[9]

Founded in 1966, the Black Panther Party for Self Defense would "conduct their *survival pending revolution programs*" which included sickle-cell-anemia medical testing and distribution of free groceries in the park.[10] De Fremery Park also hosted many political rallies, fundraisers, and physical-training sessions. Honoring one of the original Black Panther members, this park eventually became known locally as "Lil' Bobby Hutton Memorial Park" shortly after Hutton was shot to death by Oakland Police in 1968.[11] We can see that, from the mid-twentieth century onwards, De Fremery Park has served as a focal point for the local African American community's struggles against race- and class-based oppression. Below, we illustrate how this struggle continues due to Oakland's rampant gentrification. This means that there is rising tension in the community as new urban transplants, including "high tech pilgrims," are relocating into what has been deemed "the Bay Area's final economic development frontier."[12]

"The Writing Is on the Wall": The Gentrification of Oakland

"In capitalism, capital counts"

—former Oakland mayor Jerry Brown[13]

The nation often imagines that Oakland is fundamentally an African American working-class or even impoverished city with a high crime rate. During the most recent presidential campaigning, Oakland was even mistakenly portrayed as one of the world's most dangerous cities.[14] But now, riding on the metro train service, known to locals as the BART, one is confronted by a sign from a realty company proclaiming that Oakland is the place to be now, deemed as the "New Edge of Silicon Valley."[15] Oakland is unquestionably undergoing major cultural and economic shifts which we describe below.

So, what gives Oakland—for so long the quintessentially neglected American post-industrial city—so much currency now? The answer derives in part from Oakland's proximity to its neighbor San Francisco. A prominent financial center that is emboldened by a surge in nearby Silicon Valley technological industries, the city of San Francisco represents the paragon of capitalism. This financial hub has even been deemed the "capital of the new economy."[16] However, despite San Francisco's prominent financial status, the city is still "woefully over matched by other world capitals in housing capacity."[17] Thus, San Francisco has easily become the most expensive housing market in the United States, with rental prices for a one-bedroom accommodation reaching a whopping average of $3,450 per month in July 2017.[18] Consequently, increasing numbers of people doing business or living in San Francisco have turned their attention across the Bay Bridge, creating a new housing boom in Oakland.

This boom was arguably facilitated by Oakland insiders.[19] As the previous century concluded, former mayor Jerry Brown professed that Oakland needed to attract 10,000 new residents to Oakland's downtown under his "10K" plan. The choice, he claimed, was simple, as it came down to either gentrification or "slumification."[20] Speaking once with columnists from the *San Francisco Chronicle*, Brown dismissed criticism that he was going to attract "10,000 white people" because only they could afford to live in the new high-priced lofts. "That's kind of a stigmatization of nonwhite people," he eventually countered.[21]

More than fifteen years after this controversial exchange, Oakland has indeed gentrified at an accelerated rate.[22] Oakland's house-purchase prices have shot up as transplants have relocated to Oakland's western neighborhoods and city center en masse. It is therefore unsurprising that in late 2015, Oakland could lay claim to being the fourth most expensive rental market in the nation.[23] Consider a recent local story that claims "the place where prices are rising the fastest isn't San Francisco anymore—it's Oakland.[24] In fact, between July 2011 and July 2016, the median price of an Oakland home nearly doubled to $626,000, according to the popular real-estate website Trulia. And median rents went up by $1,100 during that time.[25] Still, open houses resemble "mob scenes," according to one Oakland real-estate agent featured in a local news piece.[26] And, furthermore, with San Francisco being "overstuffed with startups, to the point of exploding," companies such as Uber, Ask.com, and Pandora are leading an "East Bay tech boom."[27]

Not unexpectedly, the recent industry and population migration to Oakland has rankled some long-established residents who are concerned about the city's newfound cachet. Overt protests and other forms of resistance have begun to spring up. Oakland's new Whole Foods store, described by one local news story as a symbol of "white bohemian affluence, the kind that enjoys the 'grit' of an urban neighborhood," was recently stormed by local protesters after a twenty-seven-year-old African American man was brutalized by a security guard.[28] This piece concludes that "the store has gone from a symbol of progress to one of exclusion." Another people's protest blocked private buses procured specifically for tech workers. According to this protest group, "The rich have begun colonizing North Oakland, West Oakland, and Downtown. Their tech buses, their pricey cafes, and their luxury apartments have begun to appear with alarming frequency."[29] Even recent fires appearing on Oakland construction sites have been attributed to a disgruntled local. According to a local news report, the fires were likely "the work of an arsonist angry about the rapid and dramatic gentrification of sections of the East Bay, where long-time residents are being forced from their neighborhoods by rising rents."[30]

We can see from these compelling examples that some established residents are frustrated by official policies that have brought about seismic cultural and economic shifts. Many locals feel left behind due to lack of affordable housing. In this regard, a recent feature story, titled "Activists, Entrepreneurs Fight for a Place in West Oakland's Future," provided the following account about the locals' plight:

> Neighborhood activists complain that city officials haven't offered much leadership in addressing the area's issues, let alone managing them. "They're going to get [Oakland] ready. But who are they getting ready for?" he says. The neighborhood is simmering with activity and more development is coming. The writing is on the wall, Coleman says.[31]

This extract indicates the reality of how certain Oakland residents have been marginalized by aggressive development policies. It is to the point that many people are moving to adjacent areas. In fact, the population of African Americans in the city declined by 24 percent from 2000 to 2010, representing 34,000 people.[32] What's more, while residents making over $150,000 tend to remain, one report suggests that between 2010 and 2014, 28 percent of those leaving Oakland were making less than $30,000, which is considered a disproportionately high and unexpected leaving rate for this latter group.[33] This pattern of economic displacement touches upon local youth sport families, too. According to Ben Gucciardi, a leader in Oakland's "Soccer Without Borders" youth program, "In the past year, we have seen seven of the families we serve leave Oakland, citing cost of housing as the primary reason for moving. There is an increasing sense within the communities we work with that the cost of living in Oakland is prohibitive." Of course, there are some established residents that actually value the changing conditions in Oakland. An article in *Sunset Magazine* from 2016 provides the following commentary from one established

African American resident. "Back in the day, you'd see people of all ages, colors, backgrounds milling around. . . . That's why when I hear people saying that Oakland is gentrifying and becoming this or that, to me it doesn't ring right. The way I look at it, what's really happening is that Oakland is returning to what it used to be."[34]

However one weighs in on the current situation, it cannot be denied that Oakland, with its distinct urban attributes, is poised to become yet another creative and professional hub in the area, which will bring forth an influx of new people and ideas.[35] We shall see that in this context Town Park functions as an *Urban Platform for Capital* that strategically aims to benefit neighborhood youth and other established residents who have been historically neglected.

The Rise of Skateboarding in West Oakland: Evolution of Tha Hood Games and Town Park

The creation of West Oakland's Town Park was largely due to K-Dub; in this regard, he wears many hats, so to speak, combining the roles of artist, educator, father, skateboarder, youth mentor, and community activist.[36] K-Dub has been referred to as the "Godfather" of the Oakland skate-park scene and he was recently awarded the City of Oakland Community Person of the Year award.[37] And, in fact, when the mayor needs help with getting kids to stay in school, she calls on K-Dub to get them there.[38]

Much of K-Dub's current inspiration to be a community skate leader derives from his own upbringing. K-Dub's personal influences and experiences greatly shape the nature of Town Park's skate activities. K-Dub's actual roots in skateboarding trace back to the late 1970s, when he began skateboarding with other youth in his South Central Los Angeles neighborhood and also in nearby Orange County. K-Dub participated in traditional youth sports and skateboarding, as we can see in this interview comment: "Well, I would say growing up [in] South Central L.A., I played sports, every kind of sport, basketball, football, yada yada yada, but a buddy of mine . . . he like, 'Man, let's try this [skateboarding].' And it was cool because nobody skated where we were. It was different. Didn't need a coach, didn't need a uniform. My mom said 'just come back in one piece.'"

K-Dub later went on to attend California State University, Long Beach, where he graduated with an arts degree. Eventually he relocated to the San Francisco Bay Area and became the advisor to a skateboarding

Keith "K-Dub" Williams. *Courtesy of Todd Fuller.*

club, the O-High Playas, while teaching art at Oakland High School.[39] At that time, K-Dub noticed that local youth of color were beginning to skateboard. He subsequently attended the 2004 X Games taking place in Los Angeles and noticed a contradiction: the diversity of the crowd was not reflected in the event's actual skaters:

> Well, I was teaching at Oakland High School from 2000 to like 2007, 2008, so I started seeing some kids coming to school with skate-boards that looked like Latino and Asian and Filipino and African American, and I said, "What you guys know about that?" Like, "Yeah, we do this in our neighborhood." So at that summer, I go home to L.A. every summer and the X Games happened to be in L.A. and so I went to the X Games and I saw the diversity in the crowd, but I didn't see it amongst the athletes that were competing. So and I said, 'You know, when I come back to, you know, up to the Bay, and we'll start a skateboard club for the kids, and then create an event for them in their own community.'

K-Dub later recounted another motivating factor for starting his skate program in a newspaper story: "The industry got healthy based on a lot of kids of color purchasing [stuff] that weren't even skaters."[40] Seeing this gap, whereby youth of color were largely peripheral participants even as they were key supporters of skate events and the industry, K-Dub developed the first iteration of his social-enterprise network. He partnered with his retired social-worker mother, Barbara "Adjoa" Murden, and a professional African American skateboarder, Karl Watson, to produce an event called Tha Hood Games in East Oakland.[41] K-Dub also received support from the East Oakland Youth Development Center. He was explicit that Oakland was the unique inspiration and home base for this "punky" and "rag tag" urban festival, as he characterized it during our conversation. Tha Hood Games were originally created in order to bring quality grassroots entertainment to inner-city communities. The events themselves were festival-like, with a hybrid mix of activities that gave youth "an opportunity to showcase and nurture their skills in skateboarding, music, dance and the visual arts in their own communities."[42] However, even as Tha Hood Games events were gaining traction across the West Coast, there was still no permanent skateboarding site in Oakland.[43] Previous skate spots, as we once discussed, were mostly organically created and often shut down by government officials.

Consequently, in 2007, Williams began to scout locations for a permanent skate site to serve local youth.[44] It was during this time that a vacant lot within De Fremery Park was identified.[45] K-Dub quickly ascertained that this location had potential to benefit Oakland youth. He subsequently reached out to the City of Oakland in order to utilize this undeveloped location to build a skate park. But K-Dub made it clear to us during our interview that he was not working for the city government. He said, "I approached them about, you know, just given this space has been empty, there was nothing going on here, you know." During the recent Oakland Skatepark Summit, which we described earlier, K-Dub stated that he wanted to create accessible city park spaces for youth because he had grown up in the parks of Los Angeles.

At the same time, we must remember that city parks for sports have always been hard to come by, especially in Oakland. "Oakland is historically, chronically under-resourced," one local news report claims.[46] And parks that have existed, including ones for skateboarding, have not been safe or well-monitored. For instance, according to the same news report, another Oakland skate-park site has been maintained by "a homeless couple in their twenties" who allegedly live there. This story recalls that a seventeen-year-old runaway girl was shot and killed near this skate park. Furthermore, an interview with Eddie, a local skate coach, highlights this lack of safe, accessible skate space in Oakland.

> The reason why I stopped skating in Oakland—well . . . the reason why I stopped skating at the skate park down the street is because the area is kind of dangerous. I stay over on 90th and McArthur, and a few times—there was a few times I would be at the skate park because I was staying at the skate park until like nine o'clock or something at night and stuff. There were a few times I would leave late or something like that and people would try to rob me on my way home or something like that.

For a long time, Oakland has had an issue regarding the existence of safe and functional parks, including those designated for skateboarding. Thus, to redress this situation, the first iteration of Town Park came into existence in 2008. At this time, we learned from an interview, K-Dub and his supporters relocated donated wood and other materials from an unused skate park thirty minutes away. Donated paint was used to decorate the space. He recalled this effort and the difficulties of building a skate park from scratch.

> [We] put like two inches of asphalt on there to resurface it. And then we started getting the ramps. They were donated from a skate park in Pleasant Hill, and they were getting rid of them. They said, "You can have them, you just got to come get them," so every day after work me and [a helper] chip away till we get it to the point where they're small enough to fit into a container or into a truck, back and forth so many times.

The City of Oakland provided help in the form of a new fence and pavement.[47] Operating under K-Dub's desire "to give [youth] a home," as he once said, Town Park eventually became a safe, functional skate spot. The various efforts of K-Dub and his "beatnik crew" of local supporters, as he once called them, transformed Town Park from a "no man's land," as he put it, into a professionally designed skate park.[48] Given all of these contributors and the scope of their involvement, it is not surprising that K-Dub once referred to this skate park as "a Do-It-Yourself piece on a public property" during one of our discussions.

K-Dub subsequently moved Tha Hood Games events to Town Park. Tha Hood Games were also linked with the Karl Watson's Skate Day at

Town Park.[49] Tremendous grassroots, communal energy thus pervaded K-Dub's vision of Oakland skateboarding. And with word on the street being complimented by regular promotion on social media, the popularity of Town Park inevitably grew, to the extent that increasing usage required the makeshift wooden ramps and obstacles to be repaired and eventually replaced. K-Dub consequently began to enlist even more support from his various private social and economic networks. He bolstered his social-enterprise coalition in anticipation of Town Park's next phase.

"We Hit It While It's Still Hot": Town Park's Transformation and the Levi's "Mothership"

As the proverb states, necessity is the mother of invention. Town Park needed a makeover in order to achieve K-Dub's dream of creating a sustainable youth skate space. It was at this juncture, in 2014, when K-Dub met with Kent Uyehara. Uyehara is the owner of the iconic For the City (FTC) skateboard shop on Haight Street in San Francisco, featured in chapter 1. Through this meeting, Uyehara connected K-Dub with the skate-philanthropy division at Levi Strauss and Company, commonly known as Levi's. Discussions with Levi's eventually led to the idea of a concrete version of Town Park, requiring two renovation phases, each costing approximately $300,000. K-Dub's suggestion to the city at the time was simple, as he recalled to us: "Just give me this piece of property and let me build a skate park." However, with Town Park residing on city land, this plan remained in the fledgling stage pending formal city approval. Before renovating the skate park, K-Dub was being asked to obtain a temporary permit to dig and build on this site.

K-Dub eventually got his big chance, as he was invited to speak in front of city officials in order to explain why Oakland should accept in-kind services from Levi's to rebuild Town Park. The following extended field note reveals the tense moments as K-Dub and a packed room heard the case being made for a new, concrete skate spot:

> On this weekday afternoon in the late summer, we are at the Lakeside Park Garden Center next to Oakland's Lake Merritt. There are eight panel members present to weigh up the decision regarding whether to grant a temporary building permit to K-Dub on the De Fremery Park location. Roughly thirty people are in attendance, and most are here to testify on the need to build Town Park, including the four authors of this book. A comment comes from a woman who is

signing up for speakers to talk: "Wow, there are a lot of people here to talk about the skate park."

The first speaker talks. He is a business and property owner in Oakland. He says that Town Park is an amazing place, and his son started skating there. Amazing energy, an eclectic group is there, according to him: "Friends and buddies of all types, man this is what Oakland is all about." Then a writer, also a parent, whose son is nine years old, says his kids love it.

Another man, working on behalf of Levi's to push this project through, wants to see K-Dub's dream realized, since what he's done the last six or seven years in this space is already amazing. This will be first skate park that Levi's is building on U.S. soil. He says it is Oakland's turn to get a great skate park. He continues, saying that this will be a large marketing piece, and a big community action project. Levi's will tell K-Dub's story and those of the kids that have grown up in the park. These youth, he adds, look at K-Dub as a mentor. He finishes by stating that everyone will see these promotional materials featuring West Oakland—across the world.

At this point, K-Dub starts talking: He created Town Park because kids asked him. Oakland High School was where it started. The skate park, he says, has already attracted skaters, artist, musicians —it is a destination site. Now, he wants to keep this platform amazing so the kids are proud. San Francisco opened a new park July 1 and half the kids are from Oakland. He wants to bring these kids back to Oakland and have them be proud of this local spot. It would mean so much to the community where local people can come and parents can bring them.

The panel asks if any others want to speak. A guy comes up who is twenty-five and has been skating at Town Park, transitioning out of the military—that process was very hard and the skate park helped him deal with stress and lots of things going on in his head. The skate park keeps him motivated to do the right things. He then says it is great that he can talk with young people at the skate park about how to do a trick on a skateboard. He really appreciated all the work that K-Dub does—says he is starting to get choked up (and he is).

Next, a seven-year-old boy speaks: he likes to be with his friends, it's fun, the ramps are cool, and now it'll be concrete—new and better, he says.

Then, his dad comments, "We've skated all over the U.S. and see how strong the community is here and a lot is due to K-Dub and what he's done there." He comments that if someone is working on a trick, someone else will come over and help, "it's just this mix, this vibe. . . . It's just an amazing place." His son is able to skate all over the world, but his favorite spot is here because of friendships. The dad wants to see these friendships continue through the creation of a concrete skate park.

A young Asian woman steps up to the microphone—she is quite nervous and emotional when she begins to speak. She claims to have known K-Dub since she was in high school. Through tears, she says that he taught her how to skate; took them every Monday to go skate.

K-Dub closes the conversation: "Any question you need, I'm ready, let's do this."

Council Member Peterson: "I move that we approve."

Council Member Flores "seconds" the motion.

A minor use permit is being asked to vote on. It is stated that construction needs to be completed by November 1, 2014. The motion passes unanimously—huge applause erupts in the room. Outside the building, lots of hand-shaking and pats on the back between K-Dub, his supporters, and even us. K-Dub looks exhausted, but relieved.

"We Got Some Jewels Like That": Privatized Social Networks Supporting Town Park

With the necessary permit secured, the California Skateparks design firm, which has constructed over 350 skate parks in ten countries, was commissioned to work with Levi's and a local hardware company, Martinson's. This latter company, as we will see, played a prominent role in the Town Park story. While helping to build Town Park, the owner of this company, Andy, concurrently supported his son, Mark, who skateboarded here regularly. Mark had been skateboarding since he was only two and half years old. He has already won numerous skate competitions and been featured in a skate team video.

K-Dub later quipped in a media interview that locals did not usually purchase Levi's jeans. But a fruitful partnership had been established with this corporation anyway. This link reveals how unique relationships underpinning social-enterprise missions reflect stakeholders who might normally be unconnected. "You can't even buy a pair of Levi's in Oakland, and here they were offering a free skatepark," said K-Dub. "It's good, we hit it while it's still hot. The thing is, you get a mothership of a company like that, and they still want to complete what they started. That shows you that there's heart there, and they can see what this park means to the community."[50] In addition to cultivating corporate involvement, K-Dub was also willing to tap into the resources of parents. He told us, "Parents have always been very supportive. I have parents who come up and give me gift certificates to Home Depot for materials. Parents have different companies. . . . We got some jewels like that."

The fact is that Town Park's second phase required support from local parents to top-up private-sector investment, because the city's parks-and-recreation department played a very limited role in the skate park's development. In fact, Peter Whitley from the Tony Hawk Foundation once stated in the media that, in essence, "what the city is doing by their support is telling skaters they'll take a half-million-dollar donation to the city. Who wouldn't support that?"[51] Thus, reflecting upon his social-enterprise coalition, K-Dub said that he was "trying to build bridges" with the private sector rather than eschewing this type of contribution. "But my whole thing is like, okay, well I could try to fundraise myself, but if a company was to come right with it then let's just get it done and then let's go do some other goodness, you know."

K-Dub even went on to claim that *more* multinational corporations should contribute to Town Park in order to support local youth. Rather than shunning this type of corporate influence, as one might expect in skateboarding, K-Dub actually lamented the general lack of investment made by the major players in Oakland's blossoming corporate scene. In conversation with us he said, "And then Pandora's here, you know, Clorox is here, Waste Management's here, Kaiser is here, you know, they don't do nothing. They don't do anything. . . . You don't see any presence from any of them. I'm not going to even mention the shipping companies. All of them are multi-billion-dollar industries up there. Oakland doesn't get anything from those guys." The idea being expressed here was that neighborhood residents in need were being ignored by those with power and resources. As we showed earlier, this was a long-held perspective that underpinned numerous social activist activities throughout the area's history.

But with Levi's now on board, as well as local, grassroots assistance in place, it was finally time to break ground. Rob "Skate" Ferguson, introduced in chapter 2, often worked closely with K-Dub in Town Park by supporting his community events. Ferguson explained that the first step in the renovation process entailed tearing down Town Park's original structures. Highlighting the unique cultural ethos of this space, he said this process was going to be like "a punk rock scene." "It's going to be a little

The renovation of
Town Park. *Courtesy
of Keith Williams.*

punk show and skating." Blank spaces, he told us, were going to be left for
local artists to repaint. The intention was therefore to maintain "that same
good colorful vibe that we had before," he said, while incorporating "the
grassroots cultural aspect." At one point in the rebuild process, a former
Black Panther Party member delivering concrete deemed the overhaul an
"evolutionary and revolutionary act."[52] In a nod to Oakland's homegrown
sports heroes, paintings of local stars Bill Russell and Frank Robinson
soon adorned the skate-park walls.[53] The ribbon was finally cut by K-Dub
on July 11, 2015, as the skate park was unveiled to a crowd of skateboarders, including a few famous ones, that flooded in to use the ramps and
rails, with an MC cheering them on.[54] *TransWorld SKATEboarding* magazine's coverage suggested that Oakland now, finally had "a fresh, top of
the line cement skatepark."[55]

Town Park as an *Urban Platform for Capital*

In his youth, K-Dub was nomadic. He skateboarded constantly between
spots in South Central Los Angeles and Orange County, as we mentioned
earlier. K-Dub thus seemed acquainted with the fluid nature of this activity; he thus saw those who came to Town Park from elsewhere as enhanc-
ing skate park life, while also contributing to the local community. Thus,
while other tight-knit ethnic urban communities in California facing

gentrification have deliberately tried to keep outsiders away, K-Dub believed differently.[56] He once declared to us "I want the platform and everybody's welcome." As a matter of fact, K-Dub felt that visitors substantially contributed to the skate park and the local community, once claiming, "I have skaters that come all the way from Petaluma [Sonoma County]. I have skaters come from Sacramento, like, once a week [saying], 'Dude, we got to skate this spot.' And it's cool because when they're here then they hit other spots, too. Then they buy something from the store here or something like that, so they're kind of contributing to the city in a way, you know?"

However, insofar as Oakland's gentrification was gaining speed, K-Dub also recognized the need to provide established neighborhood kids with opportunities to benefit. He was cognizant that others from outside Oakland were already capitalizing on their use of the city and Town Park.

> Kids come here from other places just to say they skated in Oakland. They go back to Walnut Creek [wealthy suburb] with some hood cred. 'I skated in West Oakland. Made it out, you know, went to the liquor store, bought a soda,' you know? 'Better than getting jacked,' you know? So how do we capitalize, how do our own youth capitalize on that? You know, just like everybody else is capitalizing on it. That's the bigger political piece.

The quote above reveals how K-Dub wanted the local youth to "capitalize" from using Town Park, too. It would be fair to say that the influx of new capital coursing through Oakland is still not reaching many locals who really need it. As a matter of fact, it has been found that local youth, in particular, still negotiate entrenched poverty, lack of educational and work opportunities, and live in high-stress neighborhoods.[57] And recall how, in this chapter's opening narrative, two local boys could not even afford to pay a five-dollar skate contest entry fee. Given these circumstances, K-Dub wanted to ensure that local youth skateboarders could substantially benefit from using Town Park. He also wanted to enhance the presence of urban-based youth of color in skateboarding culture. "If they can't see themselves in it, then what? Because usually in skateboard culture you don't see yourself in it if you're from around here."

Throughout *Moving Boarders*, we analyze new skate parks and their users, attending to the question "who has the right to exist and benefit in the city?" In this case, making Town Park permanent through concrete served as a metaphor for cementing the place of the local culture in this neighborhood. In one local news story, K-Dub was even quoted as saying "There is a lot of history here, my whole thing is to create a time capsule that will be here for a while."[58] What's more, the Facebook page for Town Park featured declarations such as "It's time we create our own, For Our Own," "For the Town (FTT)," and "Oakland belongs to the kids."[59] K-Dub even once claimed during a media interview that "as much as we built a park, it's about the culture."[60]

In terms of local youth specifically gaining capital, a select group of skateboarders from Town Park, including Terrell "Poohrail" Newell, have already acquired the necessary skills and styles to become sponsored.[61] However, K-Dub's broader agenda is to help local skateboarders enter the creative industries supporting urban and youth skate cultures. In fact, the urban is already considered "an incredibly lucrative economic tool for marketing to broad audiences," according to scholar Sarah Banet-Weiser.[62] An example of this is when skateboarding in urban areas became branded as *skurban* in the mid 2000s, reflecting a mash-up of race and ethnicity, inner-city life, and cool masculinity; this scene, which we revealed in chapter 1, was heavily marketed by corporations such as Nike and Reebok.[63] Regular participants in urban skateboarding, often young males of color, exemplify recent brand-marketing trends. Moreover, these individuals' lifestyles and ways of working are considered valuable within today's global economy.[64]

K-Dub clearly understands the popular urban phenomenon. In fact, he once told us, "the young independent cats are all wearing skateboarding stuff, a lot of them all skate. And it's just really interesting to see it kind of come to the inner-city and have them be hip and be considered cool." Consequently, K-Dub sought to place Oakland's own men of color amidst the lucrative private industries promoting youth and skateboarding life. In the following extended remarks, K-Dub discusses his rationale for using this practice.

> Well, how do they know about getting—they can still be a part in this industry, but how do they know about even getting into those jobs? How do they know what's required? How do they know what's that step you take? What's an intern? So eventually I want to be able to have that because one thing about skateboarding culture and that's a sports culture, videos are still just as important as it was back in the day from like when a new video comes out from a skate team it's still a big thing in the industry. Photography, I mean having it— now you can take your iPhone and make a complete skate video and

upload it in five minutes, you know? So, they have the opportunity now to be more creative than ever. And then there is a website called Malakye.com and it's an action-sports job listing. All the jobs for all the companies, you know, LRG (a clothing company that supports skaters and artists), Oakley, Nike, everything that these kids' brands that we're consumers of, all the brands, it's an actual website that has all those, you know, job listings: line designer, fashion designer, videographer, GoPro, this, this, and that. So, my whole thing is maybe a lot of our kids won't be able to be pro skaters, right? But they still like the industry.

Action-sports culture is now "fueled by a buoyant transnational consumer industry" with participants "being embraced as creative entrepreneurial neoliberal citizens."[65] With this view in mind, K-Dub created Town Park in order to help local youth of color develop their "entrepreneurial labor" so that they could eventually obtain "cool jobs."[66] Scholars in fact suggest that the new creative industries are hallmarked by "the cultural quality of cool, creativity, autonomy"; these are attributes that K-Dub deliberately wanted to instill and promote in his local skaters. In this way, we can see that K-Dub's approach departs from the practice of promoting traditional sports achievement as the only way for city-based youth of color to be successful.[67]

K-Dub's philosophy had already influenced one African American young man we met named Roberto. Out skating one day with his friends, Roberto talked to us and referred to Town Park's corporate sponsorship, as follows. "I feel like that bridge, it's nice to have, that connection with Levi's," he told us. "That's dope that they even reached out to us." When asked about his skateboarding goals, he said that, like "everybody," he wanted to become a professional. But he also had another plan: " [to] keep my life in the skateboarding industry, in the business, just because I love skateboarding so much. . . . There's so much you can branch off from this industry." Roberto said that his dream was to be on a traveling skate team. Another option, he said, was to create his own industry niche: "[I want to] have some grip tape out and maybe skate lessons as well . . . teaching kids, give them a real business card, still keeping it in the skate business as well."

Private-sector mechanisms and connections increased Town Park's overall value and capacity to benefit to the local community. But we also began to wonder if K-Dub would personally benefit from his growing popularity. He had extensive private-industry and community connections from which he could potentially profit. However, K-Dub told us that he did not want to create a marketable brand for himself. He felt that this branding approach would not lead to meaningful and lasting social change, as we can see in the following comments from our interview:

> I told my friends I don't want a skateboard brand. I don't want to create a skateboard company. They're asked to come here and do demos, do events. If I had a brand it'd be all about my brand, you know? I don't have that. I don't need that.
>
> I'm old enough. I've seen how the brands do, and go and come and go, and what are [they] really doing?

K-Dub personally tapped into various private industries surrounding youth and skateboarding. Yet he only used this social-enterprise approach to support his goals of mentoring youth of color and giving them new life opportunities.

According to research, committed and caring mentors like K-Dub play a vital role in promoting youths' psychosocial development.[68] And this type of adult practice is especially crucial within urban parks where older "community heads," like K-Dub, can draw from their own experiences to help youth living in tough circumstances.[69] In this regard, another quote from the skateboarder Roberto revealed the strong impact of K-Dub's mentoring: "[He is] one of the people I look up to, just because of his big heart. He has such a big heart for his community, and he backs what he loves, and that's just the biggest role model, one of the biggest to me."

Local Youth Ownership and Social Awareness

Continuing with this idea that K-Dub was a consistent mentoring presence in the lives of local youth, we now delve into further types of youth practices found within the skate park. We heard on numerous occasions, from K-Dub himself, that his mother, a former social worker with the Los Angeles County Department of Children and Family Services, had strongly influenced his actions. "Mom's going to make sure I show up and anything else that needs to be done," he told us in conversation, before adding "I just 'do,' you know what I mean? There's so many people that just don't do, they talk. . . . I knew I could trust me. I know I'm going to show up." Under this type of commitment, K-Dub wanted to promote what has been described as "a social justice model of youth development."[70] This model purports that youth impacted by racism, poverty, and

Young male skateboarders and mentors congregating around Town Park.
Courtesy of Todd Fuller.

unemployment can "take control" over their surroundings by developing critical consciousness to engage with "the conditions that shape their lives."[71] Reflecting this idea, K-Dub once commented in a documentary video that he wanted local youth to understand their unique stake in the skate park and community.

> In Oakland with how sensitive things are especially now, new people are coming in and nobody is having that conversation with the established community that's been here, so that was one of the first things I did, right? The conversation started like "whoa what are you doing with the skate park?" Like it was theirs all of a sudden. Now

the conversation I am getting is like, "Wow, you did this." I'm like, "No, we all did this."[72]

Town Park youth were thus expected to develop a sense of ownership that could improve life in their skate space, as well as the surrounding community. Activities such as constructing and repairing the skate park became important components within this vision. What's more, by performing these activities, K-Dub believed that youth of color could gain hands-on skills that might lead to work opportunities.

> It's nice because the kids get a chance to help out. I'll have kids, even teenage kids who've never held a drill before. And now they know how to drill and measure and do things, you know, because they took all the shops and things out of the school, so where they going to learn that from? If the parents aren't there teaching them where are they going to learn it from? So there's a whole trade effort in it as well, but there have been people coming through, there have been different folks who skate, but also do construction, you know, do some woodwork.

The Levi's video documentary showcasing the evolution of Town Park indeed features local youth with drills and leather gloves working on the wooden ramps that they skated upon.[73] In conversation, K-Dub further articulated that he wanted to engage youth so that they would become more socially responsible. He contrasted his approach with the tactics of other social protest groups, such as the Occupy movement.

> You know, sometimes to make the most meaningful changes you just need to do. So, I chose—or not try to sound all altruistic or anything, but my whole thing is like I saw a need [in] young people that I was in touch with that said, "Okay, you're an adult. We trust you. Our parents trust you. Let's see what you can do old man." But just, you know, sometimes you just got people, just like the Occupy stuff, people come in and they vandalize and cause all this mayhem, but they don't have any connections to the community. It's easy just to shit on Oakland just because everybody else feels like it's okay if you get away with it.

It becomes increasingly clear that Town Park was set up by K-Dub and his support network to promote youth trust and self-determination. In fact, like Danny Sanchez from SJ 180, K-Dub also allowed youth here to inhabit skate space without making critical judgment on their behavior or being authoritarian. For instance, describing one "punk crew" that

A youth helping to rebuild Town Park. *Courtesy of Keith Williams.*

frequented the skate park in the afternoons, he mentioned "They do their thing. They hang with the little punk foes, they drink a little beer, and my whole thing is 'do your thing.'" Although K-Dub is "not a police officer," as he once reminded us, there were still some basic rules that he used to ensure youths' safety and a welcoming atmosphere. He would remind skaters, "If you see a little kid and their parent, put [beer] away for me and make sure you clean up." K-Dub mentioned that he occasionally checked in on social-media platforms to see what was happening in Town Park. But in general, we observed that he provided quite limited forms of control and intervention when it came to daily proceedings.

We can thus see that Town Park often functioned as a youth-driven scene where local young men of color, in particular, were entrusted to determine codes of behavior and social ethics. Life in Town Park thus came to mirror the belief that youth skateboarders can directly contribute to their communities rather than simply being troublemakers. It has been suggested elsewhere, by scholar Susie Weller, that social capital is created when skateboarders contribute to society by "developing skate parks, revitalizing new spaces to hang out and maintaining old facilities."[74] Certainly, Town Park encouraged local youth to act in similarly civic-minded ways, in order to generate social capital in this skate park and its surrounding neighborhood.

The Interests and Motivations of Skateboarding Parents

Given Town Park's contextualization above, largely through the efforts of its main supporter, K-Dub, it also became incumbent that we understood how families actually envisioned and negotiated this social space. In this regard, parents here provided important windows into the actual operation of this skate park, as with all other skate parks featured in this book. A pattern that we noticed was that parents were not often present during daily skateboarding here. Sometimes we saw them hanging out in Town Park, or they sat in their vehicles outside, watching and waiting. But we saw more parents at programmed events such as fundraisers, the girls' skate sessions, and Rob "Skate" Ferguson's Cali Am Jams. Over time, we were able to recruit and interview some parents. We learned that a few of these parents were steeped in skateboarding culture. But we also registered that most parents here were new to this activity, as we found in Bay City. For example, one mother, Mary, who had a seventh-grade skateboarding son, told us, "I didn't know any skaters [when growing up]. It was very tangential to my experience." Another mother of a young female skateboarder admitted to us, "I don't know too much about skateboarding."

To show how K-Dub's overall vision impacted parents, we now illustrate the variety of interests and motivations that underpinned parental engagements in Town Park. The first idea presented here is that Town Park incorporated historical and communal values, in terms of how people assisted each other when necessary. Subsequently, we will hear parents explain that both local and non-local youth were able to mix and learn from each other. We will then highlight that many parents believed that Town Park enabled youths to develop vital character and life skills.

We then add to this parenting conversation by outlining how a routine female presence in Town Park was often lacking during our first phase of research. However, we later discuss how this space eventually became much more intentional in attracting female skateboarders. Providing evidence from a father-daughter skate day as well as several programmed female events, we speculate how Town Park is becoming more central to local female skaters' experiences of skateboarding.

"I Don't Have an Organization but We Would Still Feed 'Joe-Blow'": A Legacy of Neighborhood Support

Former residents Jimmy Ray and Suzanne, both twenty-eight-year-old Asian Americans, often came to Town Park to support their eleven-year-old daughter Jaxon, who skateboards. They now live in a nearby city after leaving West Oakland. They moved out, like many others in Oakland, because of rental prices that had risen beyond their reach. Still feeling connected to this area, though, Jimmy Ray and Jaxon regularly returned to skate together in Town Park. Jimmy Ray explained during an interview, "Skateboarding is one of the things that is one of our outlets." Jaxon began to skate when she was seven, outside of her uncle's house, while watching her dad ride his board.

Like many other families that we spoke with at Town Park, Jimmy Ray alluded to an integrated, helpful community that was pivotal to his family's participation: "Down here it never mattered about the color of your skin, so we'd always help each other out. . . . If you're low on food and your neighbor had food, they always shared." Jimmy Ray further explained how people here cared for and looked out for each other. He thus wanted his daughter to be exposed to West Oakland's sense of community: "This idea of a community of people coming together and helping you out is a great thing for my daughter to be around. . . . That way she's never, ever judgmental about what somebody has or what they don't have." Jimmy Ray then added, "It's family oriented. . . . They try to help you out. I like going because if I'm skating, I had a couple of occasions where other people would try to teach my daughter how to go down a ramp."

Another set of parents, Samantha and Lamar, corroborated this idea that the neighborhood and skate park were both family-like in nature. We met Samantha, a middle-aged, African American woman working as a retail office manager, when she was outside of Town Park loading her car's trunk with a bag of aluminum cans she had collected. After a brief exchange about life in Town Park, where her thirteen-year-old son Stephen frequently skates, she agreed to meet for an interview one week later. Like Jimmy Ray and Suzanne, Samantha talked earnestly about her roots in the neighborhood, recounting her memories of De Fremery Park when she was young. "I've been to many birthday parties there," she recalled, and further reminisced that she "went to De Fremery Park as a kid." Samantha went on to assert that West Oakland was "like a family community" in which people helped each other even when everyone was struggling.

> Well, I consider the West Oakland community to be like a family community. There's a lot of opportunity here. For those who don't have clothing, who don't have health, who don't have food, there's a lot of organizations and churches that really participate in the community to help the people of the community stay afloat. So, that's appreciated—not just on the receiving end but also on the giving end.

When probed further about what she meant by "the giving end," Samantha noted how oftentimes the people giving were also the ones receiving assistance. This type of reciprocal practice was typified by her comment, "Well, because everyone helps everyone, to me. I don't have an organization or nonprofit organization but we would still feed 'Joe Blow' that sat on the corner having his beer daily."

"It Takes a Tribe to Raise a Child": Diverse Skateboarders Helping Each Other

Along with finding that Town Park was part of a nurturing and accepting community in which residents regularly aided those in need, we also discovered that this skate park was valued by parents because it had an evolving, diverse group of users who would help each other skateboard. This was one outcome from the emerging gentrification trend, as the skate park became more integrated. This recent integration of youth seemed to foster new racial, ethnic, and social-class relationships that resembled findings from sociologist Sherri Grasmuck's study of Philadelphia's neighborhood baseball.[75] Grasmuck recounts, "with gentrification, came new class and racial encounters on the local baseball field," with many of these being beneficial for both parents and their children.[76]

In a similar sense, then, many Oakland parents we met felt that gentrification actually fostered the creation of a supportive, diverse peer culture. One late afternoon we met Trent, an African American factory worker who said he lived down the street from Town Park. He was skateboarding with his son. He came to the skate park after putting in a full day's work; he had greasy fingernails and appeared weary after just finishing his shift. Trent told us that he was once a skateboarder himself.

"Not in a skateboarding 'ring,'" he explained, "but on the street." Trent's observations reflect someone who had experienced difficult times. He spoke about Town Park's new demographics in a positive manner: "That [diversity] part, that's a beautiful part that I like. How all different cultures can be in one area and get along with doing something that they like, without no confusion. No negativity. It could be something, running into somebody or something, but you know you all got to forgive and forget." With a stern look suddenly on his face, he repeated this idea. "You never forget but you can always forgive."

The same day we interviewed Trent, we also met Roberto, the young man who we described earlier in this chapter. Watching him skating with his buddies, we could see that he had significant talent. He skated over and began to corroborate Trent's view that this skate park had diverse constituents. "Different characters have come up here, and the different vibes that are up here. So, it's pretty dope." His multicultural group of friends were perched up on a skate ramp snickering and pointing as we talked in the middle of the skate park. He observed, "Today, just a normal day at Town Park. We've got the homies here, beautiful day, and it's pretty much how it is on the daily here. I love it." Roberto subsequently reminded us that this neighborhood could indeed be a tough one. Then, he expanded on the idea that Town Park brought different people together in a positive manner.

> This neighborhood was really crazy back in the day, but like a whole bunch of places—a lot of places—has its good places and bad places, but this place, I don't really see too many problems around here. Skateboarding often gives you that mutual respect towards people because we're our own little, how do you say it, I don't want to say community again, but we're our own little team, kind of. We kind of feed off of each other's energy. So, that's dope and that applies in the real world, too. . . . I see a lot of cool people at the skate park. It's nicer people at the skate park. I don't know why.

During this same visit, we also met an elderly African American woman named Camille, who had a twenty-six-year-old daughter who skateboarded in Town Park. On this day, however, she was holding the hand of a toddler, R. J., "who lives upstairs" she said. Being a helpful neighbor, Camille said that she regularly took R. J. out to the skate park since he enjoyed playing with a skateboard. When asked about the atmosphere of the skate park, she replied that it was indeed a place where diverse youth gave respect to each other, even to little R. J. "All the kids, at every age.

They respect him at his age. . . . They go around him. You know they go around him sometimes, if they want to slide on here and he's there, they'll ask him to move and he'll say okay, and they do their little jump, and he says, 'good job.' So, it's good for them to have this here. Really good."

On a different visit, we met Matt, another African American adult with roots in the neighborhood. He similarly claimed that Town Park promoted diverse social interaction for youth. Matt sometimes played basketball in De Fremery Park while his twelve-year-old son Nate skateboarded. On this day, he was watching Nate skateboard and informed us that Nate came to the park almost every day after school to skateboard. Matt remarked how skateboarding "kills the stereotype [that] every black kid wants to play basketball." He supported his son's activities at the park and commented on how, compared to the more controlled environment of school, Town Park was a more open learning context that allowed kids to grow at their own speed. Matt encouraged his son to socialize in this diverse environment. A native Oaklander, Matt pointed out that the neighborhood had changed. He commented, "Eight to ten years ago, you wouldn't see white kids here." He also observed that "some kids [white youth] probably live far from here and get dropped off in a minivan, but they bring something with them." His conclusion was that "it's way more powerful for kids to see other kids getting along."

Matt felt that the skate park was comprised of an eclectic mix of youth. Interacting with kids of different backgrounds, he believed, had opened his son up to new activities, including lacrosse. He also said that his son and his son's friends now performed better in school. Their academic success was attributed to the influence of youths from outside of the community. Seeing that there were life options available outside of their local community motivated these youths to work harder, he believed.

Another parent we met was Mary, a forty-two-year-old African American woman whose seventh grader recently picked up skateboarding. Like other parents, she valued the new type of ethnic and racial diversity found in Town Park as it impacted her son's skateboarding. Mary was originally from the East Coast and had recently moved to Oakland with her husband and two kids for her new job. As the new kid in school, her sixth-grader son started hanging around with the eighth graders, watching them do skate tricks. Mary recalled that this was when "he started getting into it." Soon after, he was asking for a skateboard for Christmas. "I got him a piece of crap on Amazon for $30. Now they are actually going to Town Park, so now they all skate as a group of fifteen boys."

Skateboarding with this group, she told us, was beneficial to his "social development," and she also admitted that the diversity within Town Park changed her perception of skateboarders. Her original conception of skateboarders was that they were "burnt out long-haireds." This belief had her thinking, "Oh, he's going to be hanging out in the parking lot smoking dope or something." Mary's perception changed as her son continued to skateboard. Commenting on the crew of close friends that her son Eric skated with, she told us, "I'm learning that it's a larger group of people. It's a very diverse racial group of people. There's everything, I'm just thinking about the group of seven boys where everybody's [race is] accounted for." She concluded that the diverse mix of youths in Town Park fostered positive experiences for her son.

Samantha and Lamar, the African American couple mentioned earlier in this chapter, seemed to offer up a more complicated view of the neighborhood's changing demographics. They were struggling to make ends meet while raising a son involved in many school leadership and sports activities. The following field note, based on an interview with Samantha and Lamar, was made in a run-down Oakland common known as Old Man's Park. This 165-year-old park was named as such because it once held gatherings of men who shared food and companionship during the Depression era.[77] Today, it is enveloped by new, trendy housing developments as well as food and beverage outlets; Old Man's Park definitely crystallizes the pronounced social disparities now apparent in the city. Samantha and Lamar were quite concerned about the gentrification occurring in West Oakland. But they still liked the new, integrated youth interactions taking place in Town Park.

> As we begin to speak while sitting at a table, Samantha gives a quick rundown on the park's name: "They call it the Old Man's Park and they call it the Old Man's Park because there used to be a lot of old men who lived here—slept here and people would feed them and clothe them. The city did clean it up but there's still, you know, people who still call it home."
>
> A black female prostitute is washing her legs in the bathroom sink while another woman peers out from inside. Guys hanging out on the park benches come over and jump into cars that pull up to the front parking lot. "You're fucking lucky I'm still here," says one of them as he jumps into the passenger side of one car.
>
> An elderly African American woman is shuffling around the park, picking up bits of cardboard near her cardboard shelter built around a picnic table. She is wearing a pair of oversized New Balance running

shoes with no laces, sliding and shuffling around, giving wary glances toward the men and women smoking drugs on the benches.

A man is sleeping in his parked car next to the park.

A man and woman are lying down on top of the playground structure writhing and grinding together in broad daylight. This "kiddie play set" was once featured in a 1999 news story describing the park's renovation as a "symbol of hope."[78]

Young, hip couples stroll past the park. They never cross through the park on their way to dinner at a new, trendy eatery just down the street. This hub of six restaurants, housed in the old "Oakland Free Market" from 1890, was recently featured on the Food Network television channel. There is also a bustling craft-beer fest being held at the nearby Marriott Hotel.

Old Man's Park feels far away from the trendy food joints and craft-beer festival. Just as we start talking, a tall, black homeless man wearing a brown, oversized blazer comes over to investigate. He stares at us constantly while mumbling something unintelligible. We seem to be intruding on his turf. He finally shouts a sexual obscenity at us before he crosses the park and hides in a large bush. Samantha and Lamar shrug and we keep talking.

In our interview, Samantha first described positive feelings about her son's skateboarding with a diverse mix of youth. Over the course of the interview, however, Samantha and Lamar strongly critiqued the influence of gentrification on the West Oakland community. Lamar began by stating, "West Oakland itself is starting to diversify." Samantha then offered the stark assessment that her own life situation was not so far from the people we observed in Old Man's Park. In a more critical tone, she added that newcomers "change the level and expectation of that area and it's no longer catered to the people that grew up there. It's now catered to the people who have come in with money. Do you know what I'm saying? So, I think it's good, but I don't think it's good when the city starts to cater the newcomers and forget the people that are there." Lamar chimed in at this point, "Our rent has gone up, too." Samantha continued, "We're renting and we can't find anywhere to rent in West Oakland or Downtown Oakland or actually, Oakland itself. . . . We're being pushed away and that's what you see with this park. . . . Yeah. I'm two hops, a skip and jump from being in this park."

Still, Samantha and Lamar went on to articulate how much their son enjoyed Town Park. They extolled the virtues of skateboarding and, referring to their son, Stephen, said it was "heaven to him." Samantha then talked at length about how skateboarding exposed him to new people and experiences. Her belief was that the diversity embedded within Town Park could really help Stephen's growth. Although she had concerns about gentrification, as noted above, Samantha still felt that nonlocal skateboarders could benefit Town Park and the established community. This belief was expressed in her next statements:

> What I was saying is that I think it's two different sides of the body. One side is how out-of-towners coming to the city, how that's affecting the city, and the people of the city, but at the same time, different groups and nationalities coming to the park, promoting the park, that is good for the community. So, I can't bunch the two different feelings, the pros and the cons of that together because they're definitely different. I think it's a positive thing. Interacting with different nationalities, [it] is always comforting to hear different experiences. I think it takes a tribe to raise a child. That means that people of all their experiences . . . so, it's a plus, plus for me.

Despite existing on the brink of homelessness due to Oakland's recent gentrification, Samantha and Lamar were still quite positive about their son's diverse skateboarding interactions. Ironically, these diverse skateboarding experiences were directly shaped by the process of gentrification that brought transplants and outsiders into the neighborhood.

Taken together, the views of parents here indicate that Town Park was a space where diverse youth, from both local and nonlocal backgrounds, could integrate and learn from one another. Next, we will see that parents also felt that their children could develop job and life skills here, much as K-Dub had intended when constructing this *Urban Platform for Capital*.

Parental Investments in Youths' Skill and Character Development

Matt is a good example of how Town Park parents conceptualized skateboarding as teaching vital life lessons to their children. This father told us that he wanted his son Nate to learn how to "do his own thing." When asked about the potential risks of skateboarding, Matt said that it was a concern for him, yet there were risks that came with being a boy. We heard that Nate's mother did not like the risk-taking aspect of skateboarding. But Matt felt that taking risks was an essential part of life. He also discussed the unique social atmosphere at this park, like the other parents did. He told us there were people of different ages, genders, races as well

Young skater being congratulated by diverse skate peers. *Courtesy of Todd Fuller.*

as the presence of marijuana and alcohol. And even though he wasn't thrilled about the prevalence of substance use, Matt said that he understood that the skate park was "a real environment" and that as parents "[You] can't lie to these kids because they know. I just let [my son] choose his path. I believe in exposing him to things—appropriate age-wise of course; [it is] like a little social testing ground." He pointed out that sometimes there were conflicts in the park, but he said these incidents did not bother him. He said that his son sometimes "gets into shoving matches [with other kids], but I don't get involved. You have to let them solve their problems." Ultimately, Matt said, "I try to plant the seeds for responsibility and accountability."

Let's return to Trent, the factory worker who used to skateboard, in order to further see how skateboarding was linked with life skills and character development. Trent said that his son had potential to become sponsored as a skateboarder. But at the same time, he thought that his son could learn certain life skills and values that would help him. "Even if you're not good at it, at least try. You know what I'm saying? Because you might find something that you have never done before, and find your—how would you say? Your peak? This is like a sport." Trent continued by making the claim that skateboarding would improve his son's "willpower" and make his "mind stronger," which would enable him to survive the hard "struggle" of life. In conversation, Trent said, "I enjoy it—it's a thrill just seeing him interact with other people, doing an individual thing, and actually like doing something he ain't never try. His willpower gets stronger as he gets older in life, because it's a struggle out there." In a more serious tone, Trent then remarked, "Economically, [Oakland] looks good on the outside, but it's hard, because so much money has got to go into living, eating."

As the interview progressed, Trent continued to speak about the intensity of life in this city. He explained that Town Park played a key role in teaching his son valuable life lessons while keeping him out of harm's way:

> The time you're in here is a time you're not out in the streets or hooking up with the wrong people. They may not be wrong, but they may not have been taught it's wrong. So, they'll be doing stuff they shouldn't be doing, and he'd follow the wrong crowd. It shortens life by all kinds of ways. Death. Incarceration. You know, if he was to be hurt from skateboarding, then you wouldn't feel so bad. But if he was to get hurt just walking down the street, minding [his] own business, then you'll feel bad.

Camille, who had brought the toddler R. J. to the skate park, further spoke about hardship and hope in the context of Oakland skateboarding. As we talked, police vehicles were constantly cruising the park area. Glancing over her shoulder, Camille remarked, "Oh they're in this community today, they're riding around." Remaining unfazed, she said that Town Park was necessary to keep youth off of the streets and out of trouble. "[It] gives them something to do other than to just go sit or stand on the street corner and do drugs, sell drugs."

Continuing on, Camille said, "[The police] are looking for someone. But this is a place that keeps [youth] off the street. It keeps them off the street, and they can come here early in the morning, afternoon, late at night. Not only are they free to do their jumps as they please, they don't have to pay to get in here." She then followed up by stressing that "this is a low-income community, even though it's starting to be gentrified." Camille then explained that this was still a poor neighborhood where opportunities for youth were restricted. She therefore appreciated that this skate park was free. In this context, youth could "practice their own jumps, their own tricks and things like that. They're free to do whatever on these things and try different things." Echoing Trent's earlier comments about resilience, Camille then commented that "sometimes they fall but they get back up and they try it again."

Regarding the idea that skateboarding could provide youths with life skills and character development, Jimmy Ray once claimed that his daughter Jaxon was becoming resilient, or "persistent," as he phrased it.

> She just keeps trying, though. I love to see it. She's persistent. It's nice to see, no matter how many times she falls or how much it hurts. At one point, she busted her knee coming down the ramp. I don't know if she leaned back or if she didn't lean forward enough, but she fell and she busted her knee. It was bleeding and she got up, she dusted it off and she went right back down that ramp. It was nice to see. That persistence is golden to look at and to know that that's instilled in your daughter.

Jimmy Ray then added that a related facet of skateboarding was learning patience, since "you're going to fall the first five hundred times before you get anything right. Nothing is always right the first time." Suzanne, Jaxon's mother, subsequently added that patience was an important attribute for a young person.

> I think she'll learn that it does take time and patience. That's something that she can learn in everyday life as well. If she's not able to go up a ramp and then do a little standstill or something and then come back down, she's always just kind of wobbly or something like that. She'll have to learn the patience to be like, "Okay, I can do this. I just have to keep trying and trying and trying until I get it right." You learn something from everything that you try to do as well. . . . I think she'll learn a lot from it.

Suzanne then continued by saying how Jaxon was learning to overcome her fears. She spoke at great length about the positive mindset that her daughter could obtain from skateboarding, by using this activity to "sail through" life and remain at "ease" rather than being stressed out. At the same time, Suzanne felt that her daughter could gain greater self-belief.

Right now, she's applying herself to it. She was really nervous about coming here at first. She was like, "Mom, I'm kind of scared," because it's not something that she's done in the open with other people. To be with her dad, I know she feels comfortable having her dad here because she's excited. At first, she's kind of shy and quiet and then to apply herself and be like, "Okay. Yes, I can do this."

Like most of the parents we spoke with, Lamar also suggested that skateboarding was good for his son in terms of learning to be resilient. In Lamar's commentary, we can once again see the metaphor of learning how to fall, "get back up," and "keep going"; these ideas framed much of our discussion with Lamar regarding the value of skateboarding.

I told him we all go through it. Boys go through it. You fall. You get back up. You're going to have a couple dings there—here. Dings here, you know? That's your battle wounds. Your battle marks. They're going to heal and you're going to get up and you keep on moving. It is what it is and he learned once you fall you get back up. We didn't have helmets and all that stuff when we grew up. You fall, you keep going.

These parents whose lives had been significantly touched by poverty and social inequalities nevertheless felt that Oakland skateboarding brought something valuable to their children. Essentially, they believed that Town Park provided their children with opportunities to learn new life skills and develop character attributes that would help them navigate everyday obstacles and hardships. But as our observations and interviews continued, it seemed to us that young men predominantly skated in Town Park and were seen to benefit from this participation. We thus wondered, how did female skaters experience life in Town Park? Were these women and girls included and considered legitimate participants? And could they likewise benefit?

The Place of Female Skaters in Town Park

We have argued that, for Town Park's parents, skateboarding was about children obtaining a range of life skills and character attributes, including self-mastery, resiliency, patience, social awareness, and tolerance. Parents also appreciated that children here could learn how to skate in the presence of racially and ethnically diverse others. As these sentiments were being expressed by the parents, we began to understand that the presence of girls and women was usually limited. In fact, Mary, who we discussed earlier in the chapter, once noted this about female skaters: "I never, ever see them [at Town Park]. Never. It would be nice to see change." The following commentary from Jimmy Ray, who skated with his daughter, Jaxon, further highlights the paucity of female youth in Town Park. He said, "Everybody looks at us." Then he added, "It's rarely any other kids, it's always teenagers and grown men. Rarely any girls also."

Our own initial observations corroborated the views of Mary and Jimmy Ray: Town Park skateboarders were mostly young men. We thus wondered how females could participate and develop capital in Town Park. During our first interview, we directly asked K-Dub, "How do you see girls in the skating scene?" He offered the following ideas:

> You know, I've had girls come through, I've had girls come through for a minute and then, you know, they don't stay with it as long. Lately we're getting a lot of older girls, like ladies who are twenty-three to twenty-seven coming out. But girls, overall industry-wise it's just a market that's tough. I think there are brands who kind of cater to young women, but it's still really kind of a surf culture. Brazil: the women skateboarders in Brazil are no joke. I mean, they're winning everything around the world and they're just, you know, they're amazing. When you go to X Games, some of the bigger events, they seem to be pretty well represented around the world. Here, I think our core sports is soccer. Soccer just kills everything. [Girls] just dominate.

During our earlier visits to Town Park, in 2014, we did not see any deliberate spatial techniques being employed to directly include women and girls. It just seemed that K-Dub would try to help *all* "shorties," as he called kids, if and when he saw them at the skate park. Yet, this broadly inclusive approach often meant that female skaters were not present or fully participating during our initial visits. For example, during the skate contest described at the beginning of this chapter, we noticed plenty of young men skateboarding with the support of event organizers, local businesspeople, and parents. Meanwhile, at this same event, we observed a lone African American girl who seemed quite hesitant to remain in the skate park. This was captured in one of our field notes.

> No girls except one African American young woman are here. She sat by the fence and watched, did a few ollies on her board. She had her bike against the fence, very much peripheral and watching. She had gone in to the park to skate earlier, but then withdrew and watched from the corner by the fence as the boys skated in the

contest and in the other sections of park, waiting for their turn. She seemed quite shy and hesitant when we tried to say hello and bring her into the skate park with us. She eventually left the premises.

However, over time, we came to see that some females were committed to skateboarding in Town Park. The skate park was gradually becoming a more common place for girls like Jaxon to skateboard. Eleven-year-old Jaxon told us that skateboarding here provided a way to challenge the perception that females could not skateboard. As her dad skated nearby, she explained to us that her skateboarding "could prove every person wrong that girls can't skateboard." She continued with this train of thought.

> Mostly, the boys in my school, they say, "Oh, you skateboard? I bet that you can't. All you can do is stand on it and keep pushing." But, I want to prove them wrong because when I skateboard, I know that I like to think when I skateboard. I like to think that, "Ha, I proved you wrong." Yeah, I just want to make a difference when I skateboard because, mostly, people think that girls can't skateboard. They just think that they like to ride bikes and stuff, but that's not true. Girls can skateboard when they want to skateboard.

Earlier in the day, we had seen Jaxon teaching some skate moves to another girl. When we were able to speak with Jaxon about this, she reflected on that moment as follows:

> [The other girl] didn't learn yet what I have learned. I just wanted to make sure that if she really likes skateboarding, she could face her fears. She didn't know what to do. She didn't have a friend to help her so I just went and asked her, "Hey, do you want to skateboard with us?" And she said, "Yeah." I was scared that she would say no because this has happened before, but I was so happy when she said yes. It was really fun to teach somebody.

As the interview progressed, Jaxon continued to articulate the importance of girls skateboarding with each other in Town Park. She echoed some of the ideas we had heard from the female skate activists: that girls were usually inexperienced in the skate park and that it was important to help them learn. "I like to skateboard with girls because it feels nice to be with people who actually don't really skateboard that often. Sometimes when girls start out, they don't know how to do it."

Later the same day, we talked with Jaxon's dad and asked him to comment on how his daughter helped another girl. Jimmy Ray told us,

"She's now a part of the community because she's teaching somebody that she doesn't know." Once again, Jimmy Ray's remark reflects the idea that Town Park existed as a communal environment. Jaxon's helpful interactions with another girl seemed to reflect the supportive ethos that was essential to neighborhood life.

As we continued to research Town Park, we could see that K-Dub was becoming more intentional about catering to women and girls through his programming. For instance, during the previously described Oakland Skatepark Summit, hosted with the Tony Hawk Foundation and MAHFIA.TV, K-Dub was asked about his plans for the future. We heard at this event that Town Park had recently partnered with SLAG and MAHFIA.TV to host regular female skate events during the year. Indeed, several of these events were promoted on social media and did take place afterwards. K-Dub also said that he was working with these groups in other Oakland skate sites, including the Montclair Mini Ramp and an indoor space in East Oakland that was being developed.

As was the case in Bay City, consistent, programmed events provided many female skaters with the means to enter Town Park. Below, we present a field-note excerpt describing a recent SLAG session held in Town Park, which reiterates the potential of these events to support young female skaters:

> There are seven female participants present: two are mothers of young girls at the park, two are women skateboarders (one from SLAG, the other independent), and three are young girls skateboarding. We were approached by Jenna, who has been skateboarding for two weeks. This was her first time at Town Park. She got into skateboarding through snowboarding, because the two activities are similar. Jenna said that she enjoys both sports for the freedom that they allow her due to fewer constraints than most other traditional sports. She mentioned that skateboarding is more about self-discovery through interacting with your environment and exploring all of the different things you can do. She was wearing knee pads, wrist guards, and a helmet: "Yeah, it makes me feel like a total noob but safety is important to me!"
>
> The female skateboarders had congregated in the far back area of the park and were, for the most part, training by themselves. They were on their own, practicing tricks.
>
> After observing the male skateboarders in the entrance section of the park, we made our way to the far side of Town Park where the female skateboarders had congregated. One leader from SLAG,

Katrina, was talking to and working with female skateboarders. Not long after arriving, she and Jenna struck up a conversation about what led them to skateboarding. They shared their experiences as described below.

Karina: I skated on and off as a kid and got back into it when I was about twenty-six.

Jenna: I just started skateboarding two weeks ago and I actually live in [San Francisco] but it's so gnarly out there. . . . There are so many really good people at the parks there. It's intimidating.

Karina: Yeah, it's a little more laid back out here.

Jenna: When I was young, my friends started boarding but they were mostly dudes. I told my mom that I wanted to start skateboarding but she told me to just do "girl" things.

Karina: Yeah, that's kind of how I got out of it for a while.

Jenna: Is it like riding a bike where when you get back on your body remembers how to do it?

Karina: Yeah! If I hadn't done this when I was a kid, I probably wouldn't be doing it now. When you're a kid you have more time to do stuff and waste time—that's what you're supposed to do as a kid. It's the only time in your life when it's ok to waste time. But as an adult you worry about so many more things like can I do my job with a broken arm?

Jenna: Yeah! Kids have more time and no fear about doing stuff. Hey—can I ask you a question?

Karina: Sure!

Jenna: I can't seem to get my shove-its [a trick where the board rotates 180 degrees without landing]. Could you show me?

Karina: Yeah, here's how you do it [demonstrates move]. I ride goofy [left foot forward] so it's a little different than if you ride regular. [Jenna attempts to replicate the skill.] You've got it! You just have to trust your instincts. Like, I do kick flips and you just have to trust that your board will be right below you.

Around 11:30 a.m., we noticed that the young girls had started riding together and helping each other out with different skills and moves. Overall, as more guys came into the park, the girls migrated toward the back corner. We noticed one mother was yelling at her daughter, "Go off the court! Get out of the way."

We can thus see how Town Park now offers females more consistent opportunities to skateboard with each other, compared to its nascent days. New opportunities for female mentoring and peer learning appear to be on the horizon as K-Dub's social-enterprise network expands to include female skate groups. And yet, if we consider the field note above, we can also see that the female skaters' experiences in Town Park became more problematic as the day progressed. In essence, the skate park shifted back to its original masculinist tendencies when the female skate event wound down. This shift reminds us that female skateboarders are not a major presence here every day. As such, gender inclusion still warrants further contemplation and intervention by adults like K-Dub and members of his social-enterprise network.

Conclusion

Over the course of our research, we saw Town Park evolve into a vibrant, popular social network that now teems with youth activity. We originally saw Town Park when it was a makeshift, wooden skate park made of donated parts housed on a vacant lot. Very quickly, through enhanced social-enterprise practice, this site evolved into a permanent, cutting-edge skate park. In its current form, Town Park evokes Oakland street life, which gives it trendy status in the highly lucrative youth skate market. Town Park has also become valued by both local and outsider skateboarders. This skate spot is one of the San Francisco Bay Area's most known skate parks thanks to the For the Town (FTT) social-media platform, as well as word on the street. Town Park also features in the Levi's global marketing campaign. As it continues to gain cultural kudos, Town Park is increasingly able to offer local youth new benefits and life opportunities.

The history, culture, and politics of De Fremery Park and its adjoining West Oakland neighborhood structure life in Town Park. The local community prioritizes trust, support, and respect among residents, and it also has a strong sense of self-determination and political activism. As gentrification gains speed, K-Dub reproduces this set of communal beliefs and attributes within Town Park, in order to sustain local youth and their neighborhood. In turn, parents' stories indicated that they saw urban skateboarding in both political and youth-development terms. Many local parents saw Town Park as a community or family-like space. They felt that it supported diverse, meaningful social interactions and peer learning practices. However, we moderated this positive outlook by indicating that female skaters initially seemed less present here. However, more recent mechanisms and events have changed our thinking. Lately, women and girls have been regularly invited to skateboard here, leading to increased instances of peer learning and friendship building occurring amongst them. It remains to be seen whether sponsored special events will translate into full, everyday female participation, as we discuss later in the book.

Looking ahead to chapter 5, the last of our case-study chapters, we will interrogate the belief systems and social techniques operating within two of San Jose's new skate parks. The next chapter's story reveals how skate life in these two skate parks was determined by government oversight and nearby Silicon Valley wealth; we demonstrate how sophisticated community redevelopment agendas strongly shaped skate life in San Jose.

FIVE

"There's No End to the Pop-Ups, the Towers, the High-Rises, the Mid-Rises, the Samsungs and the Oracles"

Skateboarding in San Jose, "The Capital of Silicon Valley"

"The City of San Jose is no stranger to the action sports scene," declared one recent news report.[1] San Jose does in fact work hard to maintain its action-sports credentials, to the extent that its Parks, Recreation and Neighborhood Services Department (PRNS) has hired a full-time employee called the Action Sports Specialist.[2] This person is expected "to put events together, activities, lessons," one city employee told us, while also obtaining sponsorships from private companies.

The presence of a full-time city employee whose sole focus is to promote, program, and fund activities like skateboarding indicates how much San Jose wants to cultivate its action-sports reputation. The city has established five smaller neighborhood skate parks as well as the massive Lake Cunningham Regional Skate Park. This latter skate park is considered to be the largest in California and, with an adjacent multi-million-dollar bike track, constitutes the city's newly branded Action Sports Park.[3]

This chapter's story thus represents how a city government has deliberately created several skate parks under its specific public-health and social-intervention goals. Given this significant investment, San Jose exists as an outlier to the overwhelming trend of government's withdrawal from youth sports, which we addressed through the concept of neoliberalism in the beginning of this book. The San Jose city government actually devised a comprehensive plan for each of its skate parks; this top-down approach largely determined how these skate parks were built and utilized. This chapter complicates this view, arguing that the city's development of skate parks also involved strategically leveraging connections with private industries in order to help promote and operate these skate spots. As such, we will see that the public-private practices of social enterprise were very much at work here, too, albeit in a different form from the other *Moving Boarders* skate parks.

Skate parks, we have argued, function according to the sociocultural, economic, and political conditions surrounding them. Here, the public-private arrangements driving San Jose's skate parks relied heavily upon the city's close proximity to the enormous wealth of Silicon Valley's technology sector. San Jose's newspaper, the *Mercury News,* recently quoted one business leader as saying, "The Silicon Valley economy is sizzling like nowhere else in the country. Its cloud, mobile devices, apps, software, social media, Internet—those are the leaders of this boom."[4] Indeed, the city of San Jose officially brands itself as "The Capital of Silicon Valley" and "#1 in Technology Expertise." This promotional tactic was obvious during one of our research visits to a local government office where, while waiting for an interview with a prominent official, we were greeted by an oversized coffee table book entitled *Silicon Valley: Inventing the Future.* The San Jose area is indeed home to the largest concentration of new technology expertise in the world, with more than 6,600 technology companies employing over 254,000 people. Cisco, PayPal, IBM, Adobe, and eBay all make the top ten list of the city's leading employers.[5]

At the same time, San Jose has a multicultural demographic that undoubtedly influences how skate parks are designed and employed. In fact, San Jose has the honor of being the most diverse city when ranked among the 100 largest metropolitan areas in the United States. Statistics clearly back up this distinction. According to *Forbes Magazine,* for instance, "San Jose is 35% White (the largest group), 31% Asian, 28% Hispanic, 3% two-or-more races, and 2% Black. In no other metro does the largest group have a share smaller than 35%."[6] In San Jose, 57 percent of residents speak another language besides English in the home; in 49 percent of those households, this other language is either Asian/Pacific Islander or Spanish. Nearly 40 percent of residents were born in other countries, with Asians and Latin Americans comprising 92 percent of this total.[7]

As well as having significant populations of immigrants and people of color, economic diversity also defines contemporary life in San Jose. The latest data indicates that information-sector employees in this area make an average of over $266,000 annually, bolstering claims that the local region has the highest median household income in the nation.[8] However, just as we saw in Oakland, many locals are being left behind economically and socially as the technology sector explodes. This fact has been deemed "an alarming situation" by one local researcher, Tracey Grose.[9] "The problem is a good share of the gains in the economy . . . aren't going to the lower half or the middle-class in income distribution," suggested Jim Diffley, another researcher who helped to prepare a study for the United States Conference of Mayors.[10]

In this chapter, we will see that this particular set of sociocultural and economic circumstances sharply implicates how skate parks were being conceptualized and managed by the city government. The city's PRNS constructed a master plan for their six skate parks that influenced how youth and parents in the city engaged with them on a daily basis. We will explain how San Jose used a two-pronged strategy to support residents' action-sports participation. In one way, it tried to use skateboarding to revive seemingly neglected urban areas with a high percentage of people of color. In these areas, where five neighborhood skate parks are based, we can see that San Jose's PRNS department attempted to transform local conditions and provide youth here with a "healthy outlet" through extensive skate-park development.[11] This practice was supplemented by a non-profit group, SJ 180, that was called upon to reinforce the city's specific goals for these areas. Specifically, the mechanism of *place-making* became central to the city's work in lower-income racial and ethnic communities. Research in the recreation and leisure field suggests that this practice of place-making reflects a unique way of designing and managing public space: "The focus of place-making is on creating spaces that promote livability, health, and well-being. Developing place is about fostering social and cultural meanings and emotional attachments to a setting."[12] We consequently illustrate life in one neighborhood skate park, Roosevelt, to demonstrate how the city of San Jose attempted to install a new set of social relations, experiences, and civic identities within this community.

Concurrent with its development of five neighborhood skate parks such as Roosevelt, the city's PRNS also constructed the Lake Cunningham Regional Skate Park facility. We soon learned that this latter skate park was unequivocally treated as an action-sports-industry trendsetter. The Lake Cunningham Regional Skate Park has in fact been touted as a global tourist destination, and even hosts a World Cup Skateboarding event. We subsequently demonstrate how California's largest skate park clearly factors into the practices of a city based next to *the* global hub of technological innovation, Silicon Valley. We will explain that cities such as San Jose are considered to be key sites within global financial networks, leading to their enactment of neoliberal policies that emphasize control over urban space.[13] Moreover, urban studies scholar David Madden argues that this approach signifies "the pacified city's receptiveness to local and global capital," meanwhile helping it to "capitalize on various sectors of the tourism industry."[14] Taking up this idea, our contention is that Lake Cunningham Regional Skate Park clearly factored into San Jose's desire to be known as a receptive focal point in the global economy.

This chapter consequently reveals how San Jose utilized dual missions in order to serve the city's skateboarding needs. This city, we argue, endeavored to promote itself in terms of its social responsiveness and capacity to reinvigorate certain local neighborhoods; yet it simultaneously showcased its economic and innovation capacities in order to create a major action-sports destination. To begin our analysis, we briefly outline the city's main goals that ultimately determined how these urban skate parks were collectively resourced and programmed. This also means exploring what types of strategies and techniques underpinned each spatial project, as we did with the other three skate parks in this book.[15]

We interviewed city officials that ranged from those in the higher echelons of government to those working at the ground level. We will hear from Steve Hammack (the former deputy director of the PRNS), Cindy Chavez (now county supervisor and a former city council member), and Paul Murphy (former aid to Cindy Chavez with the county, also a former member of a skate-park supporter group). Conversations with these government officials revealed that they conceptualized skateboarding as directly contributing to youths' development. This discussion thus returns us to the idea that skate parks, operating as *Urban Platforms for Capital*, provide youths with specific participation benefits.

Adding further layers to this discussion, we describe the viewpoints of social activists, parents, and children responding to the city's rationales and methods of programming. Like others featured in *Moving Boarders*, these individuals held certain beliefs and motivations that influenced how they valued and invested in urban skate parks. The stories in this chapter, derived largely from interviews and observations, once again demonstrate how youths and adults envision the usage and benefits of skateboarding. To contextualize these analytical ideas, we must first understand how skate parks became so important to San Jose's governing strategy. We now turn to describe the most recent wave of skate-park construction in San Jose.

"Alex Was Our Entry Point": How San Jose's Skate Park Legacy Became Reinvigorated by the City Government

Chapter 1 briefly mentioned that San Jose has a historical reputation when it comes to urban skateboarding. Here we provide more context in order to set up the spatial politics and practices underlying the current skate scene. San Jose's skate-friendly landscape was originally facilitated by massive amounts of poured concrete that appeared during the post-World War II era, as the city's aggressive growth policies during this time took effect. By the 1970s, when the city's population actually overtook Oakland's, the area became rife with youth-driven, DIY skate spots housed in buildings, under freeways, and inside warehouses.[16]

Moreover, in addition to these DIY street-skating haunts, San Jose has had some renowned skate-park predecessors. This includes spots such as Winchester Skate Park in the late 1970s, where young boys in this "cement heaven" could snake the pink Keyhole, a ten-foot vertical drop; then in the next decade, there was the horseshoe-shaped Raging Waters Boomer Ramp.[17] These were definitely "epic" times, of "just hanging out in San Jose," as skate legend Christian Hosoi later reminisced.[18] But these halcyon days of San Jose's skateboarding scene eventually came to an end because of liability issues. Winchester alone had 200 skate injuries in its first year of operation, and skate parks then began the curious practice of enrolling participants in the Boy Scouts to obtain affordable insurance coverage.[19] The end of this skate era was summed up by one fifty-three-year-old father we interviewed, who once told us, "Actually, a lot of skate parks were being built around that time [late 1970s], but after a few years they all, all the skate parks were torn down. I think due to insurance concerns. Yeah, they just basically all went away."

Skate parks in San Jose have made a huge comeback. Since the turn of the twenty-first century, several new skate parks have been funded and constructed by the city, albeit for much more specific political purposes, as we have already intimated in this chapter's opening statements. Below, we provide the backstory of how city officials first became interested in skate-park building. This story revolves around how a male teenager, someone who did not even skateboard, lobbied the city to construct safe places for his friends to skateboard.

The title of Bryce Courtenay's famous novel *The Power of One* refers to the capacity of a young individual to spark immense social change.[20]

Cindy Chavez, now County Supervisor and a former city council member, recalled certain events during her interview that directly speak to the moral of Courtenay's book. From her county office, she told us how one young man—a "theater" person, not a skateboarder—jumpstarted the city's trend of building skate parks.

Not many people know this story. So, in about, maybe 2000, 2001, and I actually can't remember the exact year, and I should; I was at a city council meeting, and at the city council, I don't know how they do it now, but what we used to do was, people could come, you'd have an agenda, and it's hours and hours long, but people could come at the beginning or the end of a meeting and they'd get two minutes to talk about any subject they wanted, whether it was on the agenda or not. This kid came forward, his name was Alex. I think he was maybe a sophomore or a junior in high school, and he came and spent two minutes talking about the importance of having places for people to skate. I was really moved by him.

So, I got off the dais and went out the back door, and I stopped Alex. . . . I went out and I said, "Hey. I just want to say how impressed I was with what you said." My first question was, how long have you been skateboarding? He says, "Oh, I don't. It's that my friends don't have any safe place to do it, and I don't think that's okay." So, I was really struck. Here's this kid who comes to talk on behalf of his friends to tell the city they should do something for something that he does not do. I just thought it was such a grown-up act that maybe that should be met with a grown-up response. It made me start to look at it, because I represented the downtown.

So, I represent all the nice hotels, all the buildings here, and that was a problem. Kids were skating, or not just kids—of all ages, were using the sidewalks and the stairwells and the rails. It makes sense that—I started to look at it a whole different way. I started to look around, and that really is kind of the revealing thing about social justice is when, all of a sudden, your eyes are open and you see something that looked like something else before and now it looks like an opportunity; now it looks like a way to really help young people be physical, have fun, get to know other people. It just changed the way I thought about it. So, after that, I decided that we were going to pursue skate parks, and that's how it started. Alex. Adorable . . . here's the other thing. He was into theater arts, so this wasn't even close to his—it wasn't like he had done it.

It was really Alex. He saw a need. He spoke up for other kids.

What person wouldn't respond to a kid speaking up for other kids? It still makes me emotional.

We can thus see how one teenager was the impetus to resurrect the city's defunct skate-park scene. This local momentum coincided with the trend of skate-park construction that was already occurring nationally. Recalling this national trend, the former deputy director of PRNS, Steve Hammack, once told us that "it doesn't matter if you're a city of 10,000 people, you were going to have a skate park. Pretty much that's been built. I don't care where, everybody's got one!" Given this convergence of local events that dovetailed with a national parks-and-recreation trend, the city soon embarked on its systematic strategy to construct skate parks, as we discuss below. In fact, Paul Murphy, county employee, told us that, at the time, the city developed a master plan which "committed the city of San Jose to building multiple skate parks" and also allowed the city to get more funding from the state of California.

Like the other *Moving Boarders* skate parks, San Jose's new skate parks were not just meant to be safe and legal spots where youth could skate. The city and its PRNS division wanted these skate parks to develop youth in quite specific ways and also revitalize certain neighborhoods. Ultimately, it seemed that skate parks were intended to help promote the city's unique vision and status.

Resources and Programming for San Jose's Skate Parks

San Jose operates a very extensive, ambitious, and well-funded PRNS department. Recently, the city has intentionally incorporated skateboarding into its public service to local people and neighborhoods. In the quote below, Steve Hammack explained to us that San Jose has one of the largest park systems in the United States, with over 200 parks in the city's vicinity. These parks range from "farm parks to golf courses to a zoo to an amusement park" and of course also include several skate parks, which are considered important to the city's operations. Hammack commented, "There's a whole series of things that we do and provide to the community, but skate parks are interesting and skateboarding is an interesting concept."

The PRNS's commitment to the skateboarding "concept" is supported by a significant stream of public funding, the source of which is further explained by Hammack below:

We also have a very nice park trust fund which is monies derived from capital projects and development projects. We have the ability and the state law helps us derive park fees for renovation and development of new parks. And, of course, look at San Jose. There's no end to the pop-ups, the towers, the high-rises, the mid-rises, the Samsungs and the Oracles. It goes on and on. We're able to take $3 million and build a bike park. Yes, so that's a nice benefit to have.

The PRNS utilized over $67 million in operating funds in 2015–2016 alone, which was augmented by $174.6 million spent in capital improvement money.[21] Yet, despite this department's healthy funding, one recent PRNS annual report still highlights the use of a cost-recovery approach for recreational services and facilities as well as the establishment of a financially sustainable approach to delivering services.[22] Thus, while the PRNS has an enviable amount of public funding in relation to other local cities, we can see that there is clear impetus for this department to work closely with the private sector to finance key operations. Private-industry connections are in fact extensively drawn upon to drive the city's skate-park improvements and services. Steve Hammack next describes the value of partnering with the private sector in order to support the city's skate-park mission.

We're in the Silicon Valley, there's a lot of great value and all of the partners you can build here. You just have to ask and most of the time people love to come forward because, not only is it good for their brand, but most of the time it's good for the youth, the kids. And that's who they want to be centered around helping in that way. I don't think enough parks-and-recreation departments actually do that kind of thing.

We eventually learned that the city solicited private funds from local businesses, hospitals, and even soft-drink corporations to support its skate parks. These privately sourced funds were used to enhance other income streams, such as skate park entrance fees, and came under the cost-recovery and cost-neutral models employed by the city.[23]

The city also looked to the private sector in terms of how it created and then branded its action-sports facilities. Private-industry mechanisms were greatly admired by city staff and were actually incorporated into the city's skate-park model. This was meant to integrate private-industry best practices, according to Hammack.

Well, we know these things really from the customer. The private industry, the private world is usually way ahead of it before we are.

Usually governments are way in the rear on just about everything. For the most part, the private industry has been doing it long before you. Don't they have the Specialized road bikes or Santa Cruz bikes or Santa Cruz skateboards? They have groups of people that sit in an office thinking about what the next trend is going to be. So, I try to keep myself tied in closely with those people so I know what's going on.

As part of its services to the entire community, San Jose has also embarked upon several ambitious programs aimed at improving the lives of youths of color and their families based in underserved and even gang-infiltrated neighborhoods. In this regard, Steve Hammack noted that skate parks were useful to address the issues found in these areas.

> The fact is that we also have [skate parks] in kind of youth risk-prone areas, if you will, and we also do a gang-prevention program with the city. It's a nationally recognized program that we do. We have gang-intervention specialists that do weave their way into the school community, the gang communities that are influenced by gangs and try to pull those kids out that are not totally committed to a gang yet, but could be close, and try to get them redirected. The skate parks act as a good tool for redirection.

One of the key city projects that Steve Hammack likely refers to here includes the Mayor's Gang Prevention Task Force. Complementing this program is another neighborhood intervention that the PRNS directly administers called the Safe Summer Initiative Grant. This latter initiative offers funding to local physical-activity organizations working with at-risk youth.[24] In these "risk-prone areas," as Hammack called them, San Jose also subsidized the work of SJ 180, the nonprofit outreach program run by local pastor and skater Danny Sanchez. The use of SJ 180, which we introduced in chapter 2, reflects how the city implemented specific skateboarding outreach devices to curb gangs, crime, and violence.

Once again, SJ 180 operated in conjunction with the city's Viva Parks! program. This latter program is made up of "a series of free public events focused on health and wellness resources, physical activities, and community engagement" in neighborhood park locations such as Roosevelt, Plata Arroyo, and Mayfair.[25] Notably, each of these three sites have skate parks in which the city hosted summer contests during the Viva Parks! events. In conversation, program leaders often cited a philosophy of space reclamation when talking about these neighborhood skate contests. One event manager from this program told us, "Basically what we do, man, is we come out and we repurpose open space, bringing in a different approach mainly to bad neighborhoods, right? Rather than having police come in and kind of clean that area, it's basically tailored to have the community kind of take back their park. So, this is part of that movement— involving the skate parks."

Repurposing existing park spaces, in order to change the local cultures based in them, can be considered an intentional, politicized practice enacted by the city. With its substantial public-private resources, the city had the power to devise and implement new types of social space that aligned with its own preferred political ideologies.[26] This practice also implies that the city had specific theories about who the intended participants were and what their needs were; certain social mechanisms, as we shall see, were then used to operationalize these ideas in each skate park.[27]

The next section addresses these lines of thought by illustrating how the city conceptualized the impressive Lake Cunningham Regional Skate Park as its action-sports showpiece. This skate space underpinned the city's claims of being a global action-sports hub even as it was concurrently seen as integral to East Side community renewal.

"A Full-Blown Family Atmosphere": Lake Cunningham Regional Skate Park

> *"You have to go there. It's a destination."*
>
> A San Jose city manager

Lake Cunningham Regional Skate Park is indeed a major attraction housed within "California's premiere action sports facility."[28] This skate park first opened in April of 2008 at a cost of $6.4 million. The city contributed $4.8 million while the state covered the remaining cost.[29] This skate park opened under high expectations, as we can see in comments from local native and global skate legend Steve Caballero.

> The one thing special about San Jose in the skate industry is that we've always had something going over time to bring people to San Jose. . . . I believe this skate park will once again be an attraction for our industry, where people will come in and out of our city. The park's at that level of attracting people to the city and the sport as well.[30]

Mother with toddler son, on skateboard, at Lake Cunningham.
Courtesy of Todd Fuller.

Parents we met often believed that Lake Cunningham was a great skate park because it had lots of different technical elements. They also felt that it was a family-friendly environment. The skate park itself is located within a larger regional nature park on the edge of San Jose. Encased in barbed wire, access to the skate park is controlled by city staff who monitor behavior and enforce rules such as required helmet- and pad-wearing.

Furthermore, there are specified hours of operation that carry threat of banishment if breached. Entry into the park costs youth $3 per day, with adults paying $5. Parking typically costs $6 per day.

We soon realized that parents we spoke to were not exaggerating about the expanse and quality of this skate park. At 68,000 square feet, the park is massive. Key features include "the world's largest cradle, tallest vert

Aerial view of Lake Cunningham Regional Skate Park.
Courtesy of SJ action sports, http://www.sjactionsports
.com/wp-content/uploads/2012/01/i.jpe.

wall, and largest full pipe," and it also "offers a wide variety of terrain for all skill levels to learn and enjoy."[31] The skate park also provides private and group lessons, camps, birthday parties, and a shop that sells everything from snacks to equipment. Steve Hammack from the PRNS even told us that Lake Cunningham would host overnight skate camps and events. "[It's] very exciting because they can then skate at 12:00 midnight and we'll throw lights on for them and then they skate. They feel pretty privileged, as they are, as campers to be able to do that," he said.

Taken together, this extensive range of programming techniques utilized by the city government created a family-centric atmosphere to a greater degree than any other *Moving Boarders* skate park. This type of environment is noted in the following field note description:

> As you walk in, Rolling Stones music is blaring over the speakers. A boy named John is riding in the pool. Four middle-aged guys, with one guy in his twenties, are riding in the pool taking turns. John goes down in the pool with the older guys. The guy in his twenties is taking turns trying a ramp trick now, as John skates with him.
> *Lots of "Yeahs!" being shouted out. "Powerslip!" is overheard.*
> John falls over in a heap trying a trick on a curved hill: "I am over it, I can't do it." He sounds resigned. Mom: "You can do it." John:

"I can't." She is in the pool bowl next to him, working on some of her own turns in her purple helmet. She comes up out of the pool and exclaims "Yeew!" and sits down under an Independent skate logo on the wall. John: "No, Mom, you can already tell I wasn't going to pull that." Mom: "You're so close."

"Don't give up, they're easy!," "Yeah," and "HAHA!" are overheard from the other skate pool with the older guys and woman.

Scooter kids move around everyone, shrieking and chasing each other. "Guys, get her!" one of the boys screams, as they are playing tag on their scooters.

A woman in a red tank top rolls by. "It's my birthday skate," she says to a dad who just sat down at a table. We can now tell that the commotion in the skate park today is largely due to her birthday party. "Could I ask you to take a group photo?" she asks the dad.

The dad goes over to take the group photo in the pool bowl. Two of the guys in the photo sit down in the bowl with their hands doing "hang ten" signs for the photo. The tent with the snacks and bags is also for the birthday-party group.

The dad taking the photo comes back to the table and talks to me. With admiration he says "This place is insane" several times. He subsequently raves about the layout and design. We tell him about our study. Then we ask him about other skate parks in San Jose. He doesn't know many of them. The guy then rants about people not picking up the trash in other skate parks. He says that here they have a ranger patrolling, the hours are controlled, and there is a barbed-wire fence. He thinks this is good, keeps out the "punks" and the "riffraff."

Van Halen and Mötley Crüe blast out from the skate park's speakers. One tall, gangly, teenaged boy on skateboard with two shorter friends says he likes the Ozzy Osbourne playing now. "I am going to throw down some moves, but let me get my safety gear on first," he says.

There is an angry dad in black shades who now drags his kid over to an older guy with tattoos—another dad—wearing a red shirt. The guy in the red shirt is with the birthday party group that was taking the photo.

Angry dad says, "What's going on with my son? [his son is crying] You need to apologize to him."

The dad in red shirt tells the kid that it was an accident. Then red-shirt dad gives the angry dad a weak pat on the back and slinks away. Red-shirt dad goes back to the birthday party and then shares the story with the group, they all laugh about it. Angry dad has a phone gripped in his hand and is closely following his son around everywhere. He watches intently with his elbows jutting out and hands on hips, very aggressively. He looks quite intense about his son's skateboarding.

A couple of parents have set up lawn chairs near a table with a tent over it. Their boys stop in and speed back out, riding BMX bikes. Meanwhile, a couple of teenaged boys are in the main clubhouse. Suddenly, one of them rushes out the door with a microwaved Hot Pocket snack.

Observations like this one led us to conclude that this skate park had many participants reflecting all ability levels. Beginners come here in droves, but at the same time, due to its size and range of concrete elements, professional and amateur skate contests are often held here, too.

During one of our visits we ran into well-known local veteran skater Jim "Bug" Martino. He was lacing up his shoes at a picnic table, preparing to skateboard with a friend. Sitting down at a picnic table with us, he directed our attention to his unique helmet and skateboard. On this equipment, he pointed out the numerous California-based companies that he supported, including Apple. Talking about this particular skate park, he offered the following candid assessments: "The more, the merrier in skateboarding"; "If we can't facilitate a kid's dream, we've already locked that door"; "I want to make sure all kids can have a shot."

And yet, despite this skate park's current popularity with youth, families, and even famous skateboarders from San Jose's past, the picture here has not always been so idyllic. In fact, three years after this skate park opened, it almost closed down. By 2011, the global economic crisis had hit California, eventually forcing the San Jose city government to rethink how to pay for its skate-park operations. Low attendance numbers at the time, around 40,000 per year, meant that not enough fees were being generated to keep the park running. Also, the city's desire to keep this skate park constantly supervised meant that it became quite expensive to operate. It thus became untenable for the city to run this skate park because of a $61,000 budget shortfall.[32]

A private citizens group that incorporated parents, other community adults, and youth was organized to keep the park alive. Beginning in 2011, this group called itself Save our Skatepark (SOS).[33] SOS worked to gain media attention, petition the city council, and leverage its industry and political connections to attain new resources. The SOS devised numerous press releases that focused on how this skate park was needed in the city because it provided a safe place for youth to skateboard. To make its case, the group highlighted that this skate spot was fully staffed and adult-regulated. Local parents involved in the citizens group, including one named Carol Kruger, were adamant that the skate park needed to be supervised, according to one news story at the time.

> All the unstaffed skate parks in San Jose are filthy, there's drug sales going on, there's graffiti everywhere. Our park is pristine. You don't hear F-bombs every other word. The great thing about Lake Cunningham is it's staffed. Everybody has to wear helmets and pads. Nobody's smoking dope around the full pipe because there's cameras. If the staffing went away, I probably would not be going to that park anymore.[34]

One news piece, during the campaign to save Lake Cunningham, even characterized this skate park in family-friendly terms: "While they fight for the park's future, parents continue to take their kids to skate at Lake Cunningham. It has become a full-blown family atmosphere."[35]

Paul Murphy, the county staff member for Cindy Chavez, became an integral part of the SOS. Murphy told us how the SOS made its case to the city council and the mayor:

> We formed a coalition of parents and adult skaters at the skate park. We started having regular meetings. We approached and joined with a city council member who represented that part of the city. We testified at city council meetings, we wrote op eds. . . . We made it a big campaign. Kids testified at city council meetings with their skate boards, helmets, and pads, saying, "Please don't close where we are." We worked with the mayor, Chuck Reed, who said everything has to be cost recovery to show him that mathematically it could become cost recovered quite easily.

SOS campaigning, in large part, convinced San Jose's government to keep this skate park open and search for new financial streams. Major private donors eventually played a key role in the skate park's survival. "Everyone was able to tie this one-time funding to the missions of their organizations," recalled Murphy. Steve Hammack also told us how a consortium of new private donors was pulled together by the city in order to keep the skate park open. Once again, we can see how the city overtly turned to the private sector in order to enhance its skate park operation. City-run camps were also developed to keep the skate park running, as revealed in the following comment by Hammack:

We had Valley Medical [Center], First 5 San Jose,[36] Coca Cola even, some independent funders came, stepped up and said, "Here, we'll help you become cost recovery or a neutral, that's zero." Since that funding model—this was three or four years ago—and since those people came forward we've also done some more efficient operational changes. Because of our revenue and our camps, our camps become a really, really big attraction, all of the skate camps. And we charge for camps just like any camp that we do in our department. Because of all of that, we've become cost neutral and, in fact, the revenues are exceeding our expenditures now at the skate park.

With a more sustainable funding model in place, due to the usage of social-enterprise practices connecting public and private stakeholders, Lake Cunningham now operates in a family-friendly manner. This idea, that this space is family-friendly, has in fact become ingrained in the belief systems of local parents, as shown in the next section.

"It Just Seems Nicer, More Comfortable, Safer": Parents' Views of Lake Cunningham

Many parents at Lake Cunningham told us that they appreciated how other families could often be found in this skate park. They also strongly emphasized the sense of safety and regulation that permeated youth skateboarding here. What's more, the layout of the skate park was appreciated by parents because it had several technical elements that could be utilized by everyone from beginners to professionals, as we also saw in Bay City Skate Park.

Juan, whose son and daughter skated in Lake Cunningham, explained that this skate park was appealing because it was supervised to a high degree. This level of supervision meant that he could leave his children alone and go jogging in the nature park.

> Well it's huge. It's a huge park and they have so many different bowls, it's a skate world, basically. . . . So yeah, I love it there. Well, he loves it there. I'm able also to drop off the kids and go on a little jog. They supervise them there. They have their first-aid kit and they are trained to deal with situations like that; so not only that but there are cameras, there's surveillance twenty-four hours, I mean whatever hours they are opened. Yeah, that makes me feel a lot more comfortable. So, it's a drop-off park which is what I love about that park.

Alexa, a thirty-seven-year-old fitness trainer, has a seven-year-old daughter. Alexa alluded to the notion that the skate park was "cleaner" and "safer" than other skate parks that her family had visited so far. Like Juan, she also appreciated how she could leave her daughter alone without fear.

> I feel like Cunningham has like a really nice—one, it's a great park in that there's great things for beginners. And then there's amazing things for the super advanced, and so I see a huge range of skating there. Well, I just feel like, you know, you get a little higher quality, caliber. It's cleaner. I don't know. Yeah. It just seems nicer, more comfortable, safer. I think I might, I wouldn't leave her there by herself, but I might let her go into the park and run down, there's a parking lot there, and that trail there, so maybe do some stuff nearby. Like let her go in there alone, skate around. Probably the only park we've been to that I might consider doing something like that.

Then we spoke with Manny, whose young daughter skated in the park. Manny concurred with the view that this skate park had a range of quality elements that could be skated by both novices and experts alike: "You know what, I actually loved it because of layout, it's got some cool stuff. Oh, I find plenty of value. It's a huge park, there's some awesome riders there." This design and usability facet of skateboarding, which parents here appreciated, has been referred to elsewhere by scholars as the concept of *trickability*.[37]

We also heard comments from Carl, a father of a teenaged son who skates. Carl said that this skate park promoted healthy behavior and was a safe space for youth to interact in a positive social manner. "It's just a healthy environment. For his age, he was eight or nine, there wasn't drinking, there wasn't smoking, there wasn't graffiti, there wasn't fighting and all of those things." Brenda, a fifty-three-year-old skater and mother of a son who skates, felt that this skate park was mostly designed and programmed for families. She worked as a legal professional, and trekked over fifty miles to San Jose with her son. When asked why she traveled so far, she said that her son was advancing in skill and that elements like full pipes offered him new challenges. Then, as a skater herself, Brenda also appreciated how she felt included in this seemingly safe and comfortable space. "I'm an old lady. They're all very helpful with me, too. I know I get in people's way because I'm not that good. . . . It's just always a positive experience for me."

In further conversation, Brenda also mentioned that the skate-park participants were diverse in age, but not in terms of race and ethnicity.

"Well, there would be more young kids with parents. . . . They have an area for parents to sit. I've actually been down there and there was a birthday party there and they closed the park for that. So, I know they do that kind of thing. As far as demographics, age-wise they're from three years old to fifty-five. Mostly white and there's, in terms of race, there's not a whole lot of diversity."

Brenda's statements, corroborated by our own field observations, indicate how this skate park attracted a narrower cultural demographic compared to other *Moving Boarders* skate spots. Given the expenses required to use this skate park, including parking and entrance charges, it is not surprising that a suburban white clientele often skated here. In fact, youth from poorer neighborhoods consistently told us that this skate park was too far away on public transit and that it was expensive to visit because of the fees.

We also met Bernie, an engineer who skated with his two young boys. He listed a range of reasons why he enjoyed visiting the skate park, mostly related to its controlled social environment. Families could interact here, he said, before giving his opinion that the atmosphere of the skate park was friendly and supportive. For him, the entrance fee was essential to creating this type of skateboarding experience.

> Lake Cunningham is a little different because it's a paid park and so there's a generation of—early morning there's a lot of, mainly fathers with their boys. They come out and skate. There's one distinct family that I recall—the whole family; the dad, the mom, and their younger sons come out and they'll just hang out. You know, at least, the morning crowds are usually just very encouraging. Very interactive. Friendly.

It became obvious to us that Bernie appreciated the surveillance and screening processes that determined who could enter and use this skate park. In essence, he liked that this was an exclusive place to skate. Bernie told us that this spot maintained a certain preferred clientele compared to other local skate parks. He clearly favored Lake Cunningham Regional Skate Park over San Jose's neighborhood parks, especially Roosevelt, as we can see in this commentary: "So, every skate park has its own, kind of, personality and I have not seen any family at Roosevelt just because the way the place is set up. So the most family-friendly or kid-friendly parks are Cunningham and partly because it's completely enclosed or it's hard to get in." When we followed up about Bernie's concerns about who might get in, he simply replied, "Gangs."

In general, parent commentary in Lake Cunningham Regional Skate Park suggested that this was a safe, highly regulated, well-designed, and family-friendly destination. The exclusivity of this skate park, particularly in terms of race, ethnicity, and social class, resulted from specific spatial techniques that were implemented. These techniques included the use of a "pay-to-play" model, its location on an isolated natural park site, and the physical layout (e.g. enclosed with barbed wire and having one main entry point). In addition, the city installed a regular, paid staff presence.

Altogether, the use of various adult techniques here created a *themed space*. This characterization of *themed space* follows a trend whereby city governments directly program public leisure spaces to be like theme or amusement parks. Writing in the Netherlands, Rianne Van Melik and colleagues argue that these "safe" spaces reflect the "tendency towards greater control and predictability of activities in public space."[38] Thus, even as this type of space can provide elements of "entertainment and surprise," the prevailing experience in this type of themed space is one of "riskless risk."[39]

We also found that some participants here used this skate park to isolate themselves from other city residents whom they considered undesirable. This arguably promotes a "clusterisation" demographic effect across cities like San Jose.[40] Next, we examine skate-park life in a local space that was often sharply contrasted with Lake Cunningham. In comparison, Roosevelt Skate Park has a notorious reputation across the city, mainly due to its heavy Latino gang presence and recent high-profile crimes that have occurred in the surrounding park area. For example, in 2012 fourteen-year-old Heriberto Reyes was murdered there. Playing basketball with his older brother one afternoon, after their father had dropped them off, he was brutally killed on Roosevelt's own basketball courts right behind its skate park.[41] And yet, despite its notoriety as a dangerous, unregulated space, we will see that Roosevelt still served as a popular neighborhood youth "hangout." Youth participants and even adults valued skateboarding there for a variety of reasons.

"I Thought This Park Was Going to Be Like Totally Crazy": Adult and Youth Views of Roosevelt Skate Park

In contrast to Lake Cunningham, San Jose city staff did not try to leverage Roosevelt Skate Park in an entrepreneurial or promotional manner for several reasons. This was not a skate scene that had popular cultural acceptance; nor did it gain purchase with private industries, the way other

Moving Boarders skate parks did. Instead, the city tried to use its substantial resources to impart economic, social, and cultural forms of capital to neighborhood youth, through a classic social-interventionist approach.

Roosevelt's neighborhood skate park was constructed next to a bustling community center that sits inside a larger park location. Coyote Creek runs through this park, and this space also contains handball and basketball courts, a children's playground, open grass areas, and soccer fields. Recently, we noticed that a new skate shop had opened across the street, catering to local participants. The name of the skate shop, "Shark City," is a play on the name of the local National Hockey League franchise the San Jose Sharks.

During our observations, we saw adults of color, often Asian and Latino/a, regularly flowing through the community center and occasionally past the skate park. There was a consistent homeless presence situated near the playground and some park tables. We regularly noticed police cars driving in the parking lot or on the pavement near the skate park, because, as we had been told, there was an obvious gang presence in the park that could be observed most afternoons and weekends. Many of these gang-affiliated men played on the handball court. One city employee, Marco Hernandez, in fact explained that "Norteños [gang], they've had a stronghold in this neighborhood. It's a beautiful park as you can see in the days. The daylight is out, it's a safe park, but you'll see it transform in the night." And according to an adult female skateboarder we met in a different skate park, "some parks have weird, different vibes to them. Some are just straight up dangerous, like you might get stabbed at Roosevelt in San Jose."

The following statement from Carl, the father of a teenaged male skater featured earlier, illustrates how parents here picked up on the differences between Lake Cunningham and Roosevelt skate parks.

> Whereas Lake Cunningham is seen as family-friendly and attracts both locals and tourists, Roosevelt is focused on the neighborhood community. So, Cunningham, you have to wear pads and helmets. It's really well-lit at night. So, a lot of older guys go there, and a lot of little kids go there. Roosevelt's the people that live around Roosevelt. It's really people that live downtown.

Danny Sanchez, from SJ 180, often worked directly on the ground in neighborhood skate parks like Roosevelt. He once compared Lake Cunningham to Roosevelt in the following manner:

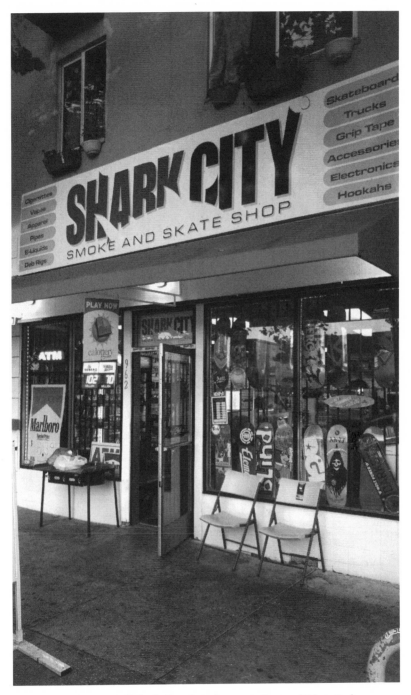

Recently opened Shark City skate shop near Roosevelt Skate Park.
Courtesy of Matthew Atencio.

The difference also is there's not the graffiti, there's not the same environment of drugs and alcohol and people that are involved in the gang lifestyle hanging around at Lake Cunningham. Out here [at Roosevelt] it's a lot different. You have a little bit of skateboarders, a little bit of gangsters and a little bit of people that are just hanging around, you know, getting high.

Admittedly, based on our observations, there were indeed regular individuals that came here to hang out and/or skate while drinking forty-ounce beers ("forties") and puffing on joints. However, these were often racially and ethnically mixed men in their twenties. Occasionally, men who were more middle-aged also came here to skate. Taken together, these men were older than the youth that we eventually met and studied. These youth, usually high school aged or recently graduated, are featured in this chapter. As we shall see, these youth seemed to be quite invested in this skate park, as it provided a supportive social network and even friendships.

Our research visits allowed us to see that groups of local teenagers and their older male counterparts mostly constituted Roosevelt's daily activities. Participation seemed to rise greatly when youth did not have school commitments; it seemed busier after school, during summer vacation, and on the weekends. The skateboarding youth here were mostly in their mid-to-late-teens, rather than being young children. Thus, even though we saw adults or parents here on occasion, it was nothing like Bay City or Lake Cunningham, where parents regularly watched or actually participated. In addition, Roosevelt did not have formal social gatherings such as girls' skate days, birthday parties, or overnight sleepover sessions. There were just a few times when the city hosted neighborhood skate contests in the summer through their Viva Parks! event series. Taking these facts into consideration, it is obvious why skaters in this park say that it most often felt like a neighborhood hangout. Indeed, we regularly saw young people talking to and watching their friends, often for several hours, and sometimes without even skateboarding. There was one Latino teenager whom we noticed regularly riding his bike around the skate park. He did not skateboard, but instead just hung out with the skaters, often keenly watching them from outside or inside the park, for hours at a time. This skate park could thus be defined as having high *sociability*, by which scholars mean the "social characteristics of a spot beyond time on the board."[42] Scholars have suggested that "activities such as chatting, eating, skateboard maintenance and watching others skate are noted as key in a spot with a high sociability, all of these relying on space to sit or stand away from the action. This might also include room for non-skating friends."[43]

Alongside this attribute of sociability marking the Roosevelt scene, youth seemed to develop a true sense of belonging here. Within the skate park there exists a makeshift memorial, complete with Modelo beer bottles, some candles, and written testimonials for a Roosevelt skater that recently died. One afternoon after school, we saw several boys and girls sitting around this memorial while drinking beer, talking with and watching the skaters, and sometimes skating themselves. Throughout the day, we would ask different locals if they knew how the skateboarder died. About half of them said they knew him. Apparently, this young man was hit by a car while standing on a freeway after he had stopped his car and gotten out. One informant told us that the youths subsequently held their own memorial for him at the skate park. During this event, we heard, people smoke and drank during the day and told stories about the skateboarder. The informant told us that the skate park was packed with "one hundred to two hundred people" and that several police cars were in the park closely monitoring the event. He recalled that there was significant tension and suspicion between the police and skateboarders; it felt much like a standoff, he said.

"Repurpose the Space": Roosevelt's Place-Making and Space-Activating Practices

During one of the Viva Parks! events held in the summer, a city employee commented to us, "We come into these parks specifically just, to come in and repurpose the space, give people the opportunity to be constructive in the community. That's why these parks have been chosen." City government definitely has a less consistent presence here compared to the regularly staffed Lake Cunningham Regional Skate Park. But the Viva Parks! events, SJ 180 program, and police presence altogether demonstrate how the city still used specific techniques to define the purpose and intended occupants of this social space.[44] Although Roosevelt served as a youth hangout spot, the city implemented certain mechanisms that largely targeted teens of color in order to direct them into new, seemingly constructive activities. In this regard, the city's assumption was that this skate park, with its own youthful behavior and identities, required transformation. Later on, we will examine how participants actually responded to the city's interventionist vision of Roosevelt skateboarding.

City officials at the top level and those working in the field both felt that making social change in this skate park necessitated attracting

Youth memorial in Roosevelt Skate Park. *Courtesy of Matthew Atencio.*

new clientele. Cindy Chavez, for instance, told us that skate parks such as Roosevelt benefitted when adults passed through them. She felt that increased adult traffic here would also serve to attract more families. Eventually, it was hoped that new demographics would deter antisocial behavior and crime in neighborhood skate parks. This was, incidentally, similar to the view held by the Tony Hawk Foundation and what we saw occurring in Bay City. In this case, Chavez specifically referred to this practice as *park activation*: "I do think, again, activating parks, when you have lots of different kinds of people and doing lots of different kinds of things, it makes a better environment." In fact, Roosevelt Skate Park was originally anchored next to a community center for this precise reason. Chavez told us in this regard, "You have eyes and activity in a park. It's really, the way a park is safest and cleanest, is people being out there consistently. I've been somebody who's, I've not been really excited about standalone skate parks, meaning that that's the whole park, because I just think that a mixture of activity in any environment is better than just all one age."

Of course, there were other city officials working in the field that held this same view. Before one summer Viva Parks! event, we caught up with Marco Hernandez, who was in charge of the day's activities. He was organizing his support staff and setting up information booths in front of the community center. Taking a short break to talk with us, he reiterated that it was important to have an influx of families that would "fight for their park." Attracting more residents and "having them take some ownership into their parks" was crucial, he said. In addition, Hernandez explained that it was important for families to be present in the park to show "they're not intimidated." What's more, as we discussed the upcoming skate contest that evening, Hernandez admitted that skateboarders could sometimes be associated with negative or "outlaw" behavior. Thus, Hernandez wanted the city to help skateboarders become more positive members of the community.

> Well, we all know the culture of skating unfortunately has sometimes a bad rap. A lot of the youth that are involved in skating are kind of seen as people that are kind of outlaws or they break the law; that kind of stuff. So, what we're trying to do is, you know, we're trying to bridge that and basically have them be positive in the community. Bring positives into their community by participating, by giving them a sense of ownership.

Hernandez, much like Cindy Chavez, wanted to incorporate more adults into Roosevelt Skate Park in order to change the existing skate culture. In this case, he believed that public safety officers could be useful. "That's my vision now, to be able to get police and fire involved more in this stuff. That also changes that culture perception."

After talking with Hernandez, we attended the Viva Parks! event to see the city's *activation* and *place-making* strategies in action. We noticed that many informational booths were set up in the park, albeit closer to the community center rather than the skate park. These booths featured local politicians, sports programs such as the San Jose Sharks professional hockey team, as well as health and nutrition programs. There was also free Mexican food and activities for children. In the actual skate park, we could see several nonlocal families juxtaposed with the local skateboarding youth who were there as usual. Lake Cunningham Regional Skate Park representatives were also present, helping to organize and promote the contest. We also noticed that young men at the back of the skate park, both skaters and non-skaters, would regularly walk down to Coyote Creek and then return shortly thereafter. But we never investigated this practice, for our own safety. Even though the back of the skate park was near all the proceedings described above, our regular observations and parent discussions suggested that this was essentially a "no-go" zone for outsiders, which included our research team.

Danny Sanchez from SJ 180 was also at this particular skate event. During our conversation, he directly referred to the city's plan for neighborhood change through place-making and activation practices. "This is called, I believe, it's called place-making. I love how they [city government] are activating the parks. I love how they are getting people to get out to the parks and have fun—just building the community relationship." But, unlike the city officials we mentioned, Sanchez was in touch with these youths on a more frequent basis, much as we saw with K-Dub in Town Park. Sanchez obviously knew the kids personally, as we first noted in chapter 2. This familiarity, as well as his own skateboarding experience, seemed to give him a more nuanced perspective of how to become immersed with the youth, in order to enact social change. Sanchez indeed articulated that his approach to helping young skateboarders was molded by his own experiences and his Christian faith.

> The reason I also have a passion to work with these guys is because I went from skateboarding to being involved in a gang lifestyle, to being involved in drugs and just leading a very negative lifestyle.

When my life was radically changed by my faith in Christ, instead of being destructive, I wanted to give back to my community. I think one of the ways for me to give back is through investing in the skate community.

Even though he was an adult coming into what was essentially youth territory, we observed that Sanchez was comfortable and accepted by youths during his visits to the skate park. Indeed, he would often sit and counsel with the skaters as they chilled and drank beer. Sanchez wanted to eventually give the local youths access to a social network outside of their regular skate-park group. In essence, he wanted to integrate them within a seemingly more normative type of community.

Well, we're here [at Roosevelt] to help to make this park a family-friendly park and you know, the skateboarders, they're like family. They are a part of this community family and we want to engage them and let them know, "Hey you're not there by yourself and it's not just this group here and that group here, we are a family." SJ 180 plans that time to connect the city in different areas, this park particularly, to let these kids know "you guys are not just off to the corner doing your skateboarding."

These comments and others by Sanchez clearly indicate that skateboarding was seen as a starting point, or hook, in order to create new forms of social capital for youth of color. Sanchez, working with the city government, wanted to expose these youth to more mainstream groups and opportunities, in order to benefit them, but also to create new types of social identities.

In general, our talks with city officials often gave us the impression that these adults were earnest in their attempts to create a potentially more normalized, family-friendly skate scene. The city's reliance on place-making and activation activities, such as the skate contests, arguably attempted to transform youth into citizens that would be considered acceptable within the neoliberal society and economy. Even Danny Sanchez, who was deeply immersed within the skate scene, wanted youth here to become more integrated within the mainstream. Sanchez was caring and respectful toward the youths; but he also seemed concerned that local youth could become enmeshed in self-destructive behaviors that would jeopardize their aspirations.[45] He thus seemed quite supportive of the city's mission to bring these youths into new community contexts, whether religious or municipal, that could potentially benefit them.

Marco Hernandez from the Viva Parks! program further outlined the city's systematic approach to transforming youth by bringing them into contact with new social networks.

> We have the [skate] competition, but what we do is we take their names down and emails and contact information and then we start. We make a little announcement about how to basically contribute to the community, be a positive role model. We'll have—our plans are to have guest speakers come out and basically, I would say, relay a positive message to them so they can be positively influenced. From there on out, what we do is we reach out to them via email. The program is called Work to Future, which is like job opportunities, like the same program we have. We also have Sounds and Works, which is also another youth job-opportunity-readiness program. So, we would look to target them in that aspect to kind of get them here to continue coming out, be positive when they're coming out, and build a relationship with the community center and with their community, but at the same time to give them opportunities to succeed as well.

We can see from the above statements that new types of capital were purportedly being generated here by the city government and Sanchez. Skateboarding was supposed to give youth access to new social groups and relationships, mainstream cultural knowledge and ways of being, as well as economic benefits such as potential job wages. This mission to provide capital is laudable since neighborhood youth of color have frequently been ignored and underserved in American society. But it also seemed problematic, because it did not necessarily reflect what youth themselves actually wanted from skateboarding in Roosevelt. By contrast, what we found was that these youth, given their compelling day-to-day lives, foremost enjoyed the immediate sense of autonomy and camaraderie that came from using this neighborhood space. And, although it was somewhat hard to contact parents here, the parents that we did eventually meet emphasized that their children appreciated the skate park's inherent social diversity and admittedly riskier circumstances. This type of commentary, from youth and adults, is provided in the next section.

"It's the Best Park in the World": Youths' Constructions of a Supportive, Autonomous Skate Network

It should now be clear from our discussion that Roosevelt Skate Park functioned as yet another *Urban Platform for Capital* set up by adults.

Roosevelt skateboarders hanging out together on a weekday afternoon.
Courtesy of Matthew Atencio.

Addressing this idea of capital generation, however, we wonder how these youth were perhaps already "doing it for themselves."[46] As a matter of fact, an issue with the capital-generation theory is that this process is often viewed through an adult lens and can ignore "the capacity of young people" to create capital in their own ways and for their own reasons.[47] Keeping this critique in mind, we now turn to explain the perspectives of youth in Roosevelt Skate Park.

Youth in this skate park were quite aware of the strong gang presence and violence that sometimes occurred here. They were careful not to overstep gang territory and contravene certain social codes, essentially telling us that they knew how to "mind their own business." This understanding was necessary to negotiate the social realities of the park. A skater named Maria told us that she had spent several years skateboarding at Roosevelt. Maria went on to explain how outsiders considered this a dangerous skate spot, although she was unfazed when coming here.

> People say, "Oh, it's bad here, especially at night. And you shouldn't be here." Like, for me, sometimes my dad doesn't even want to let

me come. It's like one or two o'clock he doesn't want to let me come because, "Oh, no. You're a girl. It's ugly over there. Especially at Roosevelt. People get killed." It's like, "calm down. I know. I understand. You're worried."

Maria further explained that one could use the skate park safely by understanding the social environment and its informal codes of behavior. "Well, actually when you come here and get to know the people and everything, I don't think it's like that at all. I mean, if you don't do anything bad, then you don't get—right? If you don't bother them." At this point in the interview, we noted that some gang members were present right next to the skate park. She continued, "But, they don't do anything if you don't do anything. Don't act stupid. I don't know, but yeah. Just mind your own business. That's it."

Trevor was a teenaged white male skater who lived in a different part of the city. But he often visited Roosevelt to skate with the locals from the neighborhood. He corroborated the importance of minding one's own business and being respectful of others amidst the threat of random violence. This practice has been famously referred to as the "code of the street" by sociologist Elijah Anderson.[48] Trevor suggested that insider understanding of the social landscape allowed one to safely engage in the skate park. "Well, like my parents and people I've told about it. They all think it's really sketchy. Like, gang affiliated. But I don't really see a problem. There's different gangs and stuff that hang out around here, but they don't really bother us and we don't bother them so . . . it's really not bad. I think it's a nice park." Indeed, we saw that Trevor appeared quite comfortable and even confident skateboarding in the confines of Roosevelt Skate Park and traversing the nearby park areas.

As long as youth kept to themselves and did not intervene in the park's other adult activities and social groups, then things seemed to be relatively calm. This meant that skate-park youth here could continue to work on their moves, hang out, and make friends. Consider the following exchange we had with several youths that were sitting on a skate ramp during one weekday afternoon:

Interviewer: Why do you like this park?

Skater One: It's the best park in the world.

Interviewer: How come it's the best park in the world?

Skater Two: Because everybody goes here.

Interviewer: What is the scene like here?

Skater Three: Pretty chill.

Skater Four: Yeah. Pretty dope. Everybody knows everybody else.

Skater Five: It's motivating, like, if somebody's trying to learn a
new trick, everybody else will, like, motivate them to do it.
Help them and give them tips and pointers and stuff.

We soon came back for a visit on another weekday afternoon. During
the previous week, someone had been shot next to the park, according to
Danny Sanchez. He explained, "There were shootings here last week. I was
with the family." Despite this recent tragic event, there was no noticeable
sense of fear in the park, and we observed the regular safe, relaxed social
scene involving local youth. Peer learning was taking place as several
young men were playing a game of S-K-A-T-E, which is akin to playing
H-O-R-S-E in basketball. We saw them repeatedly try to jump over a
garbage can laid down on its side on the pavement. For over one hour, we
observed them take turns while offering positive comments and sugges-
tions, with several young men entering or leaving the game. Toward the
end of our visit, we spoke with a white twenty-eight-year-old male skateboarder named Ryan. He told us that he had been coming to Roosevelt
since he was twelve. In the parking lot after his skate session had finished,
he pointed across the skate park and said, "That's one of my friends from
high school and he still comes here, too." They are both fathers now, he
added. Roosevelt, he reminisced, was once "the place to hang out and
party" when they were teenagers. With a Thrasher hat perched on his
head, he sat on the hood of his car and told us that this was his second
skate session today. He told us that he enjoyed the physicality and feeling of stoke (or having a thrill or buzz, while being in the moment) in
skateboarding.[49] Indeed, we had previously observed him skateboarding
quite expressively, and he was drenched in sweat when we talked to him.

Skateboarders like Ryan felt a strong attachment to Roosevelt
because it was where they congregated with their friends. We could tell
that Roosevelt was a popular youth space. It was where youths seemed
to gain a sense of place in the neighborhood and construct their own
skate identities. Maria highlighted these ideas, telling us about her deep
attachment to the skate park:

> I grew up downtown, and I actually would just hang out at Roosevelt
> when I was in high school with my friends. And I would watch all my
> friends skate, and I really loved skateboarding and I enjoyed watch-
> ing it, so I decided to try it myself. It's also a really good place because

Roosevelt Park is kind of known for the gang activity, so it takes away from that and it put the focus on skateboarding, and I feel like it keeps a lot of people out of trouble, and people are out there exercising, having fun, so, yeah, Roosevelt is just a really great place to have fun. Well, I have a younger brother that is much younger than me, and I bring him to Roosevelt. So, my parents know that we all love to skate, and that's our neighborhood park, so that's where we go.

The view that Roosevelt was a meaningful, enjoyable youth space was reinforced over many conversations we had with skaters. Trevor, for instance, compared his experiences here with those he had in Lake Cunningham's skate park. In the statement below, he explained that lack of adult supervision was the key to Roosevelt's positive, "free" vibe:

[Lake] Cunningham, I don't really like it as much even though it's more of like a—it is kind of more like a preppy, you wear all this safety equipment. It's just, it doesn't have as good of a vibe as, let's say, here. Here is just like—it feels so much more free. Even though it's kind of in a little bit bad of an area, I guess, because there's—by the handball court, there's some sketchy people sometimes and police coming through all the time. But it doesn't really matter because, to me, I really like being free. I want freedom. So, it's like this is really nice because I just feel like I can just do whatever.

While adults, including city staff, were less frequent inhabitants of the skate park, except for Danny Sanchez, they were sometimes present in other ways. And this presence was definitely noted by the youth in the skate park. We once observed that those who were drinking beer at the skate park would play cat and mouse with the police who were passing by and monitoring the park. Consider the following field-note extract:

One of the young Latino boys with a Modelo beer bottle snickers, "I love playing this game, when the cops come through." Just then, a policeman slowly rolls through the park in an SUV, and the boy is talking about being underage and drinking in public and not getting caught. Sometimes, according to the youth, police would stop directly in front of the park in a "face off" position to observe skaters for nearly an hour at a time. Although, the youth said that the police never came into the skate park itself.

In general, the youth skateboarders we met seemed circumspect about the place of adults in or near this skate park. But these youth occasionally offered more thoughtful and even conflicted views about adult intervention. The presence of Danny Sanchez as well as the Viva Parks! summer skate contests lead by city staff seemed to be appreciated. It was also interesting that some of the skaters told us that they wanted adults from the city to take an interest here and get involved by doing maintenance and upgrading the facility. All the skaters we spoke with knew about Lake Cunningham and its state-of-the-art design elements, even as many of them did not skate there on a regular basis for various reasons. Some skaters interpreted the obvious differences between these two facilities as resulting from a lack of adult support. Thus, although these youths generally wanted freedom from adults in their everyday skateboarding, they still wanted adults to support this skate park. This perspective was articulated by several skateboarders during a group interview:

> "The city just leaves them [graffiti tags in Roosevelt]. The city doesn't care about this park [because of graffiti here]."

> "The city does care, but they think it is out of their control, they can't handle this park. They just have to paint over it."

> "I want someone to come in here [from the city] and do murals in the bowl. People just tag graffiti in it. I want something like that. Like the bottom of the pool, with an eight-ball [symbol], something like that."

"I'd Be a Lot More Worried if She Was Associated as a Pokémon Go Player": Parents' Views of Diversity, Autonomy, and Social Knowledge

As noted above, very few parents stayed at Roosevelt Skate Park to watch their children, except during special events like Viva Parks! The parents that we did find to interview were quite aware of the existing culture, including its contradictions. We thus noted a tension in the views of parents. That is, they appreciated the youth-centered nature of the space but were also generally concerned about the illegal activities and random violence inside Roosevelt.

In conversation, Chas, a former skater and father of a son and daughter who both skate, described Roosevelt's unique social scene; once again, we can see it being contrasted with other skate parks, including, presumably, Lake Cunningham. "I like [Roosevelt Park]. I think it does have a little bit different feel. It definitely has more of an inner-city vibe than the parks that we've been going to. You've got the tagging and the various graffiti all over. The other parks are very—there's really none of that." But, perhaps surprisingly, the parents we met felt somewhat comfortable in the skate park and were advocates of their children using it.

Chas talked about the positive feelings he had felt when visiting the skate park with his son. He felt that there was evidence of social diversity, as well as peer support and lack of conflict. "The people that we've met, that I've met with him—I love that it doesn't seem to be a whole lot of age barrier. You know? He's thirteen, but some twenty-year-old guy who is ripping it up will say 'Hey, that was killer. Try that again' and egg him on and just—it seems like there haven't been hardly any problems. Everybody gets along with everybody." This skate park had a "good vibe," Chas concluded.

The next narrative was provided by Manny, who lived in the suburbs but came to Roosevelt when his daughter Mia wanted to skateboard. We can see from his commentary that the skate park had a very socially diverse participant base, especially when compared to Lake Cunningham. Manny gave this next commentary in response to a question about the typical social environment at Roosevelt:

> So, what you normally see at the park, there's one guy that normally parks himself, he's been there about three times before. He's got a lot of shit, a lot of stuff, it looks like he almost lives there. He's got some old boards and things, and he kind of leans against there. There's some more gnarly-looking skateboarders, maybe in their forties, who look like they have been through some tough stuff. Let's see, there's like a group of younger kids sitting on one of the bowls doing bong hits. There's a group of maybe late-teen guys, who are pretty good, who just come in for maybe twenty, thirty minutes and do a little bit and then leave. I don't have the feeling that, you know, we haven't been there enough yet to feel like we're completely accepted, but when you're out there skating, people respect you. They seem to have an easier time with her than they do with me, because I don't skate, I just kind of walk around to try to find a place in the shade. But yesterday was different. So, okay, so yeah, so the groups, there's some who look like they're almost homeless, some who look like they might be in gangs, some just teen kids smoking pot, some other kids. Some people who look like they're old skateboarders. There's a good mixture of people. But no rich white kids. No middle-class parents, that kind of thing.

Manny's daughter, Mia, subsequently remarked that this was her favorite place to skateboard. She said that she preferred skating at

Roosevelt to her own suburban town's skate park, which was quite safe and monitored by adults. Her local skate park, she explained, had lots of skate coaches and parents present. But while this father-and-daughter combo felt positive about skateboarding in Roosevelt, Manny was also aware of this social space's more complicated aspects. Like us, he knew that there were certain areas to avoid, especially in the back of the skate park. He said that this knowledge was based on his previous time living in one of the East Coast's big cities: "If you sit by certain groups of people, there's just—not hostility, but just sort of a coldness or discomfort. So yeah, and you know, I grew up in the city. I think you can tell sometimes where things feel a little tenser than they should be."

As our research progressed, we continued to tease out how Roosevelt skate parents perceived their children's skating in this highly diverse and unquestionably grittier skate park. We wondered whether these parents believed that their children could benefit from skateboarding here. We eventually found that, for many parents, Roosevelt stood out because it provided opportunities for children's autonomous development. The essence of this view was that children could learn to skateboard largely on their own amidst the social diversity and potential risks. This finding strongly contrasts with the "riskless risk" perspective that we explained was largely held by Lake Cunningham parents.[50] For example, Manny explained that he avidly supported his young daughter's skateboarding here because it was more "organic." That is, it offered her chances to skate without heavy adult intervention. Manny told us in conversation, "She is pacing herself and picking up the skill that she needs so she can do harder things. And that's what I see good skateboarders do. And it's not driven, it's not controlled by adults. Kids do it. She is making those decisions herself, and it's just happening organically."

Manny felt his daughter's skateboarding here was much better than her playing a popular mobile phone game. "But I'm fine with her being part of that scene, being associated as a skateboarder. . . . I think especially now, I'd be a lot more worried, and I don't mean this as a joke at all, if she was associated as a Pokémon Go player." He went on to explain how skateboarding in Roosevelt could increase one's awareness of immediate social surroundings. By contrast, he felt that video games were a distraction from experiencing and learning from one's actual social environment. Manny also said that games such as Pokémon Go did not promote meaningful, authentic forms of social interaction. Manny considered Roosevelt's unique social dynamic valuable because he wanted Mia to learn how to engage and share community space with diverse others. This meant that she would understand and abide by the previously identified social codes required to use this urban space, and others.

> But overall, I think that people skateboard with a fair amount of awareness of where they are, so that they don't collide with people, they don't annoy people. She seems to connect with the parts of the culture that are really functional, which is accessing the urban landscape, things like that. So, for that reason, I think it's really good.

Manny was thus highly positive about his daughter's capacity to learn about handling risks and engaging with diverse social behaviors and individuals during Roosevelt skateboarding.

This kind of parental investment in diverse social engagement was also expressed by Alexa. Her husband initially opposed their daughter's skateboarding in Roosevelt after reading a negative Yelp review. Alexa recalled that he once said, "Eh, I don't know if I would take her there," adding, "sometimes it's kind of sketchy." But, like Manny, Alexa felt that Roosevelt skateboarding could be productive, as it provided a potential opportunity to teach her daughter about different social behaviors, people, and interactions. Indeed, she was quite aware of the risks generally associated with urban skateboarding. In conversation, she mentioned, "I have seen very, very, very young children using substances that I think probably shouldn't be used at that young of an age, like twelve." But since her daughter "loves skateboarding," exposure to this type of social practice was going to continue, she said. Alexa concluded that this type of experience could in fact be used as a teachable moment. "I don't know if it's necessarily concern, like we're worried about it or anything like that, I just think we have to present it to her in the right way, and make sure she knows what's going on."

In general, the parents who came to Roosevelt felt positive about the types of social interactions and learning practices that took place in this diverse environment. They were fully aware that skateboarding here involved potentially risky or dangerous situations. Yet, as the commentary above shows, they did not avoid or attempt to change this skate spot. Instead, these parents believed that Roosevelt was the perfect environment to teach their children valuable life lessons. As Carl, the father of a seventeen-year-old male Roosevelt skateboarder once told us, "If you can navigate Roosevelt Skate Park, you can navigate the world."

The views of youth and parents, when taken together, indicate that

Roosevelt, although often negatively portrayed elsewhere, could serve as a useful space to foster youth development. It was the kind of skate spot where youth could "experiment with new identities and behaviours, and develop a sense of autonomy," as scholar Nicholas Nolan observes about skateboarding in the Australian context.[51] This attribute of skateboarding, Nolan argues, often contrasts with official "planning and management" practices found in skate spaces.[52] In our own case-study, we learned that the city's official vision of neighborhood place-making and community activation was not necessarily what these parents and youth had in mind when going to Roosevelt.

Conclusion:
San Jose Skateboarding as a Tale of Two Skate Parks

This chapter illustrated how the San Jose government's well-funded and privately supported PRNS utilized two distinctive models for their various skate parks. This meant that there were two sets of purposes and mechanisms underlying skate-park life in the city. Given this two-pronged approach to social-enterprise practice, we ascertained how local participation on the ground would match up or not with the vision of city leaders for each skate park. It soon became obvious that Lake Cunningham and Roosevelt were quite different from each other in socioeconomic and cultural terms. Consequently, each of these parks had its respective set of parent supporters. On one hand, many parents in Lake Cunningham appreciated the extensive use of formal adult surveillance to control youth activity. The exclusivity of these practices resulted in safe and comfortable opportunities for a wealthier, suburban demographic of youth to interact with like-minded peers. Meanwhile, on the other hand, parents we spoke to in Roosevelt preferred more autonomous methods of social control and youth development. This space was seen as giving youth opportunities to connect with diverse others while providing unique social lessons in a riskier and more complicated environment. Youth themselves mostly enjoyed the supportive, family-like community found in Roosevelt and consequently gained a strong sense of identification with this space. This occurred despite the potentially more dangerous social conditions surrounding them in the park.

Altogether, the findings in this chapter help us to further understand how Bay Area families take up distinct views when it comes to engaging with *Urban Platforms for Capital*. And furthermore, we can see that skate parks are often conceptualized, resourced, and programmed in quite different ways from one another, according to prevailing social-enterprise agendas. In our final chapter, we bring San Jose skateboarding into conversation with the other *Moving Boarders* skate parks in order to collectively explore the meanings and experiences found across all four *Urban Platforms for Capital.*

SIX

The Use of Skate Park Spaces to Create New Values for Youth, Families, and Communities

Introduction:
Bridging Two Dimensions in Modern Urban Skateboarding

Mike was once considered a top name in the sport of skateboarding. Known for his wild antics yet clean skating style, he was featured in famous videos and had his share of photo shoots. Now, Mike devotes tremendous energy to coach youth, and he was one of the community leaders featured in Bay City Skate Park. The tone of our interview, held in a bustling local coffee shop, was highly reflective, as Mike recalled his formative years of riding skate parks in California alongside a young Tony Hawk, among others. Mike turned professional in his mid-teens, giving him entry into the core skateboarding industry at a young age. Mike's comments below are important, because he explains a link between the traditional iteration of skateboarding and its current refashioning as a family-focused activity.

> I had this exposure early on to the real essence of skateboarding and to the industry. Yeah, that's like the endorsements and brands, and having your skateboard out, doing skateboard demonstrations, and contests, and videos, pictures, that's just kind of that whole world of self-promotion and being kind of on a team or . . . the industry basically just all these things go into, everything that goes into basically building your own brand up. You're solidifying your name. That's like a constant battle in the industry. Coming here now into the Bay Area, I wanted to find a way I can sustain being involved in skateboarding, not so much in the industry but I knew I lost a little bit of time stepping away from it, and I wanted to basically get more in touch with kind of my own self with the board again and also

get in touch with the community and ultimately, I saw that there's such a need now, there's been a need, for young kids. I was always passionate about trying to mentor kids in such a way where to help them kind of avoid what pitfalls and mistakes I made in the past or others have been making.

Mike now operates a flourishing youth-training program in Bay City Skate Park, with other coaching projects in the pipeline. Similarly, he has published a skateboarding guide for parents and was recently featured on a national talk show. Summing up the visible presence of families in skateboarding, Mike told us that skateboarding is "becoming divided into two distinct industries . . . a young-person industry and another industry." He subsequently offered the view that these two key demographic groups now have a rightful "place" within skateboarding culture.

> Let us old guys do all the stuff our old guys want to do, but then let's think about having the magazine for twelve-and-under kids. Let's think about having the videos for twelve-and-under kids, I'm not saying the Nickelodeon version of skateboarding, but how can we make it so that when parents come into skateboarding or our kids come into skateboarding, there's a place for them? It's not that they're just thrown into the whole other realm and the parents have to kind of do damage control. Does that make sense?

Mike's words perfectly sum up how modern urban skateboarding has two elements; one that is core and another reflecting a more family-friendly outlook. From his vantage point, Mike sees the need to account for both elements. Using Mike's ideas as a frame of reference, this last chapter demonstrates how subcultural and mainstream influences both have currency in contemporary urban skateboarding. The distinction of authenticity has been critical to skateboarding's subcultural, competitive male street identity, especially in renowned scenes such as the San Francisco Bay Area. But, we argue, this core aspect of skateboarding now coincides with an influx of new adult participants who are changing this sport's status and social dynamics. The involvement of more and more adults in urban skateboarding follows a broader trend whereby youth sports are being intensively privatized during neoliberal times.

The State of Urban Youth Skateboarding in Neoliberal Times

"Apart from mandatory schooling, youth sports are the most popular adult supervised activities for children and young people in the United

States."[1] Nuancing this assertion from sociologist Jay Coakley, we opened *Moving Boarders* by calling attention to a trend whereby American youth are now leaving in droves from many traditional sports, often because of adult intervention and structuring. Simultaneously, we noted that skateboarding has historically provided a place for those dissatisfied with mainstream youth sports. We can see this in the words of one of skateboarding's biggest innovators, Rodney Mullen.

> As a kid, I grew up on a farm in Florida. And I did what most little kids do. I played a little baseball, did a few other things like that, but I always had the sense of being an outsider, and it wasn't until I saw pictures in the magazines, that a couple other guys skate, I thought "wow, that's for me," you know? Because there was no coach standing directly over you, and these guys were just being themselves. There was no opponent directly across from you. And I loved that sense, so I started skating.[2]

Mullen's comments indicate how skateboarding has always been in tension with the idea of being an actual sport. In fact, this was once described as the "icky question that has stuck to skateboarding like gum on a sneaker."[3] But these words are also quite powerful because they identify a paradox that guides this entire book. *Moving Boarders* has provided many examples that highlight skateboarding's resonance with more traditional types of youth sporting practice. And this shift has undoubtedly been facilitated by "encroaching adult intervention."[4] This means American adults are getting increasingly involved in contemporary youth skateboarding. Addressing this phenomenon, the previous chapters collectively illustrate a wide spectrum of parent values and investments, that either resonate or do not, with typical youth-sports parenting.

In this final chapter, we outline the central themes that cut across all of the previous three case-study chapters (3, 4, and 5). Revisiting the findings presented in the case-study chapters, we first return to the idea that neoliberalism has a strong influence on modern skate-park life. Clearly, there is a paradigmatic shift under neoliberal conditions toward the use of public-private relationships to guide youth skateboarding. This social-enterprise practice, as it has been called, often fundamentally structured the versions of youth skateboarding that we researched.

To explain this prevalence of social-enterprise interests shaping specific skate parks, we fashioned together a conceptual lens deriving from sociological and geographic scholarship. This lens conceptualizes urban space as a socially dynamic network and was used to explore how skate parks operated as politicized spatial projects. Using this lens, we came to view skate parks as constituted by the visions of particular stakeholders who implemented certain resources and techniques to engineer urban change.[5]

Our case-study chapters highlighted diverse ways in which community leaders, private citizens, nonprofits, and industry groups *collectively* leveraged urban spaces in order to address perceived needs in their respective communities. From this understanding, we subsequently contend that urban skateboarding fits closely with the increasingly privatized reconceptualization of American youth sports. Now, urban skateboarding is instrumentally valued by many adults as a vehicle to develop youth. As in other youth activities, these adults usually want to instill youth with certain free-market citizenship ideals, including entrepreneurialism and self-regulation. This adult perception aligns with the idea that benefits, or "capitals" as they are called in sociological scholarship, are generated by skate parks. These spaces thus work as *Urban Platforms for Capital*, as we have argued. Using this conceptual cornerstone throughout our chapters, we showed that urban skateboarding provides youth with various benefits that are social, cultural, and economic in nature. Ultimately, these capital platforms were created by complex and evolving social-enterprise networks beholden to a *variety* of stakeholders, such as those listed above, and their differing societal-change agendas. The provision of skate-park platforms in the Bay Area was therefore not centralized or standardized, because social-enterprise networks in each skate park had unique sets of people with their own preferred goals and processes.

Synthesizing the findings of the case-study chapters below, we explain how *Urban Platforms for Capital* were originally designed by well-intentioned adults in their communities. These skate parks eventually fostered unique social networks that were clearly intended to provide new values and meanings to American families in line with certain public-private interests. We consequently explain the proclivity of *Moving Boarders* parents to directly participate in urban skateboarding in an unprecedented manner. We go on to dissect how broader American parenting trends, pertaining to life-skill acquisition as well as social diversity, profoundly shaped the *Moving Boarders* parents' engagements with specific skate parks.

Altogether, what this means is that parents and other adults representing corporate, government, and social-activist interests consistently understood that urban skateboarding could be used as a new developmental tool for youth. That being said, the overall portrait of adult intervention also provokes new thinking around the place of youth to construct their own values and identities through urban skateboarding. This chapter concludes with critical discussions regarding the potential for enhanced youth agency and social diversity in urban skateboarding.

Neoliberalism and the Rise of Urban Skate Parks

The discussion in chapter 1 first signaled how neoliberal practice is substantially infused within youth sports. Participation in youth sports, we showed, is now being greatly shaped by the fundamental socioeconomic shift toward privatization. Neoliberal policies and belief systems have undoubtedly ushered in a greater role for the private sector instead of the state. Consequently, we documented the trend of decreased public funding for youth sports. Although the concept of youth sports used to be conceptualized almost monolithically, as a public service offered by state entities such as parks-and-recreation departments or the Police Athletic League, it has since been reenvisioned under the neoliberal worldview. This means that, in general, "low-cost, public, neighborhood-based youth sports have . . . been replaced by more expensive private programmes."[6] Private stakeholders now bring forth new agendas in line with their own needs and requirements. These stakeholders also utilize new ways of creating infrastructure and providing resources.

Our chapters concomitantly demonstrated that skateboarding is being greatly influenced by this contemporary, privatized vision of youth sports. Skateboarding has been widely and perhaps romantically known for its DIY and nonconformist ethos. But researchers now believe that skateboarding's value system easily merges with private-sector ideologies and mechanisms. In fact, it has been found that skateboarding reflects the broader trend whereby "countercultural values have become significantly marketable within contemporary post-Fordist economy."[7] The words of one cultural observer, Adam Arvidsson, indeed frame how certain values, which we often associate with skateboarding, are considered useful in today's world.

> The new values, practices and moral visions that emerged with the counterculture have served to legitimize a general transformation of the ways in which production and consumption are governed and organized. Concepts like "anti-authoritarianism" and "self-realization" have been appropriated and translated into central

catchwords of the "new economy" such as "flexibility" or "lifestyle choice."[8]

What this means is that activities that are imbued with the above attributes have gained immense private-sector attention. Of course, urban skateboarding culture has often historically fit with Arvidsson's criteria. As such, urban skateboarding mirrors the desired attributes of living and working in the new economy.

Simultaneously, the private sector is now unabashedly making money from skateboarding, to the point where it cannot be denied that "skateboarding has a complex relationship with commercial culture."[9] As one scholar explains, "The encroachment of big business into skateboard culture is increasingly regarded in positive terms."[10] On a regular basis, the private sector has participated in mainstream product marketing and sponsorship via skateboarding. And it is obvious how the private sector's desire to reach a mainstream audience has led to major investment in family-friendly skateboarding.

Our chapters consequently revealed how the private sector's profound interest in skateboarding manifested in each skate park. The case chapters explored how urban skateboarding, often misperceived as shunning mainstream ways, actually involved numerous profit-making groups, along with their specific agendas and ways of working. And it was intriguing that these private interests fluidly spanned *both* core and family-friendly skate contexts; these twin contexts were delineated by Mike the skate coach earlier in this chapter.

The Levi's sponsorship of Town Park was perhaps the most overt instance of private-sector involvement in the more traditional, core skate market. Here, we saw that urban skateboarding had strong appeal within the youth-branding market. Town Park was valued because it reflected the type of skateboarding more often associated with an edgier, male street style. Participants in this type of "cool" and "hip" urban skate scene are usually given cultural kudos.[11] We observed that this street-style connotation permeated West Oakland's evolving social scene; as we said in Chapter 4, Oakland's gritty authenticity was even acknowledged by the mayor as being the "special" element that attracted new visitors and residents.[12] We therefore suggest that Town Park's urban, masculine skate style came to resemble a new, desirable social "taste," signifying multiethnic, West Coast "street cultural cool."[13] It is thus unsurprising that a major multinational corporation like Levi's came on board and decided to make such a large, unprecedented investment in this skate park.

We pointed out earlier in the book that major public disinvestment is occurring within youth sports. Likewise, in Oakland, it became apparent that private-sector support from Levi's and other supporters was necessary for Town Park's existence. Indeed, this skate park's development was overwhelmingly a derivative of the Levi's urban, masculine-themed branding strategy, which merged with K-Dub's mission to develop a skateboarding space for local young men. Assistance from the City of Oakland was quite limited, in this regard, and perhaps for good reason. Public funding for Oakland's parks-and-recreation services was recently considered "in peril," with the department said to be facing "lean times."[14] And, we have personally met with several youth-sports groups in Oakland that have fundraised in order to create their own facilities. The leader of one local youth soccer program, known as the Futbolistas, has even openly wondered, "What does it mean to have space to play?"[15] Eventually this group initiated a social movement that led to the creation of their own soccer field.

Therefore, a private citizen, K-Dub, and his private supporters came to the fore and mostly created a new, vibrant skate-park scene. We argued in chapter 4 that there was a clear rationale for K-Dub's network to evolve in one of Oakland's most historic, politicized neighborhoods. Together, K-Dub and his social-enterprise group of supporters addressed the city's chronic lack of youth-sports spaces and resources.

Town Park's concrete makeover thus clearly illustrates how private capital and business expertise can be systematically infused into local-level youth sports. Meanwhile, when this type of investment occurs, the private sector greatly benefits, too. The efforts of Levi's were promoted through a documentary film and numerous social-media outlets. Town Park was also featured within the Levi's spring 2015 collection roll-out.[16] We can therefore see how this type of corporate support in urban youth sports also promotes and sells products. Coinciding with this type of major corporate investment, we observed that local companies, such as Martinson's hardware company, were also brought into the fold to support Town Park's mission. These companies were often enlisted through personal connections and they further contributed expertise, materials, and labor. We found that, as a result, these companies received positive exposure and kudos both in the skate scene and in various social-media outlets.

Broadening our scope now, we can see that when private investment in the other *Moving Boarders* skate parks occurred, it often followed the belief that skateboarding could reach a wider audience that included families and women. Places like Lake Cunningham and Bay City actively courted and received additional private-sector support in line with newer ideas about skateboarding being a more mainstream activity. Often, key stakeholders in these skate parks, identified below, felt that *even more* private-sector support would benefit their services and causes. Public funding shortfalls had major impacts on both of these skate parks and their capacity to operate in a more inclusive, family-friendly manner.

In chapter 3, we described how Bay City's new skate park was jump-started with a slew of public funds exceeding $2 million. While this seemed to indicate a strong municipal commitment to skateboarding, we also learned that private-sector help was still desired and needed. This seemed necessary given Bay City's front-loaded public-funding approach; this meant that subsequent programming required private support. For instance, upon construction, a skate academy, camps, and lessons were soon installed and run by the city, as well as Mike, the skate coach. We learned that these youth programs were well-attended, and thus became lucrative sources of funding. Then, we once overheard a city official declare during a town-hall meeting that a rich private donor, a "Daddy Warbucks" type, would be useful to fund further infrastructure. Furthermore, Jane told us that the city expected the Bay City supporter group to secure its own private funding to host progressive social events. This was not always feasible. For instance, we learned that the group's plans to host a nonprofit event with A.Skate, an autism advocacy group, was unsuccessful due to insufficient funds. Lack of sustainable municipal funding for skate programming became further apparent to us when we saw one female skate group cease operations here. Thus, despite substantial public funding to build the skate park, Bay City still required private-sector assistance and in some cases fell short in its mission to support various youth skateboarding causes.

San Jose's numerous skate parks, two of which we analyzed in chapter 5, further exemplify the key role of private investment in youth skateboarding activity. San Jose's skate parks initially benefitted from significant city-government funding, too, reflecting capital-development funds derived from nearby Silicon Valley. Silicon Valley's economy contributed major funding for the city's Parks, Recreation, and Neighborhood Service (PRNS) department; this meant that the PRNS could take on a proactive role in programming and resourcing its youth sports. Yet despite this apparent prosperity, the PRNS openly utilized the private sector to support its urban skate projects. In fact, according to one San Jose city employee, "With a lot of infrastructure across the United States, like there's money to build it, but hardly to maintain it. Driving up and down the freeways of California, okay they built it, but where is [the money] to fix all this stuff? Same thing in our city."

Recall from chapter 5 that San Jose went on to solicit private funding from a range of corporations, foundations, and citizens in order to rescue the Lake Cunningham skate park. One comment provided during the 2011 campaign to save the skate park from closure crystallizes this desire to privatize urban space. According to one district councilwoman at the time, "That's not our forte, running amusement parks." She then suggested, "I think we can turn it into a profit center. From a business perspective, I think that park could really be a star."[17]

After this skate park was saved, the city hired an "Action Sports Specialist" to program skate events while simultaneously developing new private funding streams. What's more, a consultant was hired to identify a branding strategy that could be pitched to companies, "to seek sponsorship," as one city manager suggested. This practice of privatizing action sports was subsequently used to build a new bike park adjacent to the Lake Cunningham skate park site, at a cost of over $3.2 million. The city instituted a "fund development strategy" to generate "sustainable sponsorships and donations annually" to build up its new action-sports park, comprising both skateboarding and biking.[18] We can thus see how public money alone was deemed insufficient by San Jose to drive its lofty action-sports goals. At the same time, it is noteworthy that neighborhood skate parks like Roosevelt were not promoted and privatized to a high degree. We later discuss how these skate parks served a different purpose within the city's action-sports portfolio.

Given certain gaps in public funding, it is no coincidence that private-industry contributions and mechanisms were relied upon by Town Park, Bay City, and Lake Cunningham. And with the intake of new participants in urban skateboarding, which includes more youth of color, families, and women and girls of all ages, the private sector has acknowledged the potential benefits to be gained by working together with city leaders and nonprofit organizations. Thus, it cannot be denied that the private sector has seized upon skateboarding's expanding popularity and now steers significant investment toward urban, youth-centric skateboarding. This private investment helped to create infrastructure and/or sustainably run local operations. We thus introduced the concept of social enterprise to conceptualize how new, innovative public-private networks emerged to advance skate parks; these groups blurred the traditional boundaries that previously existed between the free-market economy, government bodies, and civil society.[19] Next, we further delve into how the *Moving Boarders* skate parks incorporated specific social-enterprise groups that were committed to making specific social changes across various communities.

Social-Enterprise Networks: How Multiple Interests Create Social Change

We will now take a closer look across the range of social-enterprise groups featured in our case-study chapters. In fact, *all* of the skate parks that we researched were built and/or operated through specific coalitions representing for- and non-profit sector interests. At the same time, the regular integration of social-enterprise groups in skate parks made us wonder about the impact and sustainability of their social contributions.

Perhaps unexpectedly, we discovered that nonprofit social-activist organizations focused upon youth skateboarding had a major impact upon the *Moving Boarders* skate parks. These organizations actively created new values and opportunities for families and youths in Bay Area communities. This trend of nonprofit groups working to make social change in fact exists on a national scale. There are over one million nonprofit organizations in the United States; these groups take in a range of different funding sources in order to provide community and social services.[20] It is therefore unsurprising that in 2010 nonprofits together accumulated funds that would reflect the world's seventh largest economy.[21] And in today's neoliberal climate, these types of organizations are now "increasingly relied upon to provide social services in the United States" in a "system that has come to be known as the Nonprofit Industrial Complex."[22]

What is most important here, however, is how these numerous nonprofit organizations mix in with other forms of public and private resourcing to comprise social-enterprise coalitions. This is necessary, as scholar Daniel Bjärsholm reminds us, since "organizations within all sectors of society, and particularly those within the nonprofit sector, have been encouraged, and in many cases forced, to compete for a diminishing governmental budget while simultaneously minimizing their excessive dependence on government funding."[23] Profoundly impacting skateboarding in our research sites, several nonprofit organizations utilized private-sector models and partners to make social change through skateboarding; their social-enterprise approach exemplifies the changing landscape of urban youth sports in neoliberal conditions.

As a matter of fact, some of these nonprofit groups, which we detail below, were quite savvy in terms of cultivating relationships with the private sector. This happened frequently with the nonprofit groups working at more national or even international scales. In this regard, sport sociologist Holly Thorpe reminds us that nonprofit groups such as these closely align themselves with private industries in order to remain operational.[24] Globally, she explains, these groups ally themselves with action-sports companies, hold fundraisers, and in some cases, may even try to become a marketable brand. Skateistan, which we introduced earlier in this book, has "developed highly creative, collaborative relationships with global action sport companies," according to Thorpe.[25] What this means, then, is that nonprofit-type organizations working at this macro level actually "survive, and indeed thrive, within a neo-liberally-dominated world."[26] They tend to work hand-in-hand with private businesses and multinational corporations, rather than shunning or appearing "disinterested" in this type of support.[27] Clearly, then, nonprofit groups such as the Tony Hawk Foundation (THF), featured in chapter 2, rely upon regular infusions of private-sector funding. The THF, for example, is in fact set up in sophisticated ways to accommodate this type of resourcing. It has major corporate sponsors, including Kohl's department stores, Chipotle Mexican Grill, as well as Sony and many others.[28]

In terms of social contribution, we found that the THF seemed to promote ideals of social inclusion in through research, resourcing, and design expertise that filtered down to local levels. The THF's investments in local-level skateboarding followed its conviction that skate parks should be open, visible community spaces rather than restricted and formally monitored. One of the THF's explicit aims was to create permanent "third spaces" for youth, which means that these skate spots should represent neither home nor work but instead provide another social option available to all youth.[29] The THF supports skate park projects intentionally and through local-level consultation, although it is mostly left up to community members to reinforce specific social codes and values that reflect the THF's skate vision. With its vast name recognition, major corporate sponsors, and a significant track record of building community relationships to construct skate parks, the THF thus helps to fuel unique social-enterprise coalitions. Operating in this public-private manner, the

THF and its support networks will no doubt continue to support the provision of community skate parks.

The previous chapters also illustrated how three female-focused social-activist groups were responsible for well-considered and systematic interventions at the local level. The depth of their commitment often stemmed from personal experiences they had in the male-dominated skate world. We will analyze their specific missions and social outcomes in more depth later in this chapter, when discussing the state of gender relations in urban skateboarding. For now, it suffices to say that these social-activist groups were quite explicit about how and why they promoted female participation in skateboarding as their main goal. In general, they sought to increase the number of women and girls using local skate parks. The idea here was that female skaters could act as role models to entice newcomers, and over time, create a scene built upon female inclusion and support. This followed the belief that "you can't be what you can't see," as Kim Woozy from MAHFIA.TV and SLAG once told us.

From what we saw and heard in skate parks, leaders affiliated with these female skate groups worked countless days and evenings to support their skateboarders. Early on, it became apparent to us that their work often took place on weekends, when girls and their parents were most likely to be present. Most of these leaders told us that they were essentially volunteers. In most cases, these individuals working on behalf of nonprofit female skate groups toiled extensively in the public eye and then behind the scenes. We learned that they personally promoted their organizational agendas and projects, planned and hosted skate events, gave lessons and offered tips, and also canvassed for additional funds and resources. Simultaneously, a critical activity constituting their leadership involved engaging regularly with social media.[30]

Given this extensive range of mostly unpaid work, it was not unexpected that a consistent issue arose when local chapters of social-activist groups such as Skate Like a Girl (SLAG) and Girls Riders Organization (GRO) *did not monetize* their free community-clinic models. Their largely volunteer operations had severe ramifications on their capacity to achieve their goals. At times, their efforts seemed disjointed, because of irregular programming and staffing. Thus, while these groups and their leaders worked hard to make social change in skate parks, we saw that program sustainability was a major issue especially for the local chapters of SLAG and GRO. Missing an affiliated big-name celebrity or entrepreneur, lacking profitable funding streams, and having limited public resourcing and institutionalization available to them, the activities of these groups ebbed and flowed over the duration of our research study. These volunteer-led programs thus seemed inconsistent even though the skate sessions and special events undoubtedly made a positive impact upon female skaters and their families. We will see, however, that SLAG was eventually able to develop a more sustainable model once Woozy came on board with her private-industry connections and expertise.

The MAHFIA.TV organization, led by Woozy, was more deliberately set up to generate income streams based upon the founder's sports-industry ties and knowledge. MAHFIA.TV appeared more successful both in terms of regular operation and sustainable impact on female skaters. Based on her own introduction to skateboarding through SLAG programming, Woozy definitely values ground-level projects and supports these efforts through her other media and consulting projects in the female action-sports world. Unsurprisingly, then, we recently learned that the local SLAG chapter co-hosted events with MAHFIA.TV. And, as of November 2016, SLAG's new local leader in fact became Woozy. Woozy recently told us that she was working with Town Park and other Oakland skate spots in order to promote the mission and values of SLAG. Because of her private-industry approach and connections, Woozy has in a short time been able to add many more volunteers to the SLAG chapter. Crucially, she has formed useful working relationships with several skate parks and industry partners, including GoPro and Volcom; this latter company recently provided jackets for SLAG skate coaches. Further exemplifying how Woozy utilizes private-industry links, the 510 Skate Shop, Meow Skateboards, Gnarhunters, The Skate Witches and MAHFIA.TV all teamed up during one event in 2017 to fundraise for SLAG. Famous female skateboarders such as Vanessa Torres, Elissa Steamer, Alex White, and Van Nguyen also came on this day to support the SLAG cause. It is thus unsurprising that a Facebook post from 2017 indicated that event attendance for SLAG had significantly grown over the previous few months.[31]

In chapter 2, we highlighted another local version of skate activism working in a privatized manner, in the case of Rob "Skate" Ferguson. Utilizing a highly entrepreneurial approach to social enterprise, Ferguson corralled disparate entities ranging from energy-drink companies to the Make a Wish Foundation to underpin his community work. In this regard, Ferguson went so far as to depict himself as a modern-day industrialist. In true social-enterprise fashion, Ferguson drew upon numerous government, corporate, and business sponsors in order to sustainably support his projects in underserved urban neighborhoods. We saw that his widespread youth-coaching academy and private lessons also generated considerable revenue ($60 per hour for a private lesson and $280 for six hours of camp) to support his work with free Cali Am Jam events and other community causes.[32]

We can see how Ferguson and even Woozy were both quite entrepreneurial in scope, and thus "reinvested, wholly or in large part" back into their projects to fulfill social-change missions.[33] Ferguson and Woozy also favor the "traditional characteristics associated with business entrepreneurs," like youth activists elsewhere who attempt to use profit as a means to support socially progressive agendas.[34] In her study of hip-hop youth culture, Kara-Jane Lombard characterizes such youth leaders as being "driven, determined, ambitious and creative"; as such, they are capable of galvanizing people around their organizational visions and causes.[35]

In terms of his actual social contribution, Ferguson's affiliated projects had life-skill, community-renewal, and social-inclusion goals. Our belief is that Ferguson's upbeat personality and dedication to youth mentorship enabled him to bring together many diverse stakeholders in his various projects. We glimpsed how this worked when attending feel-good and community-pride events such as the Cali Am Jam. In this type of context, which Ferguson created himself, we saw that youth, mostly urban males of color, really enjoyed themselves. They were able to showcase their abilities in front of large crowds and received accolades and prizes for their performances. What's more, Ferguson's skate lessons promoted technical skill development in a supportive, safe environment for any interested, paying parties. Ferguson has recently acknowledged that females are an important element of skateboarding, and his skate lessons definitely cater to this emerging market demographic.[36] Yet it remains to be seen how his various entrepreneurial and philanthropic activities will translate into sustainable, intensive youth development. Sometimes, as scholar Kara-Jane Lombard found in hip-hop youth programming, we felt that Ferguson's various projects provided intangible benefits by increasing the visibility and reach of skateboarding to new audiences; as such, it is difficult to ascertain any far-reaching social effects.[37] Giving skate lessons to female skaters alone does not profoundly alter the ideologies and structures that marginalize them, even though it may foster confidence and enhance physical skills in a positive learning environment. We also wonder how occasional skate contests in urban, underserved neighborhoods will translate into long-term, meaningful improvement in the lives of targeted participants. In addition, we noticed during one skate jam that only young *men* of color from the local area participated and were rewarded, thus raising concerns about gender inclusion. Buoyed by his social network, or "pipeline" as he calls it, which includes community organizations, private sponsors, and paying families that attend his skate camps and lessons, Ferguson will remain active in the local youth skateboarding scene. Looking ahead, we wonder if Ferguson can more systematically provide personal and social benefits to youths, families, and in the local communities where his projects are based.

Our concluding belief here is that social-enterprise networks and their leaders are multifaceted and fluid in terms of their make-up and approach to work. As such, they can have belief systems and processes that resonate with or diverge from each other. Interestingly, the diverse involvement of private entities in local social causes provoked divergent opinions among some of the skaters we met. For instance, one African American young man, Roberto, referred to the Levi's investment in Oakland's Town Park as "a blessing." In contrast, we spoke to a female skateboarder at Town Park who expressed conflicted feelings about the presence of this corporate intervention. She liked that the skate park was there and that it created opportunities for people of different backgrounds to discover and enjoy skateboarding. Though she was supportive, she was still concerned about how corporations and their brands might have a superficial relationship to skateboarding, as they were still using this sport in order to make money. Going mainstream gave local skateboarding immediate credibility and assistance, she admitted, but were corporations like Levi's going to be around to support local skateboarding in the long term? We thus contend that there was a spectrum of beliefs held by social-enterprise leaders and skate-park participants in relation to privatization practices.

At this point, we have demonstrated how skateboarding in our study was harnessed, in different ways, by social-enterprise practitioners in order to support both profit-making and socially progressive ends.[38] Across all of the case chapters, we saw the rise of new social-change groups that were underpinned by distinctive financial relationships and mechanisms.[39] We articulated that these groups attempted to provide certain benefits to local skate-park participants, albeit by using various methods and to different degrees of effectiveness. Next, we articulate how the cross-pollination between public and private entities in skate parks could lead to urban capital generation, by using case examples involving skate leaders, parents, and youth.

Skate Parks Serving the Social Good: Urban Platforms for Capital

Skate parks were directly established by social-enterprise groups to provide new opportunities for sets of youths, parents, and other community members. On a consistent basis, skateboarding was promoted and taken up, in essence, as a good thing for society. The specific belief that skateboarding benefits youth in terms of life skills and character development was invoked in all of the skate parks. This perspective is not new, as "the assumption that playing a sport builds character has been part of American culture for many years."[40]

To better understand the perceived benefits on offer through skateboarding, we highlighted the specific usage of action sports for character and citizenship building. This belief system is distilled by the concept of "Action Sports for Development and Peace" (ASDP). Indeed, it has been suggested elsewhere that action sports may provide "empowering learning experiences, encouraging self-expression and creative thinking and developing a different set of physical and social skills among children and youth from different socio-economic and cultural backgrounds."[41] Given these purported benefits, the theoretical ideas developed by French sociologist Pierre Bourdieu became very pertinent to our work. His scholarship provided a conceptual link between urban skateboarding's framing as a positive youth-development tool and ideas about capital creation. Bourdieu's framework gave us the impetus to analyze how individuals in skate parks invest in a set of shared meanings and practices in order to maximize social, cultural, and economic benefits for youths.[42] Consequently, *Moving Boarders* illustrates how urban youth sports participation is reliant upon how people and programs perceive the creation, usage, and conversion of these benefits, which Bourdieu characterizes as capitals.[43]

Keeping this link between youth development and capital generation in mind, we investigated how urban skateboarding was offered to families and communities through *Urban Platforms for Capital*. As shown above, skate parks have a unique constellation of stakeholders, including citizens, community leaders, city governments, private-industry representatives, and families. And, once again, key social-activist groups have conducted their work across multiple locations. Together, all of these stakeholders attempted to serve their communities through skateboarding; they consequently influenced the social activities and behaviors, belief systems, and identities that we found in skate parks.

If skateboarding has now been set up to serve the community good, then we must critically understand how skate parks, with their mixture of supporters, could actually achieve this mission. How did the eventual creation of these new urban spaces and social networks actually provide capital? The answer to this question is not straightforward. It has been extensively argued that private-sector interventions in sports, used to promote various forms of social development at the micro level, need more clarity and evidence in terms of their intended outcomes.[44] Going further, it has been said that urban youth sports do not work as a "magic bullet or miracle elixir" when it comes to developing youth and their neighborhoods.[45] Despite "massive expectations," then, it is problematic to simply assume that sports can solve urban youths' social problems, provide them with social mobility, or give them access to transferrable capitals.[46] Sociologist Jay Coakley thus concludes that we should carefully analyze "the evangelistic promise that sport participation produces positive development among young people."[47]

Therefore, although action-sports programs may "often proclaim positive outcomes" for individuals and communities,[48] we need to carefully examine the key assumptions, as well as processes, priorities, and contexts, that undergird actual programs.[49] We know that action-sports programs, including skateboarding ones, must be "well-designed and critically considered" in order to fulfill quite complex social missions.[50] Given that skateboarding interventions, like other sport programs, do not automatically have positive, linear effects on youth and society, we now pay closer attention to how each skate park "platform" actually worked toward their goals.[51] We first explain that key leaders and organizations imprinted their beliefs on individual skate parks, while attempting to create and reproduce several forms of capital. Families and youth were eventually drawn into these *Urban Platforms for Capital*. We accordingly pull together analyses from the case-study chapters to specifically illustrate parents' perspectives about capital accrual as it impacted their children. Crucially, this discussion reveals how social-class backgrounds influenced parents' decision-making processes as these led to certain types of investment. The voices and practices of youth that we encountered are then revisited, revealing how they actually navigated missions that were constituted for them by various adults.

SKATE PARK LEADERS' VIEWS ON YOUTH AND COMMUNITY DEVELOPMENT

Looking across all the chapters, we examined the workings of youth development in terms of how this was addressed by well-intentioned adults. In some cases, skate parks were designed to specifically accommodate family-friendly skateboarding. In chapter 3, for example, we explained that Bay City Skate Park was set up by its primary leaders, Jane and Mike, to mirror the social attributes of Bay City that were emerging at the time. Bay City, we explained, increasingly attracted a diverse range of professional immigrants, many of whom were newer technology-sector workers, while white middle-class residents lived in certain established areas including the neighborhood by the skate park. As such, there was an explicit attempt here to create a multicultural, family-friendly skate scene catering to the individual aspirational requirements of youths from this evolving community.

We can recall that Jane, the citizens' group leader, developed an extensive social-media community campaign based around a popular Facebook group. The Facebook group allowed a committed group of parents working alongside the skate park's leaders to promote a strong sense of adult engagement. This approach was instrumental in creating the narrative that skateboarding was a safe and healthy activity, with the family-friendly aspect being particularly accentuated. Gaining community traction, then, these Bay City adults became interested in offering programming that went beyond targeting only "core" male teenagers. Instead, they deliberately attempted to ensure that newcomers, including females, had a viable space to skateboard. Equally important, adults in the community, including those from the supporter group, continued to provide direct, ground-level oversight in the skate park. Under this adult presence, Bay City was designed to foster appropriate types of social behavior reflecting Bay City's evolving civic identity. This was further accomplished by having "authentic" skateboarders such as Mike, his coaches, and the park's rangers present in the skate park on a regular basis. These individuals were all steeped in skate culture, yet they understood and supported Bay City's family-friendly mission. These adults, too, became embedded into the skate park's social fabric and encouraged a regular parent presence.

Youth skater talking with an adult mentor at community event.
Courtesy of Todd Fuller.

And as with all skate parks in *Moving Boarders*, physical layout aligned with social-change missions. Just as the THF preferred, this skate park was in an open, visible community location that would attract a wide range of clientele. These aspects parallel Mike's own viewpoint, presented at the beginning of this chapter, that skate parks should offer something for everyone; indeed, he was involved in the skate park's design process. The deep pool in the back of the skate park attracted more veteran, core male skaters, including those who were often fathers. These men could regularly be found congregating in the back while an occasional young male might also use this space. The design of Bay City's skate park provided easy access for both beginner and advanced youths so that they could regularly and comfortably participate. It was an unbounded space, without fencing or walls, which allowed new skateboarders to freely move in and out. This enabled them to use the skate park in a "trial and error" manner. Their parents could also look inside or even enter the skate park without being right in the midst of skate maneuvers. This type of design, with plenty of newcomer-friendly elements and attributes, was not nearly as prominent in other *Moving Boarders* spots such as Roosevelt and Town Park; not surprisingly, those skate parks were much more popular with unattached, established teens and older males.

As explained in chapter 5, San Jose adults working in the government hierarchy, from city leaders down to project managers, significantly structured the local skate scene. Bolstered by a well-resourced PRNS department, we saw that, on one hand, the Lake Cunningham Regional Skate Park was designed to present the city of San Jose as a global innovation hub. Lake Cunningham was conceptualized by the city government as a preeminent action-sports destination that was appealing to the private sector. Envisioning the park as a family-friendly and healthy activity spot, the city implemented regular, intensive forms of adult control. Practices that were enacted by adults, described in chapter 5, included programmed events such as camps, overnight sleepovers, and birthday parties. This was accompanied by the implementation of entrance fees, select hours of operation, and safety requirements. Together, these practices generally provided for a family-friendly aura, albeit one that represented only a narrow slice of San Jose's overall demographics.

Just a few miles down the road, Roosevelt Skate Park, by contrast, was envisioned quite differently by the leaders and associates in San Jose government. As presented in chapter 5, we saw that this skate park was fundamentally used by the city to engage with local residents who were considered as being at-risk and in need. As a matter of fact, it could be said that Roosevelt Skate Park, of all the skate parks that we researched, most closely incorporated the long-held belief that sports can recuperate urban youth deemed underserved and "at risk."[52] The story of Roosevelt Skate Park was thus unique among the skate parks we researched. This space was refashioned to resemble late-1990s sport-based social interventions, such as Midnight Basketball, which used sports as a "hook" to attract and inspire low-income young men of color.[53] Likewise, the city's view of Roosevelt was that skateboarding could help these "hard to reach" youths become more productive, connected citizens; it was assumed that this approach would concurrently reduce danger, crime, and risk in the neighborhood.[54]

We noted earlier that, in contrast to Lake Cunningham, San Jose did not leverage Roosevelt to gain additional private-sector funding or sponsorship. Through our discussions with city leaders, we quickly understood that Roosevelt was never set up to function in this manner. Instead, Roosevelt, like San Jose's other neighborhood skate parks, was subjected to an interventionist practice called *place-making*. This agenda was deemed necessary in order to transform existing social dynamics, including youth delinquency, homelessness, and gang activity. Context is indeed crucial here, as it frames the city's motives to target the youth and their neighborhood. We said in chapter 5 that high-profile shootings and even murders in this area meant that the city of San Jose was quite avid in its attempts to transform this area by increasing adult foot traffic. The city used Viva Parks! events and the SJ 180 program to increase the adult presence and hopefully construct a family-friendly environment which seemed necessary to monitor and control youth behavior. The case of Roosevelt is thus compelling as it shows how San Jose's adult leaders sought to use sports programming in order to counter youths' seemingly "at risk" lives and identities. Yet we sensed a gap between this intervention model and the youth we met. Often, it seemed to us, youth here just wanted to hang out and decompress from other pressing life concerns and situations. Their motivation to skate also seemed to reflect desires to be part of a supportive peer group. And in this skate park they could have fun and learn while maintaining a neighborhood identity. It was also noteworthy that some youth that came to Roosevelt from other surrounding areas, including wealthier and whiter ones, were actually drawn to this type of urban youth scene.

We feel that San Jose's neighborhood skateboarding intervention model was well-intentioned and reflected a first step in terms of connecting the city government with local youths. But it also seemed simplistic in terms of how these youth of color were categorized and supported. Going forward with its skateboarding programs, the city also needs to comprehensively address existing structural issues in the local neighborhood that contribute to youth marginalization, crime, poverty, and other social concerns. In this regard, scholar Douglas Hartmann suggests that urban social interventions must balance both sports and non-sports elements, "where sport is just one part of a whole package of resources and social supports" employed to help youth on an everyday basis.[55] All too often, Hartmann contends, sports programming alone is relied upon to inexpensively address major urban social concerns, as a replacement of other social services, especially in neoliberal times.[56] Therefore, San Jose's use of skateboarding to counteract complex, entrenched social issues should be complemented by closely tying in long-term educational and social services with the sports programming. Moreover, to ensure these programs actually fit the needs and identities of youth, our belief is that the city should pay closer attention to the actual lives of Roosevelt youth, using even more embedded, day-to-day work as a starting point to obtaining this knowledge.[57]

With a growing legacy based on its status as the "Capital of Silicon Valley," San Jose positioned youth of color in Roosevelt as a focal point for its neighborhood revitalization agenda. We have concomitantly shown that the city's adults wanted youth here to be socialized into the broader community and also become job-ready. These goals became a priority for the city, in order to create a seemingly more desirable urban environment within the Roosevelt location. But, we wonder, for whom and for what reasons was the city so invested in urban neighborhood change? In one sense, we speculate that the transformative youth-development agenda in Roosevelt could perhaps be a precursor to yet another trendy city district, as we saw in West Oakland. It is not far-fetched to believe that, in its urban "core" neighborhoods, San Jose will create new social conditions that will invite gentrification, much as we saw with Oakland's 10K Plan. We believe this to be true especially given Roosevelt's close proximity to San Jose's downtown amenities and university campus; already, adjacent neighborhoods have been identified as prone to gentrification and subsequent resident displacement.[58] What's more, the Google corporation is now making "serious" investments into downtown San Jose areas, seeking to create a village of new residences, retail stores, and buildings for several thousand workers.[59] So, does this mean that Roosevelt may come to resemble Town Park in the future? That is, will it constitute another edgy-yet-cool urban space that can be branded and promoted? And how might this shift come under the city's desire to embrace what scholar Nicola De Martini Ugolotti refers to as "cosmopolitan urbanism?"[60] Ugolotti's concept encapsulates how "politicians, planners and boosters" have initiated rebranding processes in post-industrial urban centers as part of their neoliberal "urban regeneration" missions. She suggests that those advancing urban-change agendas want "to attract 'global talent,' financial capital and tourism by revaluing urban space." What this means is that cities often present a progressive image of cultural and ethnic diversity to attract new capital-rich and creative professionals. Indeed, as we have seen in Oakland, these latter individuals seem to have a "taste for difference." Or, as scholars Richard Florida and Gary Gates simply put it, "Talent powers economic growth, and diversity and openness attract talent."[61]

While Oakland is also undergoing city-led urban change, Town Park illustrates how an adult-facilitated skateboarding intervention can generate meaningful, sustainable youth capital by directly tapping in to an existing neighborhood culture and identity. Just like in San Jose, youths in Oakland have been historically underserved. Despite Oakland's recent makeover as a "hot" and "welcoming oasis"[62] it has been identified that local youths still experience entrenched poverty and high exposure to crime. We also showed in chapter 4 that Oakland's youth lack sports infrastructure, too. This reality was the impetus for adults like K-Dub and his social-enterprise network to create a new skate spot that could benefit youths' lives and futures.

As gentrification materialized, adults here became concerned about the number of new people coming into the local area. There seemed to be a circulating belief that the established African American community, along with its youth, could be supplanted. Indeed, as one African American father, Matt, declared to us, "You don't see any black kids in the neighborhood. . . . Now there are lots of young professionals with no kids." With the proverbial writing on the wall, K-Dub's intervention sought to make Town Park youths more socially aware and active members in the established neighborhood. At the same time, Town Park enabled these youths to follow their own unique pursuits and dreams involving sponsorships and/or work in private creative industries. K-Dub thus imparted the need for youth to leverage their urban capital or "hood cred"; because other, outsider youths were already doing this. K-Dub, as the leader of Oakland's *Urban Platform for Capital*, had close knowledge of the local culture and its youths in terms of their needs and identities. Indeed, he effectively merged his own social-work background with the political-activist practices that have hallmarked life in this neighborhood since the end of the Second World War.

Meanwhile, given the capital being reproduced in this skate park, it might be tempting to think that K-Dub, with his artistic, skateboarding background, as well as intimate knowledge of the cultural scene, would seek to profit himself. In fact, this "punky" and "rag tag" skate scene, as K-Dub called it, was becoming popular and trend-setting; this gave it access to more capital within the neoliberal economy. This resonates with Richard Lloyd's ideas about how creative and street cultures carry attributes that are highly sought after "in a changing urban economy," as they align with "the entrepreneurial imperatives of neoliberal capitalism."[63] We have seen many other skate-park leaders, including celebrities, entrepreneurs, and coaches, use private-sector mechanisms to obtain various forms of personal capital. However, we explained in chapter 4 that K-Dub explicitly rejected the practice of creating a personal brand from which to profit. Instead, alongside this skate park's growing cultural reputation and value, K-Dub positioned underserved youth of color at the forefront of Oakland's rising skateboarding scene.

Reflecting organic street culture, Town Park was designed to generate youth capital based on spontaneous and unsupervised youth activity.[64] Here, there was no formal adult or even government presence working to consistently transform youths' conduct and identities. And Town Park abstained from using regular surveillance and entry mechanisms found in other skate parks such as Lake Cunningham. Furthermore, K-Dub did not envision himself as being a police officer, as he once told us. Although, as he said, it was important for him to show up and serve as a role model. Testifying to this belief, we often saw K-Dub making "his rounds," that is, doing routine maintenance and cleaning up while greeting and talking with skaters. Sometimes, when he appeared, youths received money to do light maintenance jobs, as one recent news story observed: "On a recent afternoon, Williams paid two boys $20 to sweep and clean up trash. He makes sure he gets his money's worth. 'That only looks like 11 so far,' he yells across the park."[65]

This form of adult presence seemed to reflect an ethic of care, even as it was limited in scope. It seemed intended to facilitate a self-regulating atmosphere amongst youth (as explained later in this chapter). Rather than emphasizing a more deficit-oriented, recuperative viewpoint, as found in San Jose's neighborhood skate parks, K-Dub considered these local youths as having intrinsic assets and backgrounds that they could use to help each other generate much-needed forms of capital. K-Dub did not want to "place-make" or "repurpose" space like city officials in San Jose did. Rather, his goal was for African American youths to preserve existing elements of the local neighborhood culture in order to solidify their collective right to remain in and benefit from Oakland.

Altogether, we have shown that skate parks were constituted by government and citizen leaders in alignment with existing micro-conditions found within each city and its neighborhoods. Local context thus gave strong connotations for how *Moving Boarders* skate parks were designed to offer capital to local youths, both individually and collectively. Next, we frame our discussion of *Moving Boarders* skate parks around parents' viewpoints to see how they engaged with *Urban Platforms for Capital* set up in local communities.

PARENTS' USE OF URBAN SKATE PARKS FOR CAPITAL REPRODUCTION

Throughout this book, we have argued that skate parks are essentially "lived" social spaces that are negotiated by various people developing new meanings and ways of using them.[66] This concept has ramifications for how parents experienced these skate parks. Parental involvement in these skate parks, we contend, reflected the general belief that these spaces were prime sources of capital for children. We saw in our case-study chapters how many skate parents, like parents in other youth sports, perceived that their children could develop new physical and life skills, social networks, and cultural traits. The hope, then, was that this type of developmental experience, via skateboarding, would in time benefit youths in their broader lives.

At the same time, when taking into account all of the parent voices about youth development, we can see that there actually were some nuanced aspects of skate parenting that indicated diverse approaches, backgrounds, and interests. Next, we turn to discuss how each set of skate-park parents were specifically beholden to certain youth-development beliefs in line with their particular parenting identities and values.[67] Social-class distinctions, we shall also explain, played a key role in distinguishing parental views and expectations and determined their subsequent investments.

In Town Park, some parents had views that at times resonated with their peers in other skate parks we researched. There was some commonality, then, in terms of how these parents were invested in youth-development attributes such as patience, resilience, cooperation, self-confidence, and work ethic. Town Park was seen by these parents as a safe, supportive, and even community-oriented youth network that was guided by K-Dub. This type of social space was valued by local parents, many of whom had little time or resources to be active in their children's everyday skateboarding. In this way, these Town Park parents, like many others in *Moving Boarders*, appreciated the adult presence and sense of oversight, although this attribute was more implicit here when compared with Bay City and Lake Cunningham.

But in Town Park these positive youth-development ideals, highlighted above, were sometimes contextualized by parents according to the specific, compelling conditions of low-income, urban poverty. Life here could be a struggle even involving death and incarceration, as one African American father, Trent, once suggested. A few statements from Trent illustrate how youth development was seen as crucial in this neighborhood: "Be like, 'Okay. Yes, I can do this. Get back up. Keep going.' As long as you say, 'I got up and tried,' you win. Got to keep that mind in motion." Comments like these reflected an intensity forged by tough urban circumstances not found in some of the other skate parks we researched. In fact, we heard this type of view expressed by several other Town Park parents, as when Camille observed that youth in this "low-income neighborhood" needed skateboarding to stay clean and not be on the "street corner and do drugs, sell drugs." She thus seemed to be referencing how youths here got caught up in street life sometimes; to counter this, she said that skateboarding taught resilience: "They fall but they get back up and they try it again." Our point here is that these Town Park parents strongly supported Town Park because they wanted their children to gain survival traits like resilience and determination. Attributes like these were considered necessary to navigate the everyday realities of Oakland life, which could be "really crazy," as one youth, Roberto, said in chapter 4. This type of parental viewpoint resonates with the work of scholars Tom Martinek and Don Hellison, who believe that sports and physical education can promote youth resiliency and persistence, in order to counter life in underserved, urban neighborhoods.[68]

At the same time, Town Park parents seemed to frame youth-development ideals in the context of West Oakland's unique community ethos. It was said by many parents that people from this area, with means or not, historically supported each other to get through hard times. Youth skateboarding was considered an extension of this practice. In this regard, peer learning practices, involving locals and even "out-of-towners," as one mother called them, were considered vital as these supportive interactions directly exemplified West Oakland cultural values. Town Park stood alone in this sense, as parents wanted youth to develop capital according to historical and community factors, instead of just individualistic ways.[69] And in fact, research indicates that few sports programs working to develop youth actually take up this type of approach, of strengthening community ties and cultural institutions; nor do they usually empower youth to be agents of social change.[70]

Another key finding is that some parents that we met in Town Park and Roosevelt wanted their children to engage with both social risk and diversity in autonomous ways. They felt that youths' independent engagements were necessary for true development to occur, within skate contexts that were generally less regulated by adults. In these spaces, some parents felt, youth could socialize and learn about the realities of urban life. Roosevelt dad Manny, for instance, stated that he appreciated this skate park because "it's not driven, it's not controlled by adults. Kids do it. She [his daughter Mia] is making those decisions herself, and it's just happening organically." This was a practice that he deemed navigating the "urban landscape." We also recall the words of Matt, an African American father, who said that Town Park was "like a little social testing ground" where children could learn to solve their own conflicts. These poignant examples from the case-study chapters illustrate how some parents wanted their children to traverse open, socially diverse urban environments in a more independent manner.

In comparison to these latter viewpoints, parents going to Lake Cunningham and Bay City usually held to more traditional ideals of youth development often found in other youth sports. Once again, the idea of a skate park being serviced by knowledgeable adults is important because this invites parents beholden to the more traditional forms of youth development. In conditions marked by high states of adult monitoring, including the regular presence of expert coaching, parents seemed quite happy to let their kids skate. Meanwhile, these parents were able to take a more hands-on role with the intention of ensuring children's personal safety and growth. These parents, not unexpectedly, often came from more middle- to upper-class, professional backgrounds. Available research suggests that these parents often conceptualize their children as being developmental projects. This means that parents with more resources and time look for opportunities where their children can obtain specific abilities and attributes that will purportedly help them.[71]

In this regard, many parents appreciated Bay City Skate Park

Locals describe Town Park as having a family-like atmosphere. *Courtesy of Keith Williams.*

although some still had reservations about potential antisocial behavior being a negative influence. In fact, within this skate park, there were some times when more traditional skate culture was observed. We learned that youth behaviors such as swearing, drinking, and smoking could occur at certain times. And yet, Bay City Skate Park still regularly functioned as a safe, family-friendly environment due to its strong adult presence. In fact, this space was regularly supervised by a park ranger, coaches, and parents, and it was also well-lit, with "thirty-four lights!" as proclaimed by one community leader. In this space, there were formal coaching lessons offered by Mike, while other informal mentoring practices were enacted by the older male skate crowd in the back bowl. In fact, as mentioned in chapter 3, these men often had children themselves. Altogether, these adult-led practices were appreciated by Bay City skate parents who saw them as beneficial to their own children's development of key life skills.

The skate park at Lake Cunningham was valued by parents because it was more regulated and socially exclusive, even compared to Bay City Skate Park, which had more of a mixed demographic and free-flow feel. The San Jose city government installed various gatekeeping mechanisms in Lake Cunningham to ensure a safe and controlled skate experience which became important for the parents who were interested in youth development. One mother featured in chapter 5, Alexa, gave a representative opinion amongst these parents, about why she went there, when claiming that "it just seems nicer, more comfortable, safer."

In many ways, then, these two well-designed, expansive, and expensively built skate parks were highly sought after by some parents because children could skate in a safe, monitored environment. Youth-sports parenting in this more intensive, structured manner resembles a core parenting task, once again revolving around the idea of individualized child "cultivation."[72] This type of skate parent, like many others in American youth sports, is cognizant of American neoliberal society's preoccupation with representing good parenting skills.[73] Family skateboarding in Bay City and Lake Cunningham was thus often used to exemplify ideal forms of parenting. And these parents, like those we met elsewhere, were mostly non-skateboarders or beginners themselves, usually uninterested in traditional "core" skate culture. Parents in these parks appreciated that their children could try a new sport and develop new friendship networks while learning new technical skill sets. And these parents, much like their peers in the other skate parks, felt that their children could obtain vital life skills.

Because these parents explicitly wanted their children to develop by acquiring various new capitals, they often protected their children from certain perceived risks and dangers. Recall the self-identified "helicopter" parents from Bay City's annual town-hall gathering, which we described in chapter 3's opening. These parents sought to eradicate behaviors such as swearing, drinking, and marijuana smoking. Reflecting how Bay City was a contested social space, comprising diverse demographic elements, these parents said that they took matters into their own hands by confronting offending skaters when necessary. In the case of Lake Cunningham, we also found this same practice of risk- and danger-limitation in the name of "good" parenting practice, as exemplified by one father, Bernie. He was unapologetic about his distaste for skateboarding's stereotypical outlaw attributes. His comments below are quite evocative and worth sharing here, as they perfectly illustrate this protective version of skate parenting:

> There are some aspects of skateboarding that obviously are—that can, kind of, lead people on the wrong path too because it's, by nature, a very rebel sport. So, there's people that get deep into it and fall into pitfalls. It's affected many people. Many people have, kind of, gotten deep into the culture. That pathway is something that I would actually steer my kids very carefully away from just because it's something that I think—there's a darker side of skateboarding. You don't have to be a badass to be a skateboarder, you know, but it just seems like the underlying image of skateboarding is people who just don't care and fuck rules.

This kind of extensive parent involvement and oversight reflected how some *Moving Boarders* parents wanted to demonstrate that they were "good," rather than being neglectful, bad, or even "wild," as skate mom Amy declared in chapter 3. Consequently, it is clear that, for these skate parents, one form of parenting is given credence over another. This reflects the "normalisation of concerted cultivation as a parenting strategy for all" which can then lead to the notion "that parents not able to or willing to engage in such activities will be positioned as offering inadequate parenting."[74] And, as has been pointed out in the literature, it is often poorer families that lack adequate resources and time to participate in intensive youth-sports cultivating practices.[75] This means that these types of parents can be demonized by those with more capacity to invest in their children.

What's more, in conjunction with the belief that parents should mitigate risk by playing a pronounced role in their children's development, there was a view provided in both Bay City and Lake Cunningham that skateboarding uniquely provided opportunities for the development of emotional closeness between parents and their children. Several parents that we spoke to in these two skate parks even tried to skate alongside their children. For example, one father, named Cal, in Bay City declared, "I will go with them [his kids] and do a 'rock to fakie' [a skate maneuver] and everything." Bernie, the highly protective dad from Lake Cunningham, once claimed, "It's something that we enjoy together. . . . It's something that we do—just kind of mix it in with the other fun activities that I do when I have fun with them." This parent-child bonding practice was much rarer in Town Park and Roosevelt, according to what we saw, as these were more youth-focused spaces with more older children and fewer parents around.

In regards to this type of close parenting practice, some scholars have found that traditional youth sports can support states of emotional closeness; this means that parents can foster meaningful relationships with their kids and be integral parts of their lives while sharing a common interest.[76] We certainly came away feeling that skateboarding's more fluid and open format allowed for parents to bond with their children on a regular basis. But there were some instances within Bay City and Lake Cunningham where some of these practices pointed to "over-involved, over-protective parents."[77] Here is one prime example that speaks clearly to our analysis: Cal, from Bay City, initially said that spending time skateboarding with his daughter was essentially an investment in her future. "Here I will spend all of my money on my stuff . . . and when they grow up they might do something interesting." Later in the interview, Cal claimed that he was motivated to skateboard alongside his daughter in order to control her activity. He wanted to influence her educational trajectory. "[She says], 'Will you come and let me watch my TV show?' 'Yeah, whatever.' No, we don't do that. We just focus kind of more about kid's activities. So we configure the day that I can control her, I can be with her, good guidance and then it's up to her what's a good college."

Findings such as this one resonate closely with the claim that parents, often those with more resources and professional backgrounds, envision youth sports as one component of their children's future success, amongst a host of other possible activities.[78] We found that some *Moving Boarders* parents, usually in the higher socioeconomic levels, enacted this more privatized, instrumental childrearing approach.[79] This practice was based on their own specific views of success in education and the economy. In our neoliberal society, we must again remember that many parents regularly seek out contexts where they can provide individual benefits for their own children, instead of seeing youth development as part of building stronger communities and reinforcing cultural values.[80] Town Park seemed to be the one exception where parents advocated for developing youth capital in accordance with historic, communal values found in the local community. This practice, it was hoped, would eventually give more opportunities to youth while improving living conditions in West Oakland more broadly.

The more individualized parenting approach, as commonly found in our study, often lent itself to overt, hands-on parenting practice. Certain outcomes were, of course, directly expected from this type of parental involvement. We thus contemplated how youth themselves envisioned and experienced skateboarding. What did *they* want from skate-park participation? Going forward, we now shift away from discussing adult perspectives in order to engage more closely with ideas held by youth that we met and observed in our research.

YOUTH PERSPECTIVES OF SKATE PARK BENEFITS

> Many of our loved ones had run for their lives as bullets flew. We heard our friend Terrence McCrary, aka T-Mack—who we had been hanging out with only moments before—had been shot . . . . The past week has been traumatic for young people in Oakland.[81]

These statements originated from a young person writing in the *East Bay Express*, a local weekly. The author was reflecting upon the shooting death of her friend and popular local skateboarder, Terrence "T-Mack" McCrary. Not long after his death, a "skate jam" memorial was organized and hosted in Berkeley skate park by local skaters. This skate park, which we researched on several occasions, has since been renamed Terrence McCrary Memorial Park. Testifying to the power of youth to find their own social meanings, identities, and codes through skate park life, the following written reflection was given to us by one memorial attendee:

> The skate jam I attended opened my eyes to the true essence of what love is. The jam is the first of many to come. T-Mack forever lives a part of us and he will never be forgotten. I can only imagine how many people he inspired, including myself to continue skating and BEING ABSOLUTELY DIFFERENT (BAD) in society. May he rest in peace, and roll forever in our hearts.

The T-Mack example is so poignant because it signals the deep attachment that youth may have for urban skateboarding and their peers.

The stories from *Moving Boarders* skate parks indicate how adults regularly determined the role and usage of skateboarding in youths' lives. The enactment of adult regulatory practices, across several skate parks, was often intended to alleviate conditions of risk and danger. This approach was meant to demonstrate adults' commitment to supporting skateboarding youth, to ultimately promote life-skill and character development. But, despite good adult intentions, it is critical to understand how youths themselves participated and created capital in their urban spaces.

Lake Cunningham was actually the most glaring example of adult-driven skate practice, as it came to resemble what scholars Robert Rinehart and Christopher Grenfell call a "Disneyfied" action-sports space, with its adult control mechanisms, rather than being a more youth-created context.[82] This skate park seemed to function like an irregularly used drop-in space for a range of youth and their families. This type of environment parallels the Vans indoor/outdoor BMX circuit based in a shopping mall that was researched by Rinehart and Grenfell.[83]

Bay City, because of high parental involvement, was sometimes a space where youth were heavily subjected to adult desires and belief systems. Recall that one mother, Amy, said in chapter 3 that her son should not pick up habits from the more core skateboarders, otherwise he would be grounded from skateboarding. Another mother, Toral, would confront older youth and change their behaviors in order to create better conditions for her son. Let's also return here to high-tech worker Cal, from Bay City. We can recall that Cal scheduled his daughter's skateboarding, and even skated with her, so that she could gain life skills seemingly needed to get into "a good college." But Cal's approach also had a negative impact. We asked his daughter about their skateboarding, and she confided, "Sometimes if I do something wrong or something like I had trouble doing 'rock to fakie' he'd help me then he'd get frustrated and he'd get angry at me and stuff, so. Yeah. Sometimes I like it, but then when he gets angry I don't like it." This instance of "overparenting," typifying a highly controlling parenting style, shows how adults hoping to guide youth activity can actually foster negative youth outcomes including childhood anxiety.[84]

Nevertheless, youth we met and observed in Bay City and Lake Cunningham still seemed to have fun in their controlled surroundings. But this type of skateboarding was also noticeable because it often came under the influence of parents' expectations and structuring. And, the family-friendly element that we researched in these skate parks often skated together in certain areas. This "people like us" type of sporting experience, scholar Fred Coalter contends, promotes a state of bonding whereby familiar individuals reinforce certain social values and ties, which can lead to conformity and even exclusivity.[85]

By contrast, if we return to the T-Mack memorial in Berkeley skate park, there are possibilities that urban skateboarding can serve as a context where young people can generate their own preferred types of activity experiences, relationships, and identities. Clearly, skate spaces in poorer neighborhoods with older youth were more "idiosyncratic" and "self-constructed."[86] Roosevelt, Town Park, and even Bay City at certain times fostered youthful relationships reflecting mutual respect and trust amongst diverse participants. We regularly saw youth in these spaces practicing tricks and moves together for hours at a time without adult supervision.

In some cases, youth even seemed to challenge the presence of adults in skate spaces. This practice was most apparent in Roosevelt's skate park, where we sometimes saw youth enact resistant behavior, both verbally and nonverbally, toward adult surveillance. While they genuinely seemed to appreciate the embedded presence of Danny Sanchez from SJ 180, we did observe the youth mocking the regular police patrols, with beer bottles in tow and smirks on their faces. The skateboarders almost seemed to be deliberately acting cocky and/or unperturbed as they were being surveilled. The youth obviously knew that they were being closely watched by the police; in response they seemed to deliberately present a "cool pose" attitude. This type of empowering posturing was famously described in the work of Richard Majors and Janet Mancini Billson as a dignified, confident response that inner-city young males of color regularly enact in the face of powerlessness and adversity.[87] These Roosevelt youth likewise enacted "counter-conducts" toward intensive monitoring practices.[88] In fact, the police, as we mentioned in chapter 5, often sped onto the pavement right next to the skate park, and would take up an oppositional, aggressive stance from the adjacent parking lot for long periods of time.

Town Park in some ways was similar to Roosevelt, in the sense that youth here mostly determined their own behavior and learning, with adults being more secondary to their actual participation. The difference, though, was that in Town Park youth were *authorized and indeed expected* to have a strong sense of agency. As described in chapter 4, K-Dub established a new skate scene that was reliant upon historical neighborhood values. And yet, utilizing the principles of neoliberalism rather than shunning them, K-Dub pushed for a form of youthful self-determination that has been called *indigenous governance* by scholar Kara-Jane Lombard; this means that since the city essentially governed Town Park "from a distance," the actual "responsibility for skate-park development lies with skaters."[89]

Under a more limited form of adult control, then, youth here were expected to enact what sociologist Jay Coakley deems "player control" in youth sports.[90] One example of this is that, when social confrontations occurred, it was the skaters themselves that basically handled it, according to K-Dub. He once told us, "I've had some people I had to get ugly with, but you know, I think the couple of times [I] had to do it other people stepped in like, 'Dude, you need to leave man. Don't . . . this is our guy here. He's the reason why we're here. Don't do this. You just walk.'"

Together, Town Park and Roosevelt, as well as Bay City at times, offered spaces for youth to skate mostly on their own terms. These spaces became very popular with many young men and also some women. This type of unstructured youth practice undoubtedly lent itself to social-capital generation. What this means is that, left to their own devices, youth skateboarders were able to create new friendships, a sense of camaraderie, and support for those in difficult circumstances.[91] Thus, our critique of adult-led skateboarding practices, when these were dominant in some skate parks, is that they sometimes obscured youths' capacity to engage with peers and activities in ways that were most relevant to them. By contrast, youth-driven skateboarding seems to foster new types of belief systems, relationships, and identities.

Highlighting the ways in which youth might drive their own skate park experiences can be an important way of rethinking *Urban Platforms for Capital*. This is to say, capital can also be generated by urban youth for their own reasons and through their own innovative methods.[92] However, we also do not want to imply that adult control and surveillance, with the intention to create capital, is an inherently negative element of youth skateboarding. Much like Rinehart and Grenfell's study of BMX biking in "the Flats," skaters at Town Park and Roosevelt created their own organic activity space. But these more indigenously governed spaces, just like "the Flats," also could be exclusive in certain ways. For example, Town Park and Roosevelt were identified as sites where masculine styles and behaviors still seemed to dominate participation, as historically found in more traditional street skateboarding culture.[93] By contrast, a stronger adult presence in Bay City and Lake Cunningham actually provided structured, regular opportunities for female skaters and beginners to skate. Town Park now seems to be emulating this model, with adults here now regularly programming female-specific skate sessions to promote gender inclusion. This last line of discussion, which pertains to gender as well as other aspects of social diversity, will be analyzed further in the next section.

Understanding Social Diversity Within Urban Skate Parks

Skateboarding, particularly in its urban form, has always been marked by an element of social diversity, although this attribute has not always been explicitly acknowledged or promoted.[94] Accordingly, through our research, we discovered that many adults felt that social diversity could foster valuable experiences for youth skateboarders. Diversity consequently framed how many of the *Moving Boarders* adults envisioned and supported youth in skate parks. It is crucial to note that these adults framed social diversity in divergent ways, in line with specific conditions and issues found within each skate park community. Below, we highlight some compelling issues emanating from the case chapters pertaining to race, ethnicity, social class, and gender; interestingly, and worthy of future research, other types of social diversity, including religion and sexuality, were not usually addressed by the adults and youth in our study. Thus, for many of the actual skateboarders and supporters we met, these latter aspects of social diversity seemed mostly peripheral to their belief systems and experiences, except for some of the activist groups that acknowledged the presence of diverse sexual orientations. Perhaps, too, we did not probe these latter issues adequately through our research design.

Once again, Bay City Skate Park had diverse clientele. It was, at times, a family-friendly environment that had programs used to attract female skaters and youth with disabilities. Also, because of Jane's personal aim to provide a space for her son to skate with his friends, a more traditional teen scene flourished. Simultaneously, we stated in chapter 3 that this skate park was designed to support a multicultural environment that would resemble the local community's changing demographics. As one father, Cal, said, this skate park was based in a "nice community" with "more Chinese people, more Indian people, and then there's white people." And while it often attracted middle- and upper-class established, professional families, Bay City also had recent, aspirational immigrants who blended into the scene. With the local community's diverse racial, ethnic, and social-class demographics in mind, and a desire to target teenagers, females, and people with disabilities, Bay City's leaders deliberately tried to construct safe, socially inclusive conditions. This approach eventually attracted many families.

By contrast, we have previously discussed that Lake Cunningham was mostly structured in line with the idea of being a socially insulated and tourist type of destination. While in principle this space was open to all participants, in actuality it regularly served more professional, white members of the local community and well-off skateboarding families from elsewhere. This skate park, as we have consistently mentioned, had fees and extensive monitoring practices that often seemed to inhibit racial, ethnic, and social-class diversity. Not surprisingly, it had the smallest demographic range of parents and participants compared to all other skate parks in our study. Quite simply, users of this skate park were those not deterred by the resources required (e.g., money, transport, and time) to skate here on a regular basis.

In conversation, we found that several Lake Cunningham parents held strong views regarding the practice of boundary-making. These parents often compared this skate park to others like Roosevelt. Lake

Circle of young girls and coaches stretching before female skate event.
Courtesy of Kimberly Woo.

Cunningham was often lauded by parents because it was "hard to get in," as one dad said in chapter 5, with its barbed-wire fence and checkpoint setup. Some parents said that they liked these mechanisms because they excluded the "riffraff" and "crazy" behavior, as one parent said, which was supposedly found in other neighborhoods and skate parks. In this vein, one father at Lake Cunningham said that he appreciated this spot over others because "there wasn't drinking, there wasn't smoking, there wasn't graffiti, there wasn't fighting, and all of those things." In this regard, Michael A. Messner's youth sports research in Southern California tells us that comments like these seem innocent or "off-the-cuff," yet they are used by parents to distinguish safe, kid-friendly enclaves where children can be ingrained with professional-class traits and belief systems.[95] In his study, Messner found that certain parents created a *symbolic boundary* to distinguish this type of youth scene from others that were deemed less desirable because they were considered Latino/a and working-class.[96]

Lake Cunningham was also a site where this type of symbolic boundary became enacted, in order to create an "us and them" distinction between seemingly different social groups.[97] Although, interestingly, this type of distinction was not made by Lake Cunningham parents in explicit racial, ethnic, and social-class terms, but rather in relation to crime and behavior issues.

Examining another case location, Town Park, we saw how K-Dub advocated for an "arms open" and "welcoming" multicultural network. Town Park was even once described as "a racial and socioeconomic melting pot" in a recent feature story.[98] This same piece cited one participant whose view was that "it's not just white people. It's not just Black people." But, at the same time, K-Dub primarily sought to leverage the specific social-class backgrounds and cultural attributes of local young males of color. It will thus be interesting to see how K-Dub's promotion of these underserved youth through high-profile skate documentaries and social-media platforms will continue. We wonder if Oakland skateboarding could someday come to signify "a kind of racial ambivalence," where race might actually be "presented to audiences as a commodity."[99] This potentially means that "race itself no longer matters in the same way it once did but is rather an interesting means to feature the authentic, cool, or urban," as communications scholar Sarah Banet-Weiser argues.[100] As Town Park becomes more visible and gains popular kudos, we thus wonder how K-Dub will further promote Oakland youth skateboarding in line with radical African American community-based politics. Today, sports activists raising race-based and social-class issues are subjected to severe push-back and sanctioning; this fact reminds us that politically neutral depictions of sport are generally considered more appealing in the free market, in terms of mass consumption.[101]

The parents we met in Town Park believed that this new racially and ethnically integrated space was valuable for their children. Jimmy Ray, who skated with his daughter in Town Park, told us that skin color indeed did not matter in skateboarding, as it was for "all kinds of people." "There's Asians, black people skating. My buddy of mine is Mexican," he told us. Jimmy Ray thus appreciated this diverse racial and ethnic environment and wanted to regularly skate with his daughter here. Then, we can recall Sharon, who expressed in chapter 4 that she was nearly broke and homeless due to gentrification's effects in West Oakland. Gentrification, she said, invited an influx of new white, wealthier transplants. However, her view of racial and ethnic dynamics presented in chapter 4 was that "one is business. One is social." This meant that she wanted her African American skater son to integrate with the white "out-of-towners," as she called them.

Meanwhile, we have argued that the city of San Jose created and resourced Roosevelt Skate Park under a classic community-intervention approach, that is, with an intention to help and even transform poorer youth of color.[102] However, parents we met in Roosevelt actually appreciated the socially diverse mixture of youth and the activities found there. They viewed this social-class, ethnic, and racial diversity as necessary and beneficial to their children's overall development. These parents often came from elsewhere, because Roosevelt provided a strong contrast to life back in their home communities. Roosevelt was considered authentic and useful by these parents because it represented actual city life through its mostly Latino/a and low-income population. Roosevelt's youth also felt that this was a meaningful social network where they could find value, and be valued, amidst its open, diverse conditions.

At the same time, in terms of urban skateboarding's social diversity, there were also gendered practices and relationships found in the skate parks that obviously require further scrutiny. We found that certain community missions were explicitly enacted in terms of bolstering the presence and roles of females in skate parks. Because skateboarding still fundamentally exists as an activity formulated around masculine codes and identities, despite evidence over the past decade showing more female participation alongside "girl-focused" corporate marketing.[103] Given this overriding masculine contextualization, it is no surprise that increasing females' participation and their legitimacy in skate parks, and also within media and industry domains, was prioritized by the groups featured in chapter 2.

As noted previously, social-activist groups such as GRO, SLAG, and MAHFIA.TV were attempting to change the nature of urban skateboarding through female inclusion and empowerment. The four leaders featured in chapter 2 were motivated by their experiences of sexism during skateboarding and within the affiliated private industries. These women were very upfront and passionate about the need to create safe, welcoming spaces for female skateboarders. To these women, gender inclusiveness began with increasing the number of females who skate and essentially generating a critical mass of participants in skate parks. It was also important, they said, to have established women serve as role models to younger female entrants.

Outside of these specific female skate groups, other programs and their leaders appeared more generic and limited in their approach. That is, they mostly utilized an "open door" policy to include females in their programs. During an interview, for example, Rob "Skate" Ferguson directly referred to the presence of female skaters during his lessons, events, and camps, which we outlined earlier in this chapter.

> I see a lot of girls that are definitely hungry to come out and skate. Every year, actually, I have tons of programs where it's almost 50/50 on having girls and guys. . . . So I was teaching the kids at the school how to skateboard, gave them some free product, just encouraged them. Yeah, just had a whole little set up and that's other stuff that went on in there too, as well. There was lots of girls and guys that were part of that program. It was good.

Ferguson's gendered politics thus cohere around the view that girls could be equally sourced and represented within his various events, camps, and private lessons, many of which cost money and generate income.

During our interview from 2014, K-Dub revealed his own belief that women and girls had ample opportunity to participate in skateboarding, but that they tended to select other activities. For example, in 2014, he noted that women and girls might sometimes enter the skate park. But typically, he said, they did not stick with this activity because they were drawn to other mainstream sports like soccer. K-Dub's initial stance did not lend itself to attracting more female participants on a regular basis, particularly when Oakland skateboarding was practically and stylistically shaped to showcase the participation of young men of color. In Town Park, then, we observed how male bonding and mentoring frequently occurred across different generations, as in many other American skate parks. More recently we have observed that K-Dub has been much more explicit in supporting female participants through Town Park's social-media platform and at ground level. Indeed, he has been working closely with female skate activists like Kim Woozy, who simultaneously heads SLAG and MAHFIA.TV. As such, K-Dub has lately given more attention to female inclusion concerns and is using his leadership and influence to change the gendered dynamics of Town Park.

It is apparent that the instigation of a new working relationship involving K-Dub and Woozy has increased female participation in Town Park.[104] In this regard, sociologist Cheryl Cooky's provocatively titled article "Girls Just Aren't Interested" is highly relevant to this finding. Cooky contends that more targeted and formal interventions, like those we discuss above, are needed to enhance female participation. This perspective contests the simplistic yet prevalent belief that "girls and women who do not participate choose to do so" because they find sports uninteresting.[105] Cooky rightfully questions whether providing open access contexts without disrupting male-centered practices will translate into prolonged, full participation of women and girls.

Despite some changes, much work is still required to change the dynamics of gender in skateboarding. Indeed, other scholars remind us that we should not be so quick to "uncritically accept and endorse the notion that activities such as surfing, skateboarding or snowboarding can lead to girls' empowerment and . . . improve the lives of participants."[106] We must therefore probe deeper and more critically when evaluating the nature of female participation in youth action sports such as skateboarding.

Female participation at special events, like those we described, may increase due to having a specified female space and practices of female role modeling. But we argue that female participation *on an everyday basis* is still lacking in many skate parks. In our own study, we often found that female skaters were generally tasked with entering available spaces that were, in reality, challenging social environments where masculine behavior and identities were the norm.

Furthermore, it is our hope that skate park leaders and support organizations will specifically address the needs of all female participants, including those who identify in non-traditionally feminine ways. MAHFIA.TV, for instance, has already reached out to transgendered, lesbian, and non-binary-identifying skateboarders through its Facebook site when promoting skate events such as those held in Town Park. SLAG has also provided a context in which individuals can feel empowered to take up diverse gendered identities, as revealed by Mandy, one of their former leaders.[107]

> And I feel like with SLAG, why I've stuck with them is like we're all so different and like, you know, we all present in different ways and I like that none of us are worried about our image, you know, about this girl skater image that other people want to, you know, like, "Oh if you want to do something masculine then you have to present feminine or whatever," but I don't feel that pressure with this 'cause I can just, like, be myself and like, try not to give a crap.

Essentially, as a leader from Montreal's Skirtboarders skate crew once stated in another study, it is important that female skaters can "be as girly or as not girly as they want to."[108]

In fact, while skateboarding culture has often been preoccupied with "girly" or hypersexualized versions of femininity, there are signs of change.[109] For instance, twenty-five-year-old queer skateboarder Lacey Baker has joined Nike's skate team.[110] Then, the second author of *Moving Boarders* recently spoke at an inaugural skateboarding-themed conference in London, "Pushing Boarders," that featured intensive discussions about grassroots movements to include people with various gendered identities.[111] We subsequently wonder how urban skateboarding may encourage, at the everyday level, a wider range of gendered people to participate and gain capital.

In closing this section, what can we surmise from this analysis of social diversity as it pertains to skate-park life? In the beginning of this book, we outlined how major social and economic inequalities mark the lives of residents in the San Francisco Bay Area under neoliberal conditions. This fact makes us wonder how skateboarding participants negotiate or perhaps contest dominant structures and ideologies, linked with social diversity, that certainly impact them. Clearly, sports-focused social spaces reproduce belief systems and practices related to race and ethnicity, social class, gender, religion, and sexuality.[112] Thus, how are each of these elements of social diversity prioritized, overlooked, or perhaps understood more subconsciously, with particular ramifications for youth-sports practice? Looking ahead to the future, we hope that adults and youth alike will come to utilize critical, reflective approaches to engage with social diversity. Perhaps "critical social empowerment" can occur, so that positive developmental outcomes can actually be achieved, inclusively and progressively, within youth-sports communities such as skate parks.[113]

Conclusion: (Skate)boarders on the Move

As this book was being finished, we witnessed the inauguration of this nation's forty-fifth president, Donald Trump. In terms of neoliberalism's ascendancy, this was a watershed moment. Coming into the White House on a platform squarely focused upon downsizing so-called "big government," this administration now handles its affairs in an essentially privatized manner, reflected in the escalated involvement of private influencers and corporate approaches, to handle what used to be considered public affairs. It is to the point that, even at the highest levels, government officials and their supporters now promote commercial products and make business deals through public service.[114]

In these conspicuously neoliberal times, *Moving Boarders* has traced out how modern-day youth sports, including skateboarding, have been impacted by the privatization trend. Youth sports today constitute a $15 billion industry.[115] We argue that neoliberalism drives skateboarding's mainstream trajectory and encourages its expanding participant base. A plethora of reports and books have detailed the stagnation of traditional American youth-sports practice. Yet, skateboarding remains quite popular. *Moving Boarders* has given context to skateboarding's recent popularity, demonstrating that this activity is now being integrated within many diverse realms of American life, including sports, fashion, music, art, and brand marketing. Describing how the doors of this activity are now wide open, we also had to show, in a granular way, that enhanced participation has led to new social relationships, codes, and experiences. With these attributes, skateboarding reflects a new vision of urban youth sports with growing influence upon American society.

As we now conclude *Moving Boarders*, the first key takeaway for our readers is that a wide range of social-enterprise groups representing both public and private sector interests have implemented a new way of working in modern youth sports. The urban youth-sports landscape now heavily relies upon social-enterprise coalitions that blur the borders that used to exist between private industry, government agencies, and nonprofit organizations. Often out of necessity, these integrated groups, rather than public institutions alone, are using funding and sponsorships to generate new social values pertaining to sports as well as health and well-being.[116] This means that we must continue to understand the missions and processes by which communities and their private supporters are installing new social contexts for families and youth. How are these new contexts actually making an impact on the status quo? *Urban Platforms for Capital*, when closely examined, reveal certain investments and motivations relative to specific ideals of youth and community development. But, in actuality, the benefits from these platforms exist in a continuum, reflecting different degrees of what we consider to be meaningful, sustainable social change. In certain cases, we saw that branding and awareness of urban skateboarding was most apparent, while in other programs, the case could be made that more deep-rooted and intensive social-change processes occurred, reflecting day-to-day, intentional practice in skate parks. And of course, when social-enterprise groups become involved in determining what constitutes social change, there will be blind spots toward privileging certain types of citizens in society. Certainly, these working coalitions are beholden to their own specific values and priorities. And quite simply, under the dominant free-market logic, these groups have no responsibility to benefit those that fall outside the scope of their own social-change and profit-making agendas. Going forward, this raises questions to consider about how corporations investing in youth sports will balance corporate duties to shareholders with their commitment to the public's welfare.

And yet, it is equally important to see how the infusion of private resourcing under the capitalist model may actually buffer against deep social-welfare cuts being made in the public domain. The current leadership in the United States considers the public sector and its resourcing model to be "arcane"[117] or even a "dead end."[118] As a result, public health services and community activity programming, especially for youths of color based in lower-income areas, are being slashed.[119] We therefore accede that private and even entrepreneurial support for public outlets such as skate parks may actually insulate against broader budget cuts and inevitable social disparities.[120] To be clear, if it were not for the presence of thriving public-private partnerships, then all of the *Moving Boarders* skate parks would not exist or operate as they do today. But what happens when American youths and communities in need of development opportunities do not have capital-rich benefactors such as Silicon Valley or Levi's? And, since free market choice is considered vital to neoliberalism, those with wealth are able to determine what social causes, if any, should be supported.[121] So, what if some private industries eventually determine that certain social causes are no longer fundamental to their profit models? In this regard, the next few years under our nation's government are undoubtedly precarious given the increasing lack of public oversight and investment in youth activities.[122]

The next takeaway for our readers pertains to the value of skate-boarding to help adults reenvision youths' learning and development processes. The stories from *Moving Boarders* are also instructive for those involved in more formalized contexts such as schools, after-school programs, recreation programs, and sport clubs. In our own College of Education and Allied Studies, we have presented this book's key findings during an all-faculty forum. Our recommendation to a broad spectrum of educators was that some of skateboarding's practices can influence teaching and learning processes—in both sporting and non-sporting contexts. What's more, scholar Dan Gould suggests that action sports can positively influence traditional sports, because these action sports "allow youth to make more decisions about their involvement . . . to explore and be more creative."[123] In fact, Richard Bailey and colleagues have detailed how youth are more likely to participate in sports and physical activities "when they are given decision-making and problem-solving responsibilities."[124] Furthermore, research from the *International Sport Coaching Journal* also indicates that action sports may provide useful examples of problem-solving, along with non-hierarchical, respectful instructional practices.[125]

Our own observations indicate that skateboarding can work as a participant driven activity where youth navigate the physical and social elements of skate parks in highly original and strategic ways. We often witnessed skateboarders dedicating many hours at a time to improve their skills. Moreover, they regularly helped each other learn without prompting from adults. This latter finding resonates with a study of two other American skate parks, conducted by Jasmine Ma and Charles Munter. These scholars found that skate spots can function as "communities of practice," where youth interchangeably serve as both learners and teachers with each other, with "little formal, top-down organization."[126] Ultimately, these types of educative practices from skate parks challenge us, once again, to think more expansively and thoughtfully about the fluid nature of youths' lives, and the different kinds of spaces in society where they inhabit and learn.[127]

Taken together, the youths' participatory practices that we observed reflect a high state of personal engagement, with skateboarding becoming quite a meaningful, enjoyable part of their overall lives. This type of experience speaks directly to the components of what sport psychologists call *self-determined motivation*. Research into this concept has found that youth are motivated to play sports when they have fun and feel valued by their peers, and because they have the ability to demonstrate competency and learn new skills.[128] Indeed, evidenced throughout this book are youth experiences at skate parks that reflect high states of personal enjoyment and satisfaction. Therefore, it is no surprise to us that youth now gravitate towards and continue to participate in urban skateboarding in such high numbers.

A related recommendation is that practitioners based in educational, recreational, and coaching contexts should regularly contemplate how to be more relevant and helpful in contemporary youths' lives. This would mean engaging more closely with the thought-worlds of youth themselves. And it is known that teachers and coaches, who should strive to be "career-long" learners themselves, can use this type of personal reflection

Young girls about to practice skateboarding in Town Park.
Courtesy of Kimberly Woo.

and engagement with youth to become more effective practitioners.[129] For adults working with youths on a regular basis, one practice worth considering is the usage of a more "open-ended" and less "top-down" approach, which, according to education scholar Mike Jess and his colleagues, is necessary to satisfy the needs and traits of modern youth.[130] This recommendation implies that adults can share power with youth; what seems especially important for today's youth is "being allowed the chance to do something for themselves," and where the role of adult practitioners simply becomes "offering guidance, support and access to resources."[131]

Our next concluding argument is that social diversity remains an important facet of youth sports, especially for urban skateboarding. Unlike some traditional, competitive youth sports, skateboarding can fluidly integrate a wide range of different people across numerous formats and activities.[132] With the diversity of youth and adults now entering this activity, the cliché that skateboarding is only constituted by a subculture of rebellious young white men must be reexamined. At the same time, it should not be forgotten that skateboarding, unlike most other youth sports, has long served to include society's most marginalized individuals. Youth, as Rodney Mullen noted earlier, may be dissuaded from participating in more traditionally hierarchical sporting pursuits and thus turn to skateboarding instead.

And yet, urban skateboarding can also work as a polarizing and exclusive social force, as we saw in some instances where symbolic and literal boundaries were maintained in parks. This spatial practice sometimes reflected what urban scholar David Madden calls "publicity without democracy"; here the public's participation in urban space is restricted by the neoliberal logics of "surveillance, control, commerce, and consumption."[133] For instance, we saw that Lake Cunningham was envisioned as a tourist hub and global activity destination, thus serving as a lucrative site for investment and promotion. But, in practice, this spatial model tacitly or directly excluded certain youth from using these spaces for the sake of presenting a more harmonious, homogenous, and less politicized version of youth-sports activity; in essence, one that was more acceptable in the neoliberal economy.

Furthermore, in line with the notion of "publicity without democracy," it is important to consider the social borders that appear when there is incentive and momentum to intervene in the lives of certain identified urban populations. This spatial practice can occur when cities attempt to transform both residents and their neighborhoods, in line with neoliberal social values, behaviors, and identities. We saw this process enacted when "at risk" areas with skate parks were targeted for transformation, perhaps to attract new urban developments and more professional-class residents.[134]

Taking Madden's spatial concept into consideration, readers of our book should contemplate how cities and their representatives have power to create social borders that may exclude some residents based on ideals of normative citizenship and appropriate spatial behavior. We thus question what criteria are used to determine social norms and boundaries during urban spatial activities. Furthermore, who is prioritized, or not, during city-led social interventions involving youth sports? What are the consequences for those that are considered non-normative in relation to prevailing urban spatial borders?

It is clear from our findings that adults involved in youth sports hold tremendous capacity to impact the lives of youth. As a consequence, rather than reinforcing social borders through contemporary youth sports, our belief is that adults should use their power to instigate more critical awareness around issues of social diversity and inclusion. Racist and sexist practices, for instance, undoubtedly impact sports participation; adult program leaders and practitioners should thus introduce youth to "the vocabularies and paradigms that aid in this understanding," so that ultimately we can "begin to transform lives and communities."[135] Grassroots sports programs in our area, such as Oakland's Soccer Without Borders (SWB) and the Futbolistas, have already initiated these critical discussions with urban youths, in order to enact positive social changes in their local communities.[136]

Another important takeaway from our research is that youth skateboarding is generally considered as a good thing by today's parents. Skateboarding is no longer viewed by parents as an activity that is simply dangerous and antisocial. Modern parents seem to "get" how much their kids are enjoying and learning from this inherently free-flowing and challenging activity. We should not forget, then, that skateboarding, like other youth sports, can reflect vital experiences of freedom and play.[137] Indeed, one mother of an "anxious" middle-school daughter told us that skateboarding was crucial because it made her daughter feel relaxed; it felt like she was "sailing through the skate park." We thus want to remind our readers of the belief, expressed by other scholars, that "no matter how organized and routinized the lives of kids," sports should remain important contexts of creativity and play.[138] In fact, having fun was cited in one landmark study of 10,000 ten-to-eighteen-year-old boys and girls as being *the most important reason* to participate in youth sports, while winning was barely mentioned at all.[139] Adults reading this book should therefore be cognizant that creativity, play, and enjoyment actually foster strong connections between youth and activities such as skateboarding.

Of course, there are other more instrumentalist reasons why parents are validating skateboarding and other youth sports across America. While the circumstances of these parents may differ, parents are heavily investing in these activities because they believe that these are necessary mediums to help their children grow and succeed. A book called *Coming of Age in America* shows us that today's parents serve as "launching pads" for their kids, particularly within our highly competitive neoliberal society.[140] In fact, a new article in *The Guardian* suggests that today's youth are subject to unprecedented, and even unhealthy, pressure to succeed, which means that "individual limitations are no longer acknowledged and failure is not an option."[141] Another article warns that the future economy will require workers to "become as agile as possible" and "have many forms of talent and work," otherwise the robots will take over![142] The essential belief underlying this recent commentary is that youth now experience tremendous pressure to succeed in our highly competitive and changing world; this fact is not lost on American parents. These parents are always searching for new, better ways of raising their children, including through youth sports such as skateboarding.

These parental anxieties about children's success mean that skate parks have become key sites for youths to develop in line with increasingly higher societal expectations. Skateboarding, like other youth sports, is thus being regularly used by parents to enhance their children's social status and life opportunities. This can mean that certain elements of play, freedom, and even risk-taking are mitigated through parental intervention. Consequently, we would like our readers to contemplate what it means when adults get heavily involved in youth sports, mostly to help their children obtain new life skills and character attributes. Can we claim that meaningful, sustainable youth development is occurring when intervening adults regulate sports participation to a high degree and perhaps eradicate most obstacles? It is also worth considering how all of this parental attention for instrumentalist purposes may have detrimental effects upon children's emotions, sense of self, and even future opportunities, despite parents' good intentions.[143]

Our advice, once again, is that parents need to deeply consider how and why they intervene in youth-sports contexts. And, going further, what if adults, including parents, could primarily envision sporting youths "as 'wise in their own way'"?[144] This would entail taking "more seriously the things young people want" from their activities and youth-sports cultures, according to scholar Michael Gard and colleagues, and tapping into "the techniques they use."[145] In a more "bottom-up approach," then, youths' own ideas, life circumstances, and identities could be great starting points for adults to consider when they get involved.[146] This would mean engaging with youths' ideas about social inclusion and their beliefs about capital generation, too. We thus recommend that youths' voices and their agency need to be prioritized more in skateboarding and other youth-sports endeavors. In fact, one national youth-sports observer laments that, typically, "No one ever brings the voice of the kids into the conversation."[147]

However, as sociologist Jay Coakley explains, this type of youth-focused approach is rare because it directly challenges adults who have significant power and resources in sports.[148] And then there is the prevalent idea that youth must conform to adult control of their activities within city spaces. A recent event in San Francisco, where police violently broke up an impromptu skateboarding session created largely by youth, reveals that there is still much work that remains in terms of prioritizing youths' voices, motivations, and belief systems.[149]

Closing this book, we find it amazing that skateboarding, originally a makeshift activity invented by Californian surfers, has gone on to become a global social phenomenon. Simultaneously, skateboarding is taken very seriously by families as part of their day-to-day existence. And skateboarding is considered cutting-edge practice by today's leading industry experts and technological visionaries.[150] But the roots of skateboarding, essentially as an outlet for youthful play, spontaneity, and creativity, should always be remembered by participants and supporters of this activity. We should also bear in mind that skateboarding, with its free-spirited and participant-driven inclinations, can help us reconsider the prevailing conventions, boundaries, and belief systems found in modern neoliberal youth sports.[151] One of America's most original and treasured cultural artifacts, skateboarding now has more currency than ever; it truly has power to change how we envision the place and meanings of youth sports in our society.

METHODOLOGICAL APPENDIX

In this appendix, we present an in-depth perspective of our methodology while attending to some of the issues we faced while conducting this research. While discussing the case-studies used in *Moving Boarders*, we initially outline our basic research process, followed by an extensive description of our backgrounds, as these impacted the study, and the methodological considerations we employed in this three-and-a-half-year collaborative ethnography. This appendix concludes with a discussion regarding the intricacies of researching youth and adult participants within several case-study locations.

Our Entry into Researching Urban Skate Parks

The impetus for the research study that drives the stories in this book actually came from the parent of a teenaged male skateboarder. This skateboarder was doing a project for a class at his middle school and wanted to interview an expert who had published about the sport. After he finished his interview with this book's second author, Becky Beal, the mother stayed on; she recalled that she had read one of this author's papers on gender dynamics and this encouraged her to reflect on her own gendered relationship with her son. The skateboarder's mother then suggested that it would be very interesting to do a study on other parents of skateboarders. This struck Beal as an intriguing idea on many levels, especially given the current ways that youth sports were being provided and taken up amidst broader American parenting practices.

Beal proposed this idea to the rest of us in 2013; after some initial discussion, we realized that all of us had observed and participated in the privatized, professionalized youth-sports world. We had even sometimes worked as youth coaches in soccer, track and field, volleyball, basketball, and tennis. At the same time, our social and academic interactions with skateboarding, as well as growing awareness of this activity within social media, seemed to indicate there might be something new occurring in this sport's culture.

Several sociocultural phenomena surrounding skateboarding became compelling, too. Around this time, the first two authors published

Stack of Skate Like a Girl (SLAG) organization skateboards.
Courtesy of Kimberly Woo.

a paper that revealed the heightened participation of urban young men of color in skateboarding; this trend was exemplified by two featured skateboarders: Paul Rodriguez, known as "P-Rod," who was signed with Nike, and Stevie Williams, who skated under the Reebok "Dirty Ghetto Kids" (DGK) brand.[1] Recent academic research by the first two authors also demonstrated how women, in particular, were still marginalized by men's talk and their actions within skateboarding contexts. But as a group, we began to notice the growing visibility of female professional skateboarders in popular media. And we also saw that there were large numbers of new, younger, and yet highly skilled male and female skaters who were participating in competitions such as the X Games. There were also rumblings, at this time, in the media and our academic circles, that skateboarding and other action sports were being touted for inclusion within the 2020 Summer Olympic Games; the addition of these action sports has recently been confirmed.

Overall, this increasing swell of global, societal interest around skate-boarding seemed to demonstrate a mainstream shift in an activity once considered countercultural. Thus, we thought, it was highly plausible that mainstream families would also be influencing this sport in an unprecedented way, both in terms of their participation and as consumers of various associated skate industries. As we began to frame our study, we intentionally wanted to gather the voices of families (including parents, grandparents, and children) and other adults supporting this type of activity.

To make sense of these stakeholders' voices, in line with our own personal and academic viewpoints, we came to use a critical lens that examined ideologies pertaining to gender, race, ethnicity, as well as social class as they influenced skateboarding. This would help us understand the status and value of skateboarding for families that obviously lived in quite diverse communities within the San Francisco Bay Area. Moreover, this line of thought reflected a desire to extend our previous research work, detailed later in this appendix, because, unlike before, we began to focus more precisely on the family and community elements of skateboarding.

Researching Urban Skateboarding:
A Case-Study Approach to Exploring Local Skate Parks

We situated our research in the San Francisco Bay Area of California based on the unique attributes of this well-known skateboarding scene, as well as our close proximity to it. Once this context was determined, the study was conducted between November 2013 and March 2017. We researched three communities that now host skate parks—Oakland, Bay City, and San Jose. As noted in the introduction of this book, each skate park's unique placement within the San Francisco Bay Area strongly influenced our decision to purposively research it.

The analytical method of our study can be characterized as a collective case-study involving intensive ethnographic fieldwork. Case-study, as a methodology, allows researchers to attain rich, detailed data on "real people and real situations" through in-depth observation of a group or community.[2] One of the key attributes of case-study research is that it is holistic, acknowledging that "much of what we can know about human behaviour is best understood as lived experience in the social context."[3] Case-study research also became suitable for our needs because this holistic approach allows for investigation of the various links among the phenomenon (skateboarding) and broader cultural practices.[4]

Four "individual case" skate parks constituted our eventual "collective case," and gave a comprehensive and distributed portrait of San Francisco Bay Area skateboarding. The use of several cases provided a way to look at the existence of similarities or differences among the cases' characteristics.

This also allowed us to get a better understanding of how each stakeholder valued and engaged in skateboarding, a strength of collective case-study research.[5] Each individual case was examined closely by the research team in order to develop multiple insights into the people, practices, and perspectives that underpinned skateboarding within each site.

Description of the Basic Research Process

Undertaking this case-study, we immersed ourselves in four skate parks found in the three communities. We also investigated, to a lesser degree, other neighboring skate parks not featured prominently in this book. In this role as ethnographic researchers, our aim was to understand "local knowledge, including local 'definitions of the situation' and the subjects' working conceptions of the world," in order to provide an in-depth, systematic portrayal of skate park culture, that represents the "local knowledge."[6]

We conducted fieldwork, specifically in line with our key research idea, although we will discuss later that our original idea evolved. From the beginning, we wanted to learn more about skateboarding families. In terms of parents, we consequently examined their time commitment and involvements in their child's skateboarding, as well as the values and meanings they attributed to participation. We also interviewed children and older youths, including teenagers, as we were interested in learning about the nature of their skateboarding (e.g., basic history, places they skate, who they skated with, use of technology and brands), their goals, as well as motivations and values related to their skateboarding. Crucially, we also wanted to know how youths' felt about their parents' involvement in skate park life.

In terms of methods, we frequently observed and recorded skatepark families and their associates through field notes. This enabled us to understand their patterns of using skate parks. These visits also served to establish working relations with the various case stakeholders which increased our research sample and overall knowledge of park life. During these observations, we were able to speak to more individuals than we had intended, and we were sometimes able to conduct interviews on the spot and also set up future interviews. Furthermore, our research team attended a variety of community events held outside of skate parks. Often, we noted that the interactions and conversations in these other visits were just as rich as those done within the skate parks themselves. In many cases, it was easier to have an extended talk at a public event as opposed to

Four Researchers and One Narrative: Using Collaborative Ethnography in Action-Sports Research

Reflecting back over the various phases of the study made us realize that using four researchers to explain one evolving phenomenon is a complex undertaking. Collaborative ethnography, it has been said, involves a coordinated effort in the gathering, analyzing, reporting, and presenting of research between two or more ethnographers, who oftentimes have different roles or responsibilities in these stages.[7] Looking back on the *Moving Boarders* study, we each contributed different academic lenses as well as personal backgrounds and viewpoints to approach the emerging study, as described further in the following paragraph. We were, as a group, adaptable in terms of how we used this approach, drawing upon each person in strategic ways to make sense of the study and emerging ideas and data; this procedure became necessary to investigate the complex, diverse nature of local skateboarding practice. The book chapters, in their final presentation, thus reflect a range of scholarly and personal ideas that came from all four authors; these ideas were raised and then discussed by the group during the study in order to create this book.

Given the above discussion about our collaborative research approach, it was important that we also reflect upon our own "subjective" backgrounds and viewpoints that influenced the entire project. In our second research-team meeting, back in the fall of 2013, we sat down and reflected for over an hour about our knowledge (or lack thereof) regarding skateboarding culture. Our discussion eventually revolved around our beliefs and experiences related to: (1) participating in different types of sports and activities; (2) our parents' roles and values in sports and our resulting experiences in sport as youths living in the 1970s, '80s and '90s; and (3) our understanding of how gender, race, ethnicity, sexuality, and social class have influenced our sport experiences. Being reflective, then, we were able to acknowledge that our individual life experiences would influence how we collected, analyzed, and presented our data. We also acknowledged that we might be perceived differently by our participants when conducting fieldwork. It was felt that our socialization, reflected in our outward appearances, styles, and demeanors, or essentially our "habitus," as Pierre Bourdieu would say, was going to influence how we were "read" by others;[8] this, we believed, would affect how we each of us could access the different skate parks and participants.

Furthermore, at this initial meeting, a key point was raised: we had minimal experience with actually skateboarding or being part of skateboarding cultural groups. We had only dabbled in skateboarding during our childhoods, with limited success or skills attained. Some of us had studied skateboarding in an academic way, while others had experiences studying other youth sports. These facts, along with our own unique identities and experiences, would predispose us to certain ideas about skateboarding practice. For example, Matthew Atencio knew about "street" or "pickup" ball-sport cultures like soccer, because of research and being an actual participant in these activities. But, lacking the ability to skateboard and being unable to identify key maneuvers that were being performed made him feel like a researcher looking in from the outside, in many instances. As a man of color with extensive experience living in several different multicultural and international contexts, Atencio enjoyed frequenting skate spaces that had higher levels of racial, ethnic, and social-class diversity. His background in female sports coaching also meant that he specifically looked out for gender participation and inclusion. Becky Beal, because of her academic experiences since 1989, had stronger knowledge of skate culture, technical moves, and social cues. She also appreciated and was a fan of this activity. Thus, Beal felt quite comfortable with skaters and their environment. She further reflected that, especially in the past, her whiteness and gender nonconformity helped when interviewing young males in a predominately male-oriented sport (in simple terms, males tended to see her as just "one of the guys"). Beal also felt that she had an instant ability to connect with white people around her same age, which helped when meeting some parents and adults in Bay City. Now that she is in her fifties, there is more of a generational gap with younger skaters, she noted, and she resonated more with adults. For example, she could link with older parents and community leaders through this generation's cultural references, including music and activities like nature hiking.

Missy Wright came from a traditional competitive-sports background, having played and coached tennis at a national level. She admittedly was not always comfortable within certain unregulated male skateboarding scenes. There were times, for instance, when visiting skate parks on a weekend evening, when males would be visibly present and in control, that she would become uncomfortable and feel quite out of place. ZáNean McClain came into this research without any preconceptions about skateboarding, as she, too, was steeped predominately in traditional sports, participating in softball and basketball throughout her childhood and early adult years. She also coached a variety of team sports (e.g., soccer, ultimate Frisbee, volleyball, basketball) in both recreational (youth-sports programs) and extracurricular (school) settings. McClain was mostly concerned about how others would perceive her researcher role, as a black female academic. Because she had experienced prejudice from parents, teachers, and administrators previously while conducting physical education research. She reflected that these previous negative experiences continued to affect her, resulting in her being slightly reserved as she entered into this skate-park project. During *Moving Boarders* research, McClain felt that her ability to collect data by interacting with adults was dependent on the specific racial and ethnic makeup of the location. For example, McClain was able to walk into Oakland's Town Park and greet individuals and/or stand in the corner with a clipboard taking field notes without feeling uncomfortable or without feeling that others were made uncomfortable by her presence. However, in more suburban skate parks, she felt that these adults would closely and even suspiciously watch her research activities.

Reflecting Back Upon the Data Collection Process

The next discussion pertains to what might typically be classified as study limitations, although we believe that these insights from the research process actually reveal useful ideas about how this book was created. This also provides guidance for those interested in future research. These discussions should therefore help the reader make sense of the stories that were provided throughout *Moving Boarders,* and some elements that were perhaps limited or absent for the reasons articulated below.

Initially we provide some insights from our experiences conducting research with youth, in particular. Lastly, we highlight our interactions with adults in the research process. This final discussion includes addressing how we sometimes directly intervened in our adult study participants' lives and projects. At times the boundaries between researcher and participant became inevitably blurred, which raises questions about how to respect and value participant knowledge while jointly addressing the issues that confronted adults and their communities.[9]

RESEARCHING YOUTH: DIFFICULTIES OF RECRUITMENT AND INTERVIEWING

There was a major adult presence in Bay City's skate park. To collect data there, we quickly found that the best way to gain access to families at Bay

City was through the skate-park leaders and their connections with the supporter group, the Bay City Skate Park Group (BCSPG). Once we talked with a few parents from this group, they then vouched for us to speak with their counterparts. This word-of-mouth approach with the large, organized supporter network resulted in individual and group interviews with fifteen children. Perhaps not surprisingly, interviews resulted in us predominantly attaining accounts from younger children instead of adolescents (eleven children were nine years old or younger, while only four children were in the ten-to-fifteen-year-old range), as these youths were often accompanied in the skate park by a parent or guardian, which facilitated the informed consent process. It is thus important to consider that the strategies and concerns of parents of younger children may differ from those parents who have older teenagers; parents obviously have a less direct role in children's sports experiences as they move through life into adolescence and young adulthood.[10]

We attempted to use a similar process of recruiting youth by relying upon skate-park leaders in Oakland and San Jose. But while leaders and city staff in these skate parks spread the word, in the end, this did not help us find many youth. For Bay City, having an organized supporter group, mostly made up of Bay City parents, obviously made a tremendous difference in terms of finding parents that were comfortable in bringing youth into our study. In the end, our direct research visits to the other skate parks proved to be the best means of talking with youth and recruiting them into our study. The youth we eventually recruited from these three locations tended to be slightly older, on average between the ages of eight to fifteen. They were easier to approach during skateboarding, as they were more experienced and comfortable, and they tended to be more interested in our study topic, perhaps due to their more advanced age. But as we discuss see below, making plans to attain informed consent and meet with these older skateboarders could sometimes be difficult. There were several youth whom we wanted to research but never became part of the study.

Over the course of interviewing youth, it became very clear that there is a major difference between young children and teenagers in terms of the research interaction. As it turned out, it was difficult to talk with very young children, as their attention spans for undergoing interviews in skate parks were short; they often seemed quite focused on their own skateboarding or socializing with friends, which is understandable. This impacted our ability to generate extended and in-depth responses to our questions. For example, at Bay City skate park, near the beginning of an interview with a seven-year-old boy, he asked if he could take a break and skate for a while before completing his interview. Upon returning to the interview, the boy was able to complete the interview, although it ended up being quite brief. This experience surprised us, since we had mostly worked with older youth who were more attentive and expansive during interviews. Accordingly, researching in places like Bay City, we tried to implement a variety of grouping strategies to interview these children. These strategies included interviewing children alone, in pairs, and in small groups (pairs and groups were both homogeneous and heterogeneous with regard to gender).

When conducting interviews in pairs or small groups, children sometimes fed off of one another and expressed their perspectives quite well, while at other times children just said very little. Another example from the Bay City skate park was an interview with both an eight-year-old girl and a nine-year-old boy. Although the girl was talkative to a certain point, the boy just repeated what the girl had stated previously or nodded his head in agreement. When the interviewer would look in his direction, it was noticed that the boy was constantly looking in the direction of the skate park. At the conclusion of the interview, the boy took off as fast as he could with his skateboard toward the skate park.

Older youth, of course, were able to express themselves more when interviewed, but it was more difficult to schedule interviews with them compared to children. Older youth, including teenagers, tended to have a variety of reasons why they avoided interviews, unless they happened to take place during actual skateboarding time when we first met them. For example, when one author saw two teenagers at San Jose's Roosevelt skate park whom he had been trying to contact for three weeks, one of the teenagers named Ricardo said that he did not confirm the meeting because, as he said, "I can't do it anymore." He shared that he was depressed about being back in school and not being able to skateboard regularly. He mentioned this while slumped against the skate-park fence. Once more, within Roosevelt, two researchers ran into a female teenager who had previously agreed to do an interview, but had for a while been playing "phone tag" to the point that she seemed uninterested. At a Mexican restaurant next to the skate park, this teenager saw the two researchers talking and eating, so she quickly turned to go the other way, which was noticed by the researchers. The teenager eventually came by later and said a quick "hello" and had dinner with her parents at an adjacent table, without speaking to the researchers again. In San Jose, one father we spoke to continually told his older son, who went to both Lake Cunningham and Roosevelt, to get in touch with us. Despite repeated attempts on our behalf, the son never followed through. This skater might have been an interesting interviewee, given his comprehensive knowledge of San Jose's underground and sanctioned skate spots. Together, these examples speak to the fact that teenagers can have other life priorities and circumstances, and they may be more hesitant to speak with adult researchers, especially when it involves scheduling future meetings and giving consent outside of the skate park.

RESEARCHING WITH PARENTS AND SKATE LEADERS

While it was generally easy to conduct meetings with city leaders and skate-park advocates, who were used to organizing and attending meetings themselves, researching parents was at times a more arduous task. Both San Jose's Roosevelt skate park and Oakland's Town Park, in particular, had skate parents that did not frequent these locations on a consistent basis. It was thus more difficult to find parents to speak with in these places, compared to Bay City and Lake Cunningham, where parents were ever-present. We did meet a few parents from these skate parks during specific events (e.g., Tha Hood Games, MAHFIA.TV and SLAG sessions, town-hall meetings, Viva Parks! events, and skate contests). Interviews with these parents from lower-income, socially diverse areas were therefore conducted on a mostly spontaneous, rather than prearranged, formalized basis.

It was easier to conduct interviews with these parents if we saw them hanging out in the skate park or at events, and we could speak right then and there. Like youth from these same skate parks, it was harder to fill out consent forms and schedule future interviews, and these proved cumbersome tasks in many cases. In one instance, after having a great initial talk with the mother of a son who skateboarded in Oakland's Town Park, two researchers called and texted multiple times to set up further interviews. The mother was also going to recommend other parents to meet for interviews. Although the mother answered calls and texts regularly, while claiming to still be working on a date and time to connect person to person, the two researchers eventually gave up, as this was taking several months and many proposed meetings had fallen through at the last minute. Language barriers could also be a problem, as some youth in the Roosevelt community, in particular, mentioned that their parents would not want to be interviewed due to perceived language and even cultural barriers. It is important to remember that both Town Park and Roosevelt were based in communities with many people of color, and where there was more concentrated poverty compared to Bay City and Lake Cunningham. We know from both youth sports and education research that parents from communities like these often lack time and resources to actively participate in their children's activities, and thus being involved in our research study about youth skateboarding may not have been feasible or appealing.[11]

"CSUEB IS HERE TO SUPPORT A SKATE PARK?! IT'S SO ANTI-ESTABLISHMENT AND YOU GUYS ARE THE ESTABLISHMENT!"

This exclamation came from a woman who had just learned about our research team's presence at a City of Oakland Parks and Recreation meeting. This proclamation, discussed more below, provides a great example of how we sometimes directly engaged with and supported the work of our participants whenever we could. As we explain below, and in line with the section's title, this was not always a straightforward process. We attended and supported different events and fundraisers which often had specific social causes. Then, we sometimes brought in community skate leaders to speak at university events, and in some cases they were also guest lecturers in courses that we taught. Over time, we learned more about their concerns, barriers, and needs going forward. These practices also resulted in both formal and informal partnerships being made between our university students and these organizers, with some university students eventually volunteering in local skate parks.

These practices aligned with our own academic and personal interests in social justice and enabled us to gain trust with these research stakeholders. In some cases, our expertise as academics and coaches was explicitly requested. One skate leader wanted help with monetizing and promoting his skate program. In another case, a mother of a skateboarding son, after some discussion, also asked if one of the authors could give her son a coaching lesson in a different sport. This lesson never materialized since this mother became unreachable by phone as the study progressed.

Although we tried to work collaboratively to help certain community causes, we could still be seen by some local individuals as being "academics" from the outside or as the "establishment." While two of us are people of color, and while we all work in one of the most diverse university campuses in the United States, we could still be read as elite experts because of our academic backgrounds.[12] Earlier, we mentioned that recruiting youth in certain areas could be difficult because we were seen as intervening, outsider adults from academia. This may have also played a part in some parents' reticence to follow up with our initial contacts. Then, as shown at this section's opening, we were considered "so establishment" by one local woman, who exclaimed this in front of everyone attending an Oakland meeting where K-Dub was testifying for Town Park to be renovated on public property. In this case, K-Dub had told us about the meeting, and we assured him that we would support this cause for the sake of helping Oakland youth. It surprised us that despite our plans to vouch for K-Dub and this skate park, which we eventually did, we could still be considered outsiders to this community. This made us reflect further about how people in established yet historically marginalized communities, in particular, would view us, our project, and even this book, when completed.

As the data-collection and analysis phases of our study progressed, we had to consistently discuss how this type of close, mutually beneficial research interaction would influence our views and eventual presentation of findings. Although we directly supported some skateboarding social causes, when we felt compelled to do so and/or when people seemed to want our help, we have tried to offer critical accounts of these projects in order to improve practice and highlight key issues for our readership.

We were obviously not neutral or passive researchers in the study; instead, our research was regularly conducted with participants who resembled collaborators. Often, our own subjective interests and backgrounds gave us impetus to support the aims and missions of many local skate leaders featured in this book, even the ones that we have critiqued.

Conclusions About the *Moving Boarders* Research Project

Now, at the conclusion of this study, we realize that research in skateboarding is not at all a straightforward endeavor. The act of skateboarding itself is a naturally fast-moving and often unpredictable youth activity; this activity gets much more complicated when taking into consideration the social dynamics, reflected in the sheer number of diverse stakeholders and resources now supporting this popular activity. We thus believe that researchers must constantly search for innovative ways to comprehensively investigate this type of action-sports phenomenon. In fact, coming from largely traditional qualitative research backgrounds ourselves, we learned much over the course of our research study, as we tried to capture what was occurring in current-day skate parks. Based on the research journey of *Moving Boarders*, we now want to leave the reader with a few recommendations that may support future investigations with skateboarding and other action sports.

Action-sport researcher Jason Laurendeau has written about using a flexible approach in a research context by employing different methodologies to appropriately address certain research questions.[13] Being adaptable, as Laurendeau advocates, was indeed one of the biggest lessons we learned during our study. For example, we soon figured out that it was best to bring a note pad, consent and information forms, as well as a voice recorder to the skate park each time we visited, even when we only intended to conduct observations. This is where the best opportunities arose to meet people and talk to them "on the spot." This approach yielded many brief yet highly compelling conversations, providing rich insights into daily life within these neighborhood skate parks. Furthermore, unannounced and spontaneous visits conducted on a whim or during a break in our teaching commitments yielded important field notes, thus deepening our findings. At other times, we were more deliberate with our visits, getting emails or Facebook updates from organizations about special events that we ultimately attended. In these different ways, we contend that skate-park research requires preparation and strategizing, but alongside a creative and flexible approach.

In the sections above, we acknowledged some of our limitations in terms of data collection with adults and especially youth. Many of the insights we share here focus on best practices for conducting research with youth, given the issues we faced. We concur with the scholarly belief that "it takes commitment, time, and creativity to gain access to kids' groups."[14] Many of the difficulties that we experienced in fact have been documented by other researchers as they have discussed everything from the difficulty of obtaining permission to access children,[15] to how hard it can be to gather and include youth voices. There are certain methodological tools that researchers have implemented in recent studies with youth participants that aided in their attaining in-depth data. The use of visual methodologies has been suggested as a tool to engage young people in our type of research.[16] One such visual methodology, mental mapping, was successfully employed by Adam Jenson and colleagues in a recent study with youth skateboarders.[17] Participants were asked to draw a map of their local skate world, which provided significant information to the researchers. It would be interesting to try out this mental-mapping approach directly in the skate park, using either electronic or print materials, while remaining unobtrusive. Similarly, the use of mobile methods, where youth take researchers directly through the various spaces they inhabit, can lead to better understandings of youths' daily embodied, multisensory experiences; this is therefore another flexible, open strategy that has been successfully used to generate data with young people.[18] Overall, these types of approaches could be used to attain greater engagement with youth participants during the research process.[19] These methods could potentially support in-depth future research with skateboarders and other action-sports participants.

Our final recommendation is that, given the complex nature of skateboarding, as well as all action sports, a variety of theoretical lenses can be useful to design studies and work with collected data. Indeed, theoretical lenses directly inform the methodological approach being implemented in this type of research. Our three-and-a-half-year intensive collaborative study relied upon, and perhaps required, our diverse academic knowledge of sport sociology, physical education and sports-coaching pedagogy, as well as sport psychology to provide an in-depth and micro-level analysis of urban skateboarding. This type of collaborative, interdisciplinary work has its challenges, however, as we found that different fields of study may have conflicting paradigms and outlooks. Researchers working in teams within an ethnographic approach should therefore also take into account goals such as establishing and maintaining reciprocal trust and respect regarding contentious positions and values.[20] This means being able to communicate, compromise, and attain resolutions at all stages of the research process.[21] At the beginning of our study, we had no idea "how challenging such reflexive, contextualized interdisciplinary work truly is," as other researchers have discovered, too.[22] Yet it is our hope, despite the numerous challenges we faced, that our research labor has made a unique contribution to the literature on families, communities, and action sports.

LIST OF INTERVIEWS AND OBSERVATIONS APPENDIX

Listing of Interviews

Name of interviewee (Pseudonym). Date conducted. Location.

PARENTS AND GRANDPARENTS (n = 26 interviews)

1. Nori and Paul. 11 December 2013. Bay City, California.
2. Robert. 31 January 2014. Bay City, California.
3. Ashley. 1 February 2014. Bay City, California.
4. Michael. 1 February 2014. Bay City, California.
5. Gloria. 18 April 2014. Bay City, California.
6. Amy. 19 April 2014. Bay City, California.
7. Toral and Mark. 24 April 2014. Bay City, California.
8. Kelly. 15 May 2014. Bay City, California.
9. Jeff. 16 May 2014. Bay City, California.
10. Cal. 6 September 2014. Bay City, California.
11. Karen. 7 March 2015. Bay City, California.
12. Jimmy. 26 March 2015. Bay City, California.
13. Rex. 15 February 2016. Bay City, California.
14. Mary. 26 January 2016. Oakland, California.
15. Jimmy Ray. 13 February 2016. Oakland, California.
16. Suzanne. 13 February 2016. Oakland, California.
17. Samantha. 1 June 2016. Oakland, California.
18. Camille. 25 August 2016 Oakland, California.
19. Trent. 25 August 2016. Oakland, California.
20. Carl. 24 November 2015. San Jose, California.
21. Chas. 4 June 2016. San Jose, California.
22. Bernie. 7 June 2016. San Jose, California.
23. Brenda. 18 July 2016. San Jose, California.
24. Manny. 1 August 2016. San Jose, California.
25. Juan. 17 August 2016. San Jose, California.
26. Alexa. 23 August 2016. San Jose, California.

YOUTH (n = 19 interviews and focus groups)

1. Austin. 11 December 2013. Bay City, California.
2. Elise. 11 December 2013. Bay City, California.
3. Brady. 2 February 2014. Bay City, California.
4. Eric. 2 February 2014. Bay City, California.
5. Jack and Amber. 2 February 2014. Bay City, California.
6. Michael. 2 February 2014. Bay City, California.
7. Five Kids. 19 April 2014. Bay City, California.
8. Caleb. 24 April 2014. Bay City, California.
9. KD. 2 May 2014. Bay City, California.
10. Riya. 6 September 2014. Bay City, California.
11. Ebo. 25 January 2016. Oakland, California.
12. Jaxon. 13 February 2016. Oakland California.
13. Roberto. 25 August 2016. Oakland, California.
14. Maria. 3 June 2016. San Jose, California.
15. Several unidentified youths. 3 June 2016. San Jose, California.
16. Trevor. 17 July 2017. San Jose, California.
17. Joelle. 1 August 2016. San Jose, California.
18. Mia. 1 August 2016. San Jose, California.
19. Tessa. 23 August 2016. San Jose, California.

ADULT COMMUNITY STAKEHOLDERS (n = 17 interviews)

1. Jane. 6 November 2013. Bay City, California.
2. Rachel. 6 November 2013. Bay City, California.
3. Mike. 28 May 2015. Bay City, California.
4. K-Dub. 22 February 2014. Oakland, California.
5. Robert. 22 May 2014. Oakland, California.
6. Roy. 30 March 2015. Oakland, California.
7. Paul Murphy. 24 November 2015. San Jose, California.
8. Steve Hammack. 15 December 2015. San Jose, California.
9. Cindy Chavez & Paul Murphy. 1 February 2016. San Jose, California.
10. Danny Sanchez. 2 August 2016. San Jose, California.
11. Marco Hernandez. 2 August 2016. San Jose, California.
12. Ryan. 23 August 2016. San Jose, California.
13. Jim "Bug" Martino. 28 November 2016. San Jose, California.
14. SLAG leaders. 15 March 2014. Berkeley, California.
15. Mandy. 16 March 2014. Berkeley, California.

16. Evie. 20 April 2014. Berkeley, California.

17. Kim Woozy. 28 July 2016. Berkeley, California.

Listing of observations and informal meetings

Name of event. Date conducted. Location.

EVENTS (n = 50)

1. Skate park observation. 5 April 2014. Bay City, California.

2. Parent meeting. 15 April 2014. Bay City, California.

3. Skate park observation. 18 April 2014. Bay City, California.

4. Skate park observation. 2 May 2014. Bay City, California.

5. Art opening observation. 9 May 2014. Bay City, California.

6. Skate park observation. 6 September 2014. Bay City, California.

7. Volcom store observation. 27 September 2014. Bay City, California.

8. Skate park observation. 7 March 2015. Bay City, California.

9. Skate park observation. 15 February 2016. Bay City, California.

10. Skate scene at coffee shop observation. 18 July 2016. Bay City, California.

11. Skate park observation. 28 July 2016. Bay City, California.

12. MAHFIA.TV event; SLAG day observation. 6 August 2016. Bay City, California.

13. Skate park observation. 21 February 2014. Oakland, California.

14. Skate event observation. 24 March 2014. Oakland, California.

15. Skate contest observation. 1 April 2014. Oakland, California.

16. K-Dub, parents and children at skate park observation. 26 April 2014. Oakland, California.

17. Town Hall Parks and Recreation meeting. 20 August 2014. Oakland, California.

18. Oakland City Hall public works department Phase 2 meeting. 3 March 2015. Oakland, California.

19. Skate park observation. 13 February 2016. Oakland, California.

20. Skate park observation. 13 February 2016. Oakland, California.

21. Skate park observation. 1 April 2016. Oakland, California.

22. Skate park observation. 23 April 2016. Oakland, California.

23. Skate park observation. 14 May 2016. Oakland, California.

24. Skate park observation. 14 May 2016. Oakland, California.

25. Skate park observation. 18 May 2016. Oakland, California.

26. Skate park observation. MAHFIA.TV event. 9 July 2016. Oakland, California.

27. Skate park observation. 25 August 2016. Oakland, California.

28. Skate park observation. 25 August 2016. Oakland, California.

29. "Life is Living" Festival observation. 14 June 2014. Oakland, California.

30. Oakland Skatepark Summit. 18 March 2017. Oakland, California.

31. City Center and skate park observation. 15 November 2015. San Jose, California.

32. Skate park observation. 14 February 2016. San Jose, California.

33. Skate park observation. 14 February 2016. San Jose, California.

34. Skate park observation. 28 February 2016. San Jose, California.

35. Skate park observation. 28 February 2016. San Jose, California.

36. Skate park observation. 28 February 2016. San Jose, California.

37. Skate park observation. 17 July 2016. San Jose, California.

38. Skate park observation. 2 August 2016. San Jose, California.

39. Skate park event observation. 2 August 2016. San Jose, California.

40. Skate park observation. 2 August 2016. San Jose, California.

41. Skate park observation. 23 August 2016. San Jose, California.

42. Skate park observation. 28 February 2017. San Jose, California.

43. SLAG skate session observation. 20 April 2014. Berkeley, California.

44. SLAG skate session observation. 18 May 2014. Berkeley, California.

45. SLAG skate session observation. 15 February 2015. Berkeley, California.

46. SLAG skate session observation. 23 November 2015. Berkeley, California.

47. Rob class presentation. 20 May 2014. Hayward, California.

48. Donna classroom presentation. 12 November 2014. Hayward, California.

49. Donna graduate class presentation. 1 April 2015. Hayward, California.

50. YouthSpace Center for Sport and Social Justice event with K-Dub, 13 April 2015. Hayward, California.

NOTES

Foreword

1. World Skate, "World Skate Skateboarding," accessed August 1, 2018, http://www.worldskate.org/skateboarding/news-skateboarding/2910-world-skate-skateboarding.html.

Introduction

1. We mostly utilize the phrase "action sports" throughout this book, even though others in the past have referred to skateboarding as an extreme, lifestyle, or alternative sport. According to Holly Thorpe and Rebecca Olive, "the term 'action sports' is increasingly the preferred term used by sporting industries and governing bodies, as well as many sporting participants themselves (many of whom resent the label 'extreme sports' which they feel was imposed upon them by transnational corporations and conglomerates during the mid and late 1990s)." "Introduction: Contextualizing Women in Action Sport Culture," in *Women in Action Sport Cultures: Identity, Politics and Experience*, ed. Holly Thorpe and Rebecca Olive (London: Palgrave Macmillan, 2016), 3.

2. Emily Chivers Yochim, *Skate Life: Re-Imagining White Masculinity* (Ann Arbor: University of Michigan Press, 2010), 41.

3. Ben Detrick, "Skateboarding Rolls Out of the Suburbs," *New York Times*, November 11, 2007, http://www.nytimes.com/2007/11/11/fashion/11skaters.html?pagewanted=all&_r=0.

4. Detrick, "Skateboarding Rolls Out of the Suburbs."

5. Edward Iwata and *USA Today*, "Tony Hawk Leaps to Top of Financial Empire," ABC News, accessed August 10, 2017, http://abcnews.go.com/Business/story?id=4418514&page=1.

6. James Renhard, "Meet Skateboarding's Million Dollar Man: The Rob Dyrdek Interview," *Mpora*, 2014, https://mpora.com/longform/the-rob-dyrdek-interview#4j1TdmgF2Q7ATA6v.97.

7. Olympic Channel, "Watch Skateboarders Train for Gold", accessed October 14, 2017, https://www.facebook.com/OlympicChannel.

8. Nat Kassel, "We Asked Skaters How They Feel About Skateboarding Making the 2020 Olympics," *Vice*, August 17, 2016, https://www.vice.com/en_au/article/nny3nm/we-asked-skaters-how-they-feel-about-skateboarding-making-the-2020-olympics.

9. "Rising Popularity of Skateboarding to Drive the Global Skateboarding Equipment Market Through 2020, Says Technavio," *Business Wire,* July 5, 2016, http://www.businesswire.com/news/home/20160705005261/en/Rising-Popularity-Skateboarding-Drive-Global-Skateboarding-Equipment.

10. "Millennials Get Inspired by Adventurous Boomers: Challenging Yourself

Has No Age Limit," Featured Blog Post, AARP Media Sales, accessed September 25, 2016, http://advertise.aarp.org/50-advantage/adventurous-boomers-inspiration.

11. This trend is not unique to skateboarding, as it can be found in other action sports. Belinda Wheaton mentions "parkour for pensioners" in her chapter "Parkour, Gendered Power and the Politics of Identity," in *Women in Action Sport Cultures: Identity, Politics and Experience*, ed. Holly Thorpe and Rebecca Olive (London: Palgrave Macmillan, 2016), 125.

12. Detrick, "Skateboarding Rolls Out of Suburbs."

13. Michael Andreosky, "Sycamore Park- Skate Park (Thumbs Up)," February 16, 2018, https://nextdoor.com/news_feed/?post=76615718.

14. Paul Gilchrist and Belinda Wheaton, "Lifestyle and Adventure Sport Among Youth," in *Routledge Handbook of Youth Sport*, ed. Ken Green and Andy Smith (New York: Routledge, 2016), 194.

15. Don Sabo and Philip Veliz, "Surveying Youth Sports in America: What We Know and What It Means for Public Policy," in *Child's Play: Sport in Kids' Worlds*, ed. Michael A. Messner and Michela Musto (New Brunswick: Rutgers University Press, 2016), 24.

16. Jaquline Stenson, "Pushing Too Hard Too Young: Take Away the Fun Factor in Sports and Kids Can Burn Out," NBC News, April 29, 2004, http://www.nbcnews.com/id/4556235/ns/health-childrens_health/t/pushing-too-hard-too-young/.

17. See Jon Solomon, "7 Charts that Show Why We Need to Fix Youth Sports," Aspen Institute, September 5, 2017, https://www.aspeninstitute.org/blog-posts/7-charts-show-fix-youth-sports/. Project Play, led by the Aspen Institute, was launched in 2013 and brings together key individuals from the "realms of sports, medicine, media, business innovation, government and philanthropy" in order to "reimagine sports in America." See "About Project Play," Aspen Institute, accessed September 13, 2016, http://www.aspenprojectplay.org/about-project-play.

18. Solomon's article highlights that "only 36.9 percent of children ages 6-12 played team sports on a regular basis in 2016—down from 38.6 in 2015 and 44.5 in 2008"; also see Jacob Bogage, "Youth Sports Study: Declining Participation, Rising Costs and Unqualified Coaches," *Washington Post*, September 6, 2017, https://www.washingtonpost.com/news/recruiting-insider/wp/2017/09/06/youth-sports-study-declining-participation-rising-costs-and-unqualified-coaches/?utm_term=.be8e6ef81423.

19. Ryan Wallerson, "Youth Participation Weakens in Basketball, Football, Baseball, Soccer: Fewer Children Play Team Sports," *Wall Street Journal*, January 31, 2014, http://www.wsj.com/articles/SB10001424052702303519404579350892629229918.

20. Jeff Crane and Viviene Temple, "A Systematic Review of Dropout from Organized Sport among Children and Youth," *European Physical Education Review* 21, no. 1 (2015): 114–31.

21. Michael A. Messner, *It's All for the Kids: Gender, Families, and Youth Sports* (Berkeley: University of California Press, 2009), 101.

22. Jay Coakley, "The Good Father: Parental Expectations and Youth Sports," *Leisure Studies* 25, no. 2 (2006): 160.

23. Sean Gregory, "How Kids' Sports Became a $15 Billion Industry," *Time*, August 23, 2017, http://time.com/4913687/how-kids-sports-became-15-billion-industry/.

24. Farrey, "Sports for All Roundtable Discussion."

25. KJ Dell'Antonia, "The Families That Can't Afford Summer," *New York Times*, June 4, 2016, http://www.nytimes.com/2016/06/05/sunday-review/the-families -that-cant-afford-summer.html?_r=0.

26. Tom Farrey, "Competitive Youth Sports in Society: What President Obama Needs to Know to Get—and Keep—Kids Moving," *Current Sports Medicine Reports* 9, no. 6 (2010): 361.

27. Solomon, "7 Charts."

28. Bogage, "Youth Sports Study."

29. Messner, *It's All for the Kids*, 11.

30. Hilary L. Friedman, *Playing to Win: Raising Children in a Competitive Culture* (Berkeley: University of California Press, 2013), 32.

31. Gregory, "How Kids' Sports."

32. The current expensiveness of modern youth sports runs contrary to the historical origins of many American competitive team sports such as baseball and basketball. Scholar Kathleen Yep, for instance, has described how sports such as basketball first "appealed to the unemployed masses during the Great Depression because it required very little space, training or equipment. Ten people could play at once and only a basketball and a hoop were needed." See Kathleen Yep, "Peddling Sport: Liberal Multiculturalism and the Racial Triangulation of Blackness, Chineseness and Native American-ness in Professional Basketball," *Ethnic and Racial Studies* 35, no. 6 (2012): 974.

33. Eddie Matz, "The Kids are Alright," ESPN, February 24, 2014, http://www .espn.com/espn/story/_/id/10496416/are-youth-sports-ruining-kids-childhoods -espn-magazine.

34. "How Can a 4-Year-Old Join the FC Barcelona Academy?" Quora, answered February 2, 2016, accessed September 13, 2017, https://www.quora.com /How-can-a-4-year-old-join-the-FC-Barcelona-Academy.

35. Bogage, "Youth Sports Study."

36. David L. Andrews and Michael Silk, *Sport and Neoliberalism: Politics, Consumption, and Culture* (Philadelphia: Temple University Press, 2012), 7.

37. Henry A. Giroux, "Beyond the Biopolitics of Disposability: Rethinking Neoliberalism in the New Gilded Age," *Social Identities* 14, no. 5 (2008): 591.

38. Simon Beames, Chris Mackie and Matthew Atencio, *Adventure and Society* (Basingstoke: Palgrave Macmillan, 2018).

39. Chivers Yochim, *Skate Life*, 89.

40. Chivers Yochim, *Skate Life*, 78.

41. Chivers Yochim, *Skate Life*, 10.

42. Nina Gregory, "Tony Hawk: From Skateboard Misfit to CEO," Author Interviews—Morning Edition, NPR, October 29, 2010, http://www.npr.org /templates/story/story.php?storyId=130859155.

43. Holly Thorpe, "Action Sports for Youth Development: Critical Insights for the SDP Community," *International Journal of Sport Policy and Politics* 8 (2014): 93.

44. "Action Sports Facts and Figures," Active Marketing Group, http://www .activenetworkrewards.com/Assets/AMG+2009/Action+Sports.pdf.

45. Thorpe, "Action Sports," 92.

46. For further details, see Kailee Bradstreet, "The State of Skate 2016: Core vs. Casual Participation," Grind TV, May 25, 2016, http://www.grindtv.com

/transworld-business/features/the-state-of-skate-2016/ and "Outdoor Recreation Participation: Topline Report 2017," Outdoor Foundation, accessed September 13, 2017, https://outdoorindustry.org/wp-content/uploads/2017/04/2017-Topline -Report_FINAL.pdf.

47. Becky Beal, *Skateboarding: The Ultimate Guide* (Santa Barbara: Greenwood, 2013), 33.

48. Matthew Atencio and Becky Beal, "'Beautiful Losers': The Symbolic Exhibition and Legitimization of Outsider Masculinity," *Sport in Society* 14 (2011): 1–16.

49. Thomas Barker, "How USC's Skateboarding Business Class is Now Fostering the Next Crop of Industry Leaders," *Transworld Business*, February 5, 2016, http://business.transworld.net/features/usc-skateboarding-business-class-fostering-next -crop-industry-leaders/#XUOxOBdxQqWl7vYR.97.

50. Ocean Howell, "Skatepark as Neoliberal Playground: Urban Governance, Recreation Space, and the Cultivation of Personal Responsibility," *Space and Culture* 11, no. 4 (2008): 475–96.

51. Phil Wahba, "How Vans Skated Past a Big Retail Milestone," *Fortune*, March 31, 2017, http://fortune.com/2017/03/31/vans-vfc/.

52. Alex Tudela, "Non-Surf Wear from Saturdays, Prada's New Backpack and the Return of a Givenchy Icon," *New York Times*, January 10, 2017, https://www.nytimes.com/2017/01/10/fashion/mens-style/prada-saturdays-surf-givenchy -missy-robbins-shopping.html.

53. Amy Sueyoshi, "Skate and Create: Skateboarding, Asian Pacific America, and Masculinity," *Amerasia Journal* 41, no. 2 (2015): 2–24.

54. Sean Mortimer, *Stalefish: Skateboard Culture from the Rejects Who Made It* (San Francisco: Chronicle Books, 2008), 168.

55. We utilize the phrase "youth of color" throughout this book. This phrasing follows scholar Salvador Vidal-Ortiz's usage of "people of color," which directly refers to racial- and ethnic-based groups in the United States and their relationships with each other, as framed by popular, activist, and academic discussions. Vidal-Ortiz contends that this term expands upon and potentially challenges the notions of "race" and "racial and ethnic minority." For further discussion, see Salvador Vidal-Ortiz, "People of Color," in *Encyclopedia of Race, Ethnicity, and Society*, ed. Richard T. Schaefer (Thousand Oaks, Calif.: Sage Publications, 2008), 1037–39. For more background on the emergence of skateboarding in urban areas where youth of color often live, on both the East and West coasts of the United States, see Richard Marosi, "Skateboarders in Urban Areas Get Respect, and Parks," *Los Angeles Times*, June 18, 2001, http://articles.latimes.com/2001/jun/18/local /me-11888; and Detrick, "Skateboarding Rolls Out the Suburbs."

56. Renata Simril and Neftailie Williams, "One Small Step for Skateboarding Is One Giant Step for Diversity," Medium.com, May 12, 2017, https://medium.com /@LA84Foundation/one-small-step-for-skateboarding-is-one-giant-step-for -diversity-10b24ea56e66.

57. Margeaux Watson, "Skurban Legend," *Entertainment Weekly*, April 13, 2007, http://www.ew.com/ew/article/0,,20034823,00.html.

58. Matthew Atencio, Emily Chivers Yochim, and Becky Beal, "It Ain't Just Black Kids and White Kids: The Representation and Reproduction of Authentic 'Skurban'

Masculinities," *Sociology of Sport Journal* 30, no. 2 (2013): 153–72, doi:10.1123 /ssj.30.2.153.

59. "Ellen Berryman: Skateboarding Legend," Long Board Girls Crew, January 29, 2013, http://longboardgirlscrew.com/2013/01/ellen-berryman -skateboarding-legend/.

60. WYSK Guest Contributor, "8 Female Skaters That Changed History," *Women You Should Know,* October 7, 2014, http://www.womenyoushould know.net/8-female-skaters-changed-history/.

61. Lauren Evans, "Meet Sky Brown, Pint-Sized Badass Skating Prodigy," *Jezebel,* September 18, 2016, http://jezebel.com/meet-sky-brown-pint-sized-badass-skating -prodigy-1786776995.

62. Anna Pulley, "These Female Skateboarders Are Changing the Sport for the Better," *East Bay Express,* March 4, 2015, http://www.eastbayexpress.com/oakland /reinventing-the-wheels/Content?oid=4210451.

63. Pulley, "These Female Skateboarders Are Changing the Sport for the Better."

64. "Skateboader Minna Stess Shines in these New Lego Commercials," Girl Is Not A 4 Letter Word, January 17 2018, http://www.girlisnota4letterword .com/2018/01/skateboarder-minna-stess-shines-in.html.

65. Noah Remnick, "Sisterhood of the Skateboard," *New York Times,* July 29, 2016, https://www.nytimes.com/2016/07/31/nyregion/brujas-a-crew-of-female -skateboarders-in-the-bronx.html. For more information on the River Avenue Skate Park in the Bronx, see http://newyorkcityskateparks.com/bronxriver aveskateark.html.

66. Megan Griffo, "The 'Pink Helmet Posse' is a Trio of Skateboarding 6-year-old Girls and They're Awesome," *Huffington Post,* updated October 22, 2013, http:// www.huffingtonpost.com/2013/10/21/pink-helmet-posse_n_4137841.html.

67. Iain Borden, "The New Skate City: How Skateboarders are Joining the Urban Mainstream," *The Guardian,* April 20, 2015, http://www.theguardian.com /cities/2015/apr/20/skate-city-skateboarders-developers-bans-defensive -architecture.

68. Kara-Jane Lombard, "The Cultural Politics of Skateboarding and the Rise of Skate Urbanism," in *Skateboarding: Subcultures, Sites and Shifts,* ed. Kara-Jane Lombard (London: Routledge, 2016), 3.

69. Heidi Lemmon, "Grinding Out the Details: A Look at What's Trending in Skateparks," *Parks and Rec Business* 15, no. 10 (2017): 26.

70. Chivers Yochim, *Skate Life,* 53–60.

71. Nick Vadala, "The Past (and Future) of Philly Skate Mecca Love Park Lives on," Philly, June 21, 2014, http://www.philly.com/philly/blogs/lifestyle/The -past-and-future-of-Philly-skate-mecca-Love-Park-lives-on.html.

72. Chivers Yochim, *Skate Life,* 47.

73. "Brief History of Skateparks," Public Skatepark Development Guide, 2017, http://publicskateparkguide.org/vision/brief-history-of-skateparks/.

74. For details, see Gregory, "Tony Hawk: From Skateboard Misfit To CEO." A vert ramp is defined as "a half pipe, usually at least 8 feet tall, with steep sides that are perfectly vertical near the top." Beal, *Skateboarding: The Ultimate Guide,* 123; "Vert Skating 101 (A History Lesson)," *Transworld Skateboarding,* September 13, 1999, http://skateboarding.transworld.net/features/vert-skating-101-a-history -lesson/.

75. "Vert Skating 101."

76. Howell, "Skatepark as Neoliberal Playground," 475.

77. Carter Dennis, "The 2011 Skatepark Tracker," Skaters for Public Skateparks, January 7, 2012, accessed September 29, 2016, https://www.skatepark.org /park-development/2012/01/the-2011-skatepark-tracker.

78. "Skate Park a Home Run," *Carthage Press*, last modified July 24, 2012, accessed September 25, 2016, http://www.carthagepress.com/article/20111021 /News/310219982.

79. For more information on global skate park phenomenon, refer to Beal, *Skateboarding,* 2.

80. Holly Thorpe, *Transnational Mobilities in Action Sport Cultures* (New York: Palgrave Macmillan, 2014), 48.

81. Marosi, "Skateboarders in Urban Areas."

82. Gilchrist and Wheaton, "Lifestyle and Adventure Sport Among Youth," 193.

83. Howell, "Skatepark as Neoliberal Playground," 476. According to Howell, there is consensus that skate parks function as "zones of economic activity, where stunts are documented and distributed (in magazines and videos) by the multibillion-dollar skateboard industry."

84. Mike Redding, "Skate Park Pedagogy," Using Technology Better, http://using technologybetter.com/skate-park-pedagogy/.

85. Lisa Johnson, "Corrimal East Students Learn New Skills at Lunch Time Skate Pod: Video," *Illawarra Mercury,* July 26, 2016, http://www.illawarramercury .com.au/story/4053640/corrimal-east-students-learn-new-skills-at-lunch-time -skate-pod-video/?src=rss.

86. Douglas Hartmann, *Midnight Basketball: Race, Sports, and Neoliberal Social Policy* (Chicago: University of Chicago Press, 2016), ix.

87. Thorpe, "Action Sports," 91–116.

88. Paul O'Connor, "Skateboarding Philanthropy: Inclusion and Prefigurative Politics," in *Skateboarding: Subcultures, Sites and Shifts,* ed. Kara-Jane Lombard (London: Routledge, 2016), 32.

89. Graham L. Bradley, "Skate Parks as a Context for Adolescent Development," *Journal of Adolescent Research* 25, no. 2 (2009): 288.

90. Kenneth Bachor, "See How Skateboarding Is Changing Native American Youth Culture," *Time,* January 26, 2016, http://time.com/4163592/native-american -skateboarding-lakota/?xid=fbshare.

91. Myra Taylor and Ida Marais, "Not in My Back Schoolyard: Schools and Skate-park Builds in Western Australia," *Australian Planner* 48, no. 2 (2011): 85.

92. "Why a Plan Now?," City of Seattle Citywide Skatepark Plan, January 31, 2007, http://www.seattle.gov/Documents/Departments/ParksAndRecreation /PoliciesPlanning/CitywideSkateparkPlan.pdf.

93. Angela Akridge, "Kids Plead for a Skatepark in Newark, CA," YouTube, February 26, 2016, https://www.youtube.com/watch?v=uBdNbJHI8GI.

94. "Build a Skatepark in Newark: Petitioning Newark City Council," Change. org, 2015, https://www.change.org/p/skatepark-for-newark.

95. A range of critical sociological scholars have challenged this type of public-health discourse, which often aligns with societal (and moral) concerns sur-

rounding a perceived obesity problem across the world. See Michael Gard and Jan Wright, *The Obesity Epidemic: Science, Morality, and Ideology* (London: Routledge, 2005); Emma Rich and John Evans, "'Fat Ethics'—The Obesity Discourse and Body Politics," *Social Theory and Health* 3 (2005): 341–58; Jan Wright and Valerie Harwood, eds., *Biopolitics and the Obesity Epidemic* (London: Routledge, 2009).

96. James A. Phills Jr., Kriss Deiglmeier, and Dale T. Miller, "Rediscovering Social Innovation," *Stanford Social Innovation Review*, Fall 2008, https://ssir.org/articles/entry/rediscovering_social_innovation.

97. Anne-Claire Pache and Filipe Santos, "Inside the Hybrid Organization: Selective Coupling as a Response to Conflicting Institutional Logics," *Academy of Management Journal* 56, no. 4 (2013): 972.

98. Phills Jr., Deiglmeier, and Miller, "Rediscovering Social Innovation."

99. Vera L. Zolberg, *Constructing a Sociology of the Arts* (Cambridge: Cambridge University Press, 1990), 126.

100. Since the 1990s, many studies have translated Pierre Bourdieu's theoretical framework into the realms of both traditional sports and extreme or action sports. For one particularly clear and relevant application of Bourdieu's concepts of capital in modern sports, see Lisa Swanson, "Soccer Fields of Cultural [Re]Production: Creating 'Good Boys' in Suburban America," *Sociology of Sport Journal* 26 (2009): 404–24.

101. Matthew Atencio, Becky Beal, and Charlene Wilson, "The Distinction of Risk: Urban Skateboarding, Street Habitus and the Construction of Hierarchical Gender Relations," *Qualitative Research in Sport and Exercise* 1, no. 1 (2009): 3–20. This article, involving the first two authors of this book, highlights how "the distinction of risk," or being associated with risk-taking behavior, is something that male skateboarders want to claim and embody. Skateboarders, it is argued, traditionally obtain "authentic" status within skateboarding networks by embodying a unique countercultural ethos. Male skateboarders who most closely associate with "risk" are able to benefit in terms of dominating local skate spaces and participating fully in symbolic outlets such as skate videos and magazines.

102. City and park name changed to maintain anonymity.

103. Dan Brekke, "Hey, Bay Area: You Really Are Diverse," KQED, February 17, 2015, http://ww2.kqed.org/news/2015/02/17/san-francisco-bay-area-cities-among-most-diverse-in-united-states/.

104. Jan Wright, "Physical Education Research from Postmodern, Poststructural and Postcolonial Perspectives," in *The Handbook of Physical Education*, ed. David Kirk, Doune Macdonald, and Mary O'Sullivan (London: Sage, 2006), 59–75.

105. "Campus Ethnic Diversity," *U.S. News & World Report Higher Education*, https://www.usnews.com/best-colleges/rankings/regional-universities-west/campus-ethnic-diversity; "A $2.6 Million Federal Grant will Help Underserved Students at CSU East Bay," October 26, 2015, http://www.csueastbay.edu/news/2015/10/10262015.html.

106. Lombard, "Cultural Politics of Skateboarding," 6.

107. "About ISYS: ISYS Mission," Institute for the Study of Youth Sports, accessed June 22, 2017, http://edwp.educ.msu.edu/isys/about/.

108. Steph MacKay, "Carving Out Space in the Action Sports Media Landscape:

The Skirtboarders' Blog as a 'Skatefeminist' Project," in *Women in Action Sport Cultures: Identity, Politics and Experience*, ed. Holly Thorpe and Rebecca Olive (London: Palgrave Macmillan, 2016), 303.

ONE

1. Joe Epstein, "Pay-to-Play Leagues," KQED Radio, March 9, 2015, http://www.kqed.org/a/perspectives/R201503090643.

2. Lisa Duggan, *The Twilight of Equality? Neoliberalism, Cultural Politics and the Attack on Democracy* (Boston: Beacon Press, 2003), 22.

3. Duggan, *The Twilight of Equality?*, 12.

4. Jessica Skolnikoff and Robert Engvall, *Young Athletes, Couch Potatoes, and Helicopter Parents: The Productivity of Play* (Boulder: Rowman and Littlefield, 2014), 92.

5. Coakley, "The 'Logic' of Specialization: Using Children for Adult Purposes," *Journal of Physical Education, Recreation and Dance* 81, no. 8 (2010): 17.

6. Jay Coakley, "The 'Logic' of Specialization," 17.

7. Brad Schmidt, "Portland Picks Under Armour Despite Nike 'Disgruntlement,'" *The Oregonian*, September 28, 2015, http://www.oregonlive.com/portland/index.ssf/2015/09/portland_picks_under_armour_de.html.

8. Brad Schmidt, "Under Armour Seeking Deal for 2 Turf Fields in Portland Parks," *The Oregonian*, July 10, 2015, http://www.oregonlive.com/portland/index.ssf/2015/07/under_armour_seeking_deal_for.html.

9. Jay Scherer, Jordan Koch, and Nicholas L. Holt, "The Uses of an Inner-City Sport-for-Development Program: Dispatches From the (Real) Creative Class," *Sociology of Sport Journal* 33, no. 3 (2016): 185.

10. Douglas Hartmann, *Midnight Basketball: Race, Sports, and Neoliberal Social Policy* (Chicago: University of Chicago Press, 2016).

11. Hartmann's case-study of Midnight Basketball found that this program, largely targeted at urban, underserved African-American male youth, "appealed to the most libertarian impulses of neoliberalism—freeing programs and services from state regulation and offering nonstate actors the chance to compete for the opportunity to serve communities in new, innovative, and cost-effective ways." Going further with this viewpoint, Hartmann surmised that this program "was at the forefront and leading edge of the reconfiguration of social policy in the neoliberal image—a near ideal-typical model, a microcosm, of neoliberal social policy in late twentieth- and early twenty-first-century America." Hartmann, *Midnight Basketball*, 49–50.

12. Jay Coakley, "Youth Sport in the United States," in *Routledge Handbook of Youth Sport*, ed. Ken Green and Andy Smith (London: Routledge, 2016), 84–97.

13. Emily Chivers Yochim, *Skate Life: Re-Imagining White Masculinity* (Ann Arbor: University of Michigan Press, 2010), 8.

14. Matthew Atencio and Becky Beal, "'Beautiful Losers': The Symbolic Exhibition and Legitimization of Outsider Masculinity," *Sport in Society* 14 (2011): 1–16.

15. Brendan I. Koerner, "Silicon Valley Has Lost Its Way. Can Skateboarding Legend Rodney Mullen Help It?" *Wired*, January 27, 2015, https://www.wired.com/2015/01/rodney-mullen/.

16. Chivers Yochim, *Skate Life*, 173. In her book's concluding chapter, Chivers Yochim reminds us that skateboarders avidly take up, reject, and even produce the representations and products of mainstream skate corporatism.

17. Ocean Howell, "Skatepark as Neoliberal Playground: Urban Governance, Recreation Space, and the Cultivation of Personal Responsibility," *Space and Culture* 11, no. 4 (2008): 476.

18. Ocean Howell, "The 'Creative Class' and Gentrifying the City: Skateboarding in Philadelphia's Love Park," *Journal of Architectural Education* 59, no. 2 (2005): 32–42.

19. Howell, "Skatepark as Neoliberal Playground," 476.

20. Howell, "Skatepark as Neoliberal Playground," 476.

21. Chris Nieratko, "San Francisco's Best Skate Shop FTC Turns 27," *Vice*, January 1, 2014, http://www.vice.com/read/san-franciscos-best-skateshop-ftc -turns-27. FTC, in operation for nearly thirty years, has even produced a hardcover book highlighting its influence upon skateboarding culture, and it has created "certified classic" skate videos which, as one writer described, took "FTC's notoriety out of the hills of San Francisco and thrust it to international fame."

22. Nina Wu, "Skateboard Park Still a Dream in San Francisco," Coast News, accessed June 27, 2017, http://www.coastnews.com/sports/sf_skatepark.htm. Information on Kent Uyehara can be found at this website.

23. Kara-Jane Lombard, "Trucks, Tricks, and Technologies of Government: Analyzing the Productive Encounter Between Governance and Resistance in Skateboarding," in *Skateboarding: Subcultures, Sites and Shifts*, ed. Kara-Jane Lombard (London: Routledge Press, 2016), 169–81.

24. James Houser, "3 Iconic San Francisco Spots That Shaped Skateboarding History," 7X7, April 26, 2016, http://www.7x7.com/3-iconic-san-francisco-spots -that-shaped-skateboarding-history-1787343972.html#.

25. David Fischer, "The Pied Piper of Skateboarding," *New York Times*, June 27, 1999, http://www.nytimes.com/packages/html/sports/year_in_sports/06.27.html ?mcubz=0.

26. Kara-Jane Lombard, *The Cultural Politics of Skateboarding and the Rise of Skate Urbanism* (London: Routledge, 2016), 7.

27. Willy Staley, "Thrashed: Jake Phelps Has Run the Bible for Skaters for More Than Two Decades. He's Nearly Died a Few Times in the Process," *California Sunday Magazine*, March 24, 2016, https://story.californiasunday.com/jake-phelps -thrasher.

28. Cassie McFadden, "Caltrans Demolishes Bordertown Skate Park," *East Bay Express*, November 30, 2011, http://www.eastbayexpress.com/SevenDays /archives/2011/11/30/3056509-caltrans-demolishes-bordertown-skate-park.

29. Brian Krans, "Skate or DIY: Why Is It So Damn Hard to Build a Skate Park in Oakland," *East Bay Express*, March 14, 2017, https://www.eastbayexpress.com /oakland/skate-or-diy-why-is-it-so-damn-hard-to-build-a-skate-park-in-oakland /Content?oid=5719389.

30. Thrasher Magazine Year One: Issue 08, *Thrasher Magazine*, accessed June 23, 2017, https://archive.org/details/ThrasherMagazineYearOneIssue08.

31. Thrasher Magazine Year One: Issue 02, *Thrasher Magazine*, accessed June 23, 2017, https://archive.org/details/ThrasherMagazineYearOneIssue02.

32. Luis Ruano, "The Story of 510 Skateboarding," The Hundreds, June 25, 2014, http://thehundreds.com/510-skateboarding/.

33. Craig Ramsay, "Take, San Jose for Example," *Thrasher Magazine*, May 1983, 22, http://www.thrashermagazine.com/articles/magazine/may-1983/?tmpl =component.

34. Gary Singh, "Now Boarding," Metro Active, April 4, 2008, http://www .metroactive.com/metro/04.02.08/cover-sjskatepark-0814.html.

35. "True to Its Roots," *Transworld SKATEboarding,* October 8, 2002, http:// skateboarding.transworld.net/news/true-to-its-roots/#bS8UekhL5UkYkSSA.97.

36. "True to Its Roots," *Transworld SKATEboarding.*

37. Rachel Swan, "The Domestication of the Skateboard: San Francisco Battled Its Skateboarding Community for Decades. Then Silicon Valley Stepped In," *SF Weekly,* December 2, 2014, http://www.sfweekly.com/sanfrancisco/skateboards -electric-skateboards-skate-parks/Content?oid=3278135.

38. Swan, "The Domestication of the Skateboard"

39. Bill Schaffer, "No One Standing Above You: Rodney Mullen and the Ethics of Innovation," in *Skateboarding: Subcultures, Sites and Shifts,* ed. Kara-Jane Lombard (London: Routledge Press, 2016), 24–25. In a related example, Schaffer notes that "the very qualities that made LOVE Park an unlikely place to just sit and relax made it perfect for street skating. Predictably, the mayor of Philadelphia mounted a war against street skating after first trying to cash in with a corporate skate event, ordering constant police patrols to chase down skaters and confiscate their boards. When that failed, the mayor resorted to his own form of sanctioned vandalism, redesigning benches and planters in ways that he hoped would render them impossible to skate."

40. Swan, "Domestication of the Skateboard."

41. Swan, "Domestication of the Skateboard."

42. Swan, "Domestication of the Skateboard."

43. Anna Pulley, "These Female Skateboarders Are Changing the Sport for the Better," *East Bay Express*, March 4, 2015, http://www.eastbayexpress.com/oakland /reinventing-the-wheels/Content?oid=4210451&storyPage=4.

44. Alex Needham, "Acid Trips, Black Power, and Computers: How San Francisco's Hippy Explosion Shaped the Modern World," *The Guardian,* August 21, 2016, https://www.theguardian.com/culture/2016/aug/21/san-francisco-exhibition -victoria-albert-revolution-silicon-valley.

45. Dan Tynan, "Facebook's Journey 'Only 1% Done' After Surge in Revenue, Zuckerberg Says," *The Guardian,* July 27, 2016, www.theguardian.com /technology/2016/jul/27/facebook-ad-sales-growth-quarterly-results.

46. Rob Price, "RANKED: The 15 Tech Companies that Pay Interns the Most," *Business Insider*, February 12, 2017, http://www.businessinsider.com/15-highest -paying-tech-company-internships-glassdoor-google-apple-2017-2/#3-facebook -8000month-6400-13.

47. Shane Ryoo, "How Can I Survive in the Bay Area with $400k Family Income?" Quora, September 3, 2015, https://www.quora.com/How-can-I-survive -in-the-Bay-Area-with-400k-family-income.

48. Nellie Bowles, "'They Sell You a Dream': Tech Workers Protest Clooney Even for Clinton," *The Guardian,* April 16, 2016, https://www.theguardian.com/us-news /2016/apr/16/hillary-clinton-protest-george-clooney-fundraiser-bernie-sanders.

49. Joaquin Palomino, "How the Fade of S.F.'s Middle Class Affects a Slice of the City," *San Francisco Chronicle*, December 7, 2015, http://www.sfchronicle.com /bayarea/article/S-F-s-vanishing-middle-class-Dramatic-growth-6679627.php.

50. Jon Haveman, "Research Brief: Income Inequality in the San Francisco Bay Area," Silicon Valley Institute for Regional Studies, June 2015, 5, http://siliconvalley indicators.org/pdf/income-inequality-2015-06.pdf.

51. Jon Swartz, "Struggling in the Shadow of Silicon Valley Wealth," *USA Today*, November 11, 2014, http://www.usatoday.com/story/tech/2014/11/03/east-palo -alto-philanthropy-facebook-silicon-valley/16244117/.

52. Julia Carrie Wong, "Dropbox, AirBNB, and the Fight Over San Francisco's Public Spaces," *The New Yorker*, October 23, 2014, http://www.newyorker.com/tech /elements/dropbox-airbnb-fight-san-franciscos-public-spaces.

53. Wong, "Dropbox."

54. Jay Barmann, "Teen Who Protested over Mission Playground Reservations Appointed to City Hall Commission," SFist, August 24, 2016, http://sfist.com/2016 /08/24/teen_who_protested_over_mission_pla.php. This story has a new chapter, as one of the young local boys playing soccer that day, Hugo Vargas, is now at the age of seventeen, "helping advise the mayor and the Board of Supervisors on youth-related issues and legislation." At the time of the Mission Park incident, Vargas, along with "his Mexican immigrant parents, two younger sisters, and a dog were at the time all sharing a 10-foot-by-10-foot single-room-occupancy hotel room near 16th and Mission for three years."

55. Jay Barmann, "SF Native Who Fought for Soccer Field Takes Us on a Gentrification Tour of the Mission," SFist, January 14, 2015, http://sfist.com/2015 /01/14/sf_native_who_fought_for_soccer_fie.php. Information on Farina Pizza can be found at http://www.farina-foods.com/intro.php?url=farina-pizza.

56. Wong, "Dropbox."

57. Pierre Bourdieu, *Distinction: A Social Critique of the Judgement of Taste* (London: Routledge Kegan & Paul, 1984).

58. Susie Weller, "Skateboarding Alone? Making Social Capital Discourse Relevant to Teenagers' Lives," *Journal of Youth Studies* 9, no. 5 (2006): 572.

59. Adam Jenson, Jon Swords, and Michael Jeffries, "The Accidental Youth Club: Skateboarding in Newcastle-Gateshead," *Journal of Urban Design* 17, no. 3 (2012): 387.

60. Keegan Guizard, e-mail message to authors Becky Beal, Matthew Atencio, and Missy Wright, June 14, 2017.

61. Iain Borden, *Skateboarding, Space and the City: Architecture and the Body* (Oxford: Berg, 2001); Michael Nevin Willard, "Séance, Tricknowlogy, Skateboarding, and the Space of Youth," in *Generations of Youth: Youth Cultures and History in Twentieth-Century America*, ed. Joe Austin and Michael Nevin Willard (New York: New York University Press, 1998), 327–46.

62. Refer to Jenson, Swords, and Jeffries's "Accidental Youth Club," as well as Helen Woolley, Teresa Hazelwood and Ian Simkins, "Don't Skate Here: Exclusion of Skateboarders from Urban Civic Spaces in Three Northern Cities in England," *Journal of Urban Design* 16, no. 4 (2011): 471–87.

63. David Germain, "Dogtown—Film Documents Birth of the Cool in Skateboarding," CJOnline.com, June 21, 2002, accessed September 25, 2016, http:// cjonline.com/stories/062102/wee_dogtownzboys.shtml#.V-ho4pMrJTZ.

64. *Dogtown and Z- Boys*. Video format. Directed by Stacy Peralta. Culver City: Sony Pictures Classics, distributed by Columbia TriStar Home Entertainment, 2002.

65. Henri Lefebvre, *The Production of Space* (Oxford: Blackwell, 1992).

66. Doreen B. Massey, *Space, Place, and Gender* (Minneapolis; University of Minnesota Press, 1994), 127.

67. Jeremy Németh, "Conflict, Exclusion, Relocation: Skateboarding and Public Space," *Journal of Urban Design* 11, no. 3 (2006): 315.

68. Howell, "Skatepark as Neoliberal Playground," 477.

69. Writing in 1999, Cybriwsky purports that in a previous era, there was such a thing as urban public space that remained under the auspices of local government: "The familiar pattern was that in most cities, including Tokyo and New York, almost all streets and sidewalks, parks, civic squares and other such spaces were almost wholly in the public domain—that is, owned and maintained by government, especially local government, for essentially unrestricted access and use by the public." Roman Cybriwsky, "Changing Patterns of Urban Public Space: Observations and Assessments from the Tokyo and New York Metropolitan Areas," *Cities* 16, no. 4 (1999): 223, doi:10.1016/S0264-2751(99)00021-9.

70. Andrew Kirby, "The Production of Private Space and Its Implications for Urban Social Relations," *Political Geography* 27, no. 1 (2008): 74, doi:10.1016 /j.polgeo.2007.06.010.

71. Kirby, "The Production of Private Space," 76.

72. Kirby, "The Production of Private Space," 75.

73. Cybriwsky, "Changing Patterns," 225.

74. Writing from Australia in 1998, Kurt Iveson questions what remains of the "public space" concept. Considering the trend of joint public-private funding deals creating urban space in cities such as Los Angeles, he challenges the veracity of the "public space" concept by questioning what actually "constitutes 'good,' 'successful,' or 'genuine' public space" in the first place. Kurt Iveson, "Putting the Public Back into Public Space," *Urban Policy and Research* 16, no. 1 (1998): 31, doi:10.1080/08111149808727745.

75. Cybriwsky, "Changing Patterns," 223.

76. Kirby further picks up on this point, contending that public urban space has always been privatized to a certain degree: "There is an irony at the core of our usual celebration of the historical emergence of the public sphere, in that it was initially a private space." In a related argument that is particularly salient to our own study of gendered skateboarding spaces, Kirby contends that purportedly public spaces may actually be more exclusive when it comes to gendered usage, versus privately-directed spaces that may give opportunities for women to move more freely. Kirby concludes by advocating that "The assumption that private settings must inherently constitute diminished interaction and an inhibition of the public sphere is thus questionable." Kirby, "Production of Private Space," 82.

77. David J. Madden, "Revisiting the End of Public Space: Assembling the Public in an Urban Park," *City and Community* 9, no. 2 (2010): 202.

78. As a result of these changes, gentrification has sometimes been overtly resisted by established communities often based in low-income ethnic communities. Recent features stories attest to these challenges, including one recent story illustrating how an "iconoclastic" Hispanic urban neighborhood such as Boyle Heights of Los Angeles is confronting the influx of realtor tours, "artisanal treats,"

and avant-garde operas. See Rory Carroll, "'Hope Everyone Pukes on your Artisanal Treats': Fighting Gentrification, LA-style," *The Guardian*, April 19, 2016, https://www.theguardian.com/us-news/2016/apr/19/los-angeles-la-gentrification-resistance-boyle-heights. Additional information from other West Coast cities can be found in the following articles: Christopher Booker and Connie Kargo, "Iconic Portland Skate Park on the Front Lines of Gentrification," WNYC, December 24, 2016, http://www.wnyc.org/story/iconic-portland-skate-park-on-the-front-lines-of-gentrification/; Tricia Romano, "Cultures Clash as Gentrification Engulfs Capitol Hill," *Seattle Times*, March 13, 2015 (updated November 22, 2016), http://www.seattletimes.com/life/lifestyle/culture-clash-on-capitol-hill/.

79. Booker and Kargo, "Iconic Portland."

80. Jamie Peck, "Struggling with the Creative Class," *International Journal of Urban and Regional Research* 29, no. 4 (2005): 740.

81. From Chris Gibson, "Guest Editorial—Creative Geographies: Tales from the 'Margins,'" *Australian Geographer* 41, no. 1 (2010): "Creativity is said to be *the* salient feature of contemporary post-industrial capitalism, fueling innovation and investment and therefore responsible for urban economic fortunes, as well as being a somewhat intangible quality in places ('the buzz' in urban milieus)" (765).

82. Peck, "Struggling," 746. Peck goes on to say that in Florida's model of urban change, "the Creative Class generates growth, the rest live off the spoils."

83. Ocean Howell, "'Creative Class' and Gentrifying the City," 33.

84. Peck, "Struggling," 765–68.

85. Peck, "Struggling," 765–68.

86. Pete Saunders, "Regarding 'The New Urban Crisis,'" *Forbes*, June 26, 2017, https://www.forbes.com/sites/petesaunders1/2017/06/26/regarding-the-new-urban-crisis/#26ad88367706.

87. Jan Wright and Doune Macdonald, "Young People, Physical Activity and the Everyday: The Life Activity Project," in *Young People, Physical Activity and the Everyday*, ed. Jan Wright and Doune Macdonald (London: Routledge, 2010), 7.

88. Gill Valentine, Tracey Skelton, and Deborah Chambers, "Cool Places: An Introduction to Youth and Youth Cultures," in *Cool Places: Geographies of Youth Cultures*, ed. Tracey Skelton and Gill Valentine (London: Routledge, 1998), 7.

89. Valentine, Skelton, and Chambers, "Cool Places," 7.

90. Németh, "Conflict, Exclusion, Relocation," 309.

91. Cherylynn Bassani clearly addresses this concern. She discusses how social capital is an important aspect of youths' wellbeing, and yet, the social capital concept has been largely framed in terms of adults and their social lives, instead of attending to youth-based groups. Bassani eventually advocates that "youth-based social capital must be examined if we wish to improve our understanding of youths' well-being." Cherylynn Bassani, "Five Dimensions of Social Capital Theory as they Pertain to Youth Studies," *Journal of Youth Studies* 10, no. 1 (2007): 19.

92. Vicky Cattell, Nick Dines, Wil Gesler, and Sarah Curtis, "Mingling, Observing, and Lingering: Everyday Public Spaces and their Implications for Well-Being and Social Relations," *Health & Place* 14 (2008): 544–61.

93. "About Us," Changing the Game Project, 2017, http://changingthegameproject.com/about/.

94. Charlotte Faircloth, "Intensive Parenting and the Expansion of Parenting,"

in *Parenting Culture Studies*, ed. Ellie Lee, Jennie Bristow, Charlotte Faircloth, and Jan Macvarish (London: Palgrave Macmillan, 2014), 36.

95. Hilary L. Friedman, *Playing to Win: Raising Children in a Competitive Culture* (Berkeley: University of California Press, 2013), 32; Annette Lareau, "Invisible Inequality: Social Class and Childrearing in Black Families and White Families," *American Sociological Review* 67, no. 5 (2002): 747–76.

96. Carl Vincent and Carol Maxwell, "Parenting Priorities and Pressures: Furthering Understanding of 'Concerted Cultivation,'" *Discourse: Studies in the Cultural Politics of Education* 37, no. 2 (2016): 278.

97. Vincent and Maxwell, "Parenting Priorities and Pressures," 278.

98. Jennie Bristow, "The Double Bind of Parenting Culture: Helicopter Parents and Cotton Wool Kids," in *Parenting Culture Studies*, ed. Ellie Lee, Jennie Bristow, Charlotte Faircloth, and Jan Macvarish (London: Palgrave Macmillan, 2014), 203–204.

99. Barry A. Garst and Ryan J. Gagnon, "Exploring Overparenting within the Context of Youth Development Programs," *Journal of Youth Development* 10, no. 1 (2015): 5–18.

100. M. Blair Evans, Veronica Allan, Matthew Vierimaa, and Jean Côté, "Sport Parent Roles in Fostering Positive Youth Development," in *Families, Young People, Physical Activity and Health: Critical Perspectives,* ed. Symeon Dagkas and Lisette Burrows (London: Routledge, 2016), 228.

101. Evans, Allan, Vierimaa, and Côté, "Sport Parent Roles," 72.

102. Jay Coakley, "The Good Father: Parental Expectations and Youth Sports," *Leisure Studies* 25, no. 2 (2006): 160.

103. Friedman, *Playing to Win*, 49.

104. Dan Gould and Sarah Carson, "Life Skills Development Through Sport: Current Status and Future Directions," *International Review of Sport and Exercise Psychology* 1, no. 1 (2008): 60.

105. Jay Coakley, "Youth Sports: What Counts as 'Positive Development'?" *Journal of Sport and Social Issues* 35, no. 3 (2011): 308–309, doi:10.1177/0193723 511417311.

106. Jay Coakley, "Positive Youth Development Through Sport: Myths, Beliefs, and Realities," in *Positive Youth Development Through Sport*, 2nd ed., ed. Nicholas Holt (New York: Routledge, 2016), 22.

107. Friedman, *Playing to Win*, 3.

108. Friedman, *Playing to Win*, 3.

109. Friedman, *Playing to Win*, 219.

110. Onaje X.O. Woodbine, "Why I Quit Yale Basketball at the Top of My Game," *Chronicle of Higher Education*, April 1, 2016, http://chronicle.com/article /Why-I-Quit-Yale-Basketball-at/235928.

111. Friedman, *Playing to Win*, 215.

112. Coakley, "Positive Youth Development," 22.

113. Don Hellison, Teaching Personal and Social Responsibility Through Physical Activity (Champaign: Human Kinetics, 1995).

114. Michael A. Messner, *It's All for the Kids: Gender, Families and Youth Sports* (Berkeley: University of California Press, 2009), 10.

115. Douglas Hartmann, "Re-thinking Community-Based Crime Prevention through Sports," in *Sport, for Development, Peace, and Social Justice*, eds. Robert J.

Schinke and Stephanie J. Hanrahan (Morgantown, W.V.: Fitness Information Technology, 2012), 73.

116. Jay Coakley, *Sport in Society: Issues and Controversies* (Boston: McGraw-Hill, 2001).

117. For example, refer to Asa Bäckström, "Gender Manoeuvring in Swedish Skateboarding: Negotiations of Femininities and the Hierarchical Gender Structure," *Young* 21 (2013): 29–53; Becky Beal, "Alternative Masculinity and its Effects on Gender Relations in the Subculture of Skateboarding," *Journal of Sport Behavior* 19 (1996): 204–20; Becky Beal and Charlene Wilson, "'Chicks Dig Scars': Transformations in the Subculture of Skateboarding," in *Understanding Lifestyle Sports: Consumption, Identity, and Difference*, ed. Belinda Wheaton (London: Routledge, 2004), 31–54; Deirdre M. Kelly, Shauna Pomerantz, and Dawn Curry, "Skater Girlhood and Emphasized Femininity: 'You Can't Land an Ollie Properly in Heels,'" *Gender and Education* 17, no. 3 (2005): 229–48; Natalie Porter, "Female Skateboarders and Their Negotiation of Space and Identity," *Journal for Arts, Sciences, and Technology* 1 (2003): 75–80; Alana Young and Christine Dallaire, "Beware*#! Sk8 at Your Own Risk: The Discourses of Young Females Skateboarders," in *Tribal Play: Subcultural Journeys Through Sport*, ed. Michael Atkinson and Kevin Young (Bingley: Emerald Group, 2008), 235–54.

118. Tyler Dupont, "From Core to Consumer: The Informal Hierarchy of the Skateboard Scene," *Journal of Contemporary Ethnography* 43, no. 5 (2014): 19.

119. Matthew Atencio, Becky Beal, and Charlene Wilson, "The Distinction of Risk: Urban Skateboarding, Street Habitus and the Construction of Hierarchical Gender Relations," *Qualitative Research in Sport and Exercise* 1, no. 1 (2009): 3–20.

120. Pulley, "These Female Skateboarders."

121. Alana Glass, "Women's Skateboarding: Why it Matters to Skate Like a Girl," *Forbes*, July 15, 2014, http://www.forbes.com/sites/alanaglass/2014/07/15/womens-skateboarding-why-it-matters-to-skate-like-a-girl/?utm_source=following-immediate&utm_medium=email&utm_campaign=20140715.

122. For example, see Kyle Kusz, "Extreme America: Interrogating the Racial and Gender Politics of the Media Narratives about Extreme Sports," in *Understanding Lifestyle Sports: Consumption, Identity, and Difference*, ed. Belinda Wheaton, (Routledge, London, 2004), 197–213; Kyle Kusz, *Revolt of the White Athlete: Race, Media and the Emergence of Extreme Athletes in America*, (New York: Peter Lang, 2007); Belinda Wheaton, *Cultural Politics of Lifestyle Sports* (New York: Routledge, 2013), 108.

123. Wheaton, *Cultural Politics*, 64.

124. Mihi Nemani and Holly Thorpe, "The Experiences of 'Brown' Female Bodyboarders: Negotiating Multiple Axes of Marginality" in *Women in Action Sport Cultures: Identity, Politics and Experience*, ed. Holly Thorpe and Rebecca Olive (London: Palgrave Macmillan, 2016), 213–34.

125. Amy Sueyoshi, "Skate and Create: Skateboarding, Asian Pacific America, and Masculinity," *Amerasia Journal* 41, no. 2 (2015): 2–24.

126. Matthew Atencio, Emily Chivers Yochim, and Becky Beal "'It Ain't Just Black Kids and White Kids': The Representation and Reproduction of Authentic 'Skurban' Masculinities," *Sociology of Sport Journal* 30, no. 2 (2013): 153–72, doi:10.1123/ssj.30.2.153.

127. Aaron Barksdale, "How Skateboarding Became More Than a White Dude's

Sport," *Huffington Post*, December 6, 2015, http://www.huffingtonpost.com/entry/how-skateboarding-became-more-than-a-white-dudes-sport_us_55fb8f4ee4b0f de8b0cdc827.

TWO

1. Anne-Claire Pache and Filipe Santos, "Inside the Hybrid Organization: Selective Coupling as a Response to Competing Institutional Logics," *Academy of Management Journal* 56, no. 4 (2013): 972, doi:10.5465/amj.2011.0405.

2. Daniel Bjärsholm, "Sport and Social Entrepreneurship: A Review of a Concept in Progress," *Journal of Sport Management* 31 (2017): 191–206. Public-private organizations and their strategies have been given labels such as social enterprise, corporate social responsibility (CSR), social entrepreneurship, and social innovation, meaning that there have been differences noted in these hybrid models. At the same time, these concepts have sometimes been used by diverse scholars in both contradictory and overlapping ways. But what is significant for this book is that these terms collectively refer to the practice of trying to create and promote new social values through innovative public-private organizations. For consistency and relevance as it pertains to understanding the sports field, as used by Bjärsholm for instance, we refer to the social-enterprise concept throughout this book.

3. Sutia Kim Alter, "Social Enterprise Typology," *The Four Lenses Strategic Framework: Toward and Integrated Social Enterprise Methodology*, accessed September 15, 2017, http://www.4lenses.org/setypology.

4. Pache and Santos, "Inside the Hybrid Organization," 972.

5. James A. Phills Jr., Kriss Deiglmeier, and Dale T. Miller, "Rediscovering Social Innovation," *Stanford Social Innovation Review,* Fall 2008, https://ssir.org/articles/entry/rediscovering_social_innovation.

6. Belinda Wheaton and Mark Doidge, "Exploring the Social Benefit of Informal and Lifestyle Sports," *Journal of Sport Science and Physical Education* 68, no. 6 (2015): 47.

7. Bruce Kidd, "Epilogue: Cautions, Questions and Opportunities in Sport for Development and Peace," *Third World Quarterly* 32, no. 3 (2011): 603.

8. Holly Thorpe and Robert Rinehart, "Action Sport NGOs in a Neo-Liberal Context: The Cases of Skateistan and Surf Aid International," *Journal of Sport and Social Issues* 37, no. 2 (2013): 115–41, doi:10.1177/0193723512455923.

9. Kidd, "Epilogue," 603.

10. Kidd, "Epilogue," 603.

11. Holly Thorpe and Megan Chawansky, "The 'Girl Effect' in Action Sports for Development: The Case of the Female Practitioners of Skateistan," in *Women in Action Sport Cultures: Identity, Politics and Experience*, ed. Holly Thorpe and Rebecca Olive (London: Palgrave Macmillan, 2016), 133–52.

12. For an overview, see Thorpe and Rinehart's, "Action Sport NGOs," 115–41.

13. Alex King, "Bangladesh's Teenage Surf Girls are Dreaming of a Better Future: Paddling Through Patriarchy," *Huck Magazine*, accessed October 20, 2015, http://www.huckmagazine.com/ride/surf/bangladeshs-teenage-surf-girls-dreaming-better-future/.

14. Cuba Skate, ASDP, accessed June 29, 2017, http://www.actionsportsfordev.org/partners/cuba-skate-havana/.

15. Thorpe and Chawansky, "The 'Girl Effect,'" 134.

16. Holly Thorpe, "Action Sports for Youth Development: Critical Insights for the SDP Community," *International Journal of Sport Policy and Politics* 8, no. 1 (2014): 95.

17. Thorpe and Chawansky, "The 'Girl Effect,'" 133.

18. Thorpe and Rinehart, "Action Sport NGOs," 115.

19. Thorpe and Rinehart, "Action Sport NGOs," 118.

20. There are numerous other instances of celebrity involvement, even as we focus on just two particular cases. For instance, a country-music star is opening skate parks to serve inner-city youth in Nashville; Boston; San Marcos, Texas; and Annapolis, Maryland. See, Alan Poizner, "Kip Moore Opens Skateboarding Parks for Inner City Youth," *Rolling Stone*, June 4, 2015, http://www.rollingstone.com/music /news/kip-moore-opens-skateboarding-parks-for-inner-city-youth-20150604 for more information.

21. The board of directors consists of Tony Hawk (president and former professional skater); many of Hawk's family members; individuals such as Jeff Ament, of Pearl Jam fame; professional female skateboarder Mimi Knoop; Brandee Barker, the first communications executive at Facebook; and Sal Masekela, former host of the X Games on ESPN.

22. "About," Tony Hawk Foundation, accessed June 21, 2017, http://tonyhawk foundation.org/about/.

23. "FAQ," Tony Hawk Foundation, accessed July 3, 2017, http://tonyhawk foundation.org/faq/.

24. These steps include vision, advocacy, fundraising, design, and management. Peter Whitley, the Oakland Skatepark Summit Programs Director featured in this chapter's opening narrative, had these guides available at the Oakland Skatepark Summit and focused on vision and advocacy during his talk.

25. "Tony Hawk and Friends Celebrate the 12th Annual Stand Up for Skateparks Benefit in Beverly Hills," last modified October 12, 2015, accessed September 28, 2016, http://standupforskateparks.org/.

26. Tony Hawk Foundation, http://tonyhawkfoundation.org.

27. "What Are Some of the Community Benefits of Skateparks?" Tony Hawk Foundation, April 14, 2014, http://tonyhawkfoundation.org/faqs/what-are-some-of -the-community-benefits-of-skateparks/.

28. "What Are Some of the Community Benefits of Skateparks?" Tony Hawk Foundation.

29. "Rob Dyrdek, Living Amazing" last modified 2016, http://robdyrdek.com/.

30. Emily Chivers Yochim, *Skate Life: Re-Imagining White Masculinity* (Ann Arbor: University of Michigan Press, 2010), 149.

31. Bernie Wilson, "Street Skateboarding Goes Big with $1.2M Tour," *East Valley Tribune*, August 25, 2010, http://www.eastvalleytribune.com/local/the_valley /street-skateboarding-goes-big-with-m-tour/article_36e84070-b08f-11df-8690 -001cc4c03286.html.

32. "Frequently Asked Questions," Street League Skateboarding, accessed November 6, 2017, http://streetleague.com/faq/.

33. Keith Harman, "X Games Partners with Street League," XGames.com, March 14, 2013, http://xgames.espn.com/xgames/skateboarding/article/9045417 /x-games-announces-street-league-partnership.

34. *The Surf Channel*, "VIDEO: Rob Dyrdek Opens East LA Skatepark, Hazard Park," August 18, 2014, http://www.thesurfchannel.com/news/20140818 /video-rob-dyrdek-opens-east-la-skatepark-hazard-park/.

35. "Birthday Party at The Fantasy Factory in LA," Charity buzz, last modified 2014, https://www.charitybuzz.com/catalog_items/birthday-party-at-fantasy -factory-in-la-275106.

36. "The Rob Dyrdek Foundation", accessed March 28, 2014, http://robdyrdek foundation.org.

37. "The Rob Dyrdek Foundation," accessed March 28, 2014, http://robdyrdek foundation.org.

38. TWS, "Street League LA This Weekend," *Transworld Skateboarding*, July 24, 2014, http://skateboarding.transworld.net/news/street-league-la-weekend/.

39. "About," Street League Skateboarding Foundation, accessed September 13, 2017, http://streetleaguefoundation.org/about/.

40. "About," Street League Skateboarding Foundation, accessed September 13, 2017, http://streetleaguefoundation.org/about/.

41. Street League Skateboarding Foundation, "Frequently Asked Questions."

42. Street League Skateboarding Foundation, "About."

43. Joshua Tehee, "New Skate Plaza Slated for Romain Playground," *Fresno Bee*, May 14, 2015, http://www.fresnobee.com/entertainment/music-news-reviews /joshua-tehee/article21064743.html#storylink=cpy.

44. Wilson, "Street Skateboarding Goes Big."

45. A. James McKeever, "Park 'Rats' to Park 'Daddies': Community Heads Creating Future Mentors," in *Child's Play: Sport in Kids' Worlds*, ed. Michael A. Messner and Michela Musto (New Brunswick: Rutgers University Press, 2016), 221–36.

46. McKeever, "Park 'Rats' to Park 'Daddies,'" 221-36.

47. "Skateboarding CEO: An Interview with 4141 Corp Robert Ferguson of Oakland," *Smarty Girl Leadership*, last modified November 16, 2013, accessed September 27, 2016, http://smartygirlleadership.com/2013/11/skateboarding -ceo-interview-with-4141.html.

48. "Skateboarding CEO: An Interview with 4141 Corp Robert Ferguson of Oakland."

49. Paul Godfrey, "Corporate Social Responsibility in Sport: An Overview and Key Issues," *Journal of Sport Management* 23, no. 6 (2009): 698–716. Godfrey has traced the term *industrialist* back to nineteenth-century American culture.

50. "Outreach," 4141Corp, accessed September 15, 2017, http://www.4141 Corp.com/outreach.html.

51. "About," 4141Corp, accessed September 15, 2017, http://www.4141corp.com /about.html.

52. "Why Skateboarding," Rob Skate Academy: We Teach Skateboarding, accessed September 15, 2017, https://www.robskate.com/why-skateboarding.

53. Indigo Willing and Scott Shearer, "Skateboarding Activism: Exploring Diverse Voices and Community Support," in *Skateboarding: Subcultures, Sites and Shifts*, ed. Kara-Jane Lombard, (London: Routledge, 2016), 46.

54. Willing and Shearer, "Skateboarding Activism," 46.

55. "Inspiring America: Encouraging Girls to Pick Up Skateboarding," *NBC Nightly News with Lester Holt*, February 17, 2017, http://www.nbcnews.com

/nightly-news/video/inspiring-america-encouraging-girls-to-pick-up
-skateboarding-879929923850.

56. "Leave the Boys at Home," Wood Metal Rocks, last modified September 2014, accessed September 27, 2016, vimeo.com/89380197.

57. "About Us," Skate Like a Girl, accessed September 28, 2016, http://www
.skatelikeagirl.com/about-us.html.

58. Steph MacKay and Christine Dallaire, "Skateboarding Women: Building Collective Identity in Cyberspace," *Journal of Sport and Social Issues* 30, no. 2 (2013): 182.

59. Don Sabo, Janie V. Ward, and Rachel Oliveri, "Get It Going, Keep It Going: A Resource for Sports & Exercise Programs for Urban Girls," *A Women's Sports Foundation Educational Guide*, (East Meadow, N.Y.: Women's Sports Foundation, 2009), 13.

THREE

1. Sean Mortimer and Tony Hawk, *Stalefish: Skateboard Culture from the Rejects Who Made It* (San Francisco: Chronicle Books, 2008), 23.

2. David Madden, "Revisiting the End of Public Space: Assembling the Public in an Urban Park," *City and Community* 9, no. 2 (2010): 191.

3. David Madden, "Neighborhood as Spatial Project: Making the Urban Order on the Downtown Brooklyn Waterfront," *International Journal of Urban and Regional Research* 38, no. 2 (2014): 10.

4. Madden, "Neighborhood as Spatial Project," 10.

5. A.R. Cuthbert, "The Right to the City: Surveillance, Private Interest and the Public Domain in Hong Kong," *Cities* 12, no. 5 (1995): 293–10.

6. Symeon Dagkas and Lisette Burrows, "Family Matters: An Introduction," in *Families, Young People, Physical Activity and Health: Critical Perspectives* ed. Symeon Dagkas and Lissette Burrows (Los Angeles: Routledge, 2016), 2.

7. A number of authors have explored the nature of family life as it is influenced by the sporting- and physical-activity experiences of children. For more information, see the comprehensive collection edited by Dagkas and Burrows, *Families, Young People, Physical Activity and Health*, and a recent academic paper: Jaekwon Na, "Parents' Perceptions of Their Children's Experiences in Physical Education and Youth Sport," *Physical Educator* 72, no. 1 (2015): 139–67.

8. See Messner for more about how women have tended to take on supportive roles in youth team sports while men tend to take up coaching roles. Michael Messner, *It's All for The Kids: Gender, Families, and Youth Sports* (Berkeley: University of California Press, 2009).

9. Albert J. Petitpas, Allen E. Cornelius, Judy L. Van Raalte, and Tiffany Jones, "A Framework for Planning Youth Sport Programs that Foster Psychosocial Development," *Sport Psychologist* 19 (2005): 69.

10. Ellie Lee, Jennie Bristow, Charlotte Fairchild, and Jan Macvarish, *Parenting Culture Studies* (London: Palgrave Macmillan, 2014), 36.

11. Sinikka Elliot and Elyshia Aseltine, "Raising Teenagers in Hostile Environments: How Race, Class, and Gender Matter for Mother's Protective Carework," *Journal of Family Issues* 34, no. 6 (2012): 719–44.

12. Camelia Knight, "Influences on Parental Involvement in Youth Sport,"

Special Issue: Parenting in Sports, *Sport, Exercise, and Performance Psychology* 5, no. 2 (2016): 175.

13. Hilary Friedman, *Playing to Win: Raising Children in a Competitive Culture* (Berkeley: University of California Press, 2013); Dagkas and Burrows, *Families, Young People*, 2.

14. Dagkas and Burrows, *Families, Young People*, 2; Jay Coakley, "Youth Sport in the United States" in *Routledge Handbook of Youth Sport 2016*, ed. Ken Green and Andy Smith (Routledge: London, 2016), 91; Sharon Wheeler and Ken Green, "Parenting in Relation to Children's Sports Participation: Generational Changes and Potential Implications," *Leisure Studies* 33, no. 3 (2014): 272.

15. Homan Lee, Katherine Tamminen, Alexander Clark, Linda Slater, John Spence, and Nicholas Holt, "A Meta-Study of Qualitative Research Examining Determinants of Children's Independent Active Free Play," *International Journal of Behavioral Nutrition and Physical Activity* 12, no. 5 (2015): 5–7; Kari Stefansen, Ingrid Smette, and Ase Strandbu, "Understanding the Increase in Parents' Involvement in Organized Youth Sports," *Sport, Education and Society* 23, no. 2 (2016): 8, http://dx.doi.org/10.1080/13573322.2016.1150834.

16. "Factors of Skatepark Design," Public Skatepark Development Guide, accessed August 10, 2017, http://publicskateparkguide.org/design-and-construction/factors-of-skatepark-design/.

17. "Factors of Skatepark Design," Public Skatepark Development Guide.

18. Myra Taylor and Ida Marais, "Not in My Back Schoolyard: Schools and Skate-park Builds in Western Australia," *Australian Planner* 48, no. 2 (2011): 86.

19. Taylor and Marais, "Not in My Back Schoolyard," 86.

20. Kinesiology 3300, class presentation, CSU East Bay, Nov 12, 2014.

21. "Cops Love Skateparks: Study Shows Strong Support Among Law Enforcement for Public Skateparks," Tony Hawk Foundation, accessed September 17, 2017, http://www.tonyhawkfoundation.org/content/list/(archive)/20100209/.

22. To help ensure anonymity, this reference is shared with the editor but is not provided here.

23. To help ensure anonymity, this reference is shared with the editor but is not provided here.

24. For more information, see Matthew Atencio and Jan Wright, "'We Be Killin' Them': Hierarchies of Black Masculinity in Urban Basketball Spaces," *Sociology of Sport Journal* 25 (2008): 278; Matthew Atencio and Jan Wright, "Ballet It's Too Whitey: Discursive Hierarchies of High School Dance Spaces and the Constitution of Embodied Feminine Subjectivities," *Gender and Education* 21, no. 1 (2008): 31–46; Cheryl Cooky, "'Girls Just aren't Interested': The Social Construction of Interest in Girls' Sport," *Sociological Perspectives* 52, no. 2 (2009): 259–83; Lauren Rauscher and Cheryl Cooky, "Ready for Anything the World Gives Her?: A Critical Look at Sports-Based Positive Youth Development for Girls," *Sex Roles* 74, nos. 7–8 (2016): 288–98.

25. Petitpas, et al., "Framework for Planning Youth Sport Programs," 63–80.

26. Kara Jane Lombard, "Skate and Create/Skate and Destroy: The Commercial and Governmental Incorporation of Skateboarding," in *Continuum: Journal of Media & Cultural Studies* 24, no. 4 (2010): 481. Lombard's piece provides further insight into practices of resisting security measures in skate parks: "Private policing of skateboarding entrenches the resistive elements of skateboarding as skaters try

to outwit security guards. This private crime control allows skaters to proliferate tactics of resistance, and skaters have developed far more strategies for dealing with security guards than police. Skaters resist security guards in various ways: arguing, playing cat-and-mouse, or knowing the rounds of security guards. One increasingly popular method involves filming altercations between skaters and security guards, which are then posted to Internet sites. Comments on these videos deride or criticize security guards and celebrate the outlaw ethos of skateboarding."

27. For example, see Lisa Wood, May Carter, and Karen Martin, "Dispelling Stereotypes . . . Skate Parks as a Setting for Pro-Social Behavior among Young People," *Current Urban Studies* 2, (2014): 62–73; Susie Weller, "Skateboarding Alone? Making Social Capital Discourse Relevant to Teenagers' Lives," *Journal of Youth Studies* 9, no. 5 (2006): 557–74; Adam Jenson, Jon Swords, and Michael Jeffries, "The Accidental Youth Club: Skateboarding in Newcastle-Gateshead," *Journal of Urban Design* 17, no. 3 (2012): 374.

28. See Stefansen, Smette, and Strandbu, "Understanding the Increase in Parents' Involvement,"; and Ase Strandbu, Kari Stefansen, Ingrid Smette, and Morten Renslo Sandvik, "Young People's Experiences of Parental Involvement in Youth Sport," *Sport, Education and Society* (2017): 1–12, http://dx.doi.org/10.1080/13573322.2017.1323200.

29. Thomas Quarmby, "Parenting and Youth Sport," in *Routledge Handbook of Youth Sport*, eds. Ken Green and Andy Smith (New York: Routledge, 2016), 212.

30. Quarmby, "Parenting and Youth Sport," 215.

31. Nicholas Holt and Zoe Sehn, "Processes Associated with Positive Youth Development and Participation in Competitive Youth Sport 2008," in *Positive Youth Development Through Sport*, 2nd ed., ed. Nicholas Holt (London: Routledge, 2016), 30.

32. Holt and Sehn, "Processes Associated with Positive Youth Development," 32; Margaret Nelson, *Parenting Out of Control: Anxious Parents in Uncertain Times* (New York: New York University Press, 2010).

33. Jay Coakley, "Positive Youth Development Through Sport: Myths, Beliefs, and Realities," in *Positive Youth Development Through Sport*, 2nd ed., ed. Nicholas Holt (London: Routledge, 2016), 41.

34. Toni-Larissa Gordon, "Youth Development Through Street-Sports: An Exploration of the Relationship Between Learning Styles and Fear of Failure" (master's thesis, Massey University, 2015), 66, 77, 81, https://mro.massey.ac.nz/xmlui/bitstream/handle/10179/7566/02_whole.pdf.

35. For overview on normative and over-parenting details, see Barry A. Garst and Ryan J. Gagnon, "Exploring Overparenting Within the Context of Youth Development Programs," *Journal of Youth Development* 10 (2015): 7.

36. For a comprehensive discussion on bridging capital in youth recreation, see Simon Beames and Matthew Atencio, "Building Social Capital through Outdoor Education," *Journal of Adventure Education and Outdoor Learning* 8, no. 2 (2008): 99-112.

37. Robert Putnam, Bowling Alone: The Collapse and Revival of American Community (London: Simon & Schuster, 2003), 23.

38. Holly Thorpe and Robert Rinehart, "Action Sport NGOs in a Neo-Liberal Context: The Cases of Skateistan and Surf Aid International," *Journal of Sport and Social Issues* 37, no. 2 (2013): 100.

39. Paul Gilchrist and Belinda Wheaton, "Lifestyle and Adventure Sport Among Youth," in *Routledge Handbook of Youth Sport*, ed. Ken Green and Andy Smith (New York: Routledge, 2016), 193.

40. Elliot and Aseltine, "Raising Teenagers," 720.

41. "Helicopter parents" are those that "hypermanage their children's lives and take great measures to organize all activities involving their children"; this type of parenting style often occurs within the realm of youth sports. See Jessica Skolnikoff and Robert Engvall, *Young Athletes, Couch Potatoes, and Helicopter Parents: The Productivity of Play* (Boulder: Rowman and Littlefield, 2014), 137.

42. Jay Coakley, "Youth Sports: What Counts as 'Positive Development?'" *Journal of Sport and Social Issues* 35, no. 3 (2011): 306, 309.

FOUR

1. Daniel Bjärsholm, "Sport and Social Entrepreneurship: A Review of a Concept in Progress," *Journal of Sport Management* 31, no. 2 (2017): 191–206, https://doi.org/10.1123/jsm.2017-0007.

2. Alex Salazar, "Designing a Socially Just Downtown," *Shelterforce*, April 23, 2006, https://shelterforce.org/2006/04/23/designing_a_socially_just_downtown/.

3. "The Oakland Fire: Delving into What Happened, and Why," *New York Times*, December 8, 2016, https://www.nytimes.com/2016/12/08/us/the-oakland-fire -delving-into-what-happened-and-why.html?_r=0.

4. Josh Sens, "East Side Story," *Sunset Magazine*, April 2016, 73.

5. Adam Jenson, Jon Swords, and Michael Jeffries, "The Accidental Youth Club: Skateboarding in Newcastle-Gateshead," *Journal of Urban Design* 17, no. 3 (2012): 373.

6. Chance Grable, "De Fremery Park and Recreation Center West Oakland: Historical Essay," FoundSF, 2015, http://www.foundsf.org/index.php?title =De_Fremery_Park_and_Recreation_Center_West_Oakland.

7. Chance Grable, "De Fremery Park and Recreation Center West Oakland."

8. Chance Grable, "De Fremery Park and Recreation Center West Oakland."

9. Chance Grable, "De Fremery Park and Recreation Center West Oakland."

10. Chance Grable, "De Fremery Park and Recreation Center West Oakland."

11. Dajanae Barrows, "De Fremery Park," Street Stories: Oakland, http://www .streetstoriesoakland.com/items/show/37.

12. Chris O'Brien, "Uber and Gentrification Why I'm Excited and Terrified that Tech Has Finally Discovered Oakland," *Venture Beat*, October 26, 2015, http:// venturebeat.com/2015/10/26/uber-and-gentrification-why-im-excited-and -terrified-that-tech-has-finally-discovered-oakland/.

13. Chris Rhomberg, *No There There: Race, Class, and Political Community in Oakland* (Berkeley: University of California Press, 2004), 190–91.

14. Phillip Bump, "Donald Trump Somehow Thinks Ferguson and Oakland Are Dangerous Like Iraq," *Washington Post*, May 18, 2016, https://www.washingtonpost .com/news/the-fix/wp/2016/05/18/donald-trump-somehow-thinks-ferguson-and -oakland-are-dangerous-like-iraq/.

15. Eve Batey, "Photo Du Jour: Is West Oakland 'The New Edge of Silicon Valley'?" SFist, May 4, 2016, http://sfist.com/2016/05/04/living_on_the_edge.php.

16. Farhad Manjoo, "The Care and Feeding of a Tech Boom," *San Francisco*

Magazine, September 27, 2013, http://www.modernluxury.com/san-francisco
/story/the-care-and-feeding-of-tech-boom?page=3.

17. Manjoo, "The Care and Feeding of a Tech Boom."

18. Ipek Kavasoglu, "Zumper National Rent Report: July 2017," *Zumper,* June 29,
2017, https://www.zumper.com/blog/2017/06/zumper-national-rent-report-july
-2017/.

19. In his book *No There There: Race, Class, and Political Community in
Oakland,* Chris Rhomberg notes how the housing boom in Oakland has been
spurred on since the turn of this century by previous city administrators' reluctance
to enact market-cooling measures. Rhomberg identifies the former mayor, Jerry
Brown, and his pro-development policies in this regard: "Although some of Brown's
longtime supporters were surprised by his neoliberal, prodeveloper stance, he
merely replied, 'In capitalism, capital counts, and as Mayor, I can't repeal that law'"
(190, 191). In concert with this viewpoint, the *New York Times* led with the head-
line "As Mayor, Brown Remade Oakland's Downtown and Himself" and further
reasoned that "in his quest to bring 10,000 new residents to Oakland's abandoned
downtown, he cut generous deals with developers, streamlined the approval process and pushed aside city officials who stood in the way. He also alienated some
of his traditional base, progressive and black leaders who derided his policies as
'Jerryfication' and accused him of abandoning the rest of the city for his downtown
dreams." See Zusha Elinson, "As Mayor, Brown Remade Oakland's Downtown and
Himself," *New York Times,* September 2, 2010, http://www.nytimes.com/2010/09/03
/us/politics/03bcbrown.html?_r=0.

20. Jim DuPont, Elissa Dennis, and Tom Csekey, "Oakland for the Elite Only?/
As City Officials Urge Housing Downtown, Don't Forget the Others," *SFGate,*
November 23, 1999, http://www.sfgate.com/opinion/openforum/article/Oakland
-for-the-Elite-Only-As-city-officials-2893875.php.

21. Phillip Matier and Andrew Ross, "Long March: Oakland's Philosopher/
Pothole Filler Moving Swiftly," *San Francisco Chronicle,* January 10, 2000, A17.

22. Chris Rhomberg reminds us that previous "city government policies did
affect the shape of the community," leading to the existential question "Who belongs
in Oakland?" This latter question became compelling, according to Rhomberg,
when "the rapid changes in the real-estate market stirred widespread fears of gentrification and displacement of working-class and minority residents. Indeed, for
the first time in fifty years, the 2000 census showed an absolute increase in the city's
white population." See Rhomberg, *No There There,* 190, 191.

23. Anna Marie Erwert, "Oakland Ascends to Nation's 4th Most Expensive
Rental Market," *SFGate,* December 21, 2015, http://blog.sfgate.com/ontheblock
/2015/12/21/oakland-ascends-to-nations-4th-most-expensive-rental-market/.

24. Alison Vekshin, "San Francisco Housing Frenzy Shifts Across the Bay
to Oakland," *Bloomberg,* August 23, 2016, https://www.bloomberg.com/news/
articles/2016-08-23/san-francisco-housing-frenzy-shifts-across-the-bay-to-oakland.

25. Olivia Allen-Price, "How Many Are Being Displaced by Gentrification in
Oakland?," KQED News, February 9, 2017, https://ww2.kqed.org/news/2017/02
/09/how-many-are-being-displaced-by-gentrification-in-oakland/.

26. Carolyn Jones, "Gentrification Transforming Face of Oakland," *SFGate,*
April 9, 2014, http://www.sfgate.com/bayarea/article/Gentrification-transforming
-face-of-Oakland-5387273.php.

27. O'Brien, "Uber and Gentrification."

28. Joel Anderson, "How a Brutal Beating Became the Symbol of Oakland's Gentrification Struggle," BuzzFeed News, October 17, 2015, http://www.vyrtex.com /article/how-a-brutal-beating-became-the-symbol-of-oakland-s-gentrification -struggle-4177fed6-371f-4a1f-b1be-4690b54a4ade. "When it opened in September 2007, this Whole Foods was celebrated as the first new grocery store in Oakland in 20 years. But in a city of about 414,000 where little affordable housing is being built, and poorer residents find themselves unable to find a home, the store has gone from a symbol of progress to one of exclusion."

29. "Protesters Plan to Block Google, Apple & Facebook Shuttle Buses in Oakland Friday," CBS SFBayArea, April 27, 2015, http://sanfrancisco.cbslocal .com/2015/04/27/protesters-plan-to-block-google-apple-facebook-shuttle-buses -in-oakland-friday-tech-may-day/.

30. Patrick May, "Oakland Blaze at Construction Site Looks Suspiciously Like Previous East Bay Fires," *Mercury News*, Updated July 7, 2017, http://www.mercury news.com/2017/07/07/oakland-blaze-looks-suspiciously-like-previous-east-bay -fires/.

31. Devin Katayama, "Activists, Entrepreneurs Fight for a Place in West Oakland's Future," KQED News, August 25, 2015, http://ww2.kqed.org/news /2015/08/25/west-oakland-activist-wants-to-create-a-cafe-for-everyone.

32. "Oakland's Displacement Crisis: As Told by the Numbers (2016)," Policy Link, accessed September 17, 2017, http://www.policylink.org/find-resources /library/oakland-displacement-crisis.

33. Mark Uh, "Priced Out: Big Cities Are Becoming Too Costly for Lower-Income Residents," Trulia's Blog, Trulia, April 28, 2016, https://www.trulia.com /blog/trends/priced-out-migration/.

34. Sens, "East Side Story," 70.

35. A recent article reported in *Forbes* contends that Oakland "has high densities, historic buildings, an industrial aesthetic" as well as cheaper rents than San Francisco. As such, the article speculates that this city, having already attracted a raft of smaller tech companies, is poised to become a "tech hub." See Scott Beyer, "After Uber's Move, Will Oakland Become a Tech Hub?" *Forbes,* September 26, 2015, http://www.forbes.com/sites/scottbeyer/2015/09/26/after-ubers-move-will-oakland -become-a-tech-hub/#5ef20a9e4ea2.

36. Em-J Staples, "Meet K- Dub: The Hard-Hustling Visionary Behind Oakland's DIY Skate Park, Town Park," Huck Magazine, October 1, 2015, http:// www.huckmagazine.com/ride/skate/meet-k-dub-hard-hustling-visionary-behind -oaklands-diy-skate-park-town-park/; "Keith 'K-Dub' Williams: Community and Education Ambassador," Know Yourself, accessed July 15, 2017, https://know yourself.com/pages/keith-k-dub-williams.

37. DuPont, Dennis, and Csekey, "Oakland for the Elite Only"; Matier and Ross, "Long March: Oakland's Philosopher/Pothole Filler Moving Swiftly."

38. A recent story in the *Mercury News* went on to describe how K-Dub's reputation is such that the Oakland mayor calls him personally to get truant kids back into school:

> Mayor Libby Schaaf saw a couple kids riding around downtown
> Oakland on skateboards, using office structures as the canvas for their
> X Games dreams. But there was a bigger problem: It was the middle

of the day, and the middle of the week. They should have been in a classroom. The knuckleheads weren't cooperative, so she pulled out her phone and called Keith Williams. All it took was a first name and a few descriptions and the voice on the other side of the phone had identified the kids and where they were supposed to be. She put Williams on the phone with them. A minute or so later, they were apologizing to the mayor and heading back to class.

See Marcus Thompson II, "Oakland Skateboarding Mecca a Beacon for East Bay Youth," *Mercury News,* August 11, 2016, http://www.mercurynews.com/marcus-thompson/ci_29769923/oakland-skateboarding-mecca-beacon-east-bay-youth.

39. "Town Park in Oakland," *Heckler* Magazine, October 27, 2012, http://www.heckler.com/town-park-in-oakland/.

40. Marcus Thompson II, "Oakland's New Skate Park Is Fitting, Worthy Home and the Legacy of Youth Advocate 'K-Dub,'" *Mercury News,* April 15, 2016, http://blogs.mercurynews.com/thompson/2016/04/15/oaklands-new-skate-park-fitting-worthy-home-legacy-youth-advocate-k-dub/.

41. Eric K. Arnold, "Town Park Ribbon-Cutting Brings Smiles, Kickflips to West Oakland," Oakculture, November 6, 2014, https://oakulture.com/tag/town-park.

42. "Tha Hood Games: Kids. Community. Comrades," Indybay, July 18, 2011, https://www.indybay.org/newsitems/2011/07/18/18685136.php.

43. Since its inception, Tha Hood Games has snowballed into over forty-nine youth skateboard and art festivals across Oakland, San Francisco, Los Angeles, and Las Vegas.

44. Arnold, "Town Park Ribbon-Cutting Brings Smiles."

45. Know Yourself, "Keith 'K-Dub' Williams."

46. Brian Krans, "Skate or DIY: Why Is It So Damn Hard to Build A Skate Park In Oakland," *East Bay Express,* March 14, 2017, https://www.eastbayexpress.com/oakland/skate-or-diy-why-is-it-so-damn-hard-to-build-a-skate-park-in-oakland/Content?oid=5719389.

47. Staples, "Meet K-Dub."

48. Staples, "Meet K-Dub."

49. "Life Is Living: What's It All About?" Life Is Living, accessed July 15, 2017, http://youthspeaks.org/lifeisliving/.

50. Staples, "Meet K-Dub."

51. Krans, "Skate Or DIY."

52. Thompson II, "Oakland Skateboarding Mecca."

53. Thompson II, "Oakland Skateboarding Mecca."

54. Brian Blakey, "Park Spotting: Levi's Town Park Build in Oakland," *Transworld Skateboarding,* July 22, 2015, http://skateboarding.transworld.net/news/park-spotting-levis-town-park-build-in-oakland/#D4yOaVfxQhDZWj7J. 97.

55. Blakey, "Park Spotting," 97.

56. On resistance to gentrification and ethnic enclaves, see Rory Carroll, "'Hope Everyone Pukes on your Artisinal Treats': Fighting Gentrification, LA-style," *The Guardian,* April 19, 2016, https://www.theguardian.com/us-news/2016/apr/19/los-angeles-la-gentrification-resistance-boyle-heights.

57. "Past OFCY Evaluation Reports," Oakland Fund for Children & Youth, accessed July 15, 2017, http://www.ofcy.org/past-ofcy-evaluation-reports/.

58. Katayama, "Activists, Entrepreneurs Fight."

59. "For the Town Skateboarding," Facebook, https://www.facebook.com /For-The-Town-Skateboarding-153235964782006/.

60. Thompson II, "Oakland Skateboarding Mecca a Beacon."

61. Thompson II, "Oakland Skateboarding Mecca."

62. Sarah Banet-Weiser, *Kids Rule!: Nickelodeon and Consumer Citizenship* (Durham: Duke University Press Books, 2007), 143, 144.

63. Matthew Atencio, Becky Beal, and Emily Chivers Yochim, "'It Ain't Just Black Kids and White Kids': The Representation and Reproduction of Authentic 'Skurban' Masculinities," *Sociology of Sport Journal* 30, no. 2 (2013): 154, doi:10.1123 /ssj.30.2.153.

64. Michael Nevin Willard, "Séance, Tricknowlogy, Skateboarding, and the Space of Youth," in *Generations of Youth: Youth Cultures and History in Twentieth-Century America,* ed. Joe Austin and Michael Nevin Willard (New York: New York University Press, 1998), 339.

65. Belinda Wheaton and Mark Doidge, "Exploring the Social Benefit of Informal and Lifestyle Sports," *Journal of Sport Science and Physical Education* 68, no. 6 (2015): 45.

66. Gina Neff, Elizabeth Wissinger, and Sharon Zukin, "Entrepreneurial Labor Among Cultural Producers: 'Cool' Jobs in 'Hot' Industries," *Social Semiotics* 15 (2005): 307.

67. Matthew Atencio and Jan Wright, "'We Be Killin' Them': Hierarchies of Black Masculinity in Urban Basketball Spaces," *Sociology of Sport Journal* 25, no. 2 (2008): 263–80.

68. Albert J. Petitpas, Allen E. Cornelius, Judy L. Van Raalte, and Tiffany Jones, "A Framework for Planning Youth Sport Programs that Foster Psychosocial Development," *The Sport Psychologist* 19 (2005): 69–70.

69. A. James McKeever, "Parks 'Rats' to Park 'Daddies': Community Heads Creating Future Mentors," in *Child's Play: Sport in Kids' Worlds*, eds. Michael A. Messner and Michela Musto (New Brunswick: Rutgers University Press, 2016), 229–35.

70. Shawn Ginright and Julio Cammarota, "New Terrain in Youth Development: The Promise of a Social Justice Approach," *Social Justice* 29, no. 4 (2002): 82–95.

71. Ginwright and Cammarota, "New Terrain in Youth Development," 87.

72. Katayama, "Activists, Entrepreneurs Fight."

73. Levi's, "Skateboarding in Oakland—Town Park Documentary," February 12, 2015, https://www.youtube.com/watch?v=DdYahLP1tH4&t=593s.

74. Susie Weller, "Skateboarding Alone? Making Social Capital Discourse Relevant to Teenagers' Lives," *Journal of Youth Studies* 9, no. 5 (2006): 572.

75. Sherri Grasmuck, "Something about Baseball: Gentrification, 'Race Sponsorship,' and Neighborhood Boys' Baseball," *Sociology of Sport Journal* 20, no. 4 (2003): 307–30, https://doi.org/10.1123/ssj.20.4.307.

76. Grasmuck, "Something about Baseball," 307.

77. Rick DelVecchio, "Lafayette Square's New Look Preserves Neighborhood Oasis/ Everyone welcome at 'Old Man's Park,'" *SFGate*, September 21, 1998, https:// www.sfgate.com/bayarea/article/Lafayette-Square-s-New-Look-Preserves -2989760.php.

78. Christopher Heredia, "Lafayette Square Celebrated as Symbol of Hope/

Oakland Park Reopens After Renovation," *SFGate*, June 14, 1999, http://www
.sfgate.com/bayarea/article/Lafayette-Square-Celebrated-As-Symbol-of-Hope
-2924631.php.

FIVE

1. Scott McClain, "San Jose Breaks Ground on the Lake Cunningham Bike
Park," Pink bike, May 24, 2016, http://www.pinkbike.com/news/san-jose-breaks
-ground-on-the-lake-cunningham-bike-park-2016.html.

2. This position is further supported by two other full time staff.

3. Angel Rios Jr., "City Service Area: Neighborhood Services," Parks, Recreation
and Neighborhood Services Department, accessed July 17, 2017, VIII—193, https://
www.sanjoseca.gov/DocumentCenter/View/56277.

4. George Avalos, "Silicon Valley's Inequality Intensifies Even as Job Market
Booms," *Mercury News*, August 12, 2016, http://www.mercurynews.com/business
/ci_25060057/silicon-valley-job-market-booms-but-wage-equality.

5. "Economic Development," Sanjoseca.gov, 2014, http://www.sanjoseca.gov
/index.aspx?NID=194.

6. Jed Kolko, "America's Most Diverse Neighborhoods and Metros," *Forbes*,
November 13, 2012, http://www.forbes.com/sites/trulia/2012/11/13/finding
-diversity-in-america/#47ad7cd712f2.

7. "San Jose, CA," Census Reporter, accessed July 17, 2017, https://census
reporter.org/profiles/16000US0668000-san-jose-ca/.

8. "Fact Sheet: History and Geography," Sanjoseca.gov, accessed July 17, 2017,
https://www.sanjoseca.gov/DocumentCenter/View/780; George Avalos, "Santa
Clara County Has Highest Median Household Income in Nation But Wealth Gap
Widens," *Mercury News*, August 10, 2014, http://www.mercurynews.com/2014/08
/10/santa-clara-county-has-highest-median-household-income-in-nation-but
-wealth-gap-widens/.

9. Avalos, "Santa Clara County Has Highest Median Household Income."

10. Avalos, "Santa Clara County Has Highest Median Household Income."

11. Paul Murphy, personal communication, November 24, 2015.

12. Amanda J. Johnson, Troy D. Glover, and William P. Stewart, "Attracting
Locals Downtown: Everyday Leisure as a Place-Making Initiative," *Journal of Park
and Recreation Administration* 32 (2014): 30.

13. David J. Madden, "Revisiting the End of Public Space: Assembling the
Public in an Urban Park," *City and Community* 9, no. 2 (2010): 190.

14. Madden, "Revisiting the End of Public Space," 190.

15. David Madden, "Neighborhood as Spatial Project: Making the Urban
Order on the Downtown Brooklyn Waterfront," *International Journal of Urban and
Regional Research* 38, no. 2 (2014): 471–97.

16. Craig Ramsay, "Take, San Jose for Example," *Thrasher Magazine*, May 1983,
22–26, http://www.thrashermagazine.com/articles/magazine/may-1983/?tmpl
=component.

17. Bruce Newman, "Former Winchester SkatePark Kids Relive Cement
Heaven," *Mercury News*, July 29, 2011, http://www.mercurynews.com/bruce
-newman/ci_18579497.

18. Christian Hosoi and Lance Mountain, "Caballero and Hosoi," *Juice*, April 1,
2006, http://juicemagazine.com/home/steve-caballero/.

19. Newman, "Former Winchester SkatePark."

20. Bryce Courtenay, *The Power of One: A Novel* (New York: Ballantine Books, 1989).

21. San Jose Parks, Recreation, and Neighborhood Services, "Annual Report 2015: Building Community through Fun," Sanjoseca.gov, accessed September 15, 2017, http://www.sanjoseca.gov/DocumentCenter/View/53755.

22. Rios Jr., "Cirty Service Area," VIII—193.

23. Scott Herhold, "Rose Herrera: Advocate for a Village in a City of a Million," *Mercury News*, April 14, 2014, http://www.mercurynews.com/scott-herhold /ci_25565963/herrera-advocate-village-city-million. This practice can be controversial. The Vice Mayor, Rose Herrerra, once "acknowledged that Coke had given a donation to save the [Lake Cunningham] skate park. Then, noting her battle with her weight, she said, 'I don't drink any Coke products, never will.'"

24. "The Safe Summer Initiative offers grants to nonprofit organizations, governmental entities, and faith-based organizations that provide safe programs and activities that engage at-risk youth and encourage healthy play and positive relationships. Emphasis is placed on services benefiting youth in Hot Spot areas— locations determined annually as experiencing the most gang activity and youth violence." "Safe Summer Initiative," Sanjoseca.gov, accessed July 17, 2017, http:// www.sanjoseca.gov/index.aspx?NID=646.

25. "It's Happening" Sanjoseca.gov, accessed July 17, 2017, http://sanjoseca.gov /index.aspx?NID=4928.

26. Madden, "Revisiting the End of Public Space," 191.

27. Madden, "Revisiting the End of Public Space," 191.

28. "SJ Action Sports Park," http://www.sjactionsports.com.

29. John Woolfolk, "San Jose Delays Closure of Popular Lake Cunningham Skate Park," *Mercury News*, October 1, 2011, http://www.mercurynews.com/ci _19019822.

30. Gary Singh, "Now Boarding," *Metro Active*, accessed July 17, 2017, http:// www.metroactive.com/metro/04.02.08/cover-sjskatepark-0814.html.

31. "Facilities," Sanjoseca.gov, http://www.sanjoseca.gov/facilities/Facility /Details/355.

32. Bruce Newman, "Skatepark, a San Jose Hidden Gem, Fighting for Survival," *Mercury News*, September 14, 2011, http://www.mercurynews.com/2011/09/14 /skatepark-a-san-jose-hidden-gem-fighting-for-survival/.

33. Keith Hamm, "San Jose Skatepark Avoids Closure," ESPN, February 3, 2012, http://www.espn.com/action/skateboarding/story/_/id/7538202/fundraising -efforts-keep-lake-cunningham-regional-skate-park-open.

34. Newman, "Skatepark, a San Jose Hidden Gem."

35. Singh, "Now Boarding."

36. According to First5 California website information, "Since 1998, we have invested millions of dollars to design comprehensive programs that address the needs of children ages 0 to 5 and their families. Currently, our programs are centered around the child, parent, and teacher to improve early childhood outcomes in the areas of health and nutrition, early literacy and language development, quality child care, and smoking cessation" (http://www.ccfc.ca.gov/).

37. Adam Jenson, Jon Swords, and Michael Jeffries, "The Accidental Youth Club:

Skateboarding in Newcastle-Gateshead," *Journal of Urban Design* 17, no. 3 (2012): 374.

38. Rianne Van Melik, Irina Van Aalst, and Jan Van Weesep, "Fear and Fantasy in the Public Domain: The Development of Secured and Themed Urban Space," *Journal of Urban Design* 12, no. 1 (2007): 30.

39. Van Melik, Aalst, and Weesep, "Fear and Fantasy in the Public Domain," 29. Van Melik and colleagues summarized these ideas, citing John Hannigan's *Fantasy City: Pleasure and Profit in the Postmodern Metropolis*, (London: Routledge, 1998) for "entertainment and surprise," and for "riskless risk," they cite Russell Nye, "Eight Ways of Looking at an Amusement Park," *Journal of Popular Culture* 15, no. 1 (1981): 63-75.

40. Simone Tulumello, Fear, *Space and Urban Planning: A Critical Perspective from Southern Europe* (Switzerland: Springer, 2017), 56.

41. Chris Harris, "Gang Members Convicted of Stomping Eighth-Grader to Death, as His Big Brother Tried to Help," *People*, August 3, 2016, http://www.people.com/article/san-jose-gang-members-convicted-heriberto-reyes-death.

42. Jenson, Swords, and Jeffries, "Accidental Youth Club," 374.

43. Jenson, Swords, and Jeffries, "Accidental Youth Club," 374.

44. Madden, "Revisiting the End," 187-207.

45. Sanchez's apprehension about these youths mirrors the concerns expressed about urban youths and street-life influences in Elijah Anderson's classic sociological study. See Elijah Anderson, *Code of the Street: Decency, Violence, and the Moral Life of the Inner City*, (New York: W. W. Norton, 1999).

46. Susie Weller, "Skateboarding Alone? Making Social Capital Discourse Relevant to Teenagers' Lives," *Journal of Youth Studies* 9, no. 5 (2006): 567.

47. Weller, "Skateboarding Alone?," 558.

48. Anderson, Code of the Street.

49. For more information and background regarding the feeling of stoke, see Belinda Wheaton, *The Cultural Politics of Lifestyle Sports* (London: Routledge, 2013), 29.

50. See Van Melik, et al., "Fear and Fantasy," 29.

51. Nicholas Nolan, "The Ins and Outs of Skateboarding and Transgression in Public Space in Newcastle, Australia," *Australian Geographer* 34, no. 3 (2003): 312.

52. Nolan, "The Ins and Outs of Skateboarding and Transgression," 312.

SIX

1. Jay Coakley, "Youth Sport in the United States," in *Routledge Handbook of Youth Sport*, ed. Ken Green and Andy Smith (New York: Routledge, 2016), 91.

2. Rodney Mullen, "Rodney Mullen: Pop an Ollie and Innovate!" TED video, 1:37, February 2, 2015, https://www.youtube.com/watch?v=3GVO-MfIl1Q.

3. Sean Mortimer and Tony Hawk, *Stalefish: Skateboard Culture from the Rejects Who Made It* (San Francisco: Chronicle Books, 2008), 10.

4. Paul Gilchrist and Belinda Wheaton, "Lifestyle and Adventure Sport Among Youth," in *Routledge Handbook of Youth Sport*, ed. Ken Green and Andy Smith (New York: Routledge, 2016), 193.

5. David J. Madden, "Neighborhood as Spatial Project: Making the Urban

Order on the Downtown Brooklyn Waterfront," *International Journal of Urban and Regional Research* 38, no. 2 (2014): 471–97, 10.1111/1468-2427.12068.

6. Coakley, "Youth Sport in the United States," 91.

7. Matthew Atencio and Becky Beal, "'Beautiful Losers': The Symbolic Exhibition and Legitimization of Outsider Masculinity," *Sport in Society* 14 (2011): 4.

8. Adam Arvidsson, "From Counter Culture to Consumer Culture: Vespa and the Italian Youth Market, 1958–78," *Journal of Consumer Culture* 1 (2001): 48.

9. Kara-Jane Lombard, "Skate and Create/Skate and Destroy: The Commercial and Governmental Incorporation of Skateboarding," *Continuum: Journal of Media & Cultural Studies* 24, no. 4 (2010): 478.

10. Paul O'Connor, "Skateboarding Philanthropy: Inclusion and Prefigurative Politics," in *Skateboarding: Subcultures, Sites and Shifts*, ed. Kara-Jane Lombard (London: Routledge, 2016), 40.

11. Atencio and Beal, "'Beautiful Losers,'" 10.

12. Josh Sens, "East Side Story," *Sunset Magazine*, April 2016, 73.

13. Jonathan Ilan, *Understanding Street Culture: Poverty, Crime, Youth and Cool* (London: Palgrave, 2015), 105.

14. Nate Seltentich, "Parks in Peril," *East Bay Express*, January 19, 2011, http://www.eastbayexpress.com/oakland/parks-in-peril/Content?oid=2372824.

15. This group has been featured in a locally produced documentary film titled *Futbolistas 4 Life*. The documentary follows the story of a group of teens in Oakland, the Fubolistas, who campaigned to transform their prison playground into a soccer field that they could use to reject violence, discuss immigration and financial concerns, and also come up with ways of helping their local community (http://futbolistas4lifefilm.com). In the documentary film, the leader of the group raises the following lines of questioning that further illustrate how the lack of youth sport facilities have severe social consequences: "What does it mean to have space to play, what does it mean to have your parks overrun by crime or violence, what does that do to a community, and what does that do to young people?"

16. "Levi's Skateboarding—Spring 2015 Collection Video," The Berrics, May 2, 2015, http://theberrics.com/news-levis-skateboarding-spring-2015-collection/.

17. Bruce Newman, "Skatepark, a San Jose Hidden Gem, Fighting for Survival," *Mercury News*, September 14, 2014, http://www.mercurynews.com/2011/09/14/skatepark-a-san-jose-hidden-gem-fighting-for-survival/.

18. Angel Rios Jr. and Barry Ng, "Approval of Actions Related to the Lake Cunningham Bike Park Project," *City of San Jose Capital of Silicon Valley Memorandum*, August 10, 2015, accessed September 26, 2016, http://sanjose.granicus.com/MetaViewer.php?view_id=52&clip_id=8431&meta_id=530874.

19. Daniel Bjärsholm, "Sport and Social Entrepreneurship: A Review of a Concept in Progress," *Journal of Sport Management* 31 (2017): 192.

20. Jennifer Ceema Samimi, "Funding America's Nonprofits: The Nonprofit Industrial Complex's Hold on Social Justice," *Columbia Social Work Review* 1 (2000): 20, https://doi.org/10.7916/D8QC0DC7.

21. Samimi, "Funding America's Nonprofits," 20.

22. Samimi, "Funding America's Nonprofits," 17.

23. Bjärsholm, "Sport and Social Entrepreneurship," 191.

24. Holly Thorpe, "Action Sports for Youth Development: Critical Insights for

the SDP Community," *International Journal of Sport Policy and Politics* 8, no. 1 (2014): 97.

25. Thorpe, "Action Sports for Youth Development," 97. "For example, skateboarding companies—Blackbox Distribution and TSG—have provided Skateistan with skateboarding equipment (e.g., skateboards, wheels, trucks and bearings) and safety gear (e.g., helmets and wrist-guards) and host various awareness- and fund-raising events in an array of countries (i.e., Australia, Germany and the United States). Skateistan has also been working with some of these companies to establish their own brand by coproducing, marketing and distributing helmets, skateboards, T-shirts, scarves and knee-pads worldwide; many of the graphics featured on these products are designed by Skateistan students during art classes."

26. Holly Thorpe and Robert Rinehart, "Action Sport NGOs in a Neo-Liberal Context: The Cases of Skateistan and Surf Aid International," *Journal of Sport & Exercise Psychology* 37, no. 2 (2013): 115, 10.1177/0193723512455923.

27. Atencio and Beal, "'Beautiful Losers,'" 11.

28. "Tony Hawk Foundation: Annual Report 2014," accessed September 28, 2016, http://tonyhawkfoundation.org/wp-content/uploads/2016/01/THF_AR_2014.pdf. The Tony Hawk Foundation, for instance, broke down its 2014 revenue report accordingly: 50 percent private donations, 23 percent foundations, and 27 percent corporate funding. Major corporate donations were reported by Kohl's Department Stores ($50,000-99,999), MINI USA, Skate One Corp., Activision, Chipotle Mexican Grill ($25,000-49,999), as well as Clif Bar, Vans, Sony Action Cam, ESPN, MovieTickets.com, Nixon Watches and others putting money into the THF coffers ($10,000-24,999).

29. Brian Krans, "Skate Or DIY: Why Is It So Damn Hard to Build a Skate Park In Oakland?" *East Bay Express*, March 14, 2017, https://www.eastbayexpress.com/oakland/skate-or-diy-why-is-it-so-damn-hard-to-build-a-skate-park-in-oakland/Content?oid=5719389.

30. The prevalent use of social media to support skateboarding groups has been documented by Steph MacKay and Christine Dallaire. See Steph MacKay and Christine Dallaire, "Skateboarding Women: Building Collective Identity in Cyberspace," *Journal of Sport and Social Issues* 30, no. 2 (2013): 173–96. For other "action" sport groups invested in activities such as parkour, see Holly Thorpe and Nida Ahmad, "Youth, Action Sports and Political Agency in the Middle East: Lessons from a Grassroots Parkour Group in Gaza," *International Review for the Sociology of Sport* 50, no. 6 (2015): 678–704.

31. From an August 3, 2017, post on their Facebook site, "Thanks to everyone for coming out to our Town Park session last Sunday and bringing the positive energy! The turnout was amazing, we are so hyped and thankful for our community! Huge shout out to Keith K Dub Williams & 510 SKATEBOARDING for the continued love and support." "Skate Like a Girl SF Bay Area," Facebook, accessed September 4, 2017, https://www.facebook.com/SkateLikeAGirlBayArea/.

32. "Rob Skate Skateboard Academy"; "Our Private Services"; accessed August 13, 2017, https://www.robskate.com/book-online.

33. Daniel Bjärsholm, "Sport and Social Entrepreneurship," 191–92.

34. Kara-Jane Lombard, "Social Entrepreneurship in Youth Culture: Morganics, Russell Simmons and Emile 'XY?' Jansen," *Journal for Cultural Research* 16, no. 1 (2012): 3.

35. Lombard, "Social Entrepreneurship in Youth Culture," 7, 8.

36. "Rob Skate Skateboard Academy," accessed August 13, 2017, https://www.robskate.com/.

37. Lombard, "Social Entrepreneurship," 6.

38. Lombard, "Social Entrepreneurship," 18.

39. Lombard, "Social Entrepreneurship," 14.

40. Suzanne Le Menestrel and Daniel F. Perkins, "An Overview of How Sports, Out-of-School Time, and Youth Well-Being Can and Do Intersect," *New Direction for Youth Development* 115 (2007): 16.

41. "About ASDP: The Value of Action Sports for Development," Actionsportsfordev.org, accessed July 20, 2017, http://www.actionsportsfordev.org/about/.

42. Pierre Bourdieu, *Distinction: A Social Critique of the Judgement of Taste* (Cambridge: Harvard University Press, 1984).

43. To see a related Bourdieusian study, read Ramón Spaaij, "Sport as a Vehicle for Social Mobility and Regulation of Disadvantaged Urban Youth: Lessons from Rotterdam," *International Review for the Sociology of Sport* 44, nos. 2–3 (2009): 249.

44. Roger Levermore, "The Paucity of, and Dilemma in, Evaluating Corporate Social Responsibility for Development through Sport," *Third World Quarterly* 32, no. 3 (2011): 551–69.

45. Douglas Hartmann, *Midnight Basketball: Race, Sports, and Neoliberal Social Policy* (Chicago: University of Chicago Press, 2016), 207.

46. Spaaij, "Sport as a Vehicle," 248.

47. Jay Coakley, "Youth Sports: What Counts as 'Positive Development'?" *Journal of Sport and Social Issues* 35, no. 3 (2011): 306, doi:10.1177/0193723511417311.

48. Holly Thorpe and Megan Chawansky, "The 'Girl Effect' in Action Sports for Development: The Case of the Female Practitioners of Skateistan," in *Women in Action Sport Cultures: Identity, Politics and Experience*, ed. Holly Thorpe and Rebecca Olive (London: Palgrave Macmillan, 2016), 136.

49. Fred Coalter, *A Wider Social Role for Sport: Who's Keeping the Score?* (London: Routledge, 2007).

50. "About ASDP: The Value of Action Sports for Development," accessed July 20, 2017, http://www.actionsportsfordev.org/about/.

51. Douglas Hartmann articulates that when it comes to sport-based youth interventions, "development and change is far from automatic." See Hartman, *Midnight Basketball*, 198.

52. Douglas Hartmann, "Re-thinking Community-Based Crime Prevention through Sports," in *Sport, for Development, Peace, and Social Justice*, ed. Robert J. Schinke and Stephanie J. Hanrahan (Morgantown, W.V.: Fitness Information Technology, 2012), 81–85.

53. Hartmann, "Re-thinking Community-Based Crime Prevention," 84.

54. Hartmann, "Re-thinking Community-Based Crime Prevention," 75–85.

55. Hartmann, "Re-thinking Community-Based Crime Prevention," 84.

56. Hartmann, "Re-thinking Community-Based Crime Prevention," 82.

57. Zeno Nols, Rein Haudenhuyse, and Marc Theeboom, "Urban Sport-for-Development Initiatives and Young People in Socially Vulnerable Situations: Investigating the 'Deficit Model,'" *Social Inclusion* 5, no. 2 (2017): 211.

58. Indeed, this concern is becoming a reality, with two of the neighborhoods

most at risk of gentrification and displacement bordering on the Roosevelt community, according to a recent fair-housing report. This report was explained in one recent news story from *San Jose Inside*:

> "Due to rising housing costs over the last several years, residents in low and moderate income neighborhoods have experienced displacement," according to the report authored by San Jose's Housing Department, which is helmed by Jacky Morales-Ferrand. "The displacement is expected to continue, particularly in neighborhoods with accelerating growth and new development." In the report, Morales-Ferrand points to data from the Urban Displacement Project at the University of California, Berkeley, which found that more than half of low-income households live in gentrifying neighborhoods. In San Jose, the neighborhoods most at risk of displacement include Japantown, Luna Park and Little Portugal."

Jennifer Wadsworth, "Following Historic Vote on Rent Protections, San Jose Considers Ban on Voucher Discrimination," *San Jose Inside,* April 24, 2017, http://www.sanjoseinside.com/2017/04/24/following-historic-vote-on-rent-protections-san-jose-considers-ban-on-voucher-discrimination/.

59. George Avalos, "Exclusive: Google Adds Huge Site to Downtown San Jose village Proposal," *The Mercury News*, April 3, 2018, https://www.mercurynews.com/2018/04/03/google-adds-huge-site-to-downtown-san-jose-village-proposal/.

60. The quotes in this sentence and in the following two sentences come from, Nicola De Martini Ugolotti, "'They Are Just Trying to Contain Us': Parkour, Counter-Conducts and the Government of Difference in Turin's Urban Spaces," *Osservatorio MU. SIC Working Paper Series* 02 (2016): 7.

61. Richard Florida and Gary Gates, "Technology and Tolerance: Diversity and High-Tech Growth," *Brookings Review* 20, no. 1 (2002): 36.

62. Matt Haber, "Oakland: Brooklyn by the Bay," *New York Times*, May 2, 2014, http://www.nytimes.com/2014/05/04/fashion/oakland-california-brooklyn-by-the-bay.html?_r=0.

63. Richard Lloyd, *Neo-Bohemia: Art and Commerce in the Postindustrial City* (New York: Routledge, 2006), 244–45, 241.

64. Lloyd, *Neo-Bohemia.*

65. Krans, "Skate Or DIY."

66. Michael Todd Friedman and Cathy van Ingen, "Bodies in Space: Spatializing Physical Cultural Studies," *Sociology of Sport Journal* 28 (2011): 95.

67. Charlotte Faircloth, "Intensive Parenting and the Expansion of Parenting," in *Parenting Culture Studies*, ed. Ellie Lee, Jennie Bristow, Charlotte Faircloth, and Jan Macvarish (London: Palgrave Macmillan, 2014), 36.

68. Thomas J. Martinek and Donald R. Hellison, "Fostering Resiliency in Underserved Youth Through Physical Activity," *Quest* 49 (1997): 34–49.

69. Jay Coakley, "Positive Youth Development Through Sport: Myths, Beliefs, and Realities," in *Positive Youth Development Through Sport*, 2nd ed., ed. Nicholas Holt (New York: Routledge, 2016), 23. Coakley provides two models here in terms of defining youth development; mid-twentieth century to 1980s being more collective and community-oriented, and 1980s to present being more focused on individual.

70. Jay Coakley, "Youth Sports: What Counts," 313.

71. Annette Lareau, "Invisible Inequality: Social Class and Childrearing in Black Families and White Families," *American Sociological Review* 67, no. 5 (2002): 747–76.

72. Kari Stefansen, Ingrid Smette, and Åse Strandbu, "Understanding the Increase in Parents' Involvement in Organized Youth Sports," *Sport, Education and Society* (2016): 9–10.

73. Jay Coakley, "The Good Father: Parental Expectations and Youth Sports," *Leisure Studies* 25, no. 2 (2006): 160.

74. Carl Vincent and Carol Maxwell, "Parenting Priorities and Pressures: Furthering Understanding of 'Concerted Cultivation,'" *Discourse: Studies in the Cultural Politics of Education* 37, no. 2 (2016): 278.

75. Vincent and Maxwell, "Parenting Priorities and Pressures," 278.

76. Stefansen, Smette, and Strandbu, "Understanding the Increase," 5.

77. Barry A. Garst and Ryan J. Gagnon, "Exploring Overparenting within the Context of Youth Development Programs," *Journal of Youth Development* 10 (2015): 13.

78. Michael A. Messner, *It's All for the Kids: Gender, Families, and Youth Sports* (Berkeley: University of California Press, 2009), 13.

79. Faircloth, "Intensive Parenting," 36.

80. Jay Coakley, "Positive Youth Development," 23.

81. Nastia Voynovskaya, "Reflections on the 15th Street Tragedy," *East Bay Express*, August 23, 2016, http://www.eastbayexpress.com/oakland/reflections-on -the-15th-street-tragedy/Content?oid=4947666.

82. Robert Rinehart and Christopher Grenfell, "BMX Spaces: Children's Grass Roots' Courses and Corporate-Sponsored Tracks," *Sociology of Sport Journal* 19, no. 3 (2002): 303.

83. Rinehart and Grenfell, "BMX Spaces," 310.

84. Nicholas L. Holt, Katherine A. Tamminen, Danielle E. Black, Zoë L. Sehn, and Michael P. Wall, "Parental Involvement in Competitive Youth Sport Settings," *Psychology of Sport and Exercise* 9, no. 5 (2008): 663–85; Garst and Gagnon, "Exploring Overparenting," 13.

85. Coalter, *Wider Social Role for Sport*, 53, 59.

86. Rinehart and Grenfell, "BMX Spaces," 303.

87. Richard Majors and Janet Mancini Billson, *Cool Pose: The Dilemmas of Black Manhood in America* (New York: Lexington Books, 1992).

88. Ugolotti, "'They Are Just Trying to Contain Us,'" 22.

89. Kara-Jane Lombard, "Trucks, Tricks, and Technologies of Government: Analyzing the Productive Encounter Between Governance and Resistance in Skateboarding," in *Skateboarding: Subcultures, Sites and Shifts*, ed. Kara-Jane Lombard (London: Routledge, 2016), 174, 175.

90. Coakley, "Youth Sport in the United States," 91.

91. Myra F. Taylor and Umneea Khan, "Skate-Park Builds, Teenaphobia and the Adolescent Need for Hang-Out Spaces: The Social Utility and Functionality of Urban Skate Parks," *Journal of Urban Design* 16, no. 4 (2011): 496, dx.doi.org/10 .1080/13574809.2011.586142.

92. Alison L. Nelson, Doune Macdonald, and Rebecca A. Abbott, "A Risky

Business? Health and Physical Activity from the Perspectives of Urban Australian Indigenous Young People," *Health, Risk & Society* 14 (2012): 327.

93. Matthew Atencio, Becky Beal, and Charlene Wilson, "The Distinction of Risk: Urban Skateboarding, Street Habitus and the Construction of Hierarchical Gender Relations," *Qualitative Research in Sport and Exercise* 1, no. 1 (2009): 3–20.

94. Amy Sueyoshi, "Skate and Create: Skateboarding, Asian Pacific America, and Masculinity," *Amerasia Journal* 41, no. 2 (2015): 2–24.

95. Messner, *It's All for the Kids.*

96. Messner, *It's All for the Kids*, 194–97.

97. Messner, *It's All for the Kids*, 197.

98. Krans, "Skate Or DIY."

99. Sarah Banet-Weiser, *Kids Rule!: Nickelodeon and Consumer Citizenship* (Durham: Duke University Press, 2007), 144.

100. Banet-Weiser, *Kids Rule!*, 144.

101. Lulu Garcia-Navarro and Wynne Davis, "How the NFL's New Rule On Protesting Is Being Perceived By Players," NPR, May 27, 2018, https://www.npr.org/2018/05/27/614810127/the-nfls-rule-new-on-kneeling.

102. Bianca J. Baldridge, "Relocating the Deficit: Reimagining Black Youth in Neoliberal Times," *American Educational Research Journal* 51, no. 3 (2014): 440.

103. Paul Gilchrist and Belinda Wheaton, "The Social Benefits of Informal and Lifestyle Sports: A Research Agenda," *International Journal of Sport Policy and Politics* 9, no. 1 (2017): 6.

104. "Skate Like a Girl SF Bay Area," Facebook, accessed September 4, 2017, https://www.facebook.com/SkateLikeAGirlBayArea/.

105. Cheryl Cooky, "'Girls Just Aren't Interested': The Social Construction of Interest in Girls' Sport," *Sociological Perspectives* 52, no. 2 (2009): 260.

106. Thorpe and Chawansky, "'Girl Effect," 137.

107. A sample Facebook post that demonstrates this approach, from SLAG's Facebook page, August 1, 2017: "Check out these rad photos Sariah Adviento took at our last Stoked To Skate session! Join us again THIS Saturday from 1-4pm for a Girlz sesh at the sickest indoor park in the Bay! All ages / all abilities / women, non-binary and trans folks always welcome!" "Skate Like a Girl SF Bay Area," Facebook, accessed September 4, 2017, https://www.facebook.com/SkateLikeAGirlBayArea/.

108. MacKay and Dallaire, "Skateboarding Women," 182.

109. MacKay and Dallaire, "Skateboarding Women," 182.

110. Cole Louison, "Meet Skateboarding's Stylish, Boundary-Breaking New Star," *Vogue*, April 27, 2017, http://www.vogue.com/article/lacey-baker-nike-skate-team-interview.

111. "Pushing Boarders: Talks," accessed June 15, 2018, https://www.pushingboarders.com/talks/.

112. Cathy van Ingen, "Geographies of Gender, Sexuality and Race," *International Review for the Sociology of Sport 38*, no. 2 (2003): 201–16.

113. Coakley, "Youth Sports: What Counts," 317–18.

114. For examples, see Annie Linskey, "Conway Faces Ethics Review After 'Commercial," *Boston Globe*, February 9, 2017, https://www.bostonglobe.com/news/politics/2017/02/09/kellyanne-conway-pitches-ivanka-trump-products-from-white-house/XGkrDFDnfb5CaHVNwKyLOJ/story.html.;

Javier C. Hernandez, Cao Li, and Jesse Drucker, "Jared Kushner's Sister Highlights Family Ties in Pitch to Chinese Investors," *New York Times*, May 6, 2017, https://www.nytimes.com/2017/05/06/world/asia/jared-kushner-sister-nicole-meyer-china-investors.html.; Ella Nilsen, "Louise Linton's Instagram Spat Is the Latest Sign of an Administration Mingling Wealth and Privilege," Vox, updated August 22, 2017, https://www.vox.com/policy-and-politics/2017/8/22/16183510/louise-linton-instagram-out-of-touch.; David Smith, "Betsy DeVos: Trump's Illiberal Ally Seen as Most Dangerous Education Chief Ever," *The Guardian*, July 26, 2017, https://www.theguardian.com/us-news/2017/jul/26/betsy-devos-education-secretary-trump.

115. Sean Gregory, "How Kids' Sports Became a $15 Billion Industry," *Time*, August 23, 2017, http://time.com/4913687/how-kids-sports-became-15-billion-industry/.

116. "Social Enterprise and Sport: A Way Forward," SENSCOT, accessed October 17, 2017, http://www.se-networks.net/downloads/SocialEnterprise&SportTheWayForward.pdf.

117. Emma Brown, Valerie Strauss, and Danielle Douglas-Gabriel, "Trump's First Full Education Budget: Deep Cuts to Public School Programs in Pursuit of School Choice," *Washington Post*, May 17, 2017, http://wapo.st/2qssqaA?tid=ss_mail&utm_term=.c91a2a01ea65.

118. Smith, "Betsy DeVos: Trump's Illiberal Ally."

119. Vann R. Newkirk II, "How Trump's Budget Would Weaken Public Health," *The Atlantic*, May 23, 2017, https://www.theatlantic.com/politics/archive/2017/05/trump-budget-public-health/527808/.

120. For more about how public-private partnerships (PPPs) may be leading the way in terms of creating new American infrastructure, see: "Can the Private Sector Solve the U.S. Infrastructure Crisis?" Kellogg Insight, January 4, 2016, https://insight.kellogg.northwestern.edu/article/can-the-private-sector-solve-the-us-infrastructure-crisis.

121. Smith, "Betsy DeVos: Trump's Illiberal Ally."

122. Brown, Strauss, and Douglas-Gabriel, "Trump's Education Budget."

123. Scott Westfall and Daniel Gould, "Youth Culture and Its Influence on Children's Sport," in *The Young Are Making Their World: Essays on the Power of Youth Culture*, ed. Yuya Kiuchi and Francisco Villarruel (Jefferson, N.C.: McFarland, 2016), 176.

124. Richard Bailey, Edward J. Cope, and Gemma Pearce, "Why Do Children Take Part In, and Remain Involved in Sport? A Literature Review and Discussion of Implications for Sport Coaches," *International Journal of Coaching Science* 17, no. 1 (2013): 63–64.

125. Anna-Liisa Ojala and Holly Thorpe, "The Role of the Coach in Action Sports: Using a Problem-based Learning Approach," *International Sport Coaching Journal* 2, no. 1 (2015): 69.

126. Jasmine Y. Ma and Charles Munter, "The Spatial Production of Learning Opportunities in Skateboard Parks," *Mind, Culture and Activity* 21 (2014): 256.

127. Ma and Munter, "The Spatial Production of Learning Opportunties," 239.

128. Bailey, Cope, and Pearce, "Why Do Children Take Part," 60–62.

129. Matthew Atencio, Mike Jess, and Kay Dewar, "'It is a Case of Changing Your Thought Processes, The Way You Actually Teach': Implementing a Complex Professional Learning Agenda in Scottish Physical Education," *Physical Education & Sport Pedagogy* 17, no. 2 (2012): 129.

130. For more information, see Mike Jess and Matthew Atencio, "The Transformational Wind of Theoretical Change: A Historic and Contemporary View of Physical Education," in *Transformational Learning in Physical Education,* ed. Malcom Thorburn (London: Routledge, 2017), 45–60; Mike Jess, Matthew Atencio, and Nicola Carse, "Introducing Conditions of Complexity in the Context of Scottish Physical Education," in *Complexity in Physical Education: Reframing Curriculum, Pedagogy and Research,* ed. Alan Ovens, Tim Hopper, and Joy Butler (London: Routledge, 2012): 27–41; Mike Jess, Matthew Atencio, and Malcolm Thorburn, "Complexity Theory: Supporting Curriculum and Pedagogy Developments in Scottish Physical Education," *Sport, Education and Society* 16 (2011): 179–99.

131. See Peter Donnelly and Jay Coakley, *The Role of Recreation in Promoting Social Inclusion* (Toronto: Laidlaw Foundation, 2002), 10. The authors reference Voyle, "Adolescent Administration of a Leisure Centre: Lessons for Sports Organizations," *New Zealand Journal of Sports Medicine* 17, no. 2 (1989): 34.

132. Australian scholar Kara-Jane Lombard's 2016 work examining the transformation of skateboarding offers a revealing, diverse list of descriptors and interests now associated with riding the skateboard: "It is a multi-million-dollar industry, recreational activity, sport, children's pursuit, fad, underground movement, criminal activity, form of transport, aesthetic practice, and much more." See Kara-Jane Lombard, "The Cultural Politics of Skateboarding and the Rise of Skate Urbanism," in *Skateboarding: Subcultures, Sites and Shifts,* ed. Kara-Jane Lombard (London: Routledge, 2016), 11.

133. David J. Madden, "Revisiting the End of Public Space: Assembling the Public in an Urban Park," *City and Community* 9, no. 2 (2010): 203.

134. Madden, "Revisiting the End of Public Space," 203.

135. Synthia Sydnor, "Cultural Pedagogies, Action Sports," in *Women in Action Sport Cultures: Identity, Politics and Experience,* ed. Holly Thorpe and Rebecca Olive (London: Palgrave Macmillan, 2016), 350.

136. For more information about these programs, both of which are based in Oakland, see "Futbolistas 4 Life Follows Youth Bringing a Soccer Field to Oakland's Fruitvale," Colorlines, accessed September 15, 2017, https://www.colorlines.com /articles/futbolistas-4-life-follows-youth-bringing-soccer-field-oaklands-fruitvale; "What we Do," Soccer Without Borders, accessed September 15, 2017, https://www .soccerwithoutborders.org/program-model.

137. Emily Chivers Yochim, *Skate Life: Re-Imagining White Masculinity* (Ann Arbor: University of Michigan Press, 2010), 78.

138. Michael A. Messner and Michela Musto, "Where Are the Kids?," *Sociology of Sport Journal* 31 (2014): 111.

139. Vern Seefeldt and Martha Ewing, Participation and Attrition Patterns in American Agency-Sponsored and Interscholastic Sport: An Executive Summary Final Report (North Palm Beach, Fl.: Sporting Goods Manufacturer's Association, 1989).

140. Maria J. Kefalas and Patrick J. Carr, "Conclusion," in *Coming of Age in America: The Transition to Adulthood in the Twenty-First Century,* eds. Mary C. Waters, Patrick J. Carr, Maria J. Kefalas and Jennifer Holdaway (Berkeley: University of California Press, 2011), 148–50.

141. Tim Lott, "Our Children Are Paying a High Price for Society's Vision of Success," *The Guardian,* October 14, 2016, https://www.theguardian.com/lifeand

style/2016/oct/14/our-children-are-paying-a-high-price-for-societys-vision-of
-success?CMP=fb_gu.

142. Arwa Mahdawi, "What Jobs Will Still Be Around in 20 Years? Read This to Prepare Your Future," *The Guardian*, June 26, 2017, https://www.theguardian.com /us-news/2017/jun/26/jobs-future-automation-robots-skills-creative-health?CMP =fb_gu.

143. Garst and Gagnon, "Exploring Overparenting," 5-18.

144. Michael Gard, Anna Hickey-Moodey, and Eimear Enright, "Youth Culture, Physical Education and the Question of Relevance: After 20 years, a Reply to Tinning and Fitzclarence," *Sport, Education and Society* 18, no. 1 (2013): 111.

145. Gard, Hickey-Moodey, and Enright, "Youth Culture, Physical Education, and the Question of Relevance," 111.

146. Nols, Haudenhuyse, and Theeboom, "Urban Sport-for-Development Initiatives," 210.

147. Tom Farrey, "Sports for All Roundtable Discussion," *President's Council on Fitness, Sports & Nutrition: Annual Meeting*, September 16, 2014, 24, http://www. fitness.gov/pdfs/2014-council-meeting-minutes.pdf.

148. Coakley, "Positive Youth Development," 29.

149. Michael Bodley, San Francisco Chronicle, and Kevin Fagan, "Officer Injured as Police, Skateboarders Square Off at Dolores Park," *SFGate*, July 12, 2017, http://www.sfgate.com/bayarea/article/Officer-injured-as-police-skateboarders -square-11282138.php#photo-13229841.

150. John Seely Brown, "The Power of Pull: An Examination of Firms in the Brave New World of 21st Century Internet Economics: Stanford Entrepreneur's Corner Talk," *Cook Report on Internet Protocol: Technology, Economics, and Policy* 19, no. 4 (2010): 18.

151. Becky Beal, *Skateboarding: The Ultimate Guide* (Santa Barbara: Greenwood, 2013).

Methodological Appendix

1. Matthew Atencio, Emily Chivers Yochim, and Becky Beal, "It Ain't Just Black Kids and White Kids: The Representation and Reproduction of Authentic 'Skurban' Masculinities," *Sociology of Sport Journal* 30 (2013): 153–72.

2. Jerry W. Willis, *Foundations of Qualitative Research: Interpretive and Critical Approaches* (Thousand Oaks, Calif.: Sage Publications, 2007), 239.

3. Julie White, Sarah Drew, and Trevor Hay, "Ethnography Versus Case Study—Positioning Research and Researchers," *Qualitative Research Journal* 9, no. 1 (2009): 21, https://doi.org/10.3316/QRJ0901018.

4. Robert Yin, *Case Study Research: Design and Methods* (Thousand Oaks, Calif.: Sage Publications, 2003).

5. Robert E. Stake, "Qualitative Case Studies," in *The Sage Handbook of Qualitative Research*, ed. Norman K. Denzin and Yvonna S. Lincoln (Thousand Oaks, Calif.: Sage Publications, 2005), 236-47.

6. Elijah Anderson, Duke W. Austin, Craig Lapriece Holloway, and Vani S. Kulkarni, "The Legacy of Racial Cast: An Exploratory Ethnography," *Annals of the American Academy of Political and Social Science* 642, no. 1 (2012): 27, DOI:10.1177/0002716212437337.

7. Robert E. Rinehart and Kerry Earl, "Auto-, Duo- and Collaborative-Ethnographies: 'Caring' in an Audit Culture Climate," *Qualitative Research Journal* 16, no. 3 (2016): 8.

8. Pierre Bourdieu, *Distinction: A Social Critique of the Judgement of Taste* (Cambridge: Harvard University Press, 1984).

9. Mary Brydon-Miller, Davydd Greenwood, and Patricia Maguire, "Why Action Research?" *Action Research* 1, no. 1 (2003): 14.

10. M. Blair Evans, Veronica Allan, Matthew Vierimaa, and Jean Côté, "Sport Parent Roles in Fostering Positive Youth Development," in *Families, Young People, Physical Activity and Health: Critical Perspectives,* ed. Symeon Dagkas and Lisette Burrows (London: Routledge, 2016), 229.

11. See Andy Smith and David Haycock, "Families, Youth and Extra-Curricular Activity," in *Families, Young People, Physical Activity and Health: Critical Perspectives,* ed. Symeon Dagkas and Lisette Burrows (London: Routledge, 2016), 186–88, for a summary, as well as Rochelle M. Eime, Jack T. Harvey, Melinda J. Craike, Caroline M. Symons, and Warren R. Payne, "Family Support and Ease of Access Socio-Economic Status and Sports Club Membership in Adolescent Girls: A Mediation Study," *International Journal of Behavioral Nutrition and Physical Activity* 10, no. 1 (2013): 50.

12. "Top National Ranking: U.S. News & World Report Scores Cal State East Bay Most Diverse University in the Country," *East Bay Today*, September 14, 2017, https://www.ebtoday.com/stories/top-national-ranking.

13. Holly Thorpe et al., "Looking Back, Moving Forward? Reflections from Early Action Sport Researchers," in *Women in Action Sport Cultures: Identity, Politics and Experience*, ed. Holly Thorpe and Rebecca Olive (London: Palgrave Macmillan, 2016), 38.

14. Michael A. Messner and Michela Musto, "Where are the Kids?" *Sociology of Sport Journal* 31, no. 1 (2014): 109, http://dx.doi.org/10.1123/ssj.2013-0111.

15. Jay Coakley, "Youth Sport in the United States," in *Routledge Handbook of Youth Sport*, ed. Ken Green and Andy Smith (London: Routledge, 2016), 84.

16. Laura Azzarito, "Ways of Seeing the Body in Kinesiology: A Case for Visual Methodologies," *Quest* 62, (2010): 155–70.

17. Adam Jenson, Jon Swords, and Michael Jeffries, "The Accidental Youth Club: Skateboarding in Newcastle-Gateshead," *Journal of Urban Design* 17, no. 3 (2012): 376.

18. Nicola J. Ross, Emma Renold, Sally Holland, and Alexandra Hillman, "Moving Stories: Using Mobile Methods to Explore the Everyday Lives of Young People in Public Care," *Qualitative Research* 9, no. 5 (2009): 605–23.

19. Evidenced in numerous studies, including Jenson, et al., "Accidental Youth Club," as well as Ross, et al., "Moving Stories," as well as in Tom Hall, "Footwork: Moving and Knowing in Local Space(s)," *Qualitative Research* 9, no. 5 (2009): 571–85.

20. Rinehart and Earl, "Auto-, Duo- and Collaborative-ethnographies," 8.

21. Rinehart and Earl, "Auto-, Duo- and Collaborative-ethnographies," 8.

22. Holly Thorpe, Tatiana Ryba, and Jim Denison, "Introduction to the Special Issue: Toward New Conversations Between Sociology and Psychology," *Sociology of Sport Journal* 31, no. 2 (2014): 137.

INDEX

A

action sports: collaborative ethnological research, 271–73; female
skaters, 59, 227, 255; learning
and development processes and
approaches, 258–60; life-skills and
character development, 230–32;
minority populations, 153–54;
neoliberal perspective, 154; nonprofit groups, 225–27; as Olympic
event, 266; popularity, 4, 5–6, 11;
positive youth development (PYD),
18–19; privatization practices, 223;
research methodology, 271–73,
279–80; San Jose, California, 27,
177, 179–80, 184, 186, 223, 234,
246; social and health benefits,
18–19; social-change models,
67–70, 230–32; terminology, 285n1;
youth sports, 230–32. *See also* Lake
Cunningham Regional Skate Park;
skateboarding
Action Sports for Development and
Peace (ASDP), 18–19, 68–70, 230
Action Sports Park, 177
Activision, 315n28
Adobe, 178
adult networking and intervention:
gender inclusions, 84–97, 175; life-
skills and character development,
246, 247, 263; neoliberal perspective, 10; positive youth development
(PYD), 56, 232–36; risk-based
learning opportunities, 263; Town
Park Skate Park, 158, 237; traditional sports, 217–22; urban space
usage, 45–46, 50, 53, 65; youth
perspective, 208–9, 211, 235; youth
sports, 7–8, 9, 99–101, 217–22,
234–37, 263. *See also* Bay City Skate

Park; Lake Cunningham Regional
Skate Park; Roosevelt Skate Park;
SJ 180 program; social-enterprise
networks
adult-organized social spaces: Bay City
Skate Park, 99–134, 137, 232–34,
241–42, 249; Lake Cunningham
Regional Skate Park, 186–95, 234,
242–43, 246, 249; participant diver-
sity, 248–49; Roosevelt Skate Park,
195–205, 208–9, 234–35, 247–48,
249; safety concerns, 246; Town
Park Skate Park, 248, 249; urban
space usage, 53
African Americans. *See* minority popu-
lations; youth of color
Airbnb, 41
Alaway, Robin, 13
alcohol use: Bay City Skate Park, 105,
129, 130, 242, 243; Roosevelt Skate
Park, 198; Town Park Skate Park,
167
Alien Workshop, 73
Ament, Jeff, 301n21
American Association of Retired
Persons (AARP), 4
Anderson, Elijah, 206
Andrews, David L., 10
antiestablishment culture, viii, ix
antisocial behaviors, 105–6, 108, 110–
13, 120, 129–33, 242, 243, 250
Armanto, Lizzie, 13
Arvidsson, Adam, 219–20
Aseltine, Elyshia, 105
Asian Americans, 59, 196, 250
A.Skate, 115, 222
Ask.com, 141
Aspen Institute, 7
Atencio, Matthew, 24, 272

at-risk youth, 57, 70–80, 185, 234–35. *See also* Roosevelt Skate Park; youth of color
autistic youth, 115, 222
autonomy, 105

B

Back to the Future (film), 37
bad language: Bay City Skate Park, 108, 109, 130, 132, 242, 243; skater reputations, 131
Bailey, Richard, 259
Baker, Lacey, 256
Banet-Weiser, Sarah, 153, 252
Bangalore, India, 19
Barcelona, Spain, 17
Barker, Brandee, 301*n*21
basic research methodology, 268–69
Bay Area, *35*; demographic changes, 40–41, 109–10; female skaters, 58–59, 85–97; skateboarding scene, 33–39, 49; socioeconomic perspective, 39–42
Bay City, 109–10
Bay City Skate Park, *101*; access and inclusion, 91, 106, 133; adult-organized social spaces, 99–101, 103–9, 111–19, 129–34, 137, 232–34, 241–42, 249; community-building practices, 106–9, 111–19; corporate support and sponsorship, 48, 222, 223; design process, 233–34; family-friendly environments, 100–101, 107–8, 112, 114–34, 215–16, 232, 242, 243, 247; female skaters, 86–87; interviewing challenges, 273–76; origins and growth, 110–11; parental support and involvement, 86–87, 99–101, 103–9, 122, 124–34, 241–47; participant diversity, 101–3, 106, 128, 232–34, 250; positive youth development (PYD), 104–6, 122–29, 216; public/private-sector support and partnerships, 222; research studies, 22; social and health benefits, 104; town-hall meeting, 107–9, 132–33,

243; youth perspective, 247. *See also* female skaters
Bay City Skate Park Group (BCSPG), 101, 107, 111–19, 134, 274
Beal, Becky, 23–24, 265, 272
beer consumption, 66, 79, 131, 158, 161, 198–99, 203, 208, 248. *See also* alcohol use
Berkeley, California, 22, 35–36, 246, 247
Berkeley Skate Park, 91
Berra, Steve, 17
Berryman, Ellen, 13
Billson, Janet Mancini, 248
Birdhouse, 70
Bjärsholm, Daniel, 65, 224
Black Panther Party, 138, 139–40, 151
Black Power Movement, 138, 139–40
blogs, 25
BMX circuit, 246, 249
board sports. *See* skateboarding; surfing
bonding experiences, 122–23, 244, 247, 254
Bones Brigade team, 34
Bordertown, 35
boundary-making practices, 250–52, 261
Bourdieu, Pierre, 21, 43, 230, 271, 291*n*100
Boyle Heights, 75
Boys and Girls Club, 79
brand-name marketing trends, 153–55
Brazilian female skaters, 171
Brenes, Chico, 34
Brevard, Samarria, 13, 60
Bristow, Jennie, 54–55, 104
brochures, 25
Brown, Jerry, 141, 307*n*19
Brown, Sky, 14
Brujas all-female skate group, 14
Buffalo, New York, 58
bullying, 72, 129
Burnside, Cara-Beth, 13
Burnside district (Portland), 15, 47

C

Caballero, Steve, 36–37, 186

Calgary, Canada, 17

Cali Am Jam free community skate events, 81, 83, 159, 228

California Amateur Skateboard League (CASL), 14

California Endowment, 75

California Skateparks design firm, 149

California State University, Long Beach, 143

capital: capital-generation theory, 39, 205, 230, 263; capital reproduction, 50, 51–58, 151–55, 239–45; characteristics and functional role, 20–21, 43; parental support and involvement, 50, 51–58, 239–45; public spaces, 44–46; social class, 14, 56–58; urban skate parks, 43–46, 55–56, 90–91, 100, 120, 218, 230–32

Carroll, Mike, 34

Carthage, Missouri, 16

case-study research methodology, 267–68

Cayman Islands, 17

celebrity-run skate parks, 70–76, 301n20

Cespedes, Kim, 13

Chavez, Cindy, 180, 182–83, 191, 201

Chawansky, Megan, 68

child-safe environments, 53, 54–55. *See also* safe environments

Chinese skate parks, 17

Chipotle Mexican Grill, 83, 225, 315n28

Chivers Yochim, Emily, 10, 11, 32, 74

Christian outreach programs, 78

The Chronicle of Higher Education, 57

Circle-A Skate, 37

Cisco, 178

city landscapes. *See* public spaces

city parks, 30. *See also* public spaces

City Peace Project, 78

Clif Bar, 315n28

Clif Bar corporation, 91

Clorox, 150

Coakley, Jay, 16, 30, 56, 217, 231, 248, 263

Coalter, Fred, 247

Coca Cola, 192

code of the street, 206

collaborative ethnological research, 271–73

College Skateboarding Educational Foundation, 44

commitment, 126, 127–28

community-building practices: Bay City Skate Park, 111–19; Oakland Skatepark Summit, 63, 64–65; research methodology, 277–78; Skate Like a Girl (SLAG), 91; skate park leaders' perspective, 232–39; Town Park Skate Park, 64, 147–51, 160–61, 201–4, 239–41

competitive capital, 55–56, 57

competitive sports, 84, 119, 124–26. *See also* skate jam sessions and contests; X Games

Cooky, Cheryl, 254–55

corporate support and sponsorship: Bay City Skate Park, 48, 222, 223; public space usage, 30; skate park investments, 16, 17, 19; Tony Hawk Foundation (THF), 225; Town Park Skate Park, 64, 136, 147, 148, 149–50, 220–24, 229–30. *See also* public/private-sector support and partnerships

Corrimal, Australia, 18

cosmopolitan urbanism, 236–37

cost of living, 40

countercultural ethos, 12, 39, 47, 219, 266, 291n101

Courtenay, Bryce, 181–82

Coyote Creek, 196, 202

creativity, 47–48, 126, 154, 262

Cuba Skate, 68

cultural capital, 43, 44

Cybriwsky, Roman, 46

D

data collection and analysis methodology, 269–70, 270t, 273–79

DC Shoes, 73
De Fremery Park, 22, 138, 139–40, 145,
160–61, 163. *See also* Town Park
Skate Park
Del Mar, California, viii
demographic diversity, 249–56
Department of Recreation and Parks
(California), 75
Dew Tour, 74
Diamond Supply Company, 75
Diffley, Jim, 179
digital media, 24–25
"Dirty Ghetto Kids" (DGK) brand, 266
DIY skate spots, 35, 181
"do-it-yourself" (DIY) ideal, 32, 76, 219
downhill skating, 36
Dropbox, 41
drug use: Bay City Skate Park, 109, 128,
130; foundation grants, 70; Lake
Cunningham Regional Skate Park,
191, 251; neoliberal perspective, 10;
Roosevelt Skate Park, 198; safe envi-
ronments, 17, 72; skater reputations,
106, 113, 131, 133; Town Park Skate
Park, 164, 165, 168, 240; unstaffed
skate parks, 191
Duggan, Lisa, 29
Dupont, Tyler, 58
Dyrdek, Rob, 4, 17, 69, 73–76, 82

E

East Bay. *See* Oakland, California
East Bay Express, 246
East Oakland Youth Development
Center, 145
eBay, 178
economic capital, 43, 44
The Ellen DeGeneres Show, 14
Elliot, Sinikka, 105
Embarcadero district (San Francisco),
15, 34, 37–38
Engvall, Roger, 30
Entertainment Weekly, 12
entrepreneurialism, 32–33, 53, 113–14,
153–55, 218, 227–29, 238
equipment development, viii, x, 16, 91
ESPN, ix, 16, 315*n*28

ethnographic research, 24–25, 58,
267–68, 271–73
external assets, 104
Extreme Games. *See* X Games

F

Facebook: Bay City Skate Park Group
(BCSPG), 112, 114, 119, 130, 232;
historical perspective, 39; as infor-
mation resource, 25, 279; MAHFIA.
TV, 94, 255; Olympic Games, 4;
Skate Like a Girl (SLAG), 227;
Town Park Skate Park, 153, 315*n*31
Fairchild, Charlotte, 104
faith-based organizations, 78
family-friendly environments: Bay
City Skate Park, 100–101, 107, 112,
114–34, 215–16, 232, 242, 243, 247;
capital reproduction perspective,
51–58; Lake Cunningham Regional
Skate Park, 187–95, 196, 198, 246,
250–51; Roosevelt Skate Park, 203;
Town Park Skate Park, 160–61
Farrey, Tom, 8
fear, 126
Fédération Internationale de Roller
Sports (FIRS), x
female skaters: access and inclusion,
63–64, 68, 70, 84–97, 115–16,
121–22, 138–39, 170–75, 253–56;
adult-organized social spaces, 249;
gendered practices, 13–14, 51–53,
58–59, 253–56; marginalized individuals, 97, 228, 266; public space
usage, 296*n*76; social-enterprise
networks, 84–97, 226–27, 253–56;
Town Park Skate Park, 138–39,
159–60, 170–75, 254
feminist social activism, 85–97, 226–
27, 253–56
Ferguson, Rob "Skate," 69, 77, 80–84,
150–51, 159, 227–28, 254
fertilizer effect, 56
financial resources, 8–9
First5 California, 312*n*36
First 5 San Jose, 192
510 Skate Shop, 35, 36, 227

Florida, Richard, 47, 48, 237
Forbes magazine, 59, 178, 308*n*35
for-profit organizations: social-enterprise networks, 20, 65; urban skate parks, 44, 76, 81–82, 113
For the City (FTC) skate shop, 34, 147
For the Town (FTT) social-media platform, 153, 175
Fortune magazine, 12
4141Corp nonprofit organization, 81, 82
Foucault, Michel, 24
foul language: Bay City Skate Park, 108, 109, 130, 132, 242, 243; skater reputations, 131
free-market model, 30, 31, 33, 39, 48, 54, 84, 258
freestyle skating, 36
Fresno, California, 75
Friedman, Hilary, 9, 55, 56, 57
Fritz, Amanda, 30
fun, importance of, 11, 25, 95, 202, 235, 259, 262
Futbolistas, 221, 262, 314*n*15

G

gang-intervention programs, 185
gang presence, 185, 195–96, 205–6, 208
Gang Prevention Task Force, 185
Gap Kids, 14
Gard, Michael, 263
Gates, Gary, 237
gender: access and inclusion, 63–64, 68, 70, 84–97, 115–16, 121–22, 138–39, 170–75, 253–56; adult-organized social spaces, 249; feminist skateboarding organizations, 85–97, 226–27, 253–56; marginalized individuals, 97, 228, 266; public space usage, 296*n*76; skateboarding participation, 13–14, 51–53, 58–59, 253–56; social-enterprise networks, 84–97; stereotypes and sexism, 58, 89–90, 96–97, 106, 253, 256; Town Park Skate Park, 138–39, 159–60, 170–75
Generation Z, 11

gentrification: community resistance, 296*n*78; local impacts, 47–48, 49, 64; Oakland, 138, 140–43, 151–52, 161, 164–66, 169, 237, 252–53, 307*n*22; San Jose, 236–37, 316*n*58; sports participation opportunities, 41
Girls Riders Organization (GRO), 70, 85, 87–91, 115, 121, 226, 253
Giroux, Henry, 10
Gnarhunters, 227
Golden Gate Park, 34
Gonzales, Mark, 34
Google, 39, 236
GoPro, 39, 154, 227
Go Skateboarding Day, 11
Gould, Dan, 258–59
Grable, Chance, 139
graffiti: Bay City Skate Park, 72, 108, 111; Lake Cunningham Regional Skate Park, 193, 198, 251; Roosevelt Skate Park, 78, 198, 209–10; Town Park Skate Park, 136; unstaffed skate parks, 191
Grasmuck, Sherri, 161
grassroots sports programs: Bay City Skate Park, 114; female skaters, 96; skateboarding, 15–16, 67, 69, 147; social diversity and inclusion, 256, 262; Tha Hood Games, 27, 145, 146–47; Town Park Skate Park, 137, 150–51. *See also* Ferguson, Rob "Skate"; Sanchez, Danny; Williams, Keith "K-Dub"; Woozy, Kim
Grenfell, Christopher, 246, 249
Grose, Tracey, 179
The Guardian, 39, 262
Gucciardi, Ben, 142
Guerrero, Tommy, 34, 62

H

Hales, Charlie, 30
Hammack, Steve, 180, 183–85, 191–92
Harris, Jerry, 35, 36
Hartmann, Douglas, 31, 57, 235–36
Hawk, Frank, 16
Hawk, Steve, 62, 73
Hawk, Tony, 4, 13, 16, 17, 34, 69,

70–71, 301n21. *See also* Tony Hawk
Foundation (THF)
Hayward, California, 22
Hayward Parks and Recreation
Department, 84
health and well-being benefits: Bay
City Skate Park, 104; bonding
experiences, 122–23, 244, 247, 254;
local youth ownership, 157–59;
positive youth development (PYD),
55–57; SJ 180 program, 77–80;
skateboarding benefits, 10–11,
18–20, 38–39, 105, 230–32, 262;
skateboarding foundations, 73–76,
80–84; social-capital networks,
297n91; social-change model, 60;
social responsibility development,
63–64, 157–59, 237–39, 247; urban
space usage, 50. *See also* female
skaters; life-skills and character
development
helicopter parenting, 132, 243, 306n41
Hellison, Don, 240
Hernandez, Marco, 196, 201–2, 204
high sociability, 122, 198–99
hip-hop youth culture, 228
Hispanic populations, 196
hood cred, 138
Tha Hood Games, 145, 146–47
Hosoi, Christian, 181
Howell, Ocean, 16, 33
Huck Magazine, 68
Huffington Post, 60
Huizar, José, 74
Huston, Nyjah, 60
Hutton, Bobby, 140
hybrid spaces, 47
hypersexualized stereotypes, 89–90,
256

I

IBM, 178
income inequality, 40
indigenous governance, 248, 249
individualism, 53
indoor/outdoor BMX circuit, 246, 249
Instagram, 25, 94

Institute for the Study of Youth Sport,
Michigan State University, 56
institutionalized racism, 139–40
internal assets, 104
International Association of
Skateboard Companies, 16
International Olympic Committee
(IOC), x, 4, 68
International Skateboarding
Federation (ISF), x
interviewing challenges, 273–76

J

Jenson, Adam, 43, 122, 279
Jess, Mike, 260

K

Kaiser Permanente, 150
Karl Watson's Skate Day, 146–47
Kelch, James, 34
Kenworthy, Bella, 14
Kerr, Sierra, 14
Kidd, Bruce, 67
King of the Groms contest, 14
Kirby, Andrew, 46
Knoop, Mimi, 301n21
Kohl's Department Stores, 225, 315n28
Koston, Eric, 17, 60
Kruger, Carol, 191

L

Lake Cunningham Regional Skate
Park, *187, 188*; adult-organized
social spaces, 186–95, 234, 242–43,
246, 249; boundary-making practices, 250–52, 261; design process,
234; family-friendly environments,
196, 198, 246, 250–51; high sociability, 198; as industry trendsetter,
177, 179–80; parental support
and involvement, 187–95, 213,
241, 242–43, 244, 246; participant
diversity, 193–95, 250–52; public/
private-sector support and partnerships, 190–91, 222, 223; research
studies, 22; safety concerns, 196,
198, 242–43, 251–52, 261

functions, 45; sports participation opportunities, 143–46

260–62; social-enterprise networks, 20–21, 32–33, 58, 60, 61–97, 224–30, 257–58; as street-based male subculture, viii–ix, 15–16, 17; use of public space, 44–46; youth perspective, 205–9, 213, 245–49. *See also* female skaters; health and well-being benefits; racial and ethnic diversity; San Jose, California; social benefits

Skateboarding Hall of Fame, 11

Skateistan project, 68, 71, 225, 315*n*25

skate jam sessions and contests, 78–80, 83–84, 228–29, 246

skate-lifestyle clothing, 12, 13

Skate Like a Girl (SLAG): mission and functional role, 91–93; Oakland Skatepark Summit, 61–62, 64; skate events, 115, 121, 173; social-change agendas, 70, 85, 95, 226–27, 253, 255; volunteer-led programs, 226–27. *See also* Williams, Keith "K-Dub"

Skate One Corp., 315*n*28

Skate Park Association of the United States, 16

skate-park rangers, 117–19

skate parks: access and inclusion, 41–42, 47, 50, 63–64, 72–73, 84–97, 114–17, 121–22, 170–75, 253–56; adult networking and intervention, 45–46, 50, 53, 61–65, 99–101, 115–19, 190–91, 217–22, 246; celebrity-run parks, 70–76, 301*n*20; as child-raising environments, 53, 54–55, 119–20; coaching and instruction, 115–17, 120–22; community-building practices, 63, 64–65, 91, 111–19, 147–51, 201–4, 232–41; construction boom, 16–18, 19, 38, 181–83; contests and events, 145, 185, 201–3; corporate support and sponsorship, 19, 48, 64, 147, 148, 149–50, 220–24, 229–30, 257–58; family-friendly environments, 51–58, 112, 114–34, 215–16; fund-raising activities, 190–91, 222–23, 227; gang presence, 185, 195–96, 205–6, 208;

government regulations, 37–38; historical perspective, viii–ix, 15–17, 36–37; insurance coverage, 181; low-income urban youth, 70–73; neighborhood intervention model, 235–36; neoliberal perspective, 216–17, 219–24, 290*n*83; nonprofit groups, 87–91, 223–27; parental support and involvement, 17–18, 50, 51–58, 103–9, 112–34, 241–45; park activation strategies, 201, 202–4, 213; pay-to-skate parks, 72–73, 187, 194, 195; peer-to-peer interactions, 120–22, 124, 129; planning strategies, 63–65; politicized spatial projects, 186, 217–21; positive youth development (PYD), 55–57, 217–22, 230, 232–39; prevalence, 14–15, 16; private policing, 304*n*26; programming and recruitment, 115–17; pro-social development, 19, 119, 258–60; public/private-sector support and partnerships, 43–46, 49–50, 61–97, 184–86, 190–92, 217–24, 229–30, 257–58; repurposing space, 186, 199, 238; research background and methodology, 21–25, 265–67; social-capital networks, 43–44, 50; social diversity and inclusion, 12–14, 51–53, 249–56, 260–62; social-enterprise networks, 20–21, 58, 60, 61–97, 101, 107, 111–19, 224–30, 257–58; sociopolitical functions, 45; urban gentrification processes, 47–48, 49, 64; youth perspective, 205–9, 213, 245–49. *See also* Bay City Skate Park; female skaters; Lake Cunningham Regional Skate Park; life-skills and character development; police presence; Roosevelt Skate Park; safe environments; San Jose, California; social benefits; Tony Hawk Foundation (THF); Town Park Skate Park

Skate Pass program, 18

skate plazas, 74–76

skater memorials, 199, *200*, 246, 247

260–62; social-enterprise networks, 20–21, 32–33, 58, 60, 224–30, 257–58; traditional-to-contemporary transition, 215–16; youth perspective, 205–9, 213, 245–49. *See also* female skaters; health and well-being benefits; racial and ethnic diversity; San Jose, California; social benefits

USA Today, 40

Uyehara, Kent, 34, 147

V

Valley Medical Center, 192

Van Melik, Rianne, 195

Vans, 12, 16, 17, 315n28

Vargas, Hugo, 295n54

Vasconcellas, Nora, 13

vert skills/vertical skating, 16, 36

VHS technology, ix

Vickers, Vicki, 13

video games, 70, 73, 211

video technology, ix

Vimeo, 25

Vincent, Carl, 54

Vitello, Fausto, 35

Viva Parks! events, 78, 80, 185, 198, 199, 201–2, 204, 209, 235

Volcom, 227

volunteer-led programs, 226–27. *See also* nonprofit groups

W

Wall Street Journal, 7

Walnut Creek, California, 152

Washington Post, 9

Waste Management, 150

Watson, Karl, 145, 146–47

websites, 25

Weller, Susie, 43, 158

West Oakland, California. *See* Town Park Skate Park

Wheaton, Belinda, 59

White, Alex, 227

white masculinity, 59. *See also* masculine subculture

Whitley, Peter, 62, 63, 71, 72–73, 76, 150

Whole Foods, 141, 308n28

Whosevers, 78

Williams, Keith "K-Dub," *144*; biographical background, 143–59; capital reproduction, 151–55; on female skaters, 171, 173, 254; indigenous governance, 248; as mentor, 27, 143, 148, 155–59; Oakland Skatepark Summit, 61, 62, 64–65; reputation, 308n38; on skateboarding benefits, 64–65; skating projects and goals, 43, 221; social diversity promotions, 252; social-enterprise networks, 134, 149–55; social responsibility development, 237–39; Town Park Skate Park, 27, 134, 135–37, 146–59, 237–39. *See also* Ferguson, Rob "Skate"

Williams, Pharrell, 12

Williams, Stevie, 12, 266

Willing, Indigo, 84

Winchester Skate Park, 37, 181

Wired magazine, 32

women: access and inclusion, 63–64, 68, 70, 84–97, 115–16, 121–22, 138–39, 170–75, 253–56; adult-organized social spaces, 249; marginalized individuals, 97, 228, 266; public space usage, 296n76; skateboarding organizations, 85–97, 226–27, 253–56; skateboarding participation, 13–14, 51–53, 58–59, 253–56; social-enterprise networks, 84–97; Town Park Skate Park, 138–39, 159–60, 170–75

Women's Skateboarding Alliance, 91

Woodward West mega ramp, 14

Woozy, Kim, 85, 91, 94–96, 226, 227, 228, 254

Work to Future, 204

World Skate, x–xi

Wright, Jan, 23

Wright, Missy, 24, 272

X

X Games, ix, 4, 34, 74, 144, 266

Y

youth of color: access and inclusion,

41–42, 57–58, 161–70, 235–37; action-sports culture, 153–54; celebrity-run skate parks, 70–76; contests and events, 145, 185, 201–3; high-profile skateboarders, 60, 153; job opportunities, 153–55, 157, 204; marginalized individuals, 60, 235, 261; pro-social urban sports infrastructure and programming, 31, 199, 201; scholarly research, 59; skate jam sessions and contests, 83–84, 228–29; social diversity, 252–53; social responsibility development, 157–59, 237–39; social welfare cuts, 258; sports participation opportunities, 41, 57–58, 138, 143–47, 152, 161–70, 185, 195–96, 237–40, 258. *See also* Roosevelt Skate Park; Town Park Skate Park; Williams, Keith "K-Dub"

youth sports: access and inclusion, 41–42, 57–58; adult networking and intervention, 7–8, 9, 99–101, 217–22, 234–37, 263; affordability, 8–9, 287*n*32; learning and development processes and approaches, 258–60; neighborhood intervention model, 235–36; nonprofit groups, 87–91, 223–27; parental support and involvement, 51–58, 103–9, 239–45; participant decline, 3–4, 7, 8, 217, 286*n*18; participation opportunities, 41; popularity, 216–17; positive youth development (PYD), 55–57, 69, 83, 104–6, 122–29, 159–70, 230–32, 239–45; prevalence, 7; professionalization and privatization, 9, 10, 29–31, 39, 49–50, 54, 257; programming cuts, 258; protective carework, 105, 243–44; public/private-sector support and partnerships, 29–31, 49–50, 61–97, 137, 184–86, 191–92, 217–24, 231, 257–58; researcher background, 271–73; social class, 14, 56–58; social diversity and inclusion, 260–62. *See also* racial and ethnic diversity

YouTube, 25, 94

Z

Zephyr Team, 13, 44
Zuckerberg, Mark, 39
Zumiez, 83